18.27

FOUNDERS OF ENGLAND

" Under the drums and tramplings of three conquests. . . ."

SIR THOMAS BROWNE.

FOUNDERS OF ENGLAND

BY

FRANCIS B. GUMMERE

(LATE PROFESSOR OF ENGLISH
IN HAVERFORD COLLEGE)

WITH SUPPLEMENTARY NOTES BY
FRANCIS PEABODY MAGOUN, JR.

McGrath Publishing Company
College Park, Maryland

1970

Reprinted by
McGrath Publishing Co., 1970

ISBN: 0-8434-0107-9
LC# 73-119295

Manufactured in the United States of America
by Arno Press, Inc., New York

PREFACE

ONE needs no longer to fetch an oracle, — *antiquam exquirite matrem*, for example, — in order to compel attention when one writes about the sources of language, literature, and institutions of the great English-speaking race. This volume aims to give an account of the founders of that race while they still held their old home, their old faith, their old customs; and the sole purpose of these "forewords" is to explain what materials and what method have been employed. The author has tried to free his text from cumbrous allusions, and to put into the notes material for wider study. These notes, as well as a portion of the introductory chapter, tell the reader what sources have been consulted in the making of the book itself. Quotations at second hand occur only where the authority from which they are taken is itself of the first class, such as Grimm on mythology, Müllenhoff on archæology, or Waitz on institutions. All quotations from the range of Early Germanic literature are at first hand, and the same statement holds good of classical

iii

sources like Tacitus or Cæsar. Translations from Anglo-Saxon and German poetry have been made by the author; those from the Edda are in the majority of cases by Vigfusson and Powell, but are always duly credited.

F. B. G.

HAVERFORD COLLEGE, 21 December, 1891.

EDITORIAL PREFACE

Thirty eight years ago Professor Gummere published his *Germanic Origins: A Study in Primitive Culture*, now reissued as *Founders of England*, — a title contemplated by the author. This classic handbook has for many years been of service to English-speaking students as an introduction to Germanic antiquities, so far, in particular, as these illustrate the intellectual and literary development of the Anglo-Saxons. Though it has long been out of print no competing work in English has appeared, and the present issue is in all essntialse a photographic fac-simile of the original edition.

Although the plan and technique of reproduction exclude extensive alterations, it has been possible to effect a few changes calculated to render the work more useful and to bring it relatively up to date. A few misprints in the body of the text have been corrected, as well as a few misstatements — in the main noted in the author's copy kindly lent by Mrs. Gummere. For all passages translated from *Beowulf* Professor Gummere's final version, as published in his *Oldest English Epic* has, through the courtesy of the Mac-

millan Co., been substituted. It has also been possible
to revise certain footnotes and to make the references
conform to later editions of works cited. The chief
instances occur in references to Paul's *Grundriss* (to
the 2d and extensively revised edition instead of to
the 1st; in the case of Karl von Amira's article "Germanisches Recht" to the 3d edition, where this makes
a separate volume); to the corpus of Anglo-Saxon laws
(Liebermann instead of Schmidt); to Victor Hehn's
Kulturpflanzen und Haustiere (to the 8th edition instead
of the 4th); and to the *Poetic Edda* (to Gustav Neckel's
2d edition instead of to Hildebrand). In the case of
the *Poetic Edda* Professor Gummere frequently quoted
or cited Vigfusson and Powell's *Corpus Poeticum
Boreale*, but since this is costly and not always readily
accessible, wherever space in the type-line permitted
references have been added to the recent English translations of H. A. Bellows and of L. M. Hollander. In a few
instances footnotes to passages quoted from *Beowulf*
have been adjusted to the revised translation of the
poem. These changes and others of a similar character
may, in a general way, be taken as alterations which
the author himself would almost surely have made, had
he lived to prepare a new edition.

But since 1892 the frontiers of knowledge in the rich
field of Germanic antiquites have enormously advanced,
especially in detail, and new facts and new finds' have
brought new inferences and new interpretations. Accord-

ingly, the editor has assumed the not altogether easy task of drawing up a set of supplementary notes as an appendix. In the main these notes are intended as a guide for further study of the varied subjects treated in the first fifteen chapters. Occasionally, it has seemed proper to suggest that a view other than that expressed in the text is current to-day. Economy of space has often made necessary the citation of a work because of its bibliographical value rather than for its general exposition of the matter in hand. A considerable number of articles in Johannes Hoops' *Reallexikon der germanischen Altertumskunde* join both qualities, and here, as elsewhere, the indebtedness of all students of Germanic antiquities to this splendid example of coöperative scholarship must long continue great.

As one reads and re-reads *Germanic Origins*, now *Founders of England*, the deeper grows one's respect and admiration for that distinguished and graceful scholar who, often as a pioneer, did so much to promote our understanding of the life and thought and spirit of the English race from the days of Tacitus to the age of *Beowulf*.

FRANCIS PEABODY MAGOUN, JR.

CONTENTS

CHAPTER I

CHAPTER II

CHAPTER III

CHAPTER IV

CHAPTER XV

CHAPTER XVI

FOUNDERS OF ENGLAND

CHAPTER I

INTRODUCTION

Germanic and Celtic in the English race — Appearance of the Germanic element in European history — Clash of Roman and German — Sources of information about the early Germans — Chronological and geographical data — *Germania* of Tacitus chief authority — The Ingævonic tribes.

WHO were the founders of our race? Working backwards, up the stream of national descent, we come to the great influx of Norman people, Norman words, Norman ways; and we stop to reckon with this fact in the development of English life. A very brief study, a few minutes of consideration, assure us that here are no founders of England, but only generous contributors; immigrants we may call them, who brought along valuable property, and furnished us with some new and desirable elements of civilization. Again, and for still stronger reasons, we reach the same conclusion with regard to that earlier conquest of England by the Northmen. The Danes gave us a few words, — the common vocable "are," for example, — a few customs, a few laws; and that is the whole

1

story. It lies, therefore, between the Celts, the people whom Cæsar found in his Britain, and the Germanic invaders and conquerors who seized upon the island when the Roman legions were withdrawn. Of these two claimants, the latter race is recognized by history and criticism as furnishing the real foundation of our national life. True, there is more or less opposition in the matter of actual descent. We are Germanic in our institutions, concedes Professor Huxley; but the race itself is at least half Celtic in its blood. "Not one half," Mr. Grant Allen is inclined to think, "of the population of the British Isles is really of Teutonic descent;" and he carries the battle into still remoter territory when he concedes our language to Germanic origins, but claims our literature, especially the imagination displayed in it, for Celtic influences. Furthermore, the greatest of our critics in literary matters, the late Matthew Arnold, has broken a lance for this Celtic influence in our national development, and is half inclined to answer the question, "What is England?" by saying, "A vast obscure Cymric basis with a vast visible Germanic superstructure."[1] In particular, Arnold attributes so high a quality of our literature as its humor — and what quality is so peculiarly its own, so triumphantly its own? — to the dash of Celtic impulse and fancy, clashing with our Germanism.[2] And he goes on to say, that our poetry probably got its turn for style, probably its turn for melancholy, and certainly its "natural magic," from the Celtism in our character. Such statements as these from a man who on his own

[1] *On the Study of Celtic Literature* (Macmillan & Co., 1883), p. 64.
[2] Ibid. p. 101.

ground had no rivals deserve most careful consideration. Arnold, however, is off his own ground when he asserts that rhyme, which he calls the main source of the romantic element in our poetry, "comes . . . from the Celts." Kluge has shown, in an article dealing with strictly scientific evidence, that our Anglo-Saxon poetry, which already possessed that form of rhyme loosely called alliteration, was in its own fashion developing that form which we commonly understand when we use the general term.[1] Now this mistake of Arnold's, trifling as it may be, shows us the need of very severe tests when we attempt to pass judgment on questions so intricate and rooted in such difficult and distant soil. It is a little too loud protesting when Mr. Grant Allen, though he may well be quite in the right, lays down the positive law that "our modern poetry"—and *a fortiori*, our prose,[2] —"is wholly Romance in descent, form, and spirit." We are tempted to ask Mr. Allen for definitions, for sources, for proof. It is just the same hesitation that besets us when he says that while our social and political organization must be regarded as Germanic, this Germanic element did nothing for our culture, which is "wholly Roman."[3]

[1] Ibid. p. 120; Kluge in Paul-Braune, *Beiträge zur Geschichte d. deutschen Sprache u. Literatur*, Vol. IX.

[2] Anglo-Saxon prose is vigorous, and sometimes, as in Ælfric, not without a certain compactness and form. But every one knows that the best qualities in the older period of English prose—as in Hooker or Milton—were Latinistic, and that the best qualities in the later period are distinctly indebted to the French.

[3] See Grant Allen, *Anglo-Saxon Britain*, pp. 106, 224, 227. For the other side, see Professor Freeman,—who opposes "the witness of speech" to "the witness of skulls," and insists on the continuity of our race from Schleswig to New England,—in his *Four Oxford Lectures*, 1887 (Macmillan & Co., 1888), especially pp. 71, 78, of the lecture on *Teutonic Conquest in Gaul and Britain*.

Granting all that these critics claim, we find in their concessions of speech, custom and law, broad enough basis for our assumption that the Germanic race is the source of English life, and that the Germanic invaders of Britain may fairly be styled founders of England. Moreover, in regard to the disputed territory, while we feel sure that Arnold has considerable justice in his claims for Celtic liveliness as a factor in the imaginative qualities of our literature, we do not wish to see the Germanic element fairly elbowed out of our poetry. We are willing to concede that Prospero found his Ariel on the island; but what shall we say of Prospero himself?

> Vom Vater hab' ich die Statur,
> Des Lebens ernstes Führen,
> Von Mütterchen die Frohnatur
> Und Lust zu fabuliren, —

sang Goethe of his own "origins"; and father Germanic and mother Celtic may have contributed the same elements in the case of English poetry. But Mr. Grant Allen says that our Germanic origin gave our literature "patience and thoroughness," and nothing more.[1]

It is little better than beating the air to argue in general terms against these random conclusions. It is a question of facts; and we must first of all inquire how we can best reach the facts. We could take that complex mass which we call English Literature, and by a grand source-hunt, such as the modern scholar loves, pursue origins and sources over every land and time. It is easy with a certain facility in tailor-lore

[1] Ibid. p. 229.

to show how oddly this literature is "suited," to trace the doublet to Italy and the round-hose to France, — pretty sport and often profitable, — but how is it with the flesh and blood of literature? Is the heart of our literature Germanic or Celtic? Or is it neither? Is it rather the result of classical or even Romance traditions? How can we so much as begin to answer these questions until we know what "Germanic" means? If we wish to know what elements in our literature or our life we ought to refer to the Germanic invaders of Britain, it is of prime importance to study this Germanic invader in his habit as he lived. He is the subject of these pages; and it is to be hoped that a view of him, in different types and periods, may leave some general impressions — we may not hope for a sharp picture — of the Germanic character.

Our knowledge of the early German must be derived from three main sources, — the accounts of his foreign contemporaries, the early literature of Germanic races, and survivals; the *Germania* of Tacitus, our Anglo-Saxon *Béowulf*, and the church festival of All Souls, are respectively examples of the three sources. In all of these classes our material must be sifted with extremest caution, but particularly in the second and third. No direct literature remains to us from the Germans of Tacitus, and the songs [1] about god or hero which they chanted in those early days have perished quite beyond the faintest hope of recovery. But heroic legend was richly developed by the Germans of the "Wandering," the period when Roman and barbarian were opposed in the hottest struggle;

[1] Tac. *Germ.* II.; *Ann.* II. 88.

and these legends have passed with more or less purity
into early Germanic literature. The Christian setting
often contains a purely heathen jewel.

Evidently, with material scattered over so great a
stretch of time, one is in danger of rescuing no old
German at all, but rather of holding up a bit of literary patchwork, a veritable scarecrow of ill-matched
garments passing for a man. The danger is real; but
it must be remembered that a type is far easier to
establish for primitive than for modern times. Facts
have wider bearings and life is more uniform of tone,
the further we go back in history. Early times lacked
diversity of employment, fine divisions in the drift of
thought and feeling. It is civilization which brings
out the individual and lays emphasis on his importance, — consider the "interview," — which creates
distinctions, and puts a thousand angles of vision
to-day for a hundred in the past. One reason why
Shakspere seems so much more modern than Chaucer is that the latter still drew types, while the former
drew men and women. The Squire becomes Romeo
and the Wife of Bath yields to Mrs. Quickly of East-
cheap. What we must particularly avoid is to con-
fuse types, to treat on one plane the German of Tacitus and the German who has absorbed elements of
classical and Christian culture. The players of the
fifth act must not be huddled in one group with the
simple and hardy characters who open the action and
set the play upon its path of development. First
of all, moreover, we must glance at the stage itself
on which our German made his rude and clanging
entrance; we must study the scene.

Civilization in the first centuries of our era revolved about the Mediterranean, where a complex of races was held together by the organizing genius of Rome. But the Roman state was in decay; its lack of moral greatness combined with certain political and physical defects to bring about what a French scholar has called the "mortal illness" of epochs which are destitute of lofty aims and firmness of conviction. The slow "death of Rome," [1] consequence of this malady, may be said to begin with the invasion of Alaric in 402, and to end with the invasion of Alboin in 568. With the latter name we touch mediæval literature; for Alboin is mentioned in our oldest piece of Anglo-Saxon poetry, in the curious medley of description and memories put into the mouth of an ideal Germanic minstrel, Widsith, "the far-wanderer."

When the historian begins to reckon the causes of downfall, he has the right to put first and foremost the general corruption of the age. But, as was just now hinted, there were other and specific causes,[2] such as thriftless administration of public and private property, excess of taxation, and high cost of living. The individual was crushed by the dead weight of imperial organization. Trade and manufactures must needs languish; science led to no practical results; and there was absolutely no material progress to keep pace with wider responsibilities. As Hehn remarks, the empire stretched further and further, and yet Roman ships remained what they always had been, coasting vessels, unable to contend with the perils of winter or the open sea. Where commerce did find

[1] Hodgkin. *Italy and her Invaders.* I. 3.
[2] Summed up by Victor Hehn in *Kulturpflanzen und Haustiere in ihrem Übergang aus Asien* (8th ed., rev. O. Schrader, Berlin, 1911), pp. 490 ff. Cited hereafter Hehn⁸.

its way, it gave no spur to invention, and accomplished little for the arts of life; like the sailor, the farmer clung to the methods and implements of his forefathers. In the world of mind it was no better, and literature gradually lost itself in rhetoric, its only remaining form. A deep scepticism prevailed, stifling all creative joy; the old gods were merely excuses for a priesthood, objects of a cult in which no one really believed.

Over and through this outworn civilization swept two great waves, — Christianity from the east, Germanic invasion from the north. In one sense, both of these movements were hurtful to literature; for the invaders doubtless annihilated a mass of precious material, and what they spared was often the prey of monkish bigotry.[1] As a piece of revenge, the answering wave of culture, the reacting civilization which carried rudiments of criticism and letters among the barbarians, went far toward destroying whatever native elements of literature were to be found. The spirit of Christianity rudely checked the development of the heathen epic poetry; and such song as had reached form and substance was put under ban. The Frankish or Saxon monk disdained in most cases the artless poetry of his vernacular; and in the hands of the monk lay all destiny of letters. Still, in that general wreck of literature, it was Christianity which

---

[1] See the famous story of the Athenian libraries which the Goths were about to burn during a raid into Greece, near the end of the third century. It is told in Gibbon's *Decline and Fall*, Chap. X. The "bigotry," by the way, was not always "monkish." Under Valentinian and Valens the persecutions on account of supposed "magic" involved the destruction of a vast amount of philosophical and classical literature; and this was a political, not simply theological persecution. See Gibbon, Chap. XXV., and Hodgkin, *Italy*, I. 40.

manned the only life-boat. Christian zeal rescued many precious remnants of classical culture, keeping them for a time that could use and value them aright. Patriotic monks were here and there found who would set down the songs and legends of the fatherland, notwithstanding occasional survivals of heathendom which crept between the lines, — so we have a *Béowulf*, a Lay of Hildebrand; or else the old subjects were treated in the new style, as where German Ekkehard sings in vigorous Latin hexameters the story of Walter and Hildegund.

This last example brings us to the greatest service which the church ever did for the cause of letters. It established a neutral ground on which classics and barbarism could in some manner join hands and so save what was best in each. Christianity inspired an international literature. Despised by the learning of a riper age, this literature nevertheless saved the classics and preserved those early records of the Germanic nations which we now value beyond price. To it we moderns owe what a great scholar owes to the simple books and lessons of his first school-days. With its universal medium of Latein[1], it controlled and shaped the beginnings of every literature which arose in the states of Europe. Its great advantage was universality; its defect was monotony. It already realized, as Ebert points out, the later dream and longing of Goethe for a World-Literature; but it lacked the vitality of a national consciousness, is everywhere the same, and has an air of saying its lesson, — not always too

---

[1] A standard work on this subject is M. Manitius, *Gesch. der latein. Literatur des Mittelalters* (Munich, 1911ff.); see also E. K. Rand, *Founders of the Middle Ages* (Cambridge, Mass., 1929).

fluently, — after its teacher.[1] This Christian Latin literature was the village-school of learned Europe; but while it trained, it could not create. The vital power of mediæval literature lay in the poetic impulses of old Germanic life, — we are speaking here of the northern nations alone, — in that joy of "singing and saying" which our forefathers brought out of their forests. The original songs have vanished. One lay about Arminius, such as Tacitus assures us was sung in his time, were worth its millions. But the later legends, which sprang up with the national consciousness in the victories over eastern and western Romans, still keep the early note and give us some of our best material for studying the ancient German. True, they are inspired by contact with civilization, but the contact calls out a national and original utterance.

It is in the first flush of Germanic conquest, in the clash of a fresh, ignorant race with a corrupt, outworn but highly civilized race, in the awakening of national consciousness, that we should like to make our picture of the ancient German. But such a picture is no easy affair. The clash of Germany and Rome lasted five hundred years; and the Goth had grown as civilized as the Romans at a time when his Saxon brother was still the barbarian of Tacitus. We must look to our historical and geographical perspective.

The pressure of Germanic invasion which finally burst the barriers of Rome was not altogether spon-

---

[1] "One feels," says Müllenhoff, "that the early middle ages wore another color and spoke another speech than we find in their chronicles and documents." *Deutsche Alterthumskunde*, Vol. I. Vorrede, p. v.

taneous. For a long time previous to the fall of the empire, there had been a restless movement in the heart of Germany; and while we find some explanation for this in the nomadic character and military instincts of the race, we must attribute no small share to the pressure of Huns and other tribes upon Germans of the east and north. The actual "migration of the tribes", or *Völkerwanderung*, is usually referred to a round century from the flight of the West-Goths into Roman territory, — they were driven by the Huns, — until the fall of the Western Empire.[1] The late Professor Scherer tells us[2] that the historic consciousness of the Germans dates from this movement; and we may say that it was during this entire period that German after German came out of his barbaric environment and took up that strange battle between an old civilization and a new race in which each is victor and each is vanquished. It is in this period that we have the real conflict between Roman and German, a struggle along the entire line and fought for life or death; but there had been many a previous encounter. Southern Aryans first heard of their kinsmen in the north, not so much by conquest, as in the peaceful way of trade. Müllenhoff is of opinion[3] that nearly all the supply of tin came from Britain, and that the trade began in times too early for computation. Tin was needed for the making of bronze; but another eagerly sought article was valued for itself. Amber — it is mentioned in the Odyssey — was in all probability the means of putting Greeks in communication with the shores of

[1] See F. Dahn, *Bausteine*, I. 282.   [3] *D. A.* I. 211.
[2] *Geschichte d. deutschen Lit.* p. 22.

the Baltic, and with the Germanic tribes who lived
there. Greek coins of the fifth and sixth centuries
before Christ have been found near the Baltic; but
in Müllenhoff's opinion, commerce at that time was
indirect, and articles were forwarded from tribe to
tribe. The first person, therefore, who brought to the
Greeks a definite knowledge of the north, was Pytheas
of Marseilles, a Grecian geographer of the fourth century before Christ, who "followed the old path of
the Phœnicians," and was an eye-witness of the tin-
mining processes in Britain.[1] He went further. We
may assume, concludes Müllenhoff, after a most elaborate investigation, "that Pytheas saw with his own
eyes the islands and shores of the North Sea, passed
the mouths of the Rhine, and the boundary between
Celts and Scytho-Teutons; but found it best to
push no further among unknown races, and so contented himself for the rest with what he heard of
them."[2]

Thus, so far as we know, came the first tidings
about our ancestors to the ancient world. Their first
actual appearance on the border of the civilized countries about the Mediterranean, is not definitely settled. Müllenhoff thinks the Bastarnæ were Germanic,
a tribe mentioned by Tacitus and Pliny; they appeared
on the lower Danube about the beginning of the
second century before Christ. A king of Macedonia

[1] Müllenhoff, *D. A.* I. 375, 472. "The Humboldt of antiquity," as
Pytheas is called, is also discussed, with less critical knowledge, by
Elton, *Origins of English History*, p. 6 ff. It should be added that
Professor Rhys, *Celtic Britain*, p. 47, says there was no direct trade
between Cornwall and the continent, and adds that there is no "scrap
of evidence, linguistic or other, of the presence of Phœnicians in
Britain at any time."

[2] *D. A.* I. 495.

is said[1] to have sent an embassy to them and to have asked them for troops as allies. According to Müllenhoff, the Bastarnæ came from the neighborhood of the upper Vistula, attracted by southern fertility; in the third century of our era they vanish utterly.

Next of Germanic races to tread the tempting but perilous path southward were the Cimbrians and Teutons. A large part of the second volume of Müllenhoff's great work on German Archæology, the *Deutsche Alterthumskunde,* is devoted to a searching investigation into the details, scanty and disconnected as they are, which Greek and Roman writers have left us in regard to this movement, — a movement which, like the battle of Marathon, though less decisively, struck into the very heart of history.[2] Müllenhoff makes[3] it strongly probable that these tribes were Germanic, and that their names — for the later term 'Germanic' was not used at Rome till about 80 B.C.[4] — were given to them by neighboring Celts. Cimbrians[5] may be translated "robbers," and Teutons "bands," or "multitudes." They came, after a succession of Celtic movements had left vacant tracts between the Weser and the Rhine, from the old home of the Germans, a region bounded by the Oder, the Harz mountains, and the Thuringian hills. Till a couple of centuries before Christ, if Müllenhoff is right, this girdle of

[1] For references, see Zeuss, *Die Deutschen und ihre Nachbar-stämme,* p. 129. Zeuss says without reservation: "Die Bastarnen sind das erste deutsche Volk welches auf dem Schauplatze der Geschichte auftritt. . . ."

[2] The author reminds us that it is now about two thousand years since that Cimbrian terror heralded the Germanic invasion of Europe.

[3] *D. A.* II. 207.   [4] Ibid. II. 189.

[5] The name has nothing to do with "Cymry," etc. Ibid. II. 116.

primeval forest [1] had separated the Germans from
the Celts. Now they broke their bounds and streamed
southward, the Cimbrians a swarm made up from
various tribes along the middle Elbe,[2] the Teutons
mainly from the coasts of the North Sea. The
Romans had a tradition that this great invasion was
caused by floods, which drove Cimbrians and Teutons
out of their homes "in the uttermost parts of the
earth." [3]

What havoc they wrought in Italy we know from
Livy and Plutarch.[4] Rome was saved at Aquæ Sextiæ by the genius of Marius; and the great barbarian
wave melted away to the northward almost as suddenly
as it had come. Not very long afterward, however,
a kinsman of Marius, bent on the conquest of Celtic
Gaul, found, across his path and intent on the same
errand, an army from east of the Rhine, the hordes of
Ariovistus the German. Cæsar was quick to see that
here was the deadliest foe of Rome.[5] The destruction
of the Suevians, the Rhine-bridge, the legions led upon
German soil, are evidences of Cæsar's greatness as
statesman as well as soldier. His achievements not
only furnished a model for the few victorious campaigns of his successors, not only saved Gaul to
the Romans, but in the judgment of competent men,
prolonged by centuries the very existence of Rome

[1] See also Kiepert, *Alte Geographie*, p. 535.

[2] *D. A.* II. 289.

[3] Dahn (see next note) finds this notion credible.

[4] A vivid account of the invasion is given by Dahn, *Urgeschichte
der germanischen und romanischen Völker*, in Vol. II. Of course, Plutarch's *Marius* is the most detailed ancient account.

[5] Read, *Bell. Gall.* I. 33, his own words upon this danger to his
country. Chapters 43–46, describing the interview of Cæsar and Ariovistus, have high dramatic interest.

itself. There is something almost theatrical in that opening clash of arms between the conquerors of the world, with perhaps the greatest of all generals at their head, and a mass of half-naked barbarians, — in this beginning of a war which lasted for five hundred years, which saw the old world with its arts and learning go down in wreck, and the new world arise in all its incompleteness and rawness, but in all its immense and eager vitality. Rude as they were, these Germans henceforth held a foremost place in the eyes of statesmen who knew how to estimate the perils of the empire. Germans were sought as soldiers, as allies; the two nations came in touch; what Germans were and what they did became a matter of interest. Cæsar fixed his keen eye upon them; a century or so later came Tacitus and studied them. Roman statecraft now bought, now fought, but always kept planning the destruction of such unwelcome neighbors. At first, Drusus and Germanicus almost completed Cæsar's policy of conquest; but later this was given up, and a system of border fortifications[1] threw the Germans back upon themselves, brought about their solidarity, checked the old nomadic driftings of the tribes, and organized them into nations. Four centuries of wars and treaties, bribes and bargains, — the Germans fighting together against the Romans, as allies with the Romans, and against one another, — must have sent a vast amount of civilization, both for good and for evil, across the

---

[1] The so-called *Limes* ran from about the junction of Lahn and Rhine to a point near the junction of the Altmühl and the Danube. This line was held by the Romans for two centuries. See Arnold, *Deutsche Urzeit*, p. 81 f.

Rhine.   Indeed, most of the early lessons which Germans learned of Rome seem to have lain in the direction of perfidy and bribes.   "We have taught them," even Tacitus could say, "to take our money;"[1] and they soon became skilled in the art of selling a treaty, and of breaking it.   Vellejus[2] says that the Germans, for all their barbarism, are thoroughly sly and seem born for lying and deceit.   But this opinion is provoked by the victory over Varus.   Large bodies of soldiers were formed who lived along the Roman border, separated from the good influences of home and family,[3] and exposed to all the vices of mercenary warfare; centuries of this life must have destroyed much of the old Germanic virtue.   The low-water mark of Germanic morals was reached by the Merovingian Franks.   Stubbs does not seem to think that much change was wrought in Germanic character during the early part of the period we have described. The institutions of our forefathers, he believes, remained practically the same for the two centuries succeeding the time of Tacitus; "nor is there any occasion to presume a development in the direction of civilization."[4]   Much of this may be true for the remote tribes, for Angles and Saxons; but the border

---

[1] *Germ.* XV.   [2] II. 118.

[3] See Loebell, *Gregor von Tours*, 2d ed. p. 75 f.   A description of certain German tribes, who were still heathen, and whose virtues are held up to the dissolute Christians of Rome and Gaul, is often quoted: "Gothorum gens perfida, sed pudica est [the Goths held the Arian heresy], Alamannorum impudica sed minus perfida.   Franci mendaces, sed hospitales, Saxones crudelitate efferi, sed castitate mirandi." That is, the Goths are faithless but chaste, Alamannians unchaste but less treacherous, Franks liars but hospitable, Saxons ferociously cruel but of admirable chastity.   Salvianus, however, has a suspicious leaning toward antithesis.   See Grimm, *Deutsche Mythologie*, 4th ed. III. 1 f.

[4] *Const. Hist. England*, I. 37.

and interior tribes of Germany must have changed greatly, and some faint ripple of these changes may have reached the north. Victor Hehn, in the admirable book already quoted,[1] says that the Romanizing process began before the movement of the tribes; and he calls attention to the great part played by Belgium in mediating between culture and barbarism.

With the overthrow of the empire we have a levelling of walls and dikes, a rush of strange elements in each direction. Barbarians sit on the throne of the Cæsars, and Roman laws are current in the forests of Arminius. Over all is the mediation of the new faith. Wattenbach reminds us that while later accounts attribute the spread of the Christian religion to individuals, apostles like Boniface or bishops and missionaries like Augustine, in reality much was done by persons of no name or fame, — merchants, soldiers, laborers, — converted men, who worked in many places and with great effect.[2] We can extend this humble but potent influence to other fields. Culture of every kind must have been carried in this fashion to all parts of northern Europe, which were open to Roman and German.

Enough has now been said to show that our typical German, like Plato's ideal horse, is a very difficult matter to define and draw; and, indeed, he has been drawn in every shade from absolute savagery to a graceful and accomplished person, as unlimited in courtesy and intellect as in muscular development, who "cultive ses jardins, les vertus et les arts." Jacob Grimm had some indulgence for this nobler

---

[1] Hehn⁸, pp. 498, 499.

[2] Wattenbach, *Deutschlands Geschichtsquellen im Mittelalter*, 5th ed. p. 37 f. See also Winckelmann, *Geschichte der Angelsachsen*, p. 22.

type; and while one would rather err with Grimm than be right with Adelung, one must nevertheless admit that love for the Germanic past has sometimes carried even the greatest scholar of our century too far. There are two assumptions. One is that the German of Tacitus was a mere nomadic barbarian, and all attributes of civilization found in him a few centuries later are the result of contact with Rome. The other assumption clothes the primitive German with these same attributes, — that is, with the virtues and mental habit, if not with the accomplishments, of civilization. The advocates of both theories can find in the chaos of material whatever facts they need. In recent times, modern savage life has been heavily drawn upon to supply pictures of early Germanic culture. It is the disciples of ethnology who depict our ancestor in such a degraded guise; while the philologists still paint a portrait that glows with too many hues of civilization.[1] Of course it is the point of view that is continually shifted with such disastrous results. What an enormous difference between the Germany of Boniface and the Germany of Tacitus or Cæsar! We turn from the idle, half-naked brawler of the *Germania*, the chieftain of Tacitus, to Theodoric the Goth quoting Tacitus himself on the subject of amber . . . " *Cornelio scribente*," he says, just as any Roman would give us a line of Virgil.[2]

---

[1] Wackernagel thought a fair mean could be obtained by taking the civilization of the Greeks as described by Homer, and assuming the same stage for Germania. See Chadwick, *Heroic Age*, pp. 432 ff.

[2] The king — through Cassiodorus — is thanking a tribe by the Baltic for certain gifts of amber. See Cassiod. Var. V. 2, quoted by Dahn, *Bausteine*, I. 17.

Basis of our description must be the *Germania* of Tacitus. But we are justified in adding to this picture those traits of Germanic temperament which were developed under pressure of the later struggle with Rome. Thus the virtues of Siegfried are not classical or Roman virtues; they are the attributes of an ideal German of the warrior type, blending with conceptions of the Germanic myth. But where are we to stop in this process? Where shall we draw the line which separates Germanic from Christianized and Romanized Germanic? The answer is involved in the question. Christian faith and Roman culture, from the time of the tribal movement on, went hand in hand; and where the German stands hostile to these, he must retain most of his primitive characteristics. Now the West-Goths were converted in the fourth century, about 375, then the East-Goths and Vandals; early in the fifth century the Burgundians, later the Franks; in the sixth, Alamannians and Lombards; Bavarians in the seventh and eighth; Frisians, Hessians, and Thuringians in the eighth; Saxons in the ninth. This is for the Continent. Anglo-Saxons were converted about 600, and took the lion's share in converting their continental brethren. Scandinavians accepted Christianity in the tenth and eleventh centuries.[1] It is evident not only that these tribes must have varied in the extent and accuracy of their heathen traditions, but also that we are at liberty to use primitive material even when we find it covered with more or less theological varnish

---

[1] Legend said that King Arthur had conquered and Christianized Norway and Iceland, and it even went so far as to make the apostles themselves carry the gospel to Scandinavia.

from the hands of a monkish scribe. Moreover, let us remember that the epoch of heroic legends was closed about the end of the sixth century, when at least half the Germanic tribes were unconverted. The Angles, Saxons, Jutes, and perhaps Danes, who conquered and settled Britain in the fifth century, were absolute heathens; and it needed three hundred years more to bring the gospel to those swamps and forests which stretched along the German ocean and into the Cimbrian peninsula. The continental Saxons had the reputation of great conservatism, and up to the time of the exodus to Britain had wandered least of all the Germanic tribes.[1] We must therefore be careful to abstract from our notion of the Germanic settlers of England whatever traits, found in the continental German, are to be ascribed to a long contact with Christianity and Roman culture.

Chronology in some wise determined, and enough historical perspective assured for our purpose, we need to fix clearly the geographical limits and divisions of Germany. All work done in this field rests, in the first instance, on the information given us by Tacitus; and we must face the question of credibility. What of the *Germania?* There have been doubts raised regarding the trustworthiness of this book, none, perhaps, going so far as a general denial, but in one instance at least, making, if successfully proved, utter havoc of all foundation for the modern historian. In Dr. Latham we have the most outspoken enemy of the *Germania;* he assails its ethnography and opposes its statements. " Much," he says, " which is

---

[1] Dahn, *Urgeschichte der german. und roman. Völker*, II. 307.

held to be German is Slavonic," and he insists that
there were "Slavonians from the Teutoburger Wald
to the Vistula."[1] These assertions of Dr. Latham
are rejected utterly by modern criticism. There is,
however, another sort of opposition, not yet silent,
which attacks not so much facts as motives. Most
energetic in this respect is the commentator Baumstark, who has somewhere spoken of the "rose-red
romanticism of the sickly sentimental Tacitus," — in
troth, my captain, bitter words! And another writer,
but of a very different school, Lippert, the follower
of Spencer, tells us that Tacitus, for the sake of the
moral effect upon his countrymen, makes out of every
German necessity a German virtue, and so gives us
a quite false picture of German civilization.[2] That
is no new accusation. The poet Heine speaks of
hearing E. M. Arndt lecture on the *Germania*, and to
our satiric young Hebrew the enthusiastic professor
seemed to "seek in old German forests those virtues
which he missed in modern drawing-rooms."[3] Moreover, the same Heine, in a less playful mood, compares the *Germania* with Madame de Staël's book
De L'Allemagne, and thinks the former "a satire on
Rome."[4] Are we, then, to regard this study of the
Germans as partly an idyl and partly a political pam-
phlet? Is it a Roman "Utopia"? There may be
some justice in this conclusion. One recent writer
has based it upon a critical study of the method employed by Tacitus, and shows, or tries to show, that

---

[1] In Kemble's *Horæ Ferales*, pp. 1–35, and especially p. 47.
[2] *Religion der europäischen Culturvölker*, p. 120.
[3] Heine, "Works," Hoffman und Campe, 1885, Vol. 13, p. 49.
[4] Heine, *Die Romantische Schule*, "Works," Vol. 7, p. 158.

in the arrangement and description of the different
races of Germany,[1] the Roman historian was governed
mainly by the idea of artistic grouping and picturesque
effect.[2] Much of this claim may be granted.   True,
so great an authority as Waitz insists[3] that Tacitus
wrote purely as a historian, and not as a moralist.
But we may concede something to the artist in Tacitus. It is likely enough that he cared more for his
coloring and contrasts than for the accuracy of his
line. He paints the Chatti ferocious to a fault, the
Chauci full of the fruits of peace. But granted that
he purposely arranges his models, and here or there
exaggerates their peculiarities, no one can doubt that
the group as a whole is true to nature. His chief
sources of information were the works of Sallust,
Cæsar, Livy, and Pliny the Elder, in addition to the
reports of officers and soldiers who had served in
Germany. It is hardly likely that Tacitus saw much
with his own eyes ; but as politician and office-holder
he had many indirect opportunities of studying his
subject. After the fiercest possible light has beaten
for centuries upon his work, the author of the *Germania* is hailed by modern criticism as a keen observer
and an accurate historian.

The name " German " has given rise to a great deal
of discussion. It seems to be of Celtic origin, and
may mean either "neighbors" or "those who shout
in battle." Tacitus explains it to be of late origin

---

[1] *Germ.* XXVI.-XLIV.

[2] G. Kettner, *Die Composition des ethnographischen Teils der Germania*, in Pfeiffer's "Germania," Vol. 19, pp. 257-274.

[3] *Verfassungsgeschichte*, 3d ed. I. p. 22. Where we find special
pleading in Tacitus, it is of a noble sort, like the fine outburst in Cap.
XXXVII.

and due to the fact that a tribe, in his day called
" Tungri," but earlier known as " Germani," crossing
the Rhine and driving away the Gauls, had brought
it about that the name of a single tribe was extended
to all the race.[1] It is reasonable enough that a race
should get its name from abroad. Jacob Grimm
remarks [2] that names of tribes, like names of human
beings, are given to them by others: " the need is
greater to name a third person than to name ourselves." Still, the Germans had a sense of relationship, even if they lacked " solidarity." [3] Long afterwards, they called their own tongue " belonging to
the people," — in Anglo-Saxon, *theodisc*, as opposed
to " Welsh," the talk " of the stranger." It was long
a favorite gibe with Englishmen that the fiends in hell
spoke this latter language ; and from a passage in the
Anglo-Saxon Life of St. Guthlac (in prose), down to
Hotspur's remark : " Now I perceive the devil under-
stands Welsh," this notion held both in jest and in
earnest. Dunbar, the Scottish poet, refines the fun
a little by making even the devil rebel against the
hideous Gælic of his followers.[4] To this day, Germans call Italy " Wälschland." The names of the
different tribes or clans were gentile, sprung from the
family system.[5]

[1] *Germ.* II., a much disputed passage, but clear in the fact, if not
in the reason for the fact. The best recent summary of criticism is by
Müllenhoff, *Deutsche Alterthumskunde*, II. 198 f. See also Baumstark, *Germania*, 100 ff.

[2] *Geschichte d. deutschen Sprache* (henceforth *G. D. S.*), p. 108.

[3] A fine defence of it in Grimm's *G. D. S.* p. 792.

[4] See his famous *Dance of the Seven Deadly Sins*, in Schipper's
beautiful edition, now appearing in Vienna, Part II. p. 133, and note.

[5] Stubbs, *Const. Hist. England*, I. 38. Compare further Birmingham, Walsingham, etc., also the names of tribes in the Wîdsîð Lay.

How much territory the Germans occupied in the
first century of our era is stated with sufficient clear-
ness by Tacitus. "Germany as a whole,"—that is,
Greater Germany, east of the Rhine, not the Gallic
provinces called Germania, — "is sundered from
Gaul, Rhætia, and Pannonia by the rivers Rhine and
Danube, from Sarmatia and Dacia by mutual fear
or by the mountains: the rest is bounded by Ocean,
which flows around broad peninsulas and huge
islands." [1] In this description it suited the political
purposes of Tacitus, so conjectures Müllenhoff,[2] to
leave Germany practically unlimited in at least one
direction; else the Vistula would have been given as
a boundary. Moreover, for artistic reasons it may
be, Noricum is also omitted from the contiguous
countries. Still, the general facts are clear enough.

Within the territory named, Tacitus informs us,
the population of Germany may be divided into three
groups: the Ingævones (or Ingvæones) who lived
nearest the ocean; the middle race of Herminones;
and in the south the Istævones (or Istvæones).
Pliny adds another group, the Hilleviones; these
Zeuss assigns to Scandinavia.[3] The fact that these
three continental tribes have names which are bound
together by rhyme — so-called "alliteration"—in the
well known Germanic fashion,[4] makes their genuine
character extremely probable. The traditions which
held together each of these groups were probably of

---

[1] He seems to think North Germany full of islands, and long after
his time Scandinavia itself passed for the greatest of them.

[2] *D. A.* II. 3 f.

[3] *Germ.* II.; Zeuss, *Die Deutschen u. die Nachbarstämme*, p. 77.

[4] Hengist and Horsa; Heorogâr, Hröðgâr, and Hâlga in *Béowulf;*
Gunther, Gîselher, and Gêrnôt in the *Nibelungen Lay*, and others.

a religious nature, and were retained in a common cult.[1] The Ingævones, our own ancestors, held Ingvas as father and founder of our race; and we find Ing mentioned, seemingly as a god, in the Anglo-Saxon *Runic Poem*. Ermanas and Istvas were similarly the founders of their respective clans. The three names, if we may follow Müllenhoff's interpretation,[2] mean "He who is come," "The exalted one," "He who is desired and honored." In ancient song, says Tacitus, our forefathers record (*celebrant*) these three as sons of Mannus, the original man, himself son of Tuisto, whom Tacitus calls "a god born of the earth," *deum terra editum*. In this way the clans about the North Sea and along the Cimbrian peninsula, though hardly a united political body, felt a close tie of kinship. It was emphatically a sea-loving race, — Frisians, Angles, Jutes, Saxons: these are our forefathers, together, it is probable, with a few of the Danes. It is significant enough that Saxons, Danes, and Normans made the three conquests of Britain.

Let us glance a moment at the separate tribes of these three groups. In the first and second centuries after Christ,[3] the Saxons were settled on the right bank of the Elbe opposite the Chauci, with Reudigni and Anglii north of them and running well up into the peninsula. Southeast of the Saxons and east of the Langobardi were the Suevi-Semnones. Scandinavia was already settled by Germanic tribes. The Goths were still on the right bank of the Vistula,

---

[1] Waitz, *Verfassungsges.* I. 15, thinks the division was based on linguistic differences.

[2] *Haupt's Zeitschrift für deutsches Alterthum*, 23. 1 ff.

[3] See maps I. and II. at the end of Müllenhoff's *D. A.* II.; also Kiepert, *Alte Geographie*, p. 537 ff.

with Slavonic and other neighbors on the east and
northeast. Such was the situation in the earliest centuries of our era. Then came the great movement
of the tribes, which changed completely the positions
of many German nations; but Frisians, Angles, and
Saxons held their ground. The latter had long been
known as desperate pirates, — in fact, as early as the
second century. They gave the name to that "Saxon
Shore " of Britain, and made necessary the appoint-
ment of a *Comes Litoris Saxonici per Britanniam*, one
of the most important officials of the empire, with his
"nine strong castles dotted along the coast from
Yarmouth to Shoreham." [1] These Saxon pirates,
with their Frisian and Anglian neighbors, clung to
the coast, while the Goths were wandering from
the mouth of the Vistula to the shores of the Black
Sea, or while the Lombards made their slow way
to Italy.[2] The sea-myths of the latter tribe were
changed to suit an inland life; what was once an
ocean legend was forced to adapt itself to the tamer
scene of a river.[3] As our forefathers had been, so
they remained; and it was no new path they sought,
when, about the time that Attila was crushed upon
the Catalaunian plains, these heathen Germans were
"driving their foaming keels " over the North Sea
towards the coast of Britain, no longer pirates, but
invaders, conquerors, settlers. Nor need we assume

[1] Hodgkin, *Italy*, I. 228.

[2] Possibly the three families of Ingævones, Herminones, and Istævones failed to keep strict lines in this general movement. Possibly some
of the later groups, like Franks or Thuringians, may have been formed
from two of these divisions. See Arnold *Deutsche Urzeit.* p. 125.

[3] The story of Lamissio, Paul. Diac. 1, 15, and Müllenhoff, *Beovulf*,
pp. 10ff. But see Malone, *Amer. Journ. Philol.* XLVII (1926), 319ff.

any pressure from enemies at home, the Danes for example, as sending our forefathers into exile.[1] They were men of their hands, and had that love for fight and adventure, that habit of seeking war afar if they could not find it at their doors, which Tacitus records of the Germans at large. Indeed, the Ingævonic race is early known in history. The Romans had no more dangerous foes and no more valued allies than the men of this same strain. Thus the Frisians, to whom we are closely related, are first mentioned during the campaigns of Drusus; with the Batavians, they dwelt on the northwestern coast of Europe, near the mouth of the Rhine.[2] They threw off the Roman yoke and were free and unmolested until the year 47 A. D. Again they fought, and were enrolled against Rome in the revolt headed by Civilis.

The large and powerful tribe of the Chauci were also first known through the expedition of Drusus.[3] They lived on both sides of the Weser, where they were seen by the elder Pliny; they stretched over a large territory which, says Tacitus, "they not only hold, but fill (*implent*)." Huge of stature, bold of heart, sound in morals, they are praised extravagantly by Tacitus [4] as "the noblest race of the Germans"; they are self-contained, dignified, justice-loving, molesting no one, always maintaining honorable peace, but ready to rise in arms upon provocation, horse and foot in multitudes.[5] Pliny, however, Pliny the

---

[1] Müllenhoff, *Nordalbingische Studien*, I. 125.

[2] Zeuss, 136 ff.; Tacitus, *Ann.* IV. 72, 79.

[3] Zeuss, p. 139. Möller, *das altenglische Volksepos*, p. 86, thinks that Chauci settled in Kent and Northumbria, and so play a decided part in our ancestral history.

[4] *Germ.* XXXV.   [5] Vellejus confirms Tacitus; see Zeuss, p. 140.

eye-witness, seems to have received a very different
impression. In his Natural History,[1] he tells us that
he saw them in their desolate swamps where ocean
claimed almost as much right as the earth itself,
forcing the miserable inhabitants to seek such high
places as can save them from the tide. "There a
wretched race of men must seek refuge on the hil-
locks or in dwellings laboriously raised above the
highest known tides. When the water covers their
neighborhood (at high tide), they are like sailors;
when it recedes, they are like shipwrecked folk. The
fish going out with the tide are caught close by the
huts. These people have no herds as their neighbors
have, and do not live on milk; nor do they hunt wild
beasts. For fish-nets they braid ropes of sedge and
swamp-grass. For fuel they use peat. . . . They
have no drink save rain-water caught in a trench
about the houses." Then Pliny adds his rhetoric
and his compliment. "Enamoured of their barbarism," he exclaims, "these men actually declare that
if they were to be conquered to-day by the Roman
people, they would call it slavery!" But evidently,
as Zeuss points out, Pliny is here, quite as much as
Tacitus, the seeker after rhetorical and artistic effect.
One wishes to emphasize the virtues of the people;
the other is bent upon a completely dreary picture of
the land and the climate.

The Saxons, whom we must not too quickly con-
fuse with the great nation which Charlemagne so for-
cibly converted to Christianity in the ninth century,
are first named by the geographer Ptolemy.[2] He
means the separate tribe which afterwards helped so

[1] XVI. 1.   [2] Zeuss, p. 150.

much to conquer and settle England. They were not only pirates; a land-expedition which they sent against the Roman province provoked the description of them as "a race who live in the trackless coastlands and swamps of ocean, and are terrible for bravery and agility." They were seated at the foot of the peninsula and by the mouth of the Elbe. Next to them were the Anglians; the traditions of this old home held long in England, and there seems no good reason to doubt the truth of Beda's statements.[1] The Anglians lived in what is now Schleswig.[2] The Jutes lived in modern Jutland and must have been close neighbors of the Danes.

We have laid more stress upon the Ingævonic tribes because they were beyond question the founders of our so-called Anglo-Saxon race. In the middle parts of Germany, however, were the Herminones, Suevi, Hermunduri, Chatti, and Cherusci: out of these tribes, not without mixings and shiftings, emerge the later Thuringians and Franks.[3] Other minor divisions are given by Pliny and Tacitus. It should be mentioned tnat philologists have divided the Germanic race into three broad groups, — the North, East, and West - Germanic. The first two include Scandinavian and Gothic; the last High and Low German, — Low German naturally covering the Ingævonic tribes.

[1] References in Zeuss, p. 495 ff.   [2] Chadwick, *Origin*, p. 193.
[3] Waitz (*Verfs.* I. 14) says the Franks were Istævones; Simrock says Ingævones; Zeuss (p. 80) as in our text.

CHAPTER II

LAND AND PEOPLE

The German in Germany — His former home — Inherited and
actual culture — Country and climate — Pastures, flocks, and
herds — Nomad or farmer ? — Boundaries.

IN a district bounded by the Elbe and the Oder,
north of the mountain ranges, and protected by the
vast forest of Southern Germany, Germans had grown
into a peculiar race, a *gens tantum sui similis*.[1] But
it is improbable that they were original inhabitants
of the land. Their forefathers must have broken,
centuries before the time of Tacitus,[2] from that mysterious East which has sent out wave after wave of
western conquest; and must have driven away, or
possibly enslaved, the primitive tribes which held the
land. No legends, no dim traditions even, seem to
have survived from this remote epoch to tell the story
of the conquest or keep memorial of an older home.[3]
Dahn, indeed, suggests that some vague recollection
of conquest may lurk in those legends of a dwarfish
folk which fled from men and sought refuge in the

---

[1] *Germ.* IV.; Müllenhoff, *D. A.* V. 1.

[2] Müllenhoff is inclined to place this date as early as the entry of
Greeks and Italians upon their respective peninsulas.

[3] " Ohne Zweifel hielten sie sich für Autochthonen."   Müllenhoff,
Schmidt's *Allgem. Zeitschr. für Geschichte*, VIII. 216.

crevices of rock and field and moor, — in other words, an indigenous race, smaller and darker than the Germans.[1] Grimm is more poetical than clear when he speaks of rumors, still faintly pulsing (*nachzucken*) among all Germanic races, of primitive emigration out of Asia, rumors that connect themselves with the legends of Alexander, of Priam and Æneas, and furnish to mediæval tradition the origins of British tribes.[2] But this is extremely uncertain. The tribes which our forefathers drove before them may have been such as the Finns, a hunting folk low enough in the scale of civilization, who " had neither wool, salt, nor wagons with wheels, and could not count to one hundred." [3]

Where the Germans parted from their Aryan kinsmen; where, moreover, all the Aryan race once dwelt, and whence the various families set out, — these are questions which bid fair to be long discussed and very late decided. The general assumption has pointed to Asiatic origin and a mainly westward course of Aryan conquest; but against such a view decided protest was made some time ago by Dr. Latham and Benfey, and lately by Canon Isaac Taylor and Professor Sayce.[4] As rivals to the

---

[1] *Bausteine*, I. 285. [2] *G. D. S.* 520. [3] Hehn, p. 18.

[4] The isolated German attacks of Penka and others became a general advance at the meeting of the British Association in 1887. In addition to the philological arguments, Huxley has thrown the weight of biological research into the scale for a European origin of the Aryans. (See *Nineteenth Century* for November, 1890: "The Aryan Question and Prehistoric Man.") His arguments arrive at much the same conclusion (see p. 766) as that reached by Dr. Latham. The best book on the subject is Dr. Otto Schrader's *Sprachvergleichung und Urgeschichte*, now accessible in an English translation by F. B. Jevons, 1890. Dr. Schrader collects the material and gives a fair summary of the arguments advanced in opposition to the old belief.

old table-lands of Asia, may be mentioned the country north of the Black Sea, modern Germany itself,
and Scandinavia. Indeed (limiting the question to
our own race), in the older generation of Germanists
there were men like P. A. Munch, the historian of
Norway, and Wilhelm Wackernagel, who believed
that our ancestors came out of Scandinavia down
upon the continent and drove the Celts before
them.

A candid critic is forced to admit that the whole
question hangs in the air, belongs to a time quite
beyond the reach of investigation, and probably will
never be settled. If there is any drift of argument
to decide the matter after we have looked at such
results as Hehn has given us, it is in favor of Asia.[1]

Easier to answer is the question of inherited culture, brought by the Germans from their earliest
home. The absurd practice long prevailed of col-
lecting all facts of culture which could be found in
older Sanskrit literature, applying these first to the
primitive Aryans, and then, by easy implication, forcing them bodily upon the early Germans. Victor
Hehn has done something to check these unbridled
imaginings, and he is sustained by such an emi-
nent philological authority as Professor Johannes

---

[1] A vivid and plausible sketch of the Aryan invasion of Europe is
given by Hehn in his monograph, *Das Salz*, p. 21 f. Referring to the
argument for an Asiatic origin which is based on the character of
domesticated animals and cultivated plants, Huxley, in the article
quoted above, says (p. 768): "But even that argument does not necessarily take us beyond the limit of southeastern Europe; and it needs
reconsideration in view of the changes of physical geography and of
climate." For our own purposes in the following pages, which have
nothing to do with origins of the Aryan race, Hehn's conclusions have
abiding value.

Schmidt.[1] In the first place let us take the primitive
Aryans, the parent stock of our race. What culture
had they as common dower for all the members of
the family, as one after another left the early home?
Conservative inference from the facts of philology
assures us that the primitive Aryan was on a higher
plane of civilization than the North American Indian.
The Aryan was no longer a mere hunter; he knew
horses and cattle, though the latter were used mainly
for the yoke. The dog was already domesticated;
but, oddly enough, the cat, most domestic of animals,
was not known to the household until modern times.[2]
The Aryan plucked — not sheared — the wool of
sheep and braided from it a sort of felt; for he did
not as yet know how to weave. He knew the use of
barley, but had little or no regular agriculture; for
the use of wild grains can be assumed where there is
no attempt to plant and cultivate. Flesh was eaten,
though probably the Aryan had no salt.[3] Milk was
a favorite, and butter; while out of honey was made
a fermented liquor, — mead. Houses, wagons, boats,
and swords were common. The state was organized
on the basis of the kin, and there were some beginnings of a legal system. The decimal system had
been invented for counting, and time was reckoned
by the moon, "the measurer"; hence the habit of

[1] In his lectures on Comparative Philology, as well as in his special
works. See also Hehn³, pp. 14 ff.

[2] Hehn³, p. 463. Against the assertion that the Romans did not have
the domesticated cat, see Thomas Wright, *Womankind in Western
Europe*, p. 18.

[3] Races still without use of salt are mentioned by Hehn, *Das Salz*,
p. 16. Hehn thinks the Aryans first found salt in the neighborhood of
the Caspian Sea.

our ancestors to count by nights (as in " fortnight ")
rather than by days.

Above this stage of culture we need not fancy the
Germans of Tacitus very far advanced; nor, on the
other hand, must we picture them below it.   Philology insists that the words brought from a common
Aryan vocabulary represent things and thoughts
brought from a common Aryan life.   Moreover, it is
well worth noting that the conclusions of archæolo-
gists, especially those of the north, make Scandinavia
emerge from the stone age about 1500 B.C.; place the
bronze age, with considerable culture evinced by its
relics, from that date until 500 B.C.; and from this
point date the iron age.   For the time of Tacitus,
therefore, savagery cannot be assumed of the Germanic races, unless we believe that some great revolu-
tion or invasion, some social cataclysm which washed
away one race and floated in another, made a breach
with the past.   It might be alleged to suit this theory that graves of the later bronze age do not contain
so many or so fine objects as the earlier burial-places,
and rarely have weapons in them.[1]   But the burning
of bodies, which came in about this time in place of
the older and simpler burial, may account for the
change; and, again, we have the hard facts of philology.   Montelius says that Southern Scandinavia
three thousand years ago had a civilization like that
described in the Homeric poems.

In the time of Cæsar and Tacitus, Germany was
covered with dense forests.   Pomponius Mela, who,

---

[1] Montelius, *Civilization of Sweden in Heathen Times*, transl.
Woods, p. 86. Some recent authorities put an age of copper between
stone and bronze.

in the reign of Claudius, wrote a sort of geography, tells us that the land was crossed by many rivers, rough with many mountains, and for the most part impassable because of woods and swamps.[1] Swamp and forest, while they held back German culture, made mightily for German independence. Without these vast and dangerous reaches of woodland and morass, the military skill of Drusus would doubtless have conquered Germany as the genius of Cæsar conquered Gaul; for Gaul had been no wilderness, and in some branches of agriculture had given lessons to the farmers and gardeners of Rome. But Germany was one vast forest, broken by swamp or meadow, with here and there a stretch of open land: nothing about it was likely to attract an Italian. " Who," cries Tacitus, " would leave Asia or Africa or Italy to come to Germany, with its desert aspect, its harsh climate, its lack of cultivation, — a dreary world!" The German swamps are often mentioned, and abounded particularly in the north; what difficulties they made for the Roman soldier may be read in the nervous Latin of Tacitus.[2] Quicksands were plentiful enough. Jordanes, the historian of the Goths, tells, in his fourth chapter, a legend of the early wanderings of his race. They had come to Scythia,[3] drawn by fruitful soil; and as they were crossing a bridge it broke, and numbers of them perished, not only in the stream but in the *tremulis paludibus* on both sides. With a touch evidently taken from old song about the tragedy, Jordanes adds that even in his time voices of cattle could be

[1] Pomp. Mela, *de situ Orbis*, III. 3. [2] For example, *Ann.* I. 63.
[3] Probably we are to think of Lithuania as the scene.

heard there, and forms of human beings could be seen. How swamp and fen and moor must have abounded in the low country northwards by the sea, the land of our Ingævonic forefathers! In their myths we find many allusions to these moors. The coast-line of northwestern Europe has changed since those days; where now is firm land was then a maze of islands, inlets, and marshes.[1] The epic of *Béowulf* deals largely with a demon of swamp and seaside; and even if, with Uhland and Laistner, we regard this monster as a fog-demon, he rises from the waters. Ingævonic poetry seldom wanders far from the scent of brine and dash of waves.

The winters were keen and long. True, the "harsh climate" of Tacitus would be echoed by a modern Italian; but swamp and forest of that day made the winter far more severe than it is now: there was more ice and snow, more fog and rain. Like land, like people. The genius of Germanic poetry is tragic, and is fain to sing the fall of empire, such as the ruin of the Burgundian house, or the collapse of Theodoric's great kingdom. But back of the tragedy lies the melancholy temperament, and back of this the gloomy world in which our forefathers dwelt. Their song echoes to a homelier note of sorrow, — to hunger and cold, howl of wolf, grinding of ice, exile and misery of friendless men, bitter toil on a wintry ocean; such is the shadow to which a fierceness of delight in battle and slaughter makes the only contrast. So far as Germanic fancy pictured an underworld of sorrow and gloom, — not, of course, of pain

[1] Müllenhoff, *Nordalbingische Studien*, I. p. 117: "Die deutschen Völker an Nord- und Ostsee in ältester Zeit."

or of punishment, — it was a world of cold and cheerless waters : a " water-hell," men have named it. In the Old English ballad of Thomas the Rymer, or Thomas of Ercildoune, we hear of these chill and gloomy waters. Thomas is led away to Elfin Land by the Elfin Lady : —

> Scho ledde him in at Eldonehill
> Undirnethe a derne lee,
> Whare it was dirke als mydnyght myrke
> And ever *water till his knee.*
>
> The montenans of dayes three
> He herd bot *swoghynge of the flode ;*
> At the laste, — *etc.*[1]

Scandinavian poetry would yield us a plenty of similar examples.

These swamps, these vast and sullen forests, made the German of fitful and passionate temper, savage, inclined to gloom or to unchecked revelry. The *furor Teutonicus* was no fiction. Yet the German loved his forest; and trees are everywhere near to his heart.[2] The grove was his temple, with dark and horrid rites that suited the scene; the dead were often buried under trees, as in old Hebrew days when Rebecca's nurse, Deborah, is said to have been buried under an oak, afterwards called " the oak of weeping " ;[3] and the boundaries of estate or mark were designated by some tree, as oak, ash, beech, thorn, elder, lime, and birch.[4] These sacred trees long continued to be a source of anxiety to the

---

[1] *Thomas of Ercildoune,* ed. Brandl, p. 83 f.

[2] See Mannhardt, *Baumkultus der Germanen,* which brings together a great mass of material.

[3] Genesis xxxv. 8.   [4] Kemble, *Saxons in England,* I. 52.

authorities of the church, and one was cut down by
the apostle of Germany, St. Boniface.   Under a tree
was held the old Folk-Moot, the primitive court and
local assembly;[1] and the Westphalian descendant of
these older courts, the famous *Vehmgericht*, not only
held its sessions under such a sacred shadow, but
hanged the victims of its process " on the nearest
convenient tree," after the manner of early Germanic
executions.[2]   The peasant still loves to plant trees
about his home, and in olden days the tree itself was
centre and prop of the house; even in our prosaic
America,[3] one can often tell from far away where
the different farm-houses stand, simply by the groups
of tall pine trees that cluster about each home.   Of
the German forests, however, we find here and there
such a picturesque periphrase as " where the squirrel
leaps for miles from tree to tree."[4]   The oak tree
was the dearest; and it has held its royalty.   It
gave acorns to the swine; and where game was
scarce and other food exhausted, the same humble
fruit kept life in man himself.   Later times inquire carefully about the ownership of acorns which
drop into a neighbor's ground.[5]   Next to the oak
stood the beech, and these two are " noble " trees;[6]
although the ash often took high rank in Anglo-
Saxon days.   The later English ballads preserve traditions of their sanctity.

[1] G. L. Gomme, *Primitive Folk-Moots*, passim.

[2] " Proditores et transfugas arboribus suspendunt. . . ."   Tac. *Germ*.
XII.

[3] Especially in New Jersey.

[4] J. Grimm, *Rechtsalterthümer* (henceforth, *R. A.*), p. 497.

[5] J. Grimm, *R. A.* 550.

[6] *R. A.* 506; *Mythologie*,[4] p. 540 ff.

Glasgerryon swore *a full great othe,*
By oake and ashe and thorne :
" Lady I was never in your chamber
Sith the time that I was borne." [1]

Punishments for injuring trees were inconceivably
harsh; and beheading is among the milder penalties.[2]
Fallen into disuse in historic times, — we find no
examples recorded of the worse punishments, — these
old laws were, nevertheless, once part and parcel of
the system and were doubtless rigidly enforced.

Inhabitants of such a land must have been more
nomadic than agricultural; but, although marsh and
forest predominated, Germany was not without fertile fields and a rude system of farming. We read
in Tacitus of good farming land offered as an induce-
ment for German tribes to make peace with Rome.
The proportion of cultivated fields to pasture and
woodland might perhaps serve as a test of civilization; and Arnold calls the German now a " nomad-
farmer," now a " farmer-nomad." Again, the bronze
sickles and the hand-mills found in graves show that
tillage was known in Sweden previous to the fifth
century before Christ.[3] Cæsar, to be sure, discovered
very little which testified of agriculture among the
Germans; but Tacitus mentions it in more favorable
terms. The increase of population acts on a nomadic
race as a stimulus to further wanderings; but when
Roman barriers threw the Germans back upon themselves, there was natural demand for some steadier
supply of food, and they learned to till the soil. The
Angles, Saxons, and Jutes, once settled in the fertile

[1] Child, Ballads,[2] III. 138: *Glasgerion*, stanza 18.   [2] *R. A.* 518 ff.
[3] Montelius, work quoted, p. 71. See also Waitz, *Verfassungsges.*
I. 16.

fields of Britain, became as outright farmers as were ever seen. Nevertheless, nomadic instincts were very strong with the German, and, on the Continent at least, he put his chief trust in flocks and herds. The German pastures were famous. Among the Ingævonic tribes especially, swine must have been raised in great numbers, and, though of an inferior breed, doubtless were a prime source of food.[1] The horse was raised or hunted, not for modern reasons, nor yet for the milk of the mares,[2] but for its flesh. Like the oak, horses had a sacred association, and were among the noblest offerings that could be rendered to the gods. White horses were used for divination,[3] and the color still remains a mark of royal ownership. Modern anthropology is inclined to associate the prominence of the horse for sacrifice with its prominence as an article of food.[4] Certainly the eating of horse flesh at feasts and celebrations was a practice which the church in Germany opposed as strenuously as possible, and drove out only after a long and hard struggle. About the year 732 Pope Gregory III wrote as follows to the Anglo-Saxon Saint Boniface in Germany: "Thou hast allowed a few to eat the flesh of wild horses, and many to eat the flesh of tame ones. From now on, holy brother, permit this on no account." Perhaps, hints Hehn,[5] the apostle of the Germans

---

[1] Tacitus does not mention them. See Hehn, p. 16; Waitz, I. 36.

[2] "Das melken der Stuten ist bei reinen Germanen nie Brauch gewesen." Hehn, p. 45.

[3] Tac. *Germ.* X.: "candidi et nullo mortali opere contacti."

[4] Lippert, *Culturgeschichte*, I. 160.

[5] *Culturpfl.* p. 22. The church also forbade the eating of storks, beavers, and hares. Cæsar says, in Britain *leporem et gallinam et anserem gustare non fas putant* — sign of sacred associations. Hehn, p. 337.

had been thus liberal because the custom was known to him in his native England, while it seemed but abomination to the Italian. The horse was cared for in droves and was watched by herdsmen. In the Old Saxon *Héliand*, a paraphrase of the gospels made early in the ninth century, the "shepherds" of the original become in Germanic rendering *ehuskalkôs*, horse-servants, who were not watching their flocks by night, but rather were guarding their horses.[1] Down to the year 1000, horse flesh was eaten in Germany; and in Poland horses were objects of the chase as late as the seventeenth century. It must be noted, however, that certain rock-pictures of the Scandinavian bronze age show the horse in regular cavalry combats; and it was doubtless used for riding, not hauling, in the earliest Germanic times.

Cattle came later than horses, and at first were used mainly for the yoke. As with the horses, which were neither fleet nor handsome, and with sheep, Tacitus notes in German cattle an inferior breed; and he points out the lack of that *gloria frontis*, the stately horns of an Italian herd. A German commentator on Tacitus murmurs in a note that the short-horns probably gave much better milk! In the year 225 of our era enormous herds of cattle are reported as covering Germany. It is a characteristic trait of nomadic times that cattle might be honorably stolen from a neighboring tribe, provided it was done openly, — just as wood might be cut and hauled away if the act was accompanied by noise and shouting. The mortality of cattle in those days must

[1] Pointed out by Vilmar in his excellent little work, *Deutsche Altertümer im Héliand*.

have been enormous: with all modern resources, a severe winter kills thousands upon our western plains, and it was infinitely worse with the Germans.

As in the case of oak tree and of horse, cattle, which entered so closely into the life of the Germans, were connected with sacrifice and rites of worship. Kemble [1] sees signs of a cult of this sort in the fact that bones of oxen and cows, as well as of horses, have been found in divers Germanic graves. He also notices the cows which drew the wagon of Nerthus, chief goddess of the Ingævonic race, and the oxen yoked to the chariot of the Merovingian kings. Cattle were of course supremely important to the nomadic Aryan. One thinks of the great part played by the cow in Sanskrit literature, of the heavenly cattle, more or less frequent in all Aryan mythology, and of the customs which we can easily revive for our imagination from such fossils as the Latin "pecunia" or the English "fee." The clouds, those fascinating objects for early myth-makers and modern myth-mongers, are represented as horses, ships, swans, — but most of all as cows, which are milked by Indra or our own Thunar.[2] There was a "holy cow, first-born of all things," in Hindu myths; and the cow remained, for the whole race, chief synonym of good. In Scandinavian cosmogony, a cow appears on the scene at the earliest possible moment; and we even hear of a certain Swedish king who was wont to take a cow with him into battle. Good reason for all this. Alive, cattle gave milk and drew loads; dead, they were useful in many ways, — flesh for food, skin for

[1] *Horæ Ferales*, p. 68.
[2] So interprets Mannhardt, *Germanische Mythen*, p. 1 ff. and p. 37, n.

clothing, sinews for bowstrings, horns for cups, bone
for needles and tools.[1] Even to-day, proverbial wisdom insists that there is "nothing like leather," and
leather is palpably a weaker avatar of the holy cow
herself.

Fowls and bees are not unknown to nomadic life;
and they were common with our forefathers. Of
fowls we meet geese, ducks, and chickens. Pliny
tells of the famous German goose-feathers, highly
valued for bed-coverings in Rome, and fetching enormous prices; though we are reminded that such use
of feathers for stuffing cushions and pillows was not
originally Roman, but borrowed from Gaul and Germany.[2] Geese were even kept as pets, and we have
a case recorded where they sympathize audibly with
the grief of their mistress : —

> Lamented Gudrun, Giuki's daughter,
> so that tears flowed . . .
> clamor'd answer geese in courtyard,
> beautiful fowls the fair one owned.[3]

As for the bee, its industry did something more
than point a moral for our ancestors and provide an
occasional luxury. It furnished them with fermented
liquor; while honey itself was prized far beyond any
standard of modern times. This is true of nearly all
nomadic races, and at first concerns only the wild
honey; later there sprang up a regular bee-culture.
In Slavonic lands, we can trace for a long while the
custom of paying taxes and tribute in honey; in Iceland, wax was used for the same purpose.[4] The old

---

[1] Hehn³, p. 14.   [2] Hehn³, p. 372.
[3] *Edda*, 2d ed. G. Neckel (Heidelberg, 1928), *Guðrúnarkv.*, 1. 16.
[4] Weinhold, *Altnordisches Leben*, p. 89.

laws were very strict and minute in their treatment
of property in bees, particularly the right to mark
and keep a tree in which the insects have taken quarters, — evidently nomadic jurisprudence:[1] a fine
was imposed on him who took the bees from such a
marked tree, " de arbore signato in silva alterius apes
tulerit." If the tree had no mark, no fine could be
levied.[2] In the Anglo-Saxon " Rectitudines Singularum Personarum," we find the functions of the bee-
churl, *béo-ceorl*, clearly defined; among others, he is
to pay so much tax in honey.[3] He is evidently an
important personage, and much in demand. In that
priceless account of the voyages of Ohthere and
Wulfstan which English King Alfred added to his
translation of Orosius' *Historia aduersum Paganos*
we have Wulfstan's description of the Esthonians (*i.e.*
the Old Prussians) as follows: " And there is very
much honey and fishing; and the king and the richest men drink mares' milk (the fermented liquor);
poor folk and slaves drink mead. . . . And there is
no ale brewed among the Esthonians, but there is
mead a plenty." Alfred's own people used honey in
all cases where later times employ sugar.[4] The older
Anglo-Saxons drank mead galore; their chief building was the " mead-hall." Indeed, as late as the reign
of William the Conqueror, a very large proportion of
the products of the country, as shown by Domesday

[1] Grimm, *R. A.* 596 ff. Agricultural races, of course, raise barley
and hops, and soon turn to beer-brewing.

[2] Homeyer, *Haus und Hofmarken*, p. 10.

[3] Fr. Liebermann, *Gesetze der Angelsachsen*, I, 448. Moreover, we
have the "bee-thief". In Alfred's Laws (Liebermann, I, 54) three
special thieves are named, — of gold, of horses, and of bees.

[4] Cockayne, *Leechdoms, Wortcunning, and Starcraft*, II. p. ix.

Book, consisted in honey, used chiefly for the making of mead.[1] There is a question in the *Demaundes Joyous*, printed after the French by Wynkyn de Worde in 1511, and quoted by Kemble in his *Salamon and Saturnus*:[2] "Whiche is the moost profytable beest and that man eteth leest of? — This is bees." Finally, bees passed into religion and superstition. He that kills a bee is the devil's own. Bees speak to one another, and understand what is said to them.[3] We "tell the bees" of a house-owner's death; and in old times people added a humble request that the bees would kindly remain with their new master. In Westphalia, they sing on such an occasion : —

> Ime, dîn här es dot,
> verlått mi nit in mîner not!

> Bee, thy lord is dead :
> forsake me not in my need !

When the bride was led to her new house, a similar rite was performed : —

> Imen in, imen ut,
> hir es de junge brut;
> imen üm, imen an,
> hir es de junge mann :
> imekes, verlått se nit
> wenn se nu mal kinner kritt !

That is, "Here is the bride and here is the groom; good bees, don't leave them when the children come." One of our old bits of English poetry is a charm to prevent bees from deserting their home.[4] They are

---

[1] T. Wright, *Domestic Manners*, etc., p. 91.   [2] p. 287.
[3] Wuttke, *Deutscher Aberglaube*, p. 109.
[4] Grein, *Bibl. d. ags. Poesie*,[2] I. 319 f.

called *sigewif*, a name of the Valkyrias, "victory-women," and are evidently not far from active myth. Like the cow, honey is a precious thing among the Germanic (or at least, the Scandinavian) gods. It is the main ingredient of their drink; it is connected with the origin of poetry, their gift to men; and Grimm reminds us that, in like manner, Grecian fable made bees carry to Pindar — or any other convenient poet — the divine gift of song.[1]

All these things point very strongly to a nomadic existence; but there was, nevertheless, a certain amount of farming practised even by the Germans known to Cæsar and Tacitus. We need not in our haste hand them over to barbarism or savagery.[2] Guizot, in his *Histoire de la Civilisation de la France*, assumes that our forefathers were savages outright, and he prints along with the *Germania* parallel passages describing American Indians and other equally barbarous races.[3] Aside from positive evidence to the contrary, we may reasonably object to this view, as confounding what the Germans call *Uncultur* and *Vorcultur*. The former is the state of tribes which never come to anything better than a raw clanship and remain mere hordes; the latter is the note of those races which are passing through the clan-stage to higher forms of national life.[4] The Germans of Tacitus are a developing, ardent, ambitious race, destined soon to become a dominant race. They undoubtedly had more or less agriculture; and this

---

[1] *Deutsche Mythologie*[4] (henceforth, *D. M.*), p. 579.

[2] A. Lang, *Myth, Ritual, and Religion*, I. 222, calls the society of the Germans of Tacitus "a higher barbarism," like that of the Scythians of Herodotus.

[3] See Waitz, I. 32.   [4] Dahn, *Bausteine*, II. 77.

is perhaps the best standard of civilization, seeing that it marks definite advances from the merely nomadic state. Agriculture among the earliest Germans has left ample proof at least of the beginnings of its existence. In the first place, we have Cæsar's account, derived from his contact with a warlike and aggressive tribe. He says the Germans do not care much for farming, since they depend for food mainly upon milk, cheese, and flesh of animals.[1] They have no individual farms, — but he goes on to tell how they cultivate their fields. Moreover, he tells us that Germanic tribes, Usipites and Tencteri, crossed the Rhine with a great mass of men, in the year 55 B.C., driven out of their homes by the Suevi, *who hindered them in their farming (agricultura prohibebantur)*. Again, Cæsar tells of Germans who went into Belgium on account of the fertile land there, and this "in ancient times." He himself burns the villages and destroys the crops of the Sigambri.[2] What the warriors whom Cæsar met would think and say of such a peaceful pursuit as farming, appeared to the Italian almost a denial of the fact. Farming was entirely a matter for slaves and women, not in any way the freeman's business. By the time of Tacitus, — and he had doubtless better information than Cæsar could elicit in the hurry of a campaign, — farming is a more important subject.[3] The description given in the twenty-sixth chapter of the *Germania* is unfortunately so brief and obscure as

---

[1] *Bell. Gall.* VI. 22. See also IV. 1.   [2] *B. G.* IV. 19.

[3] Grimm, *G. D. S.*[3] 16, believes that the Germans were mainly nomads (not, of course, savages) when they first appeared in history, but admits the beginnings of agriculture.

to remain one of the favorite skirmish-grounds of a work that furnishes opportunity for battle in almost every page. But whatever the real method of Germanic agriculture as the Roman here describes it, there is no doubt at all about the fact; there was a respectable amount of farming carried on in Germany when Tacitus wrote his book. Land, however, was plentiful, and pastures were probably much in excess of cultivated fields.

Moreover, we have older evidence, not so direct, indeed, but of a very convincing character. The best writers on Scandinavian antiquities find it probable that in the later stone age agriculture was known and practised; while for the bronze age the same assertion is made with absolute certainty. Rock-pictures of that time show scenes from the farmer's life with plough and oxen; and grain has been found in the graves.[1] Not so sure a witness is the allegory of Germanic myth; and yet, if Müllenhoff's brilliant interpretation be correct, the prelude of our own great epic, *Béowulf*, tells in mythical language the story of agricultural beginnings among our far-off ancestors by the North and Baltic seas.[2] The Anglo-Saxon kings boasted descent from Woden, the chief divinity of the Germanic race in the time of Tacitus; but the genealogies go even farther back than Woden. The remotest ancestor that appears in any of them is Scéaf;[3] for Anglo-Saxons he seems to have been the type of the oldest times, the most

---

[1] Kålund, Paul's *Grundriss*², III, 408.

[2] First developed in *Haupt's Zeitschrift*, VII. 410 ff.; then in the book *Beovulf*, printed after Müllenhoff's death.

[3] Grimm, *D. M.* III. 386. See also Müllenhoff, *Beovulf*, p. 6.

ancient of all kings and heroes. The Saxon Chronicle, with the customary confusion of two religious systems, asserts that Scéaf was born in Noah's ark. An exquisite myth is told about him, standing in evident relation to those later romances and legends about the swan-knight which are most familiar to us in the story of Lohengrin.[1] In some Scandinavian country, or possibly in the old seat of the Angles on the Cimbrian peninsula,[2] a ship without oars or rudder drifted one day to land, its only freight a new-born boy lying asleep upon a *sheaf* of grain and surrounded with treasure and weapons. It was a kingless land, and the folk hailed this omen joyfully, named the boy Scéaf (sheaf), and brought him up to be their king. We shall see more of this legend when we come to speak of Germanic ship-burial;[3] for the present we are concerned with Müllenhoff's interpretation. "If we look closer at the legend," he tells us, "ship and sheaf must evidently mean navigation and agriculture, weapons and treasure are as much as war and kingship; and thus all four gifts point to the chief elements and foundations of civilization among the ancient Germans by the sea." Müllenhoff goes on with his *deus ille fuit;* but whatever the truth may be about Freyr and the rest, it certainly seems safe to believe that our heathen forefathers held traditions of a dim past in which the first shadowy figure is the "culture-hero," the benefactor of his race, who shows them how to till the

---

[1] *D. M.* III. 391.   [2] Müllenhoff, *Beovulf,* p. 6.

[3] The prelude of *Beowulf* is translated below, p. 324. To Scyld, the warlike king, has apparently been transferred the legend belonging to Sceaf, perhaps once an agricultural or vegetation diety. On Scyld see further the supplementary notes, p. 494 below.

soil. Moreover, the myth comes from a neighborhood
where heathendom held stubbornly for long centuries
after Southern Germany had been converted.   From
all this various evidence it seems clear that the early
Germans were, to a certain extent, farmers; they
sowed and tilled and reaped; but how much they
gathered into barns is a more difficult question.

We should like to know how far the idea of individual ownership of land had become fixed, and how far
a legal and executive system had taken the place of
mere paternal or patriarchal jurisdiction; for farming
means property, and property means law.   J. Grimm[1]
points out that a nomadic race is naturally most
interested in public or common lands, but farmers in
private and divided estates.   As we go back to the
beginnings of our institutions and laws, folk-land, as
the Anglo-Saxon terms run, grows more important
than book-land, — the mark or common than the
farm.   Uncultivated land is highly important to the
nomad; he looks to it for his hunting, his grazing,
and his bee-tracking.   For this reason, we hear so
much about the mark.   Moreover, land was very
plentiful; there was enough for everybody, as Tacitus expressly tells us.   It is likely that farming tracts
were occupied by small clans or families, and land
was assigned by lot to the individuals.   We thus
have farmsteads (*Einzelhöfe*), scattered about the
country as this or that locality invited settlement.[2]
With advancing need of land for agriculture came
the increased power of single leaders and princes,

[1] *R. A.* 495.
[2] *Germ.* XVI.: "colunt discreti ac diversi, ut fons, ut campus, ut
nemus placuit."

who doubtless took up by conquest, or otherwise, large
tracts of country and let them out to tenants under
conditions which varied according to the time and
the locality; the conditions grow more complicated,
step by step, until we come to mediæval Europe and
the full-blown feudal system. The individual ownership of land seems to have found earliest and sharpest development among the Anglo-Saxons; but on
the continent it was not unknown. To own land
came to be the test of one's gentle condition; and
some writers are fain to carry back this instinct to
the most primitive times. Waitz, for example, thinks
that the individual ownership of land measured the
amount of *wergild*, and formed the very foundation
of personal freedom.[1] On the other hand, Von Sybel
denies that primitive Germans had any interest whatever in separate ownership of land. Arnold, in a
more temperate spirit,[2] simply decreases the amount
of private holdings and increases the area of common
land, the further we penetrate into the Germanic
past. Permanent, settled ownership came into full
force, he thinks, about the fifth century.[3]

This vexed question is one that we may well leave
to the historian of our institutions. Philology and
literature, however, are not altogether silent on the
subject. The names of our popular fruits and vegetables show conclusively their origin in Italy;[4] and
the same holds true of the refinements of gardening
and the processes of the vineyard. But if the rude

---

[1] Work quoted, I. 126, 133.   [2] *Deutsche Urzeit*, p. 231.
[3] There is much literature on this subject. See, among other books,
Seebohm, *Primitive Village Community*, and D. W. Ross, *The Early
History of Land-Holding among the Germans*. Ross gives a host of
references.   [4] Hehn*, p. 501.

German had no such arts or resources as these, he
nevertheless very early learned the luxury of owning
land. The warrior who served his king was rewarded
not only by the arm-rings of gold or silver or bronze,
but by land. The young clansman of Béowulf,
Wiglaf by name, who has joined his prince struggling
alone against a dragon, is overwhelmed with shame
when he thinks of the benefits the old king has
heaped upon him. —

> He minded the property his prince had given him,
> wealthy seat of the Wægmunding line,
> and folk-rights that his father owned.[1]

where Professor Scherer interprets folk-right to mean
"share in the folk-land."[2]   This is, of course, open
to question; but in our two oldest Anglo-Saxon
poems, both of them based on quite heathen traditions, we have reference to the gift of land to a person
in reward for actual service.   Widsith, "the ideal
minstrel," says that he was with a king of the Goths
and had from this monarch a precious ring: —

> and this to Eadgils then I gave,
> my helmet-lord, — when home I fared, —
> to the lov'd one in pay for the land he gave me,
> my father's heritage. . . .[3]

The minstrels, however, seem to have held their
estates by an uncertain tenure.   That altogether
charming little poem which worthily heads the list
among the Anglo - Saxon lyrics, *Déors Lament*, tells

---

[1] *Béow.* 2606 ff.
[2] See H. M. Chadwick, *Studies on Anglo-Saxon Institutions* (Cambridge, Eng., 1905) for an interesting discussion of this passage.
[3] *Widsið,* 11. 92 ff.

in the first person how a singer comforts himself for
the loss of his position as court-minstrel. After enu-
merating some cases of particularly bad fortune taken
from German heroic legend, Wayland the Smith
coming first of all, Déor tells in the last stanza all
about his own plight: —

> — To say of myself the story now.
> I was singer erewhile to sons-of-Heoden,
> dear to my master, Déor my name.
> Lone were the winters my lord was kind;
> I was happy with clansmen; till Heorrenda now
> by grace of his lays has gained the land
> which the haven-of-heroes erewhile gave me.
> That he surmounted: so this may I!

Lastly, we may appeal to immemorial custom and
the poetry of our old laws. Primitive is the fashion
prescribed in oldest Germanic laws for one who should
take possession of a piece of land. It was done by
certain symbolic acts; one must break a branch from
some tree on the property, or set one's chair in the
midst of the field, or drive a wagon across it, or
kindle a fire upon it.[1]

In regard to the whole question of nomad or
farmer, it seems most probable that the German of
Tacitus was a nomad with the beginnings of agriculture, but also with a passion for warfare that threw
all his other tendencies into the shade. He was a
warrior: his nomadic traditions and his agricultural
instincts found no expression in his own acts, but
were left to slaves, captives, and women, the old
and the infirm.[2] His farm was mainly in pastures

---

[1] Grimm, *R. A.* 109.
[2] *Germ.* XV.: "delegata domus et penatium et agrorum cura femi-
nis senibusque et infirmissimo cuique ex familia."

with a few cultivated fields, in which he raised
barley, perhaps oats, and rye, — the latter in the
north, — and, of course, flax for his linen.

It makes against the theory of mere nomadic life
among the Germans that they were so careful about
their boundaries. The main boundary of a land,
called the " Mark " in German, and in English " March,"
mostly neutral and uninhabited, was generally a forest;
at any rate, the word meant both boundary and woods.
Marcomanni can be " men of the wood," or " men of
the border." [1] Or the boundary might be a moor,
a stretch of swamp, as would naturally happen in
North Germany and in parts of England. The lore
of metes and bounds is evidently of great antiquity
in Germanic law, and particularly with regard to the
smaller estates. Boundaries are fixed by many a
curious fashion; as far as the salmon swims up the
stream, where a certain shadow falls, as a bird flies,
or an egg rolls, or a hammer is thrown.[2] Later, but
still in primitive times, rude marks, often of a sacred
character, were cut into a tree.[3] As in classical lands,
these border marks and signs acquired a sacred character, and came into touch with myths. Perforated
stones, which the ancients seem to have held sacred,[4]
served as sign of the boundary; and so did the huge
mound which marked a grave. Nay, the gods themselves were thought to have laid out the boundaries
of land and land; for not only have we the general

---

[1] J. Grimm, *Grenzalterthümer*, Kleinere Schriften, II. 33.

[2] See Hoops' *Reallexikon* under "Hammerwurf" and von Amira,
Paul's *Grundriss*,[3] p. 123.

[3] " Notæ in arboribus, quas decurias vocant. . . ." Homeyer, p. 11.

[4] Grimm, *D. M.*[4] 976. A feeble child, people thought, would gain
strength if he were made to sit in one of these holes.

testimony of such a word for "god" as Anglo-Saxon
metod, measurer, but we find everywhere bold, irregular lines of rock, or huge, isolated stones, standing
in some connection with the devil, — behind whom,
remarks Grimm, there lurks an ancient god. Such a
devil's wall the modern tourist of the Harz Mountains
may still see in the neighborhood of Blankenburg.
The Scandinavian Thor had to do with boundaries.
Often the border-line was marked by a place of worship and sacrifice; and since any legal punishment in
those days could be regarded as the offering to an
offended deity, it is quite evident why a criminal
should be punished "on the border."   Kemble[1]
refers to the well-known case in our Anglo-Saxon
poem, *Juliana*. This saint and martyr is led "to
the borders of the land, to that place where the stern
ones determined in their hatred to behead her."[2]
Other-sacred traditions of the boundary-places are
collected by Grimm in his essay on *Grenzalterthümer*.
Duels, ordeals, trials by combat, took place at the
border, or on an island, — whence was derived the
Old-Norse name for such a duel, *holmgang*. Equally
romantic and far more peaceful customs, such as
wedding or betrothal, may also have been observed
upon the boundary; certainly it was custom for a
prince to receive his bride on the frontier of the
realm, as witness *Gudrun :* —

> In fair and noble fashion they met the lovely maid
> At the border of two kingdoms. . . .[3]

Nothing, however, testifies so clearly to the anxiety
with which the German regarded the preservation of

[1] *Saxons*, I. 49, note.   [2] *Jul.* 635.   [3] *Kudrun*, ed. Bartsch, 13.

boundaries, as his excessive punishment for violating
them. The severity of these penalties reminds us of
the laws about wilful injury done to a tree ; and
where the power of earthly law was brought to an
end by the death of the offender, superstition took
up the tale and told of many a wretch whose ghost
haunted in this or that painful fashion the place where
he had done his evil deed. It is perhaps not altogether
accidental that in a bit of Danish popular tradition
the punishment for this offence is the old Germanic
horror of cold and freezing. Strande's wife had
helped her husband move a boundary-stone ; and now
she is dead and haunts the place each night, and is
heard crying pitifully to her husband — his punishment may be even worse — "O Strande, I'm freezing!"[1] Reaching down into modern times is the
custom prescribed for a new purchaser of land, for
an heir, or even for the king who has just obtained
his throne. From all of these, custom demanded a
formal inspection of bounds and borders ; as is so
often the case, even comedy and farce seize at last
upon a grave tradition, and we hear of villagers
whipping their children at the border of the hamlet
in order that this important boundary may be indelibly impressed upon the memory of future townsmen.
In fine, we conclude from all this mass of boundary-
lore that the desire to have and hold a settled territory is Germanic instinct, is original, and needed no
importing.

[1] Thiele, *Danmarks Folkesagn*, II. 126.

CHAPTER III

MEN AND WOMEN

Stature and features — A fair-haired race — Sense of personal beauty — Food and drink — Habits of daily life — Clothing — Adornments.

WE have long enough discussed the Germanic type; let us look at the individual German, his personal appearance, his home, the habits of his private and public life. About his bigness but one tale is told, from Cæsar, Quintilian, and Tacitus, down to the writers of the dying empire; all agree that he was huge of stature. To the small but wiry Roman this unspoiled son of the woods seemed a veritable giant. Even as late as Senlac, the Saxon is larger and taller than the Norman, whose Germanic blood had been crossed with a Gallic strain;[1] and for the earlier period, skeletons seven feet in length bear similar witness. The race seems to have been pure, so that these bodily traits were shared by all its members;[2] while the rigors of life and climate worked together for a very strict survival of the fittest. Puny or undersized children, pronounced weaklings, were

[1] Freeman, *Norman Conquest*,[2] III. 480, note.
[2] *Germ.* IV. See also Huxley's article, already quoted, in *Nineteenth Century*, November, 1890, p. 756 ff. The skull is of the "long" variety.

either treated as we treat superfluous kittens, or else were thrust aside into the byways of household and menial labor.

The giant was no lolling, good-natured fellow; his huge frame was easily shaken by passion, and in the hour of rage or battle, his blue eyes flashed an uncanny fire.[1] Even the Gauls, says Cæsar, were dismayed by the wild glances of their neighbors across the Rhine. Hehn is inclined to think that this ferocity is inherent in the glance of all nomads; but it was a characteristic of the Scandinavian down to recent times, and was known among them as the snake in the eye, — *ormr i auga*. Svanhild was daughter of Gudrun and Sigurd, and had all the pride and fire such blood should bring. On a false charge of dishonor, she is condemned to be put under the feet of wild horses, that they may trample her to death; and it is done. "But when she looked up at them, the horses durst not tread upon her, and Bike [Bicci, Sibich, the treacherous counsellor of the king] had a sack drawn over her eyes . . . and so she ended her life."[2] It was easy for this fearful glance to attract a superstitious terror, and pass into the domain of spells and enchantments. We read that when a sorcerer was executed in Norway, it was customary to throw a sack over his head, for his dying glances might well be big with harm.[3]

---

[1] *Truces et cæruli oculi.* — *Germ.* IV. Plutarch (in *Marius,* XI) speaks of the Cimbrian eyes as "sky-blue." The blue eye and fair or ruddy hair were admired by the Hellenic race, and may have been their original type. Certainly their epithets for gods and goddesses bear out this view.

[2] P. E. Müller, *Sagabibliothek,* II. 83.

[3] Maurer, *Bekehrung d. norweg. Stammes z. Christenthume,* II. 119.

Huge of frame, blue of eye, — often one may fancy
it a keen, hard gray, — the German rounded out the
list of his blond attractions with golden or ruddy
hair. We are not to forget that he was a cavalier,
at least in his flowing locks; to be a roundhead was
to be a slave. This long hair was the German's conspicuous feature, for he used various means to heighten
its color, and we read of a Roman army in Gaul sur-
prising certain Germans who had been making a raid
in the provinces and were engaged in the amiable
occupation of hair-dyeing. The Roman leader, says
our chronicle,[1] found them by a river, "some bathing, some, after their custom, coloring the hair red,
and many engaged in riotous drinking." When
Caligula was fain to make his Roman subjects believe
that there were Germans among the captives whom he
led in triumph, he made certain Gauls dye their hair
red. Another emperor, Caracalla, went so far as to
wear a blond "German" wig; and it became fashion-
able for ladies in Rome to dye their hair with a peculiar
German soap imported for the purpose, — that from
Batavia was the favorite, said to have been made of
ashes mixed with goat's fat, — with which they obtained either a golden or a ruddy tint. Still better
was actual German hair, — blonde wigs, — which they
often affected.[2]

We have said that the German cherished his flowing hair; it was his outward and visible sign of freedom, a precious thing. The gift of a lock of one's
hair was a symbol of submission. Among the

---

[1] Ammianus Marcell. 27, II. 2. It was in the year 367.

[2] For the popularity of yellow hair in Rome, see Wright, *Womankind in Western Europe*, p. 11.

Frisians, men who took oath to anything touched hair or beard;[1] and a story quoted by Grimm tells how those who were about to be beheaded took measures to save from stain of blood their long golden hair. Possibly some faint echo of this tradition lingered with Sir Thomas More when on the scaffold he "moved his beard carefully from the block." Particularly the kings, the *reges criniti* of the Franks, were marked by flowing hair; and if this were lost, with it went the fact and chance of kingship. Paul the Deacon, in his history of the Lombards, tells a pretty tale about one of their princes. A hostile tribe had resolved to put to death all the adult Lombards, and three of the princes escape on fleet horses. A younger brother, Grimuald, they deem incapable of keeping himself so long in the saddle, and are about to kill him that he may not pass into slavery; but as the spear is lifted against him, the boy begins to weep, and crying, "Do not kill me! I can hold myself on horseback!" is spared, and rides away with his brethren. Nevertheless, he is overtaken by a foeman and is again in danger of death; but his enemy, impressed by the noble figure, the glittering eyes, and above all by the long blond waving hair, spares him, and leads him, still mounted, to the camp. But royal blood is in the boy's veins. He chafes at his disgrace; draws a short sword, "such as lads carry," splits his captor's head to the skull, rides off, and triumphantly rejoins his brethren.[2] The long locks were sign of

---

[1] Grimm, *R. A.* 147, 285.

[2] Paul Diac., *Langob.* IV. 37. Paul in IV. 22 describes the old fashion among his race as requiring neck and back of head to be shorn, and allowing the hair, parted in the middle, to fall over the cheeks down to the mouth.

freedom in woman as in man. *Fri-wîf loc-bore* — " free woman with curly or flowing hair " — is the phrase applied in an old Anglo-Saxon law.[1]

It needs not to add that Germanic complexions were blonde, to suit the hair and eyes. The type is seldom found in modern descendants, and was broken in England by intermarriage with the native population; however, "the much debated problem of the relations of Anglo-Saxon invaders to pre-existing populations is still very difficult to follow to any reasonable conclusion, but it is often argued that the very large amount of medium and dark-brown hair in British populations is a sign of survival of pre-Saxon elements.[2] In some parts of Scandinavia and in Saxony one can still find the " white girls and black bread." Recent German school-statistics[3] of one of these favored localities gave, out of 468,763 children, 317,444 who were " blonde," and 136,014 who were " brown." Andree, however, asserts[4] that to-day the majority of that great " white " race, the Aryans, whose career of conquest helped Spencer to draw the conclusion that white races are " habitually the dominant races " in the struggle for existence, have a dark complexion; among these white families, " does not the dark-haired type," asks Victor Hehn, " always conquer the blond?" How different is the story with our Germanic ancestors, or even among those early races whose modern representatives are uniformly

[1] Fr. Liebermann, *Gesetze der Angelsachsen*, I, 7, § 73. As for color, compare tne proper names "Fairfax" (fair-hair) and its opposite "Colfax". also "Halifax".

[2] *Encyc. Brit.* (14th ed.), VIII, 462c.

[3] See Richard Andree in the *Zst. f. Ethnologie*, 1878, p. 343.

[4] Ibid. p. 335 ff. See, moreover, an essay by the present author in the *Haverford College Studies*, I. 132 ff.

dark! For in Greece the gods, Eros, for example, were represented with golden hair, just as in our mediæval miracle plays and mysteries the sacred personages were always given golden hair and beards, and the angels wore "gold skins and wings." In the purely Germanic races gold and white are the aristocratic colors, and a Scandinavian legend[1] tells how god Heimdall, "whitest of the Æsir," wandering the green ways of earth under the name of Rîgr, begets in succession Thrall and Karl (Churl) and Jarl (Earl). Thrall's complexion was black, and he was straightway a hewer of wood and a drawer of water, worked afield, fed swine, dug peat. Karl the freeman tamed oxen, raised ᐟcrops, made ploughs, built houses and barns and wagons. One of his sons is named Smith, or the artisan; and he and all his breed are of a ruddy hue, and are like their favorite god, plain old Thor. Highest of all was Jarl; when he was born he was "swaddled in silk," "his hair was yellow,[2] his cheeks were rosy, his eyes were keen as a young serpent's"; and as his complexion, so also his callings were of another color than Karl's or Thrall's. He learned to brandish the shield, to wind the bowstring, to span the elm-bow, to fit the arrow, to hurl lance and spear, to egg on the hound and tame the stallion, to swing the sword, and swim through the sea. To match this aristo-

---

[1] *Rígspûla, Edda,* ed. G. Neckel, pp. 276 ff., transl., L. M. Hollander, *The Poetic Edda* (Austin, Texas, 192?), p. 140 and Vigfusson-Powell, *Corpus Poeticum Boreale* (hereafter *C. P. B.*), I, 234 ff.

[2] Meyer, *Altgerm. Poesie,* p. 209, without special references, says that the typical Germanic hero's hair is not "blonde" but "bräunlich." The "jugendkräftige Mann" whom we have met in description of Germanic heroes, is certainly "blonde."

cratic type of earth, we find Balder, darling of the
gods, "so fair to look upon that light streams from
him, and the whitest of all flowers [or grasses] is
likened to his eyelashes." [1] So the tradition passes
down into the ballads ; and what reader of these
abstracts and brief chronicles of old time does not
remember how all the knights and all the ladies
have fair skin and yellow hair ? Even Robin Hood
has "a milk-white side." Churlish dispositions crop
out in the dusky color of face or eyes or locks ; in
some versions of *The Twa Sisters*, "the younger sister is fair, and the older dark" to suit their characters : [2] —

> Ye was fair, and I was din (dun).

Dark complexion is a badge of low birth, and then
comes to be the note of undesirableness in English
feminine beauty. Again and again Shakspere returns to this theme in his sonnets about the "dark
lady," [3] that "woman colour'd ill," with "mourning
eyes " : —

> In the old age black was not counted fair,
> Or if it were, it bore not beauty's name. . . .

In a Scandinavian saga, twins of a dark complexion
are born to a certain queen, but her husband calls
them "hell-skins" and refuses to own them. [4] It is
prejudice of race, this passion for the blonde, — at
least in modern times; and we find the Arabian proverb just as scornful of fairness as the German could

---

[1] Prose Edda, *Gylfaginning*, XXII.   [2] Child, Ballads,[2] I. 120.
[3] See, especially, Sonnets 127, 130, 131, 132, 137, 141, 147, 150, 152.
[4] Here we meet the old notion, brought out in the Middle-English
Lai le Freine, that of twins one child must be illegitimate. See K.
Warnke, *Lais der Marie de France* (3 d ed., Halle, 1925), pp. cviff.

be of the brunette: "Ruddy of moustachio, blue of eye, and black of heart," which matches a phrase in our old friend the *Arabian Nights:* "Blue of eye and foul of face."[1] An international summary of the whole matter may be found in a proverb quoted by Uhland:[2] "Beware of a black German, a white Italian, a red Spaniard, and a Dutchman — of any color!" It would seem to run counter to this doctrine that we find in all Germanic nations, from about the year 1000 of our era, a decided prejudice against red hair. The Middle-English *Proverbs of Alfred* affirm the red man to be a rogue; while

> Alder-wood and red hair
> on good soil are rare,

is a proverb found in nearly every Germanic dialect.[3] To explain this we need not drag in honest old Thor by his red beard, — not even red-haired Loki, — nor appeal to the pictures of Judas Iscariot. It is the red which verges upon black, the dusky color that is meant, like those dull flames of hell which make darkness visible. The light, ruddy color, the golden red, has always a noble and gallant connotation; of such complexion and such hair was Kaiser Friedrich Barbarossa, or the West-Goth Theodoric II., who is described by Sidonius Apollinaris as having long and curly hair, snow-white teeth, and a skin colored like milk and flushed with manly red, — evidently a pattern of kings and Germans.[4] It is not all

---

[1] Transl. Sir R. Burton, IV. 192, and note.

[2] *Kleinere Schriften*, IV. 45.

[3] R. Andree, work quoted, p. 335 ff. All witches are red-haired; trolls and nixies tend the same way. See sufficient evidence in Rochholz, *Deutscher Glaube und Brauch*, II. 223 f.

[4] Rochholz, work quoted, II. 222.

rhetoric, again, when Sidonius, describing the wedding of a young Frankish prince, arrays him in glitter of gold, in flame of scarlet, in sheen of whitest silk, — but assures us that all these were easily peered by the gold of the flowing locks, and by the fairness and flush of the complexion.[1] Add to these florid graces the power to hold us by his glittering eye, and we have a kinsman of whom we need not be ashamed. Even after we have stript the rhetoric from the description, and the robes of civilization from the prince, after we have put him into a simple dress of skins, and a bit of linen, and thrust him back into his forest, there still remains a huge, keen-eyed, florid, yellow-haired person, impetuous, melancholy, cruel, passionate, fitful, with dreams of conquest, with longings dull and indefinite, with a contempt for civilization, and an eagerness to touch and keep some of its nobler elements, — a person, in short, whom no amount of ethnology is going to put on a par with the modern African savage.

How far the sense of personal beauty was developed, how far his "lassie wi' the lint-white locks" bewitched a Germanic youth with something higher than mere physical attraction, is a question not easy to answer. We must not inject too liberal a measure of romance into that old courtship; but yet there was surely something of the grace of love even in Germanic forests. Late as the myth may be, we feel sure

---

[1] In the ballad *Willie o' Winsbury*, Child,[2] IV. 399, we have a fine match for the older figure : —

> " But when he came the king before,
> He was clad o' the red silk,
> His hair was like to threeds o' gold,
> And his skin was as white as milk."

that when the Scandinavian god falls into utter love-
madness for his longing after Gerthr, whose "white
arms lightened all the sea and land," this was no
new viking invention, but had its prototype in the
passion of many an early warrior. *Béowulf* and
the epic fragments show in their phrases a monkish
abstinence when speaking of women: "gold-adorned,"
"fair-haired," "white," "fair," are the traditional
epithets. There is more sense for manly beauty
than for that of woman. In the one simile applied
to woman, which is found in our wreckage of Germanic poetry, she is compared with the sunbeam.[1]

Unromantic but useful is the query what this glittering and florid person had to eat. For in spite of
his gigantic frame, he lacked endurance, — not so
much the natural quality as that which is born of discipline, systematic campaigns, and regular supplies.
That he could bear cold better than heat, hunger
better than thirst, is natural criticism for an Italian;[2]
and Plutarch notes the advantage enjoyed in this
respect by the Romans in their fight with Cimbrians
at Vercellæ. No doubt, however, the uncertain
amount and kind of food helped to make the Germans less patient of fatigue. Often the larder must
have been bare, often filled to excess. Their feasts,
says Tacitus, while not of great variety and exquisite,
are yet abundant;[3] — and this is concession from a
Roman of the empire. They ate the flesh of wild or
half-tamed horses and of swine, with other kinds of
game, mostly fresh, — *recens fera*, says Tacitus,[4] — but
doubtless often dried or salted. Cæsar seems to have

---

[1] Meyer, *Altgerm. Poesie*, p. 112 f.   [2] *Germ.* IV.
[3] Ibid. XIV.   [4] Ibid. XXIII.

believed a decidedly indigestible story about the habits
of a German elk and the popular mode of snaring it.
He says [1] that it does not lie down, nor can it rise if
it has fallen ; but it takes its rest by leaning against
a tree. The hunter has simply to cut nearly through
such a tree and leave it standing apparently in its
usual case; the elk leans against it, overturns it, and
falls with it to the ground.

It must be admitted that these statements about
the German larder point to nomadic life and tend to
confirm the view of Jacob Grimm, who saw "nomad"
writ very large over primitive Germany. But it is
going too far to seize upon an assertion of Pomponius
Mela to the effect that our forefathers ate raw meat,[2]
and hastily assign them to outright savagery. For
they had milk, and probably butter and cheese ; [3] as
time went on, they used more and more meal, whether
baked in bread or eaten in a thick broth. In the earliest times they had nothing save wild fruits, apples,
of an ignoble sort, one may think, and berries. All
our modern fruits and vegetables came from Italy,
and brought their foreign names along with them.
Pytheas of Marseilles, already named as the earliest
visitor to our shores who came from classic land, said
that German tribes by the North Sea had hardly
any garden produce or domestic animals such as the
Greek knew, but that they lived on millet and other
plants, on roots and berries.[4] Perhaps the earliest
vegetable which the Germans imported from their

[1] *B. G.* VI. 27.

[2] " Victu ita asperi incultique ut cruda etiam carne vescantur."
Pomp. Mela, III. 3.

[3] *Lac concretum,* says *Germ.* XXIII., which may mean these, or
simply thickened milk.　　　　[4] Hehn, p. 122.

neighbors in Gaul was the leek, a plant, it would seem, of decidedly magical qualities. Thrown into one's mead, it was a safeguard against treachery;[1] and for whatever reason, when the great Helgi is born, his father comes back from battle with "a noble leek" for gift.[2] Even among the Anglo-Saxons there were few vegetables, and chief of these was the leek; a garden is called outright "leek-enclosure," *léac-tún*, and the gardener is "leek-ward."[3] A Danish ballad quoted by Professor Child[4] speaks of the happy land where all birds are cuckoos, all the grass is leeks, and all the streams run wine. There were, however, other Germanic vegetables. There was asparagus, or something very much like it; the radish, of extremely large size; and sweet turnips that were good enough to be imported for the express use of the Emperor Tiberius.[5]

Saxons and Frisians by the sea ate fish; and of course the Scandinavians did likewise. Montelius cites King Sigurd Syr, stepfather of St. Olaf, who gave his guests fish and milk one day, and meat and ale the next. In a lay of the Edda, old Thor, who represented the homely life of days before the vikings were in vogue, says that he has been eating "herring and oatmeal porridge."[6] Salt was valued highly, not

---

[1] *Sigrdrífomál*, 9 (ed. Neckel, p. 187): "and cast a leek in thy cup: (then know I that never thou needest fear that bale in thy beer there be)", Hollander, p. 276; also H. A. Bellows, *The Poetic Edda*, p. 392.

[2] *Helgakv. Hundingsb.*, I, 7; Hollander; p. 123; Bellows, p. 293.

[3] "Holitor (for Olitor) leacweard," Wright-Wülker, *Anglo-Saxon Glosses*, 416, 30. See also Wright, *Domestic Manners*, etc., p. 294.

[4] Ballads,[2] I. 89.

[5] See references in Wackernagel, *Kleinere Schriften*. I. 23.

[6] *Harbarðslióð*, 3: so Hollander, p. 86 and Bellows, p. 123: Neckel (Glossary) translates "*hafra*" "goat" instead of "oats".

only as the best of all seasonings, but also for its antiseptic qualities. It kept the hunter's game, the coast-folk's fish. In Anglo-Saxon larders, salt meat was very prominent, and hence, as Wright reminds us, arose the custom of boiling nearly all flesh that was eaten.[1] The Germans themselves seem to have had no skill in the preparation of salt, an art first developed by the Celts; but Germany was especially rich in salt-springs, and these were the cause of many a desperate fight between neighbor tribes struggling for possession. Pliny and Tacitus testify to the extremely rude fashion of salt-making among the Germans. It seems that they piled up logs in the neighborhood of such a spring, set them on fire, and then quenched the flames by liberal application of the salt water. When the fire was out, a crust of salt was found clinging to the embers.

Once more we see the close connection between a necessary or favorite article of food and the ceremonies of primitive religion. The salt-springs were places of worship, and a story told by Tacitus about the desperate war waged between Chatti and Hermunduri for the ownership of such a prize is of interest in many ways.[2] The Germans, we are assured, held the place holy, deemed it in the immediate neighborhood of heaven, and believed that prayers nowhere else were wafted so quickly to the gods, — gods by whose grace it came about that salt was formed whenever the waters of the spring were poured upon a heap of burning logs. In the time of Emperor Julian, several hundred years later, we find

[1] *Domestic Manners and Sentiments,* p. 26.
[2] Tac. *Ann.* XIII. 57.

Alamannians and Burgundians fighting for the same
sort of treasure.[1] In short, salt and its not particularly congruent rival, honey, were the main condi-
ments of the primitive German.

How far more rich was the store of an Anglo-
Saxon franklin! Even a modern epicure might not
be displeased with such a larder as Cockayne[2] has
discovered. The Germans who conquered Britain
did *not* "stuff their bellies with acorns," maintains
this lively editor; and the Saxon descendant knew
well how to live, as witness a bewildering array of
flesh and fish, with such side-lights as "oyster patties"
and "junkets," and minor meats galore. We have
testimony, a little later, about the boy's ordinary fare
in an Anglo-Saxon monastery, — "worts and eggs,
fish and cheese, butter and beans, and all clean
things." Flesh he rarely got.[3] But we cannot argue
back from all this into the German forests. Only
what seems sanctioned by an old tradition, or has
come in touch with cult, has any value of this sort.
For example, cheese enters into cult; even in modern
times it was thrown into a sacred well in Scotland,
hence called Cheesewell, by way of propitiation and
offering.[4] Frisians and Anglo-Saxons had an ordeal
called the *corsnæd*, in which a bit of bread and cheese
was put into the mouth of the accused; if he swallowed it, good; if he was choked, it was a sign
of guilt.[5] As for milk, we have the sacred cow

---

[1] Hehn, *Das Salz*, 31; Amm. Marc. 28. 5.

[2] See his *Leechdoms*, ii., vii. ff.

[3] Colloquy of Ælfric, in Wright-Wülker, *Glosses*, p. 102.

[4] Liebrecht, *Otia Imperialia*, p. 10.

[5] *R. A.* 931 f. Rochholz, *Deutscher Glaube und Brauch*, p. 12 ff., gives
a number of cases when cheese or milk formed the staple of a myth,
and hence belonged to the tradition of cult.

already noted, or the goat which in later Valhalla
belief feeds upon the branches of the World-Ash and
gives the milk of immortality to heroes of Odin.
Here, too, belongs butter. Hehn draws a geographical line between the realm of " beer and butter " and
the realm of wine and oil. According to Pliny's
Natural History,[1] the Germans " made out of milk
an article called butter, noblest food among barbarous races and one which sundered rich from poor."
Butter was even used as a sort of ointment, northern
pendant to the oil of southern lands. Milk and its
products were of supreme importance to the nomad;
no wonder that Scandinavian goat, German cow, and
Slavonic mare should loom out of the past in such
heroic proportions. With the herd there must be a
dog, and very properly we find a magnified and non-
natural dog barking fearfully as herald of Ragnarök,
the end of all things, in a late Scandinavian myth.[2]
The tradition of nomadic times pure and simple would
seem to be preserved in Beda's explanation of the
Anglo-Saxon name for the month of May, — " Three-
Milk-Month"; that is, says Beda, the month when
the cows (*pecora*) used to be milked three times a
day: " So great was the abundance which once
reigned in Britain and Germany."[3]

With butter, as soon as any of the necessary grain
can be raised, is ranged beer, which gradually takes
the place of mead, the original Aryan beverage. On
the subject of beer Hehn lavishes his learning with a

[1] XXVII, 133; Hehn³, pp. 158, 162.

[2] The Cimbrians had watch-dogs with them in Italy.

[3] "Talis enim erat quondam ubertas Britanniæ vel Germaniæ."
See also Grimm, *G. D. S.*³ 56 f. The extract is from Beda *de temporum
ratione*, Cap. XIII.

fond indulgence. Beer, as he tells us,[1] once held far wider sway than now; Egypt knew it, and Spain, and many a land which later bore only the olive and the grape. Pytheas of Marseilles found our ancestors drinking mead and beer; while among the Celts of Gaul beer was the common drink, and only the rich and great used wine. This was the case in England, and for even better reasons. In the colloquy just quoted, the master asks our monastery-boy what he drinks. "Ale [beer] if I have it, or water if I have no ale." "Don't you drink wine?" "I am not so rich as to buy me wine; and wine is not a drink for children or fools, but for old and wise people." The Emperor Julian made a satiric epigram in Greek on this custom of drinking beer, which in his day was so common with Gauls and Belgians.[2] For Germans, Tacitus bears ample testimony; but inasmuch as beer is inseparable from agriculture, we may argue not only that our ancestors of that time had taken some steps above the nomadic state, but also that beer could not have been their original drink.[3] In earliest times mead ruled alone. Grimm sees in the name of the English river Medway a trace of the nomadic beverage; Medway would be "mead-cup," and there would be the mythical and classical whim of a stream "flowing from the horn or urn of a river god."[4] Certain is the name of an Anglo-Saxon banquet-room; it is a "mead-hall," *medo-œrn*, where,

---

[1] Hehn⁸, pp. 144, 160.
[2] Cider also was used by the Gauls. Amm. Marc. XV, 12, 4
[3] There are traces of mead drinking in Greece previous to the epoch of wine. Hehn⁸, p. 152, approves the etymology of *beer* from *bibere* and *ale* from *oleum*, but neither is now accepted: see Schrader in Hehn⁸, pp. 160 ff.   [4] *G. D. S.*³, p. 457.

however, beer-drinking, *béor-þegu*, goes on, and the
ale-cup, *ealo-wǣge*, makes its round. Wine, of course,
came later to the Germans, and in the time of Tacitus
was bought now and then from Roman merchants on
the border, — no national drink.[1] Its origin is probably Semitic. We owe this race, along with the art
of crushing from grapes the sweet poison of misused
wine, the nobler gifts of measuring, of money, of
the alphabet, and of what Hehn calls the profound
abstraction, Monotheism,[2] — a heavy balance in favor
of the Orient! But let us return to our beer. Cæsar
does not mention it, nor Pliny; it was in its beginnings, like the parent art of agriculture; but Tacitus
speaks very distinctly, and opens his twenty-third
"chapter" as follows: "For drink they have a liquor
brought into some resemblance to wine by process of
fermentation [3] from barley or wheat." [4] He gives no
name for this liquor, but it is undoubtedly beer; and
the trick of making it must have been learned from
the Celts of the lower Rhine and the Danube.[5] But
it was not by any means modern beer, and Hehn
warns the enthusiastic German youth not to fancy
his remote ancestor indulging in such a beverage as
the Fatherland boasts to-day; for hops, a most important element, were not used in breweries until the
Middle Ages. Naturally we find beer in ceremonies
of Germanic religion. St. Columbanus, about the
year 600, surprised a group of Suevi who were sit-

---

[1] It was prohibited as imported ware among the Suevi, because it
made men soft and effeminate. Cæsar *B. G.* IV. 2.

[2] Hehn ", p. 71.

[3] In the original, one word, *corruptus*, over which there has been
much throwing about of brains.

[4] *Frumento :* wheat, or rye?   ' Hehn '. p. 151.

ting around a huge keg or vat[1] of beer, which they intended to offer to their god Woden; and later, as a more indirect sacrifice, we hear of tithes paid to the church in beer.

How much did the Germans drink? This parlous question is sufficiently answered by Tacitus. The German meals, he says, are frugal, but with regard to thirst, there is not the same temperance; and it is evident that these barbaric potations dismayed the moderate Roman. Much in the fashion of our familiar laments over the weakness of the Red Man, Tacitus bewails as a moralist and exults as a Roman that this German "is conquered as easily by his own vices as by foreign arms." But even immoderate drinking has its amenities; and civilization has witnessed as much excess as barbarism itself. How far the refinements which we easily see in the banquets of later Germanic races — those, for example, described in *Béowulf* — may be assumed for earlier times, is a matter of doubt. We find certain courtesies of feasting prescribed by law for the Anglo-Saxons. A Kentish law of the seventh century ordains that if any one shall take away another's stoup (*stéap*) or cup where men are peaceably drinking, let him pay *according to the old law* one shilling to the owner of the house, six shillings to the offended person, and twelve shillings to the king.[2] As Schmid points out, to remove a man's drinking-cup was a palpable insult, and would easily precipitate a quarrel among men who were wont to plead guilty to any charge sooner than to that of being pigeon-livered. The next laws

---

[1] " Vasque magnum quod vulgo *cupam* vocant." See *D. M.*[4] 45.
[2] Liebermann, I. 11, §§ 12, 13, 14.

impose a fine of one shilling, paid to the owner of a
house where people are drinking, upon him who
draws his arms in such a company, and twelve shillings to the king; and if the house (*flet*, really the
floor) be stained with blood, one must pay to the man
his *mundbyrd*, a fine varying according to the rank
of the person in question. The law of Ine, after
fixing penalties for several sorts of fighting, goes on
to say that if the quarrel begins at a banquet (*gebéor-
scipe*) or beer-drinking, and if one of the disputants
bears it all with patience, the other is to pay a fine of
thirty shillings.[1] In a law of Æthelred, of course
much later, the various breaches of decorum taper
down from the king's peace itself to the good order of
an alehouse; the fine for breaking the latter depends
on whether you kill your man, or simply wound him.[2]
All these laws testify to the Germanic habit of drinking, quarrelling, and fighting, with quarrelling proper
as a vanishing element in the situation; words soon
yielded to blows, and the German would rather strike
than revile. Holtzmann quotes very happily from
the Nibelungen Lay: —

> . . . How fits it heroes bold,
> Like a pack of women to quarrel and to scold?

Evidently there was a certain measure of safety, if
one could do it, in following the implied advice in
Ine's law about the man who bears all in patience.
To let the tongue wag was dangerous. In an Anglo-
Saxon poem on the *Fates of Men*,[3] we are told
that the sword shall slay many a man on the ale-

---

[1] Liebermann, I, 92, §§ 5, 6. [2] *Ibid.*, pp. 228, 229, § 1, 2. [3] vv. 48 ff.

bench, many an angry tippler heavy with wine; "he hath been too hasty with his tongue."

Still, the flyting was by no means unknown at these banquets. There seems to have been a sort of formal entertainment in which first one, then the other, would hurl smart but pointed remarks at the opponent, delicacy being no object. For swing and dash, an Old Norse poem known as *Lokasenna*, " The Flyting of Loki," takes easy precedence. Loki enters a hall where all the other gods and goddesses are assembled, demands drink, and passes the time of day with each deity in turn. The following, in Vigfusson and Powell's translation,[1] may serve as example : —

Byggvi. Be sure, if I had a heritage like Frey, the Ingowin, and such a seemly seat, I would pound thee to marrow, thou ill-omened crow, and maul thine every limb.

Loki. What is the tiny thing I see there wagging its tail, snuffling about (doglike)? Thou wilt be always at Frey's hearth, yapping at the quern.

Milder, but still forcible, is the flyting between Béowulf and Hunferth, which will be found below ;[2] while the language of the dialogue between Salomon and Saturn, and of the famous dispute between Soul and Body, may be termed parliamentary. Still another fruit of the banquet was the personal boast, — in Anglo-Saxon, *gilpcwide*, — the proclamation of one's

---

[1] C. P. B., I, 107: see Hollander, p. 115, Bellows, p. 165ff.

[2] See p. 114. For a vigorous aftergrowth of this style, see Dunbar's Flyting with Kennedy; as to influence of the French *jeu-parti*, see Schipper, *William Dunbar*, p. 64 f. Schipper, by the way, in his edition of Dunbar, pp. 141, 151, thinks there is little connection of development between Dunbar's flyting and these Germanic specimens. He assumes Celtic influence and French models.

own and singular virtues, together with vigorous re-
vilings of one's foe, and promises of deeds of valor
in the next fight.

Yet the outcome of revelry was not always of this
bellicose nature. In the frankness and brotherly con-
fidence begotten of their cups, the Germans opened
heart and mouth in council and discussed public
affairs. Reserve and suspicion were banished. When
they were sober again, they made a decision upon the
question which they had debated at their feast; and
thus, says Tacitus, in admiration of so excellent an
arrangement, "they deliberate at a time when con-
cealment and deception are out of the question, and
they come to a conclusion when mistakes are impossible."[1] He omits to note the probable interval of
repose, which may have done its good service as well
as the other factors; for Germanicus surprised the
Marsi after one of their great banquets, and the legions had easy work with a mass of prone and drowsy
warriors, — " drunken," as the historian calls them.[2]

The German did not simply eat and grow strong,
but he helped nature by exercise. He also understood
the value of baths, for sanitary if not for personal and
altruistic reasons. Races which wear fur or skins of
any sort, instead of linen or similar texture, are apt
to suffer from vermin to an almost incredible degree;
so that the story which follows may well come, as
Hehn remarks, from the sincerest depths of Germanic
consciousness. A certain king, in an Old Norse saga,

[1] *Germ.* XXII. The Rev. Mr. Sterne, in his *Tristram Shandy,* ap-
plauds this arrangement. Similar practices prevailed among the Persians, and with uncivilized races in South America.

[2] *Temulentos;* and they were "stratis etiam tum per cubilia prop-
terque mensas. . . ." Tac. *Ann.* I. 50.

catches a merman, and the latter lives among human beings long enough to know their ways. The king asks him what has pleased him best of all that he has seen. "Cold water," he answered, "for the eyes; flesh for the teeth; and linen for the body." [1] When the Germans took to linen, — which meant that they first learned to raise flax, — this must have mitigated their sufferings; but even linen could not entirely protect them from the pests, and hence a passion for bathing. The Cimbrians were bathing when they were surprised by the Romans at Aquæ Sextiæ. Warm baths were a great luxury; and in later times a German house had its bath-room, even among the less flourishing classes. In Iceland the warm springs were used eagerly for this purpose; and such natural baths were everywhere coveted property and caused many a sharp struggle for possession. The Goths were plundering Thrace, says Jordanes,[2] and found on their march certain warm springs; these stayed for a while their impetuous career, and they lingered "many days" to enjoy the luxury. Of course, as Jordanes tells us in this special case, there was always more or less medicinal and healing virtue ascribed to such a well and to the divinity which protected it.

From the Germanic bath we properly pass to the Germanic wardrobe. Linen has already been mentioned; but it is doubtful whether it formed part of the German's original clothing.[3] It was introduced,

---

[1] Helin², p. 182; Weinhold, *Altnordisches Leben*, p. 160.
[3] Traces of linen, however, are found by antiquaries in remains of the Scandinavian bronze age, along with proofs of agriculture. See Kälund, *Grundriss²*, III, 409, 410.		210.

however, very early in the historical period. Goths, Franks, and the rest come upon the stage dressed in linen as well as skins; "dirty linen and short skins" is the costume in which certain West-Goths make their appearance.[1] Wool, on the other hand, is of very ancient date as an element in our forefathers' clothing. A find, described by Montelius,[2] shows excellent woollen garments in use in Denmark during the bronze age, — that is, at least as early as 500 B.C. The outfit consists of a cap, a long mantle, and a sort of covering for the legs. Another find shows the clothing of a woman of the same period; it was much like the dress of the man, and was abundant in quantity. We even find nets for the hair.

With regard to the clothing of Germans in the time of Tacitus, there are two opinions. The *Germania* tells us that the common garment of the people was a mantle or cloak fastened by a buckle or even by a common thorn. Without other clothing (*cetera intecti*) they spend whole days by the fireside. The richest people are distinguished by a garment (*veste*), which is not worn loose, in the fashion of Sarmatia and Parthia, but rather clings to the figure and the limbs. Moreover, the Germans wear skins of wild beasts, paying more attention to selection and adornment, the further they are removed from Roman influences. The dress of the women is like that of the men; only the women are wont to wrap themselves in garments of linen, which they embroider with purple,[3] but use

[1] Hehn², p. 179.

[2] *Civilization of Sweden in Ancient Times*, trans. by Woods, 1888, p. 59 ff.

[3] As the commentators point out, this is not the Roman purple, but probably a native vegetable dye.

without sleeves, leaving bare the arms, the shoulders,
and the upper part of the breast. So far Tacitus.[1]
Pomponius Mela, the geographer, follows the instincts of his kind in making barbarism very barbarous indeed. Even in severe winter weather, he says,
the German men are clad in mantles,[2] or with the
bark of trees; and it is by exposure to cold that
they harden their huge frames. Boys go naked.[3]
Lastly, Cæsar and his Suevi may give evidence.
These warlike Germans are described in the usual
Roman fashion, as undisciplined and impetuous giants,
who in that cold climate go without any clothing
save skins, and these so small as to leave large portions of the body utterly bare.[4] Cæsar says the same
thing of the Germans as a race, — they wear skins
or aprons, which leave naked a large part of the
body.[5]

It must be admitted that these accounts make for
a very slender outfit of clothing. But Müllenhoff
enters the lists for a larger Germanic wardrobe.[6] In
the first place, he bids us look at the climate; it
demanded at least a sufficient undergarment made
of woollen or linen, together with a mantle or jacket.
Instead of understanding Tacitus to say that the
richest Germans are distinguished " by *a* garment "

[1] *Germ.* XVII.

[2] *Sagis:* the same word which Tacitus uses; probably made of thick
and rough woollen material.

[3] Pomp. Mela, III. 3: "qui habitant immanes sunt animis atque
corporibus et ad insitam feritatem vaste utraque exercent, bellando
animos, corpora assuetudine laborum, maxime frigoris. nudi agunt
antequam puberes sint, et longissima apud eos pueritia est. viri sagis
velantur aut libris arborum quamvis sæva hieme."

[4] Cæsar *B. G.* IV. 1.   [5] Ibid. VI. 21.

[6] In *Haupt's Zeitschrift*, X. 553 ff.

which fits closely to the figure, Müllenhoff would
read, "by *the* garment," and would make the rich-
ness and adornment of its material the test of its
wearer's rank.   That is, he would make not only the
sagum, but also the *vestis*, common to all Germans ;
whereas many commentators understand Tacitus to
mean that the rich have a peculiar kind of garment,
an exceptional garment.[1]   This view is borne out by
the testimony of Pomponius Mela, and of Cæsar, who
does not even mention the mantle.   On the other
hand, however, the complete woollen outfit found in
Denmark, later customs, and several other considerations, go to support the claim of Müllenhoff.   The
neighboring Gauls wore trousers and shoes, — Gallia
Bracata would be nearest Germany in these respects,
— and a northern climate would force some such habit
upon the nations.   Summer and winter would naturally make a difference, and Germans may have
showed themselves oftenest to Roman eyes in scanty
raiment, such as we know they affected for the hour
of battle.   Finally, the rhetorical impulses of the
most truthful and sober Roman would exaggerate
every difference of garb between the two races.   It
may well be true, remarks Müllenhoff, that a German warrior would sit whole days by his fire in such
an undress as Tacitus describes ; but it is not said
that he went thus out of doors.   Müllenhoff gives in
good faith a somewhat amusing illustration of the
ancestral habit drawn from the ways of a modern
German professor.   "Does not many a man," he
asks, "content himself, when he rises from bed, with
dressing-gown, one other garment, and slippers, and

[1] Baumstark, *Germania*, pp. 585, 592.

so work through the morning until he arrays himself to go out?"

The question seems to hinge on the *vestis* of Tacitus, — whether it was a general garment worn by
high and low, which differed in its making and material, or whether it was a "lending" of Gallic or
other culture, foreign to the Sabine austerity of a
true primitive German. It is not an easy question
to decide, and the doctors disagree radically. On
one of the triumphal columns in Rome, German
soldiers are represented in trousers and shoes, and,
for the rest, either in a short doublet or else naked
to the girdle. Of course they fought in scanty
clothing;[1] and Paul the Deacon even tells us of
a battle between his countrymen and the Heruli,
where the latter went into the fight with nothing
but a cloth about the loins, "either to fight more
freely or else to show contempt for wounds ": the
explanation however, would seem to make this uniform an unusual one. Children at play wore little
clothing; witness Pomponius Mela above, and Tacitus
with his *nudi ac sordidi*, "naked and dirty."

Even if we take the description of Tacitus, much as
it leaves to be desired, for an authentic description of
the Germanic dress, we may fancy at least a noble or
wealthy freeman of that time in woollen *sagum*, or
cloak, woollen, or perhaps now and then linen undergarment, something like trousers, and his inevitable
arms. We may safely add shoes, made out of leather
which was tanned with the aid of bark. Clothing
was made chiefly by the women, who span and wove
steadily through the long German winter; for Egypt

[1] Tac. *Hist.* II. 22.

is the only country of old times where men did the weaving.[1] German women had great skill in this art, and may well have taken pride in the raiment of their sires and husbands, and indeed in their own garb. The priestesses who came with the Cimbrians to Italy had white robes, with a girdle, and mantles of fine linen. Men whose wives and daughters are famous websters and spinsters — Pliny waxes fairly enthusiastic on this subject — could not have been like African savages, and would hardly have gone naked for the sake of enduring the cold. A Danish variation of "carrying coals to Newcastle" is "to give white bread to a baker's boy"; and surely it is the same thing when we assert that foreign culture had to bring the merest beginnings of raiment to a race whose women were experts in weaving and spinning! The tradition held. Charlemagne, who clung to the old Frankish dress, made his daughters learn to spin and weave. Even in the time of Tacitus, rent or tribute from slave to master was often paid in clothing.[2] This, too, is hardly characteristic of the naked savage.

We may conclude our brief description of Germanic dress, just as we began it, with a notice of some garments found in a bog not far from the old home of the Angles on the Cimbrian peninsula. These clothes were in a good state of preservation, and seem to date from about the year 300 A.D.[3] They probably belonged to a wealthy man, and consist of two mantles of a square piece of woollen cloth (the *sagum* of

[1] Lippert, *Culturgeschichte*, I. 173.   [2] *Germ*. XXV.
[3] Weinhold, *Deutsche Frauen*,[2] II. 221. His description is taken from the Danish; the articles themselves are in the museum at Kiel.

Tacitus), with fringe one side and frogged on the other, and originally green in hue. There was also a coat of woollen, with sleeves of stronger material than the rest; of still heavier material were the two pairs of long trousers, to which stockings were sewed fast. There was a place for the belt. Further, there were leather sandals with attempt at ornamentation. Not unlike this fashion was the garb of those Hengists and Horsas, who, not simply "in 449," but many long years before, were wont to take ship for the tempting shores of Britain.

It is a well-known fact in ethnology that the custom of wearing clothes springs in the first instance not from the sense of decency, and hardly from the desire of warmth, but from the passion for adornment. Ornaments were familiar to our remotest ancestors. In the stone age of Scandinavia, more than a thousand years before the beginning of our era, men and women had an abundant supply of this aid to individuality, — which some philosopher has discovered to be the cause of personal adornment, — mainly articles made of amber. Some centuries later, in the bronze age of the same country, amber has yielded to metal, and rings, buckles, buttons, combs, and the like, are found in great profusion.[1] The yet later Germans were not without such adornments. Many articles, thinks the sanguine Waitz,[2] were of domestic manufacture; but the greater part were taken as booty or obtained in the way of barter. Gold, in the historic period, was furnished by the Byzantine coins sent to Goths on the Danube, and thence by the old trade-

1 Kålund, *Grundriss*², III, 410.
2 *Verfassungsges.* I. 21, note.

route through Poland to the Vistula, and so to the
Baltic Sea; and this tribute-gold may have been
worked into rings and collars by the domestic smiths.
Perhaps, however, the jewellers of Byzantium sent
actual ornaments to their northern trade, and half-
breed bagmen may have wheedled into purchase
many a chieftain and many a matron of the German
forests.[1] Like weapons, the old Germanic ornaments
had a pedigree, and in the poetry of the day are
called "work of giants," "the making of old days,"
"heirlooms of price." In *Béowulf*, the Danish king
says that he has settled a feud by paying tribute to
the enemy, —

> To the Wylfings sent, o'er the water-ridges,
> olden treasure . . .[2]

and at the end of the same epic we are told that the
hoard, watched by a dragon and concealed in a cave,
consists of —

> heirlooms old . . .
> dearest treasure . . .[3]

This mystery and this antiquity which hedge about
Germanic treasure would seem to indicate that most
of it was bought or stolen, and the making of it no
common and palpable affair, to be seen in any goldsmith's shop. The same sense of mystery induced
the poets of Christian days to talk of "heathen
gold," which had come down from the olden time.
As to the value of these ornaments in the regard of
their owners, we have the sequence of Florus, "horses,

---

[1] See also Montelius, work quoted, p. 126 f.
[2] *Béow.* 472.   [3] Ibid. 2233 ff.

cattle, and necklaces," as the summary of German
spoils made by Drusus.

Nearly all the metals seem to have been known,
but neither gold nor silver was mined by the natives;
and hence the lack of costly plate. When Tacitus
tells us that his Germans care no more for silver than
for common earthen vessels, we may certainly assume
a rhetorical rebuke meant for the Roman collectors
of such ware at fabulous prices, — German simplicity
once more a foil to imperial prodigality. Massive
articles made of the precious metals, such as those
silver vases which the historian mentions as now and
then seen in Germany, would hardly appeal to native
taste; but ornaments of these metals, as well as of
amber and glass, were freely worn by men and women.
The conventional adjective of the minstrel, when he
sings about dames of high degree, is " gold-decked,"
"gold-laden"; such is Hrothgar's queen in *Béowulf*,
and such is even the Hebrew Judith, whom the Anglo-
Saxon poet calls " adorned with rings." But the
men by no means despised such decoration, especially
kings and chieftains, who are called " gold-givers "
and " ring-breakers " from their habit of wearing upon
the arm spirals of gold, which they were wont to break
off and bestow upon a valiant clansman. Neck-rings
of massive gold — the so-called " snake-rings " — were
the rarest and costliest of these treasures, arm-rings
and finger-rings the commonest; besides, we find in
the graves necklaces, clasps for mantles, buckles, and
so on, made of gold, of silver, and of a mixture of
the two metals. Perhaps the spirals are best represented in the museums of Europe; for not only the
warrior but the singer was rewarded by these rings,

and sang the bounty of his patron from tribe to tribe.
Widsith, the ideal minstrel of early Anglo-Saxon
times, tells us : —

> And from the Burgundians got I a ring;
> there Guthhere gave me glittering treasure
> in pay for my song, — no puny king![1]

Ælfwine, too (Alboin), is generous to the minstrel,
and Ermanric gives him another ring, which he spends
for land, only to have gift of yet another from his
gracious queen : —

> Thus moved her fame thro' many lands,
> whenever chanced I was charged to say
> where under heaven I'd heard of the best
> gold-deckt queen her gifts dividing.[2]

" To have gift of red rings," as Weinhold remarks,
sounds much better than to draw wages or to take
money; but it was all the same thing. The love of
these rings was as keen as the love of money nowadays, and the appetite increased with what it fed
upon. The Chatti, who regarded the wearing of
rings as a sign of slavery, make, if the story which
Tacitus tells[3] be true, an exception. It was a franker
and more childish love of gold than our modern and
tempered affection, in days when we have so many
people to tell us of the vanity of riches. For instance,
in the Hildebrand Lay — that solitary bit of jetsam
from the wreck of strictly German heroic poetry — a
chieftain returning home after years of exile finds on
the border of his land the son whom he left an infant
in the cradle, now a warrior in arms. The son insists

---

[1] *Widsið*, 65 ff.   [2] Ibid. 99 ff.   [3] *Germ.* XXXI.

upon fighting his father, whom he deems to be an impostor, and the old hero expostulates in vain. When, finally, all persuasion fails, the sire appeals to the last infirmity of barbaric mind, and offers his arm-rings : —

> Unwound from arm winding rings
> of Kaisergold wrought. . . .

In fact, plenty of this treasure and a good wife — with flocks and herds enough, *bien entendu* — made up the domestic ideal of the German. Says Giant Thrym in the Edda, waiting impatiently for the arrival of his bride: "Golden-horned cattle go about in my yard, all-black oxen. . . . I have plenty of jewels and plenty of rings, — I lack nothing but Freyja !" [1]

Finally, as in so many cases, the thing dear and desirable to man is lovely in the sight of the gods. Rings occur in cult and in myth. In the rites of Scandinavian heathendom, an oath was sworn upon the holy ring of the altar; [2] it was smeared with blood of the sacrifice, and was worn on the hand of the chieftain at all assemblies of the people. In the myths, we find Odin taking oath upon a ring. An interesting case is mentioned by Maurer, [3] where the vikings in England during King Alfred's reign solemnly swear to leave the country. They take oath first upon the arm-ring, and then upon the Christian

---

[1] *Þrymskv.* 22 ff.; see *C.P.B.*, I, 179, Hollander, p.125, Bellows'p. 180.

[2] Maurer, *Bekehrung d. Norweg. Stämme*, II. 221; and II. 190, note; Grimm, *R. A.* 895 f.; Vigfusson and Powell, *C. P. B.* 1, 422 ff. The ring was of gold or silver, and weighed from two to twenty ounces.

[3] Work quoted, I. 68. Maurer notes that only Asser and Florence of Worcester mention the relics. See also *Anglo-Saxon Chronicle, anno* 876.

relics. Our usual "magnified and non-natural" ring is also forthcoming in the pretty Scandinavian myth — allusions to it occur in Anglo-Saxon poetry — of the necklace belonging to the goddess Freyja (or Frija), made for her by the dwarfish smiths of the hillside.[1] Grimm compares it with the necklace, and even the cestus of Venus ;[2] and the interpreters are ready with a host of explanations, — grass, crops, twilight, stars, what not. Our main interest lies in the fact that old Germans, like old Greeks, gave a necklace to their goddess of love. We may conclude the subject with a bit of Germanic paraphrase. The translator of the gospels who made the Old-Saxon *Hêliand*, with the passage before him: "Cast not your pearls before swine," puts it as follows : "Ye shall not hang your pearls on the neck of swine, the treasure of jewels, *the holy necklace*," — and this last alliterative expression, *hêlag halsmeni*, Vilmar counts as a bit of the old heathendom.[3]

[1] See Fr. Klaeber, *Beowulf* (2d ed., Boston, 1928), p. 172 and notes.
[2] *D. M⁴*, p. 255.
[3] *Heliand*, 4th ed., M. Heyne, v. 1724, and Vilmar, *Altertümer im Heliand*.

CHAPTER IV

THE HOME

Hatred of cities — Underground dwellings — Houses wooden and frail — Construction, and later improvements — The *burg*, and the hall — Descriptions in *Béowulf* — Banquet, songs, flyting, etc. — Amusements and vices — Hunting — The primitive house compared with modern dwellings.

WE pass to the Germanic house. The nomad has little need of cities, which are indeed a good index of civilization, if one bears in mind Aristotle's definition of man as "a political being," a being with gregarious instincts. Cities, we know, the German could not brook; his nomadic instincts were too strong, and these hated walls of stone, which so often set a limit to his raid and kept him from his booty, were but the *munimenta servitii*, ramparts and refuge of slaves.[1] Such confinement, cried a German orator, robs even wild beasts of their courage. Indeed, the city is in every way offspring and lover of peace. It is interesting, as Leo points out,[2] to note that among all Germanic races, the names of towns have no warlike reference such as we find in the names of people. Towns are named after races and families (Canterbury, Birmingham), or even after trees, stones, and natural

---

[1] Tac. *Hist.* IV. 64.
[2] *Rectitudines Singularum Personarum*, p. 14.

peculiarities. Not till he became at least in part a
man of peace, did the German build his towns. Such
cities as he took from his enemies were given over to
plunder, and then left to crumble away in neglect.
So fared the Roman towns of Britain at the hands of
our invading forefathers.[1]

When actual German towns are mentioned as the
seat of chieftain or king, nothing is to be understood
which could compare with the Roman city, — only a
cluster of wooden houses, convenient place for the
assembly of tribes or clans. Such may have been
Mattium, the capital town of the Chatti,[2] which Germanicus burnt on one of his raids. This was doubtless a very easy task, since here was nothing used but
wood in the construction of a German house. The
use of stone, like so many other arts, was quite foreign to the north of Europe; it is first found "by the
southeastern corner of the Mediterranean, and spreads,
like the use of wine and oil, step by step along the
coasts and peninsulas of southern Europe, and thence
over the civilized world."[3] Stone masonry meant
to the German something mysterious, uncanny, the
doing of demigods in old time; and so it easily fell
under the ban of the supernatural. This massive
solidity seemed hardly of human origin; and the earliest Englishmen called such a building "the burg of

[1] For example, the city of Anderida. Whether our Anglo-Saxon
poem, "The Ruin," is to be referred to the Roman city of Bath — as
Leo and Professor Earle think it should be — is doubtful. See Wülker,
Grundr. d. ags. Lit. p. 211 ff., for the various opinions. Green (*The
Making of England*) and Grant Allen (*Anglo-Saxon Britain*, p. 47)
hold that the Saxons left the Roman cities of Britain to decay; but
T. Wright (*The Celt, the Roman, and the Saxon*, p. 510) asserts that
such towns were not generally destroyed.

[2] Tac. *Ann.* I. 56.   [3] Hehn³, p. 138.

giants," " the giants' ancient work." In the *Héliand*,
" greatest of stone-works " is the phrase applied to
the temple at Jerusalem. However, it is not very
likely that Stonehenge and other works of the sort
are monuments of a race which preceded Aryans in
the possession of southern and western Europe, a
race which "stretched from the Nile valley along
North Africa, and so through Spain and France to
the Atlantic." [1]

In the time of Tacitus, the Germanic house was
built entirely of wood, — etymology tells us that
Latin *domus* and English *timber* are the same word,
— and was either an isolated dwelling surrounded
by cabins for slaves and dependents, like the modern
Hof in Baden and Westphalia, or else stood in a
village. The latter is the type of house in our *hâm*
or *tûn*. The house itself was not very substantial,
if we may argue from the custom of going underground in winter; and was probably even in the
time of our historian a comparatively new experi-
ment. The primitive house must be sought for the
northern tribes mainly in those same underground
dwellings which so rudely blot our picture of the
Germanic home. These are not specially Germanic; [2]
Scythians, Armenians, races from all quarters of the
globe, have used them. Hehn makes the later house
an outgrowth of this primitive burrow; from a mere
cave, the dwelling grew in size and form, and "little
by little rose the roof of turf, and the cavern under
the house served at last only for winter and the
abode of the women." Villages made up of such
houses can still be seen in Russia. We must not shut

[1] Hehn². pp. 141, 142.   [2] See again Hehn², p. 536.

our eyes to the darker side of Germanic life which
this dwelling shows us; in evading the cold of winter, our forefathers found an atmosphere foul almost
to suffocation, and abundance of every sort of vermin, — as is still the case with many places in Siberia.
Yet here sat the women of the Germanic family and,
as Pliny tells us, wove and spun, producing their
exquisite linen in spite of all the squalor. Indeed,
Virgil paints us a far cosier scene:[1] "For the people,[2] they keep careless holiday in caves delved deep
under the earth, with store of timber, nay, whole elms
pushed up to the hearth, and heaped on the blaze —
there they lengthen out the night in games, and
jovially imitate draughts of the wine with fermented
grains and acid service-juice."[3]

In later times than those which Tacitus describes,
the Norwegian farmer had a subterranean room by
his house, or even under it, with a secret passage
leading afield, which served as an escape from the
attacks of the foe or from a sudden outbreak of fire.[4]

Such was the nomadic German's winter home. In
summer he had his wagon-like house, which could be
pitched, after the fashion of a tent, for a day or two;
and which, even after agriculture had begun to tighten
its hold and fasten men to the soil, was still a very
flimsy affair. The primitive German, though led by
his fate to the forest with its abundant material for
building, set up nevertheless no substantial house, —
why should he do it? *Ubi bene, ibi patria;* all he
asked was grazing and hunting and the coveted salt-

---

[1] *Georg.* III. 376 ff.
[2] Of the north, — Scythia, Germany, — "the frozen north" generally.
[3] Conington's translation. The beverage is beer.
[4] Weinhold, *Altnord. Leben,* p. 227.

spring.[1] Tiles, mortar, and the like were unknown to the German; and he seems to have been long in learning to use actual timber. Wattled work, twigs or flexible branches woven together, seemed to give enough stability for all his purposes; and even on the column of Marcus Aurelius what we may take to be contemporary German houses are "of cylindrical shape with round vaulted roof, no window, and rectangular door; they appear to be woven of rushes or twigs, and are bound about with cords." Tacitus says the sole material for German houses of his time is wood;[2] and this we may take to include the just-described twigs and rushes of the later Quadi and Marcomanni. When the German settled down to till the fields, he began to use the heavy rough-hewn timber of his forest. Nevertheless, the nomadic trick of carrying about parts of one's house was slow to die out. The Aryan's dwelling was his temple; there hovered the souls of his ancestors, and there he had often buried their bodies. When the Norwegian emigration to Iceland was in progress, certain men arriving off the island coast, and ignorant where they ought to land, threw into the sea the house-posts which they had brought with them; wherever the timbers drifted to the shore, in that spot they built their new abode.[3] Parts of a heathen temple were also carried to Iceland.

[1] Hehn quotes Seneca *de Prov.* IV. 4 : " Nulla illis domicilia nullæque sedes sunt, nisi quas lassitudo in diem posuit."

[2] *Germ.* XVI.

[3] *Eyrbyggiasaga,* in P. E. Müller's *Sagabibliothek,* I. 189 f. For the rest, R. Henning, *Das deutsche Haus,* " Quellen und Forschungen," No. 47, Strassburg, 1882, p. 163 ff., gives examples of such a removal of houses, taken from Indian, Greek, and modern German history. See also below, p. 443.

Evidently the house which Tacitus describes must
have been a very light structure, wholly made of
wood, or with plaited work in the less stable parts.
According to William of Malmesbury, the first Christian church in England was of the wattled material
or hurdle referred to above. Foundation and floors
are of more recent date, and the Norse *flet* is simply
the earth itself stamped hard and firm. The modern
peasant-house, which best shows in survival our old
Germanic dwelling, is built directly on the earth, —
this is particularly true of Saxony, — or else on a
foundation made of posts.[1] To be sure, Professor
Moritz Heyne, in his excellent monograph on the
hall described in *Béowulf*,[2] says that all Anglo-Saxon
houses had a stone foundation, and quotes both Anglo-
Saxon and Gothic words in support of the assertion.
But the general words for " foundation " do not prove
for primitive times the existence of the specific part of
a house, being rather applied later to the imitations of
Roman architecture. Further proof of the absence
of any elaborate foundation is seen in certain old German laws which seem to us not far removed from
burlesque.   But our ancestors doubtless took very
seriously the law providing punishment for any man
who should dig his way under the walls of a house,
and so make criminal entrance. Still more suggestive is the ordinance against him who throws down or
tears apart another man's house.[3] Further proof of
frailty comes from the Anglo-Saxon, where the " tree-
wright," as a builder was called, certainly did not
make houses which would last till doomsday. Wright[4]

[1] Henning, p. 166.
[2] *Ueber Lage und Construction d. Halle Heorot*, p. 32.
[3] Hehn³, p. 141.   *mestic Manners and Sentiments*, p. 14.

calls attention to an episode in the story of Hereward, where the "bower" or ladies' room of a certain house was built in such a weak fashion, that when one day a bear broke loose and rushed for the bower, in which the lady of the mansion had taken shelter, it was only the prompt slaughter of the bear that saved her.

The roof of the Germanic house was made of reeds or straw, was steep, and projected over the sides. By the nature of the case, fire must have been a dreaded foe; and the burning of a German village is often mentioned in history as well as pictured on columns of triumph in Rome. In later times, the German lighted his hall in the long winter evenings with flaring torches, or with candles, — mere lumps of fat, — and the fire burned freely on the middle of the floor.[1] Very picturesque was the Old Norse hall with its blazing fires, of which the Sagas and the Edda tell us; but the element of danger, said always to heighten the romantic, was not far to seek. Roof and walls in this constant smoke would dry to a perilous extent; a bit of quarrel in the midst of drinking and revels, and we can imagine many an overturned torch or scattered fire, and many a banquet hall bursting into sudden flames. This wild gleam of fire lights up our old poetry on every hand. Hrothgar's palace, in *Béowulf*, is one day destined to fall a prey to "hostile waves of flame."

> There towered the hall
> high and hornéd; the hot waves biding
> of angry flame. . . .[2]

---

[1] ". . . accenso quidem foco in medio et calido effecto cenaculo. . . ."
Beda, *Ecc. Hist.* II. 13.   [2] *Béow.* 81 f.

The fine fragment of *Finnsburg* alludes to this as a common fate of castles ; while for Old Norse, Loki at the end of his famous flyting predicts a like destiny for the hall where he has been feasting.[1] In the Nialsaga, most dramatic of all the Icelandic stories, we are told how the avengers, letting "housecarls" and women and children first go out, set Nial's house in flames. Similar flames, but on a far grander scale, and with an epic splendor, light up the tragic close of the Nibelungen Lay. Moreover, even if earthly flame spared, one had to reckon with the heavens. Lightning made sad havoc, and the Saxon Chronicle tells how one year " the wild fire" destroyed a vast amount of property.[2]

The proportion of adornment to utility in the German's dress gives us a hint of what we may expect in his house. Frail as his dwelling might be, and built for the simplest need, it nevertheless showed an incipient decoration; and he began to adorn it long before he had made what we should call the merest beginnings of comfort. We learn from Tacitus that the Germanic house was painted here and there with a glistening color, which was obtained from the earth, — probably of the description still found in the "ochre-swamps" of the Harz region; but whether this painting was exterior or interior, or both, is hard to understand from the difficult passage of the *Germania*.[3] In any case, the early German painted his

---

[1] *Lokasenna*, 65; Bellows, p. 172, Hollander, p. 120.

[2] Our ballads are often as vivid as the sagas. See "Edom O'Gordon," "The Fire of Frendraught," and other songs of the border. Child, Ballads,[2] VI., VII.

[3] Cap. XVI. *Quædam loca*, he says, "certain parts."

dwelling. Later, he carved the woodwork of it into fantastic forms, an art which found its best development in certain parts of Germany and in the wooden churches and houses of Norway; and he adorned the inner walls with paintings and even with tapestry, — the latter an imported luxury. It is not unlikely that in the oldest times shield and spear and other weapons were hung upon the wall, with trophies of the raid and of the chase.

Whatever the primitive house, development was rapid; for war, and captivity, and service in Roman legions, put many a new notion under the Germanic helmet. Tricks of fortification were learnt from the imperial engineers; and it is quite certain that our Angles and Saxons made extensive use of the military improvements which Rome had given to her province. The "street" (*strata via*) and the "ceaster" (*castra*) were soon borrowed, thing and word; and in *Béowulf* we are told that the road which led up to Hrothgar's burg was "stone-variegated," — *strǽt wæs stânfâh*, — paved in the Roman fashion; although it is plain that, as with stone in houses, so with these paved roads, the Germanic instinct regarded the process as something uncanny and savoring of those mysterious giants who long ago had rolled up the huge piles of masonry. So we read in *Andreas*: — [1]

> Manful they marched by mountain-dales,
> stout of heart o'er the stony cliffs,
> as far as ran the roads before them,
> once built by giants, the burgs within,
> stone-gay streets. . . .

[1] Wülker-Grein, *Bibliothek d. Ags. Poesie*, II. v. 1232 ff.

These roads are referred to the same source as certain pillars and statues of stone which are mentioned in the same poem, and are called by this stereotyped phrase, "old work of giants," — *eald enta geweorc*.[1]

While wall and ditch were soon adopted for purposes of defence, the burg was often put upon a hill, or in some equally commanding place. In Anglo-Saxon poetry, the burg is called "lofty," "steep"; it stands on "the hoary stone."[2] A wall, of whatever material, soon encircled the place; *tûn*, "town," is like German *zaun*, a fence or hedge; and in Anglo-Saxon the word *eodor*, "hedge or wall," soon passes into the general notion of house or fortified place; while in poetical speech the prince is called *eodor* of his subjects, their shelter. We have to distinguish between the "door" and the "gate," the latter being a most important strategic point, where the hottest struggle of a siege was mostly fought. The Anglo-Saxon Chronicle, in what Sweet calls "the oldest historical prose in any Teutonic language," gives us a vivid account of the siege of a king who is visiting at a house in Merton. It is set down for the year 755. The king has come to see a woman, and is with her in her bower (*bûr*), when an enemy of his, one Cyneheard, comes up with a besieging party, breaks through the "gate" and surrounds the bower itself. The king, aware of the danger, comes to the door, fights manfully and with success, until he spies his foe, the "ætheling," and so in sudden rage, rushes out upon him, away from the vantage-ground of the door. They all set upon the king and kill him.

[1] *Andreas*, 1495.
[2] Heyne, work quoted, p. 9; Vilmar, *Altert. im Hêl.* p. 10.

Alarmed by cries of the woman, the king's thanes, who form his body-guard, come running up, — presumably from the hall, of which the bower was a dependency, — and vainly fight the besiegers, falling all of them about the dead body of their lord. Next morning the tables are turned; up ride the roused thanes and soldiers of the king; the late besiegers shut the gates, and are in turn besieged, stormed, and cut down, — all save one. It is easy to see that the English house of 755 has made considerable progress from the Germanic house described by Tacitus, for an active race does not stand still during six centuries, even to be photographed; and yet the dwelling preserves many of the old characteristics. The bower, detached from the hall, must have been fairly primitive; and very early, we may think, provision was made for the domestic animals. True, in the houses of ordinary men, as still in some peasant-dwellings of Europe, man and beast lived under one roof; but the home of chief or king must have been from the first independent of the domestic apartment and the stalls for cattle. In this case, we have to imagine the hall, with its sacred associations, its hearth and its fire, in the middle of a group of buildings;[1] nearest to it, and sometimes part of it, were the sleeping-rooms, then store-houses, bake-houses, barns, treasure-house. Such a group of houses, with a gradually increasing family to occupy them, lying in open country, and protected by a hedge or wall, was a *tûn* ("town") or a *hâm;* when it was a fortified place, high, a home of warriors, it was a *burg*. However, as Heyne re-

[1] The plural is often used in speaking of a single place: *on burgum.* See Heyne, p. 38.

marks, this distinction is not constant.[1] The *burg* might hold a single family or a whole city full; and *hâm, tûn, burg,* and *byrig* are all used indiscriminately in the names of later English towns. With the rise of towns, we bid farewell to primitive Germanic relations, and note not only the use of older walls and roads, but imitation of Roman architecture. In this imitation, Anglo-Saxons were far more apt than their brothers on the Continent; though it must be conceded that with all his borrowings, the Englishman kept a certain independence; and while his language and his verse show material taken wholesale from classics or Romance, yet the heart of his speech, and the pulse of his poetry remained Germanic. There is, however, scarcely any material left to form a basis for our judgment in the matter of oldest English houses. Of the so-called Saxon architecture, very little has come down to us; and these meagre remains, says Lübke,[2] "remind one more of the carpenter than of the mason." Elaborate buildings, such as church or palace, were erected by workmen from abroad. How many of these foreign elements had crept into the Anglo-Saxon notion of a royal burg at the time when the materials of *Béowulf* were drifting together, or even how far the poet of that epic added his own ideas to the traditional account of Heorot, is a very difficult matter to determine; in any case, we must remember that the historical events of *Béowulf* are removed from the time

[1] Work quoted, p. 9. See also Kemble, *Saxons,* II. 550 ff. He gives a list of the towns mentioned in the *Chronicle.* Significant is the word *mægburh* as used to indicate the collective notion of a family, the clan in a narrow sense.

[2] In an essay on Gothic Architecture, in the *Zeits. f. Völkerpsychologie u.s.w.* II. 266.

of Tacitus by four hundred years, although the northern heathens would naturally preserve old traditions
much longer than the converted border tribes.   Let
us assume that the burg itself, — the complex of buildings, — as described in *Béowulf*, is modernized ; but
why should not the hall be authentic?   We will
simply transcribe Heyne's account of the burg of
Hrothgar, and then return to our study of the Germanic hall.

This burg, probably surrounded with a wall, is the
home of the royal race of the Scyldings, or sons of
Scyld; and here, with thane and thrall, with queen,
children, relatives, and slaves, lives King Hrothgar.
Chief of all the buildings is the hall; and near it is,
of course, the bower of the queen, the *brŷd-bûr*, where
she and her children spend their time, whenever some
particular occasion does not call her into the hall, to
greet a guest at the banquet, or to bear the first
beaker to her lord.   " Hall and Bower " long remains
an evident metonymy for Lord and Lady, — as in
Wordsworth's famous sonnet.[1]   To this bower, moreover, comes the king at night when he has closed the
banquet in the hall : —

> Then Hrothgar went with his hero-train,
> defence-of-Scyldings, forth from hall;
> fain would the war-lord Wealhtheow seek,
> couch of his queen.[3]

Scattered in the neighborhood of this bower, and thus
submitted to the oversight of the mistress, lay those

---

[1] To Milton : —
> " Altar, sword, and pen,
> Fireside, the heroic wealth of hall and bower. . . ."

[2] Kenning or metaphor for a prince.   [3] *Béow.* 662 ff.

other domestic buildings for store and kine and cook-
ing of food, which are below the dignity of epic
mention. A special house, however, is named as
affording accommodation for Béowulf and his companions. Finally, on a cliff overlooking the sea, is a
sort of fortified watch-tower, whence the strand-ward
and his men keep sentry over the ocean approaches
and guard the burg from surprise of sud en raids.
Such is the Germanic burg as painted in an epic of
the seventh century ; but it is difficult to shut our
eyes to a certain touch of the mediæval castle in
some of these arrangements, let the background be as
primitive as one please : the " stone-gay,' path from
the sea to the palace, the courteous challenge of the
strand-ward as Béowulf's ship comes to shore, and
the highly parliamentary answer of the chieftain, —
these must be outward flourishes of the story, added
by the monkish poet who was fain to let some bit of
southern color fall upon this passing sombre legend
of the north. If when, after the song of the minstrel in Hrothgar's hall, —

> bench-joy brightened. Bearers draw
> *from their "wonder-vats" wine.*

and the revellers thus forget their Germanic beer, we
know that many other departures from the primitive
order must be reckoned with in our epic.

Such beautifyings might be tolerated in the vaguer
architecture and the unimportant details, but when
it comes to the hall itself, the scene of that struggle
between hero and monster which had doubtless
formed the subject of more than one old ballad, here,

---

[1] *Béow.* 1161 f.

in a locality connected at every turn with tradition, we may expect the primitive arrangement.

The hall Heorot or "Hart," probably named so on account of the antlers which adorn its gables, differs from the usual centre and nucleus of a Germanic home, in that it lies outside the walls of the burg. The old hall had been within; but riches and power incline the king to build a new one, which shall outshine anything of the sort ever known to man; and since within the enclosure there is no room for such an edifice, it is built nearer the sea, and probably on lower ground. The material is wood; the general plan an oblong. Massive pieces of timber are held together by iron clamps, and rest, if we are to follow Heyne, upon a stone foundation. If so, these are modern touches. We are told that the floor was gleaming, bright, of variegated colors, —

o'er fair-paved floor the fiend trod on,[1]

It would seem that there were two doors, one at each end of the building; and this is borne out by the often-quoted passage from Beda: "So seems to me, O king, man's life in this world compared with that which we do not know, as if you were sitting at meat among your thanes and nobles in the winter time, with a fire burning in the midst, and the hall full of warmth and light, but outside a raging storm of wind and snow, — and a sparrow should fly swiftly in by one door, and presently fly out again by the other. . . ."[2]

---

[1] *Béow.* 725.

[2] *Hist. Eccl.*, ii, 13; Wordsworth has put the speech into verse, *Eccl. Sonnets*, XVI; likewise Alexander Smith in *Edwin of Deira*, Bk. iv (ed. Boston. 1861, pp. 158. 159).

The hall was entered on a level, or by a very few steps; for, as Heyne points out, the horses which are presented to Béowulf as a reward for his gallantry, are led directly into the hall; and we may add the later custom mentioned in an English ballad, where, by the way, the gift of an arm-ring has a decidedly ancient flavor: —

> King Estmere he stabled his steede
> Soé fayre att the hall-bord;
> The froth that came from his brydle bitte
> Light in Kyng Bremor's beard.[1]

Professor Child gives abundant references to older literature which support the custom, the most familiar being from the Squire's Tale: —

> Whil that this kyng sit thus . . .
> In at the halle dore al sodeynly
> Ther cam a knyght upon a steede of brass.[2]

Outside of the hall and along the wall, in which was the principal door, ran a row of benches; here sit Béowulf and his men until admitted to an audience with the king, and here they stack their "gray-tipped" spears. The roof and outer walls were probably painted in gay colors, a development of the art mentioned by Tacitus, and practised in the middle ages by the builder of a German castle[3] Our poem insists on the fact that Heorot "glistens," "shines far over the land": it is once called "gold-gay," and some have thought of a tile-roof in different colors, or even that the roof was plated with actual gold. But we need assume nothing more than the

[1] Child, Ballads,[2] II. 51, 54.   [2] *Cant. Tales,* F. 77—81.
[3] Heyne, p. 44.

Germanic trick known to Tacitus. Huge antlers decked the gable. All burgs, it would seem, had such a decoration. Both the Anglo-Saxon author of *Andreas* and the Old Saxon poet of the *Hêliand* speak even of the temple and houses of Jerusalem as furnished with these "horns." An Anglo-Saxon riddle [1] has such a horn for subject. A picture of an Anglo-Saxon house, reproduced in Wright's book [2] from a manuscript of the ninth century, shows the roof of a building which must be the "hall," adorned with a stag's head and antlers. The windows of the Germanic hall had, of course, no glass; [3] they were high up in the wall, or even in the roof itself. In simpler halls the smoke of fires escaped as it could, through door or window; but there was often an opening in the roof directly over the fire, protected from rain by another and smaller roof above.

Within, the hall is supported by a single central pillar, which, as Henning tells us, [4] is one of the oldest characteristics of the Aryan house. Such was the olive tree about which Odysseus fashioned his sleeping-room; [5] such the huge oak in the hall of the Volsungs, into which Odin thrust the sword. For the king there is a special "High Seat," which in Heorot, Heyne thinks, was placed at this central pillar; [6] in Scandinavian halls it was put on the

---

[1] No. 87, ed. A. J. Wyatt, pp. 59, 120.

[2] *Domestic Manners*, etc., p. 15.

[3] It was introduced in England, for church purposes, about 676. Heyne, p. 46.

[4] *Das deutsche Haus*, p. 171.   [5] *Odyssey*, XXIII. 190 ff.

[6] Against this view, see Sarrazin, in his somewhat futile *Beowulf-studien*, p. 19. He claims *Béowulf* as a Scandinavian poem, and says Heorot is "plainly a Scandinavian tavern."

north side. A second seat or bench of distinction,
probably opposite the throne, was meant for the
prince and royal guests, like Béowulf. The High
Seat had room for two persons besides the king, —
the queen and his nephew; while at his feet, on a sort
of dais, lay the *thyle*, a combination of master of the
revels, orator, poet laureate, and jester. Inasmuch
as the kin-system was the unit of Germanic life, the
head of a house needed every conspicuous sign of
authority; and this High Seat was no kingly symbol
alone, but was used by each householder. It was
probably found in all Germanic houses, no matter how
rudimentary its grandeur; and it may still be seen
in the cottages of Scandinavian peasants. On the
death of a householder, the eldest son took possession
of this seat with all pomp and ceremony, and dis-
pensed the hospitalities of his house to relatives and
friends. If he were chieftain or prince, he would
thenceforth, sitting on this throne, called from such
associations *gifstôl*, or gift-seat, bestow on vassal or
neighbor the ring which he twisted from its spiral,
or some other piece of treasure, even the right to
hold estates in land, — and so gladden the hearts of
his retainers. Last stage of all, we find this gift-seat
in the tomb. The Scandinavian sepulchre was sometimes built like a house, the freeman's final and permanent "hall," where he is now and then found
sitting on the High Seat and ruling over his ghostly
home.[1]

About the other sides of the hall were tapestries,
of course no primitive adornment, though not neces-

[1] Weinhold, *Altnord. Leben*, p. 498. See also the description of the
tomb of Charlemagne.

sarily late in the history of Germanic decoration. In *Béowulf* they are called *web:* [1] —

> Gold-gay shone the hangings
> that were wove on the wall, and wonders many
> to delight each mortal that looks upon them.

The use of " weaving " in many figures of speech, — as " peace-weaver " for " wife," [2] — together with the analogy of ornaments in dress, allows us the inference that rude tapestries may have ornamented the Germanic hall in comparatively early times. Under the tapestries, and adorned with carvings or even with gold, ran the benches of the retainers, the trusty vassals of the king, who drank his mead or ale, feasted and sang, and shared his treasures. These treasures were doubtless kept in the hall itself under a picked guard, or else were assigned to a fortified separate building.

Bearing in mind the date of our poem, but remembering as well the conservative nature of custom and of the traditions of social or family life, let us glance a moment at the picturesque scene which the poet of *Béowulf* shows us in Heorot.

Ranged along the walls are the benches filled with vassals, warriors old and young, — as the old English phrase ran, *duguð and geogoð,* — who drink from horn or cup, replenished by servants who hasten with vessels of ale about the room. On the throne sits the king, and at his feet lounges Hunferth the *thyle.* Béowulf is announced, and his peaceful message; the king bids his chamberlain go back, see that the

---

[1] *Béow.* 994 ff.
[2] See Bode, *Die Kenningar in der Ags. Dichtung,* p. 48.

weapons are stacked without, and usher in the guests.
Leaving a small guard over spears and shields, Béowulf and his men, clad in their armor and helmets,
enter the hall.   Then Béowulf salutes the king,
tells his name with a brave deed or two by way of
credentials, and announces the purpose of his visit.[1]

Then hied that troop where the herald led them,
under Heorot's roof: [the hero strode,]
hardy 'neath helm, till the hearth[2] he neared.
Beowulf spake, — his breastplate gleamed,
war-net woven by wit of the smith: —

"Thou Hrothgar, hail! Hygelac's I,
kinsman and follower. Fame a plenty
have I gained in youth! These Grendel-deeds
I heard in my home-land heralded clear.
Seafarers say how stands this hall,
of buildings best, for your band of thanes
empty and idle, when evening sun
in the harbor[3] of heaven is hidden away.
So my vassals advised me well, —
brave and wise, the best of men, —
O sovran Hrothgar, to seek thee here,
for my nerve and my might they knew full well.
Themselves had seen me from slaughter come
blood-flecked from foes, where five[4] I bound,
and that wild brood worsted. I' the waves I slew
nicors by night, in need and peril

[1] This long extract from *Béowulf* is given not only for its illustration of the ways of a Germanic hall, but also on account of its allusions
to other parts of our subject. The author is responsible for these, as
for other translations from Anglo-Saxon which occur in the book.

[2] Reading *heorðe* for *heoðe*: see Holder, *Béowulf*, and others.

[3] Reading *hador* for *heaðor* "receptaculum," with Grein (*Sprachs.*
II. 40) and Heyne. Wülker-Grein, *Bibl.* and Holder read *hádor* = "bright-
ness." Grendel, the monster, came to plunder the hall every night, and
killed any whom he found there.

[4] Owing to discrepancy of this and the narrative below, Bugge would
read "on the monster-sea" — the sea that breeds monsters. See Paul-
Braune, *Beit.* XII. 367.

avenging the Weders,[1] whose woe they sought, —
crushing the grim ones. Grendel now,
monster cruel, be mine to quell
in single battle! So, from thee,
thou sovran of the Shining-Danes,
Scyldings'-bulwark, a boon I seek, —
and, Friend-of-the-folk, refuse it not,
O warriors'-shield,[2] now I've wandered far, —
that I alone with my liegemen here,
this hardy band, may Heorot purge!
More I hear, that the monster dire,
in his wanton mood, of weapons recks not;
hence shall I scorn — so Hygelac stay,
king of my kindred, kind to me! —
brand or buckler to bear in the fight,
gold-colored[3] targe: but with grip alone
must I front the fiend and fight for life,
foe against foe. Then faith be his
in the doom of the Lord whom death shall take.
Fain, I ween, if the fight he win,
in this hall of gold my Geatish band
will he fearless eat, — as oft before, —

my noblest thanes.[4] Nor need'st thou then
to hide my head;[5] for his shall I be,
dyed in gore, if death must take me;
and my blood-covered body he'll bear as prey,
ruthless devour it, the roamer-lonely,

[1] *Sc.* the Weder-Geats, a by-name of the Geats (Gautar), the race to which Beowulf belonged.

[2] Notice the complimentary heaping up of metaphors for the king's person.

[3] Yellow; the color of the linden bast with which the shield was covered.

[4] For "my noblest thanes" there are strong arguments, advanced by Malone and summarized by Klaeber (*Beowulf, ed. cit.*, p. 427, note to v. 445) for a rendering "the noblest Hréðmen" (Hréðmen-Geats).

[5] The general sense of the passage is clear: there will be no need of funeral rites (cf. vv. 2124 ff.). "To hide my head" refers either to interment or to the custom of covering the head of the dead with a cloth (see Herrig's *Archiv*, XCIX (1897), 417; *Anglia*, XXXVI (1912), 172 n.). This latter custom may have prevailed in England as well as in Scandinavia (Hoops in *Englische Studien*, LIV, 1920, 19—23). See also Klaeber, *op. cit.*, pp. 141, 427.

with my life-blood redden his lair in the fen:
no further for me need'st food prepare!
To Hygelac send, if Hild[1] should take me,
best of war-weeds, warding my breast,
armor excellent, heirloom of Hrethel
and work of Wayland.[2] Fares Wyrd[3] as she must."
Hrothgar spake, the Scyldings'-helmet: —
"For fight defensive, Friend my Beowulf,
to succor and save, thou has sought us here,
Thy father's[4] combat a feud enkindled
when Heatholaf with hand he slew
among the Wylfings; his Weder kin
for horror of fighting feared to hold him.
Fleeing, he sought our South-Dane folk,
over surge of ocean the Honor-Scyldings
when first I was ruling the folk of Danes,
wielded, youthful, this widespread realm,
this hoard-hold of heroes. Heorogar was dead,
my elder brother, had breathed his last,
Healfdene's bairn: he was better than I!
Straightway the feud with fee I settled,[5]
to the Wylfings sent, o'er watery ridges,
treasures olden; oaths he swore me.
Sore is my soul to say to any
of the race of man what ruth for me

[1] Battle, death in battle personified.

[2] Wayland Smith. Wayland was the Germanic Vulcan, of whom more p. 208 below; his legend is well known in early Germanic heroic legend and indeed appears conspicuously in the Anglo-Saxon lyric, *Déor's Lament.*

[3] This whole passage, stamped with primitive Germanic marks, is replete with mythologic interest, though the elegiac and mournful tone is specifically Anglo-Saxon. *Wyrd* (= that which is accomplished) is Fate, a Germanic goddess; compare "To dree one's weird."

[4] Hrothgar at once shows his knowledge of royal histories and genealogies, a great point with the Germanic chieftains. In the Hildebrand Lay, old Master Hildebrand, when he unwittingly meets his son, and asks the name of his opponent's father, says proudly: "If thou namest one to me, I shall know the rest; boy, in the kingdom all folk are known to me!"

[5] By paying the *Wergild.* See p. 178.

in Heorot Grendel with hate hath wrought,
what sudden harryings. Hall-folk[1] fail me,
my warriors wane; for Wyrd hath swept them
into Grendel's grasp. But God is able
this deadly foe from his deeds to turn!
Boasted full oft, as my beer they drank,
earls o'er the ale-cup, arméd men,
that they would bide in the beer-hall here,
Grendel's attack with terror of blades.[2]
Then was this mead-house at morning tide
dyed with gore, when the daylight broke.
all the boards of the benches blood-besprinkled,
gory the hall: I had heroes the less,
doughty dear-ones that death had reft."

With these speeches, the king and his noble guest
have put themselves on the proper terms, and Hrothgar proceeds to bid a feast.

"— But sit to the banquet, unbind thy words,
hardy hero, as heart shall prompt thee."[3]
Gathered together, the Geatish men
in the banquet-hall on bench assigned.
sturdy-spirited, sat them down,
hardy-hearted. A henchman attended,
carried the carven cup in hand,
served the clear mead. Oft minstrells sang
blithe in Heorot. Heroes revelled.
no dearth of warriors, Weder and Dane.

The songs sung to harp or zither[4] by such a minstrel were sometimes, it is true, gnomic verses full of

[1] Vassals, retainers; those who dwelt in the hall.
[2] Would await him with drawn swords.
[3] Evident parallel of our "Make yourselves at home." Other interpretations in Heyne's note. 5th ed.
[4] Symons, *Grundriss*,[2] III, 622; cf. *ibid.*, p. 570.

proverbial wisdom,[1] but mostly, as befitted a warrior throng, ballads of heroic or mythic acts done by members or ancestors of the clan; or else — for the family stock of songs would easily grow too familiar — some legend of other Germanic tribes would be eagerly greeted, like the song sung by one of these minstrels attached to Hrothgar's court as the men are riding up to the hall, after the combat of Béowulf and Grendel.[2] Personal compliment would have its

---

[1] Such are, in late guise, the gnomic verses preserved in Anglo-Saxon poetry; this proverbial poetry was very popular; see B. C. Williams, *Gnomic Poetry in Anglo-Saxon* (N. Y., 1914).

[2] Very few words will be in place concerning the nature of Germanic poetry. Its chief fault is lack of artistic finish; it has "more matter and less art" than the poetry with which we are familiar. Its development in respect of form and style was rudely checked by the conversion, and never came to maturity. I have elsewhere made bold to apply to this early poetry of ours those infinitely pathetic words of Goëthe's Mignon: —

Vor Kummer altert' ich zu frühe.

Sorrow made it old before its time. But for the facts. Of course, the material is human speech, and many words used in poetry were used in daily life. Substantives, not verbs, are the chief consideration. A certain number of words, however, constituted by their solemn and formal nature an exclusively poetical vocabulary, and these joined with certain artistic factors to make up our old poetry. Rhythm is the chief of these factors; tone-color, the second; parallelism of phrase is a third. Sievers has shown a far greater regularity in Germanic rhythm than was suspected by older scholars. With certain subordinate regulations of quantity and balance, the main law of our old poetry called for a verse which fell into halves, — in each half two accented syllables. These verse-accented syllables must also be word-accented; in other phrase, the rhythmic accent coincided with the syntactical or logical, — the distinguishing element of all Germanic poetry. Scherer says that this desire to force home the root-syllables, the sounds which bore the sense, was due to the passionately earnest character of the race. To bind together the two halves of the verse, tone-color was employed, — what we call alliteration or beginning-rhyme. The first accented syllable of the second half was standard; with the initial sound of this syllable must rhyme one, and might rhyme both, of the accented syl-

place. On this occasion in question, we may fancy
that some deed of Béowulf, or of a member of his
kin, was sung amid the enthusiasm of the warriors
and their guests, with shouts of applause and remembered delight of battle, with copious flowings of the
ale. But Béowulf has another proof to endure. The
thyle, or king's master of the revels, is not at his post
in vain; and the guest is to be put to his mettle in
one of those flytings, or contests of wit, which seem
to have been so popular, especially among the Scandinavians. Lolling at his chieftain's feet, heated with
liberal potations, the *thyle*, Unferth, jealous and
vexed, tries to jeer and scoff the guest out of countenance ; and so he calls across to the bench where
Béowulf sits : —

> Unferth spake, the son of Ecglaf,
> who sat at the feet of the Scyldings' Lord,
> unbound the battle-runes.[1] — Beowulf's quest,
> sturdy seafarer's, sorely galled him;
> ever he envied that other men
> should more achieve in middle-earth
> of fame under heaven than he himself. —
> "Art thou that Beowulf, Breca's rival,
> who emulous swam on the open sea,
> when for pride the pair of you proved the floods,
> and wantonly dared in waters deep
> to risk your lives ? No living man,

lables of the first half. In good verse, the two accented syllables of the
second half never rhymed with each other. This peculiarity of the verse
we have sought to retain in translation, as well as the parallelisms, in
which Anglo-Saxon poetry bears some resemblance to the Hebrew.
The use of alliteration is shown in the host of phrases like "have
and hold" retained by our once poetical, now prosaic laws. For list
in Anglo-Saxon, see Meyer, *Altgerm. Poesie*, p. 260 ff.

[1] "Set loose the secrets of battle," *i.e.* began to quarrel.

or lief or loath, from your labor dire
could you dissuade, from swimming the main.
Ocean-tides with your arms ye covered,
with strenuous hands the sea-streets measured,
swam o'er the waters. Winter's storm
rolled the rough waves. In realm of sea
a sennight strove ye. In swimming he topped thee,

had more of main! Him at morning-tide
billows bore to the Battling Reamas,
whence he hied to his home so dear,
beloved of his liegemen, to land of Brondings,
fastness fair, where his folk he ruled,
town and treasure. In triumph o'er thee
Beanstan's bairn his boast achieved.
So ween I for thee a worse adventure
— though in buffet of battle thou brave hast been,
in struggle grim, — if Grendel's approach
thou darst await through the watch of night!"

Beowulf spake, bairn of Ecgtheow: —
"What a deal hast uttered, dear my Unferth,
drunken with beer, of Breca now,
told of his triumph! Truth I claim it,
that I had more of might in the sea
than any man else, more ocean-endurance.
We twain had talked, in time of youth,
and made our boast, — we were merely boys,
striplings still, — to stake our lives
far at sea: and so we performed it.
Naked swords, as we swam along,
we held in hand, with hope to guard us
against the whales. Not a whit from me
could he float afar o'er the flood of waves,
haste o'er the billows; nor him I abandoned.
Together we twain on the tides abode
five nights full till the flood divided us,
churning waves and chillest weather,
darkling night, and the northern wind
ruthless rushed on us: rough was the surge.
Now the wrath of the sea-fish rose apace;

yet me 'gainst the monsters my mailéd coat,
hard and hand-linked, help· afforded, —
battle-sark braided my breast to ward,
garnished with gold. There grasped me firm
and haled me to bottom the hated foe,
with grimmest grip. 'Twas granted me, though
to pierce the monster with point of sword,
with blade of battle: huge beast of the sea
was whelmed by the hurly through hand of mine.
Me thus often the evil monsters
thronging threatened. With thrust of my sword,
the darling, I dealt them due return!
Nowise had they bliss from their booty then
to devour their victim, vengeful creatures,
seated to banquet at bottom of sea;
but at break of day, by my brand sore hurt,
on the edge of ocean up they lay,
put to sleep by the sword. And since, by them
on the fathomless sea-ways sailor-folk
are never molosted. — Light from east,
came bright God's beacon: the billows sank,
so that I saw the sea-cliffs high,
windy walls. For Wyrd oft saveth
earl undoomed if he doughty be!
And so it came that I killed with my sword
nine of the nicors. Of night-fought battles
ne'er heard I a harder 'neath heaven's dome,
nor adrift on the deep a more desolate man!
Yet I came unharmed from that hostile clutch,
though spent with swimming. The sea upbore me,
flood of the tide, on Finnish land,
the welling waters. No wise of thee
have I heard men tell such terror of falchions,
bitter battle. Breca ne'er yet,
not one of you pair, in the play of war
such daring deed has done at all
with bloody brand, — I boast not of it! —
though thou wast the bane[1] of thy brethren dear,

1 Murderer.

thy closest kin, whence curse of hell
awaits thee, well as thy wit may serve!
For I say[1] in sooth, thou son of Ecglaf,
never had Grendel these grim deeds wrought,
monster dire, on thy master dear,
in Heorot such havoc, if heart of thine
were as battle-bold as thy boast is loud!
But he has found no feud will happen;
from sword-clash dread of your Danish clan
he vaunts him safe, from the Victor-Scyldings.
He forces pledges, favors none
of the land of Danes, but lustily murders,
fights and feasts, nor feud he dreads
from Spear-Dane men. But speedily now
shall I prove him the prowess and pride of the Geats,
shall bid him battle. Blithe to mead
go he that listeth, when light of dawn
this morrow morning o'er men of earth,
ether-robed sun from the south shall heam!"[2]
Joyous then was the Jewel-giver,
hoar-haired, war-brave,[3] help awaited
the Bright-Danes' prince, from Beowulf hearing,
folk's good shepherd, such firm resolve.
Then was laughter of liegemen loud resounding
with winsome words. Came Wealhtheow forth
queen of Hrothgar, heedful of courtesy,
gold-decked, greeting the guests in hall;
and the high-born lady handed the cup
first to the East-Danes' heir and warden,
bade him be blithe at the beer-carouse,
the land's beloved one. Lustily took he
banquet and beaker, battle-famed king.
Through the hall then went the Helmings' Lady,
to younger and older everywhere
carried the cup, till came the moment

---

[1] Note how Béowulf's invective leads up through murder to the climax of Germanic sins, — cowardice.

[2] That is, " the hall will be safe after to-night's combat."

[3] King Hrothgar.

when the ring-graced queen, the royal-hearted,
to Beowulf bore the beaker of mead.
She greeted the Geats' lord, God she thanked,

in wisdom's words. that her will was granted,
that at last on a hero her hope could lean
for comfort in terrors. The cup he took,
hardy-in-war, from Wealhtheow's hand,
and answer uttered the eager-for-combat.
Beowulf spake, bairn of Ecgtheow: —
"This was my thought, when my thanes and I
bent to the ocean and entered our boat,
that I would work the will of your people
fully, or fighting fall in death,
in fiend's grip fast. I am firm to do
an earl's brave deed, or end the days
of this life of mine in the mead-hall here."
Beowulf's battle-boast. — Bright with gold
the stately dame by her spouse sat down,
Again, as erst, began in hall
warriors' wassail and words of power,
the proud-band's revel, till presently
the son of Healfdene hastened to seek
rest for the night; he knew there waited
fight for the fiend in that festal hall,

In other words, they remember that it is night-time
now, and the monster must shortly make appearance.
So the Danes leave the hall to Béowulf and his
Jutes.

... The warriors rose.
Man to man, he made harangue,
Hrothgar to Beowulf, bade him hail,
let him wield the wine-hall: a word he added: —
"Never to any man erst I trusted,
since I could heave up hand and shield,
this noble Dane-Hall, till now to thee.

Have now and hold[1] this house unpeered;
remember thy glory; thy might declare;
watch for the foe! No wish shall fail thee
if thou bidest the battle with bold-won life"[2]

Then they go, and anon the great struggle takes
place; the hall totters with the conflict between
Béowulf and Grendel and would have fallen, had it
not been so extraordinarily well built. The extract
we have just considered is somewhat tedious, and
exaggerates certain grave and obvious defects in the
style of Anglo Saxon poetry; yet the quality tire-
some to us was welcomed by the Germans, who had
a childish delight in repetition and detail; and the
defects are inherent with poets that have not attained
the self-control of the artist. This breathless hud-
dling style was dear to the brawny old warriors.
Again, where monkish learning has touched our
verses, it has not adorned. They are in many parts
tinged with Roman culture, and veneered with a thin
coating of the new religion; the speech of Béowulf
is too parliamentary for the temper of those earliest
Germans; and perhaps the queen is something too
much of a *grande dame*. But making all these allow-
ances, we are safe in looking on this description as
essentially Germanic; nor can a tolerably critical eye
fail to detect and leave out of account the touches of
a more modern brush.

The chief business of the hall was evidently such
as we have seen, — royal receptions and banquets,

---

[1] The antiquity of this legal form is proved by the alliteration, as
well as by its solemn use in this place.

[2] The passage is given in full except a few lines near the end, and
runs in the original from v. 402 to v. 661.

the latter being, of course, the more constant factor.
In these revels, men had cup or horn to hold in the
hand, — "without tables!"[1] says a plaintive German
commentator.   We have spoken of horn and cup already;[2] but we must not forget the old blood-cur-
dling habit, which has done service for so many orators
and editors, of drinking from the skulls of slaughtered enemies.   This custom was primitive and Germanic; Livy tells us the same thing of the Celts.[3]
Nor was it necessarily the skull of an enemy; one
could pay this graceful compliment to a dead friend,
and murmur, "Alas, poor Yorick!" with even a nearer
sentiment.   Grimm cites many instances.[4]   We know
that Alboin met his death because "when he had sat
too long one day at a banquet in Verona, with the
beaker before him which he once had caused to be
made from the skull of his father-in-law, King Cunimund, what must he do but send wine to the queen
and bid her drink merrily along with her father.   Let
no one" — adds the good Paul — "let no one call this
impossible; I speak the truth in Christ, and I myself
have seen this beaker."[5]   And in another place the
same writer says: "Alboin slew Cunimund, cut his
head off, and had a beaker made of it.   This sort of
beaker is called *skala* among them; in Latin, *pa-
tera*."   Older than history is the myth of Wayland,
best told in the Old Norse *Poetic Edda*.[6]   Volund, as

[1] Tacitus says these were used at the Germanic meal: "Sua cuique
mensa."   *Germ.* XXII.
[2] Many names occur in the Germanic languages to express "drinking-cup."   See Vilmar, *Deutsche Altertümer im Héliand*, p. 37.
[3] Hehn², 537.   [4] *G. D. S.*³ 100.
[5] Paul. Diac. *Hist. Langob.* II. 28.   See also I. 27.
[6] Bellows, pp. 252 ff., Hollander, pp. 186 ff.

his Norse name runs, treats in a fashion similar to Alboin's the bones of a king's two sons.

In *Béowulf* little was said about the particulars of the feast; in *Judith*, a late epic on a Christian subject, a banquet is described quite in the Germanic fashion, even if it is the doing of no less a person than Holofernes. He orders a great feast and bids to it "the eldest of his thanes," — the highest in rank and service.

> Then fared they thither at feast to sit,
> proud to the wine, his wicked fellows,
> bold mailed-warriors. Beakers tall
> were borne to the benches, bowls and flagons
> were filled for the floor-sitters : fey they took them,
> warriors stout, though he wist no thing,
> dread leader of earls. Then Olofernes,
> gold-friend of men, was glad with wine,
> laughed and was loud in larum and din,
> so that many a mortal marked afar
> how the sturdy-minded one stormed and yelled,
> mead-mad and haughty ; admonished oft
> the crowd of benchers to quit them well.
> So the worker of evil all day long
> drenched his warriors deep in wine,
> stout treasure-breaker, until they swooned,
> plied his thanes till prone they lay,
> drenched them all as if death had seized them,
> drained of life. . . .

This is Germanic through and through, — the "larum and din" agreeing with accounts given us by classic writers of the clamor and "wassail" cries of a Gothic banquet,[1] — as indeed any one may see by comparing the biblical account; and it is much more strongly

[1] In the fifth century the Alamanni had the fame of being the hardest of German drinkers. Salvianus, quoted by Hodgkin, *Italy*, I. 310.

and sharply outlined than the too shadowy description in *Béowulf*. This cheerful defiance of all local coloring is a saving virtue in the early English poets, and helps us to many a trait of their own time which they would have scorned to record of purpose. The old Saxon poet who paraphrased the gospels describes, much in the same fashion as above, the feast of Herod, and also — though naturally as a far more decorous affair — the banquet at Cana.[1] People gather in the "guest hall" of the "high house"; they grow "blithe"; while the servants "go about with bowls and cups and pitchers," till "on the floor" — that is, in the hall — "was fair pleasure of earls," and from the benches rose delight of the people. The technical term among the oldest English poets to describe this bliss of revel was "dream,"[2] — the joy that springs from drink, and song, and laughter in the warm hall, shared with one's household and vassals; then it came to mean a similar state in one's sleep, which is the only meaning now attached to the word. Song, noise, — that was the Anglo-Saxon notion, as witness the three remarkable glosses:[3] "*Concentus, i. adunationes multarum vocum*, efenhleoþrung, *vel* dream. — *Furor enim animi cito finitur, vel gravius est quam ira*, reþnes, woden, dream. — *Armonia* [= *Harmonia*], dream." A "dreamer" is a musician. However, the Germanic warrior could enjoy in hall both the ancient and the modern dream; for, save when a Grendel made the hall-night hideous, it was there, stretched on his bench, or on a rude sort of

---

[1] *Héliand*, 1994 ff.; Herod's banquet, 2734 ff. (Heyne's ed.).
[2] See also Vilmar, work quoted, p. 38.
[3] Wright-Wülker, 212, 36; 245, 7; 342, 39.

bed, that the clansman slept; and Tacitus tells us
that it was often well into the following day when
our dreamer rose,[1] took his bath — hot, if possible, —
and went off to the duties of the morning. It might
be that another feast claimed his attention, some public affair, as when a youth was graced with spear and
shield in presence of the clan, and so became a freeman, a warrior, and a pillar of the state. It might be
a town meeting, or some other function of the citizen; but it was certainly no manual labor, no care of
farm or cattle. That was not the warrior's business.
He would often, says Tacitus, lie whole days before
the fire; and if we ask what he was doing there when
not asleep, we are entitled to the suspicion that he
was gambling. This was his vice of vices; the national propensity to gamble was not a mere pastime,
but a reckless, absorbing, passionate gambling, which
often ended not only in poverty, but in slavery.
When property was gone, when wife and child were
gone, the German staked his own liberty; and if he
lost his last throw, went voluntarily into servitude,
even under a weaker man.[2] This is an old Aryan
trick. Dice are actually prayed to in the Vedas; and
dice remained prime favorite with Germans throughout the middle ages, even among women.[3] A more
innocent game, resembling our draughts or checkers,
was known to the Germans perhaps as early as the
fourth century; and the materials of the game, " bone,
glass, amber, or earthenware," are found in Scandinavian tombs, which date from the early iron age.[4]

[1] *Germ.* XXII.   [2] *Germ.* XXIV.
[3] See also Weinhold, *Deutsche Frauen*,[2] I. 113.
[4] Montelius, work quoted, p. 113.

Of course, the Germans hunted. Cæsar says it was an amusement in which they took delight, a very reasonable statement. What more natural than for this giant to rise from his lolling by the fire, like any man of muscle, sick at last of inactivity and sloth, to shake his invincible locks and course the woods for bear or boar or stag? Unfortunately, Tacitus and the *Germania* tell another story, and say that Germans do not spend much time in the chase. Holtzmann and certain English editors, with heroic remedy, simply strike out the negative, and so square Tacitus with Cæsar and with common sense. We know that the latter mentions game as part of the German larder; and since, moreover, your hunting is a war in little, we have reason to think of our forefathers as mighty hunters before their gods. How else shall we account historically for the English squire and the game-laws? Still, we must go cautiously in these assumptions. Jacob Grimm saw even in falconry an old Germanic sport, and dedicates to it a chapter [1] of his *Geschichte der deutschen Sprache;* but Hehn's opposition to such a view seems based on very solid facts.[2] All the refinements of the chase, he contends, are of Celtic origin, whence even the Romans borrowed more than one improvement. Nevertheless, we feel sure that the German, though careless of terms and methods, had plenty of plain, honest hunting, — wolf, bison, elk, bear, and boar. Something of the old spirit must assert itself in that merry scene of the Nibelungen Lay, which with conscious or unconscious art finely increases the horror of the tragedy that follows so

[1] Cap. IV.   [2] *Kulturpfl.,*[3] p. 374.

hard upon its heels.[1] We hear the horn winding
clearly through the forest, the bay of hounds on all
sides, four and twenty packs yelling after the game
in as many directions, Siegfried laughing, joking,
killing whatever is met, and at last in sheer sport
catching a huge bear alive and binding it to his saddle; he carries it to camp, where he lets it loose to
dash through the kitchen, scare the cooks and upset
half the food among the ashes; and then, as the beast
escapes all pursuit, and makes for the forest, we see
Siegfried once more in pursuit, killing it and bringing
it to the fires. It seems imbedded in our race and no
importation, even from the Celt, — this broad-hearted
joy in following the deer, this delight of hounds and
horn, which ring out so bravely in English as well as
German song, and which can still drive a London fop
into prairie or jungle that he may find " something to
kill." What race speaks in Shakspere's Theseus? —

> And since we have the vaward of the day,
> My love shall hear the music of my hounds.
> Uncouple in the western valley. . . .
> . . . My hounds are bred out of the Spartan kind,
> So flew'd, so sanded; and their heads are hung
> With ears that sweep away the morning dew;
> Crook-knee'd and dew-lapped like Thessalian bulls;
> Slow in pursuit, but match'd in mouth like bells,
> Each under each. A cry more tuneable
> Was never holla'd to, nor cheer'd with horn
> In Crete, in Sparta, nor in Thessaly. . . .

It is not without full purpose that these scenes
and doings of such a late period have been thrown in
with extracts from the *Germania* and quotations from

---

[1] XVI Aventiure, *wie Sifrit erslagen wart.*

Béowulf. It is probably true, or nearly true, when Justus Möser calls modern peasant life in Germany a fair copy of the primitive condition of the race; but we must make the important concession that parallel scenes may be rendered really different by a difference in the persons. Charlemagne doubtless lived in the midst of discomforts that would not now be tolerated by an Irish navvy; but, aside from the absurdity of comparing the persons, not a detail in the surroundings of one can be fairly appealed to for a picture of the surroundings of the other, unless we constantly insist upon this nobler element of personal character, and the relative nature of civilization. To do this, there is evident help in any bit ot epic which preserves Germanic elements in comparative purity. With such caution, we may finish our consideration of the Germanic house by bringing it into contrast with modern homes. How little of our modern home was represented in the old German dwelling is readily seen when we examine familiar names like *tile, wall, street, mortar, tower, pillar, chamber,* and many others.[1] The primitive Germanic house took different forms in plan and detail, which may be studied in Henning's monograph.[2] This author thinks that the Saxon peasant-house is developed directly from the old Germanic dwelling; and here we see a combined stable and house, entered through a door large enough to admit a wagon. Right and left of the entrance are stalls for cattle and horses. Passing by these, we come upon the *flet,* — the living-room, — answering to

---

[1] Hehn², pp. 142, 143: all Latin loans.
[2] See especially 29 ff., 56 ff., 136 ff. The Germanic hall is described 153 ff.

the primitive hall, whose occupants our Anglo-Saxon
epic called *fletsittende*. Here is the low hearth, altar-
like, by the further wall, but once in the middle of the
room, and centre of the house in every way. It was
an old custom for bride and groom, on entering their
new home, to march thrice *around* the fire.[1] On one
side of this hearth are table and bench; on the other,
a washing-place, open, with water from the outside; and
immediately adjoining the stalls was a rude platform
on which stood the beds of the family, and where the
mistress of the house could sit and spin, while she
overlooked all the house, — man, maid, and cattle.
Equally interesting is the diverging plan of dwelling
found upon the Cimbrian peninsula near the home
of our own ancestors.[2] In all these houses, for the
most ancient times, we may assume dead as well as
living tenants; the German peasant was once buried
in the house where he was born.

Henning makes it probable that this old Germanic
house was not very different from that of primitive
Italians and Greeks. All go back to a common
Aryan type. The word "hall," like the thing, is
original; it means that which protects or conceals.
"Timber," as we have seen, is Latin *domus*, the building itself. "Thatch," "door," are both original words.
It seems probable that the primitive Germanic dwelling was an heirloom of Aryan days, and that the
simple art of building house and home was learnt
before the great exodus from the birthplace of that
clan of destiny.

It seems reasonable to assume that his house at
least was felt by the primitive German to be his own.

---

[1] See Simrock, *Mythologie*, p. 600.   [2] Henning, p. 48 ff.

"Own" is a very old Germanic word — and fact.[1]
Besides his house, what did the freeman own? In
the matter of land, to be sure, we have rival theories,
individual ownership and the communistic plan; but
however that may be, the man who tilled land owned
it while he tilled it, and owned what he raised upon
it. The old German distinguished between real and
personal estate; the latter consisting in weapons,
dress, ornaments, utensils, hunted game, cattle, slaves,
and even the house itself;—for could not this be carried about from place to place? Of other kinds of
property we could find curious examples gathered
from old laws; but we shall notice only the property
in trees of the forest. In his treatise upon *Haus-
und Hofmarken*,[2] the signs or marks made on houses
or other property, Homeyer shows that proprietary
marks were put on trees, tame stags, cattle, clothes,
and what not. The *Lex Salica*, for example, provides that a man may mark a tree for felling, and no
one else is to touch it for the space of one year; after
that it becomes again public property. The property
in bees who hived in a particular tree has been
already noticed.— In fine, we may be sure that our
ancestors were not in that delightful condition of
certain African tribes where nobody owns anything
and everybody steals what he can.

[1] Von Amira in Paul's *Grundriss*[2], pp. 192 ff.
[2] Berlin, 1870, p. 8 ff.

CHAPTER V

HUSBAND AND WIFE

The husband a warrior, the wife housekeeper and farmer —
Rights of women — Germanic chastity — Woman as sibyl — Her
courage — Wooing and wedding — How far love was a factor —
Dower or price — Ceremony of marriage — Punishment for infidelity.

LET us come closer to the family life of our forefathers. The free German was essentially a warrior,
and such farming as he had was in the hands of his
wife, who was helped by slaves and the weaker members of the household. To look after the cattle and
the horses was work for the freeman so long as nomadic habits prevailed; but he had no taste for
grubbing and raking and gathering of crops. To
steal cattle — provided the theft was open, there
was no disgrace in it [1] — smacked of war; just as
the moss-troopers and raiders of the Scottish border in very late times were not by any means without allies of gentle blood. Meanwhile, farming
slipped into Germanic life under feminine escort,
and began. very modestly indeed. The primitive
German wife, says Lippert, [2] "span wool, made
clothes, cared for the fowls, and — tried her hand

[1] Grimm, *R. A.* 634.   [2] *Religion d. europ. Culturvölker*, p. 36.

at raising barley." [1] In other respects her position
in the state was pitiable enough; and Wackernagel reminds us [2] that, if we may believe Gregory
of Tours, the Franks once held serious debate in
one of their church assemblies whether or not a
woman was a human being. Yet this importance
in the household and in the farm gave her a
certain responsibility, leadership, and dignity. We
must remember, too, what an important part the
German woman played in matters of divination
and religion; add to the power of the wise woman,
like Veleda, the chastity for which Tacitus so
warmly praises the German wife, and we can imagine that this was no race of sheer barbarians. Suetonius [3] lauds the insight of Augustus, who saw how
much stress Germans laid upon noble women as hostages, caring little for men; and so Rome began to
demand this new sort of pledge from the barbarians.
But we must not let sentiment run away with us; and
the famous eulogy will bear a bit of investigation.
No part of the *Germania* is so much admired as this;
and it is the fashion to accept it as a sort of conspiracy before the fact with Goethe's *Ewigweibliche*,
— in some respects, not without reason. Women,
even in those days, were not deprived of legal protection. Legal and statutory exclusion from certain privileges is a proof that other rights exist
and are guaranteed by custom; thus we find the
Salic Law, "oldest of Teutonic codes," [4] fixing cer-

[1] Barley had for the German three distinct merits: grew quickly,
needed little care, and furnished an intoxicating drink
[2] *Kl. Schr.* I, 3.
[3] See also *Urzeit* (*Deutsche Vorzeit*, I.), p. 319.
[4] It dates from the fifth century.

tain principles of female inheritance, particularly that
women may not inherit land. Of course, as is now
well known, nothing is said about succession to a
throne. From ownership of land woman was probably excluded in all Germanic tribes, and this Salic
Law represents the general point of view.[1] Where
we find daughters admitted to equal shares of an
estate with sons, as among the Visigoths, we may
assume foreign influence. Moreover, women were
not members of the state, but were under control
of father or brother, who punished or rewarded them
at pleasure. The oldest English law is full of this
doctrine.[2] Refractory wife or daughter, where stripes
are unavailing, is sold or even given away. We shall
presently see that the Tacitean account of the punishment meted out by German custom to an adulteress
agrees exactly with this view of a woman's position
in the state. But custom is law; and custom had
very early begun to give woman a certain legal
standing. This process probably began in the rights
of inheritance; a runic inscription of ancient Norway,
highly important both for its age and for its length,
speaks "of the male heirs" (*arbija*) and "of the
female heirs" (*arbijano*). Thus, in the absolutely
heathen and purely Germanic north, we have as early
as the year 550 a definite word, corresponding to a
definite fact, and recognizing the rights of female
inheritance.[3] Traditional equity gave the daughters
ornaments and certain articles of furniture; the rest

[1] "De terra Salica nulla portio hereditatis mulieri veniat." Lex
Sal. 62, 6 apud Grimm, *R. A.* 407.
[2] Details in *R. A.* 738.
[3] Stone at Tune in Norway. See A. Noreen, *Altisl. u. altnorw.
Grammatik* (4th ed., 1923), p. 390, No. 79.

of the property followed the male line.   Not without
importance is the hint of Tacitus that among the Germans of his day traces still lingered of a primitive law
which gave all property to the sons, but only in the
female line.   He says [1] that a sister's sons stand with
the uncle as high as with the father; "some even
think this tie of blood to be holier and closer, and
they have regard to it in the choice of hostages. . . .
Still, the heirs are always the children, and wills are
unknown."   Now by the old notion of maternal
inheritance,[2] a man "would part more readily from
his wife's child than from his sister's child; for in his
eyes there was more blood-relationship with the latter."[3]   The Germans of Tacitus had long passed this
point of view, and had developed a high sense of the
paternal relationship; but survivals occurred like the
above, and gave a certain support to the position of
woman.   In slave-law the old rule held, — *partus se-
quitur ventrem*, the offspring belonged with the mother;
but even in this respect the ancient laws show considerable divergence.   Proof of woman's position is
helped, as has been already remarked, by a study of
Germanic myths.   If the ways of gods and goddesses
reflect earthly existence, — and we are sure they do, —
the worship of a Nerthus seems impossible for a community which gave no rights and paid no respect to
women.   When Tacitus tells us of a tribe of Germans in the north "which is ruled by a woman," [4] we
may, it is true, call this a fable, like the other won-

---

[1] *Germ.* XX.

[2] Obviously, in communities without settled married relations, maternal inheritance is the only certain method.

[3] Lippert, *Rel. d. eur. Culturv.* p. 60.   [4] *Germ.* XLV.

ders which his artistic instinct marshalled at the end
of his book and on the border of the frozen world,
and we may ascribe it to the misunderstanding of a
Finnish word; but for all the fable, there may be
something in the legend beyond what meets the ear
of the etymologist. We know that the lady of Mercia was no fiction; as Warton[1] says, "ladies in England were anciently sheriffs of counties!" And
lastly, let the grave itself bear witness. Antiquaries
in Scandinavia refer to 1000 B.C. the body of a
woman found buried in a tree-coffin, with a dagger
by her side. Montelius, perhaps with too much cre-
dulity, calls this and similar finds "a remarkable inti-
mation of Amazons during the bronze age in the
north."[2]

It is popularly supposed that women were lifted
to their present place mainly by the influence of the
church and of chivalry. This is in great measure
true. In the eighth century, — say a hundred years
after the conversion, — nuns in England take active
part in literature. They correspond with monks
and bishops in Germany; and one of them, living in
German cloisters, writes the life of her brothers, the
missionaries Willibald and Winnibald.[3] This Wal-
burga, however, is outdone by a nun of the tenth
century, Hrotsvith of Gandersheim, the famous mediæval blue-stocking. She wrote legends and history
in Latin verse, and actually made the first attempts
at dramatic composition, of which we have any record,

---

[1] *History of English Poetry*, II. 186.

[2] Work quoted, p. 62.

[3] See also Wattenbach, *Deutschlands Geschichtsquellen im Mittelalter*,[2] p. 97.

since the downfall of classical culture.[1] Now there must have been some basis for this in the old life. From the start, if we may believe Wackernagel,[2] knowledge of writing was largely in the hands of women; in Scandinavia women seem to know most about the making and reading of runes. The sibyl was very potent in Germany, and, as we shall presently see, united to her knowledge of divination and mystic signs a certain majesty and sanctity that must have helped her sisters in more ways than one.

Again, the care of the house and farm, onerous as it might be, gave dignity to the mother and wife. In higher walks of life she shares her husband's state, — witness Wealhtheow in *Béowulf*. We find the daughter of Hrothgar performing offices like those of the queen; Freawaru also goes through the hall, bears the ale-cup to thirsty warriors, bestows treasure and greets the guests.[3] The purity of German family life was eagerly held up by Tacitus as a lesson for his countrymen. Cæsar had already praised this feature, and it became a by-word with the later chroniclers. A writer of the fifth century [4] says that the Germans are all chaste, except the Huns and Alans, — an exception which does not affect the statement. In Rome, family relations were going from bad to worse; and Tacitus, eager to teach his countrymen that strength in man or state depends on purity, painted too bright a picture. It has the pink-and-white unreality of a Dresden-china group. In some respects it reminds us of Cooper's

---

[1] See M. Manitius, *Geschichte der latein. Literatur des Mittelalters*, I, 619—632, for an account of her life and work.

[2] *Kl. Schr.* I. 14, note.　　　　[3] *Béow.* 2020 ff.

[4] Salvianus, quoted by Hodgkin, *Italy*, I. 507.

eulogy of our red man, or of the far more grotesque savage ideals presented by French writers at the beginning of this century.

Briefly, we must not understand the chastity and simplicity of Germanic life to have been coupled with those qualities which in our own stage of culture are sure to be found among persons who are simple and chaste. This German woman, who doubtless had a plenty of rough household virtues, with her vigorous barn-yard brood of children, passed into history as a sort of Cornelia or Lucretia, ruling an ideal family, where the daughters all look rosy and firm of flesh, and spin, and sing ballads about Arminius, with a shy, downward look when a certain brave young warrior of the next village is mentioned in domestic conversation, and where the sons hurl lances and speak tumultuous truth. Romance, as in Freytag's books, has helped the picture. Leafy forest, gay greenwood, are very well; but neither in Spain which coined the proverb nor yet in Germany, is it "always May"; and the scene shifts to those underground dwellings, covered for sake of warmth with dung, where the household passed its winter, — paterfamilias in that "single garment," moody and idle by the fire, the women weaving and spinning, and all glad of the coarsest sort of food. Between the picture of romance and the squalor and savagery which certain of the modern school are fain to pour over every portion of our forefathers' existence, lies a middle ground of common sense, based neither on romantic fancies, nor on the anxiety to push a theory of ethnology to its last gasp, but on the facts of history and the hints of early literature.

Nor do we need to give up the Roman's splendid and generous eulogy. We have simply to take it out of the sphere of rhetoric and reduce it to prose.[1] In the first place, polygamy was doubtless rare; but it had no particular moral sentiment against it. Precisely because it was no great crime according to German ethics, there is little said of the matter at all. Ariovistus had two wives. In Scandinavia, unlimited concubinage was common enough;[2] but it was not a lawful polygamy, seeing that only the children of the free wife had any rights in the family. The habit held late. Even so pious and noble a man as Charlemagne had a court — and a personal record — which in this respect will not bear scrutiny. Economy, not morality or sentiment, decided the matter. There was a total absence of sentiment in Germanic life; but a householder respected the capable mistress of his home — because she was capable; and he accorded her a certain supremacy, because only thus could she do her best work and bring about the most good for the family. She had, therefore, full sway in her own realm; she could not easily brook a rival. Perhaps the best modern instance of an old German's point of view would be that of the second George of England, "Paladin George," and his devotion to his queen. She had been most emphatically "the man of the house," and the king was in despair as he

[1] Part of it seems sober fact. "Marriages are strict, and no phase of their life is to be so highly praised. Alone almost of the barbarians, they are contented with a single wife, a few excepted, who, not for the sake of sensuality, but on account of their high rank, are sought several times in marriage." *Germ.* XVII.

[2] Weinhold, *A. L.* 248 f. Grimm, *R. A.* 440. Later summaries indicate belief in polygamy among the old Germans: see v. Amira in Paul's *Grundriss,*[3] pp. 178 ff.

stood by her deathbed. Who does not remember his pathetic declaration that he would never marry again? — "Non, j'aurai des maitresses."[1]

The sanctity of the household, and in consequence the inviolable character of marriage, owed a good measure of their support to the old ceremony of ancestor-worship. It is not only Spencer and the ethnologists who insist on the wide importance of this cult; it is nearly, if not quite a settled matter in the court of scholarly opinion. Only a legitimate son, reasoned the German, can or will minister to his dead parents. To leave a son who should be head of the house, and therefore its priest, who would perform its rites according to the good old custom, and train up his own children to the same belief and practice, was one of the foundations of family life. Household gods were no fiction in those days. Now with such a sanction for the family, with such necessity for a head, for strict gradations of birth, we can see how the iron weight of custom and religious tradition, and not the feeble breath of sentiment, inclined the scale in favor of German women. If other reasons are needed for taking in earnest the main of Tacitean eulogy, we may point again to the importance attached to noble ladies as hostages, — in the Waltharius legend, heroine as well as hero is hostage at the court of Attila, — or to the honor paid to daughters of the royal blood, as among the Goths.

Again, there is the subjective side. The Germanic

---

[1] *Béowulf*, 1932 ff., describes the good and the bad type of woman in the persons of two queens, Hygd and Thrytho. The former is mild, generous, gracious; the latter remorseless, cruel, and altogether unwomanly.

woman stands out in history with a certain nobility and steadfastness of character. In the doubtful issues of battle — it is an enemy who records it — she prefers death to captivity. When Caracalla asked some German women whom he had taken captive, whether they preferred to be slaves or to be killed, they chose to die; and when in spite of this they were sold into slavery, they all put themselves to death. At Aquæ Sextiæ the women died rather than go into captivity; and the same is told of the Cimbrian women at Vercellæ. They tried to make a bargain for their captivity by which they could be slaves in temples and so preserve their chastity; and when this was refused, they killed their children and themselves. Paul the Deacon tells an odd story how the daughters of a certain Lombard duke, captives among a strange race, took heroic measures to preserve their honor;[1] we are glad to learn that these courageous damsels finally escaped and married, one the king of the Alamanni, the other a prince of the Bavarians.

Divorces and second marriages among the Germans were very rare. They were so frequent at Rome, however, that no barbarian custom could have seemed lax by comparison. It was the honorable work of the church, and that only after most desperate struggles, such as the contest between Lothar II. and Pope Nicholas I., that marriage came to be regarded as indissoluble. Among the Germans, infidelity on the part of the wife met swift and ruthless punishment, often death. Boniface[2] mentions hanging, and being whipped to death by other women.

---

[1] IV. 37. They carried putrefying meat about their own persons, in order to disgust the ardent suitor.   [2] *Epist.* 59.

Tacitus gives a vivid picture of the formal expulsion of an adulteress from her husband's home: "With shorn hair and stripped of her clothing she is thrust by her husband from his house, her relatives looking on, and so is driven with blow on blow through the whole village."[1] But all this, of course, was only for women. The church has the credit of forcing law and sentiment to take cognizance of the husband's guilt as well.

As regards that famous *sanctum aliquid et providum*,[2] we may well believe that there was abundant reverence for the prophetic and sacred character of woman; but it was a reverence based on religious tradition, and was at the farthest possible remove from mediæval or modern chivalry. We are hardly to think that the German attributed superior insight to woman as woman; the gods spoke through her. The Veleda, whom Tacitus mentions, both in this passage and in the histories, was a typical wise woman, who had prophesied the defeat of the Roman legions. From the words of Tacitus it seems that she was finally captured and brought to Rome.[3] She was chosen, along with the leader Civilis, to decide a

---

[1] *Germ.* XIX., prefaced by the general statement: "paucissima in tam numerosa gente adulteria, quorum poena præsens et maritis permissa."

[2] *Germ.* VIII. Mention has been made of the services rendered by women in time of battle, — of the ardor inspired in the warrior at sight of his mother, wife, or daughter, and the thought of what captivity would bring to them. Captivity thus becomes doubly feared. For the enemy to have noble women as hostages is a most efficient restraint upon the Germans. Then Tacitus adds: "Indeed, the German thinks there dwells in his women *something holy and prophetic;* he neither spurns their advice nor neglects their oracular sayings."

[3] "Vidimus sub divo Vespasiano Veledam." See remarks of commentators.

weighty question of state; but the messengers were
not permitted "to see Veleda face to face and speak
to her. Sight of her was withheld in order that the
reverence for her might increase. She stood upon a
lofty tower, and one of her relatives, like a messenger
of the gods, carried question and answer."[1] Costly
gifts were sent to her; a trireme, for example, captured from the Roman fleet.[2] Even the Romans
themselves sought to win her good graces, in order
to influence her countrymen. Nor were all of her
functions oracular and prophetic; she was made
umpire in civil disputes.[3]

Such a position offered attractions to the ambitious
young woman of Germany who had a soul above
marriage and a talent for ecstatic shrewdness. Indeed, we afterwards hear of a certain system of education in these matters, and find Norwegians and
Swedes sending their daughters to Finland, the chosen
country of magic and sorcery;[4] a historic basis for
the young woman of our own day who goes to Germany. Nor is this so far-fetched as it may seem.
Runes, incantations, the cunning interpretation of
various carved or written symbols, formed a good
part of the sibyl's business; but to write and read
in this way does not — under leave of Dogberry —
"come by nature," and we may certainly think of a
definite if not systematic instruction. It was doubtless such a woman's duty to etch upon the warrior's
sword-blade those potent runes of battle, or to undo
the harm of hostile runes. A Norse maiden who has
lost her brother offers to carve the runes on the

[1] Tac. *Hist.* IV. 65.   [2] Ibid. V. 22.   [3] Grimm, *D.M.*[4] 334.
[4] Weinhold, *Deutsche Frauen*, I. 105.

kevels, — pieces of wood, — if her father will make
the memorial verse.[1]

Moreover, as Grimm remarks,[2] it is women who
mediate between divine and human; and Tacitus
reminds us that such handling of holy business leads
at last to godhead itself. "Veleda," he says, "a virgin
of the tribe of Bructeri, was respected far and wide
in accordance with the custom of the Germans, who
regard many of their women as sibyls, and, with
growing superstition, as goddesses." [3] In other words,
the sibyl did not lose her power at death; we shall
see hereafter how "dead women" reveal to Scandinavian dreamers the secrets of another world, or tell
of a mortal's approaching death.[4] Chip and cut as
we will from the testimony of the ancients, this reverence for women, living or dead, stands out a stubborn fact in the Germanic character. It is one of
those nobler elements which shine all the more
clearly in the dark world of their ignorance and
ferocity. Jewish tradition knew only the prophet,
the masculine angel, who carries God's will to a
nation or to a man; but, as Grimm points out, with
the German, "men are for deeds, and women are for
wisdom." Our ancestors assigned the *providum* to
women; now it is a goddess, a Valkyria, — now it is
a mortal maiden of the Veleda pattern, a *spákona* in
Norse, the *spae-wife* of our own Scottish tradition.
It is such a woman who gathers up the past of Scandinavian myth in the *Vǫluspa*, the prophecy of the

---

[1] Ibid. I. 133 f.   [2] *D.M.*[4] 329.

[3] "Ea virgo nationis Bructeræ late imperitabat: vetere apud Germanos more, quo plerasque feminarum fatidicas, et augescente super-
stitione. arbitrantur deas." *Hist.* IV. 61.

[4] *Atlamál,* 28 (ed. Neckel); Bellows, st. 25, p. 508, 509; Hollander,
st. 25, p. 350.

sibyl, and sings the death-song of Germanic heathendom. On the border world of spirits and living men hover the forms of supernatural women warning, helping or banning. When Drusus had crossed the Weser and drew near the Elbe, there met him a woman, in form and habit more than mortal, who warned him[1] of his approaching end; and to another dreaded invader appeared a rune-maiden, and cried "Back, Attila!" to the Hunnish king.[2] Such are the Valkyrias and the Swan-Maidens of our mythology; and highest phase of all, we find, as in Greek and Roman tradition, the issues of death and life in women's hands. The Norns are governed by no god, be he Odin himself; and the vast underworld, a far older locality in myth than the Vikings' heaven of Valhalla, is ruled by the inexorable goddess, Hel.

Some are ready to affirm that this power of woman in the other world only reflects the earlier stages of actual life, — that the Valkyrias, for example, are nothing more than sublimated Amazons.[3] Instances are not far to seek of this actual fighting on the part of Germanic women. Tacitus, indeed, confines their activity to exhortations, the rallying of a disheartened army; but when all this failed at Aquæ Sextiæ, when the drum-beating and the incantations were of no avail, then the German women fought fiercely enough around their "wagon-burg." An old story of some Germanic raid into Rhætia under the reign of Marcus

---

[1] In Latin. Suetonius, *Claudius*, I.   [2] *D.M.*[4] 334.

[3] So Holtzmann. See E. Mogk in Hoops' *Reallexikon* under "Walüren"; *New English Dictionary* under "walkyrie" (also under "valyrie"); and R. Jente, *Mythologische Ausdrücke im altenglischen Wortschatz* (Heidelberg, 1921), pp. 208ff. (§ 129a).

Aurelius, says that after the fight bodies of armed women were found upon the battle-field, covered with wounds. Thomas Wright notes[1] that during the middle ages Welsh women used to go with their men in hostile excursions across the English border; and for Germanic women, Rochholz has collected[2] abundant material bearing on this matter of physical bravery. Occasionally women took their own parts in the trial by combat; at least Weinhold quotes a curious case where a woman fights an accuser for her own cause[3] Her weapon was a stone bound up in a veil or hood; while the man stood half buried in a hole and fought with a stick; but this is not without a strong savor of burlesque. Probably the noblest figure in Scandinavian poetry is Hervǫr, as she stands undaunted before the flaming tomb of her father and demands the dead man's sword. Here is evidently the later Norse ideal of high-born womanhood.

It would be pleasant to suppress the final chapter of a story that begins so nobly; but if truth be told, the last state of this *sanctum et providum* in Germanic women was its worst. Christianity banned the old sanctities and mysteries, and the prophetic maiden — "*ea virgo*" — grew little by little into a woman who clung to the disgraced divinities, had dealings with Satan, was guilty of the lowest vices and the most disgraceful motives, did nothing but harm, caused storm, ruin, pestilence, and death. The much-abused "Dark Ages," however, went no further than bans and curses; it was reserved for the dawn

---

[1] *Womankind in Western Europe*, p. 5.
[2] *Deutscher Glaube u. Brauch*, II. 289 ff.
[3] *Deutsche Frauen*, I. 205.

of our modern epoch to muster in a last attack all the old mummeries and superstitions; and the *sanctum et providum*, taking lead of the rest, deluged the age with that mass of cruelty, blasphemy, and obscenity which we now include under the half-harmless name of witchcraft.

So much for the general position of woman; we must now consider the household of which she was no unimportant member. The family, the kin, and so to the clan, is obvious progress of civilization, which at last reaches the point where private family life works to strengthen the state, and the state works to protect the family and guarantee individual rights. In early Germanic times the family, or rather the kin, is by far the most powerful factor in public as in private life. The family proper comprised the six relations of father, mother, son, daughter, brother, sister;[1] a wider circle began outside of this limit, and could be extended at will. These outer degrees of relationship were called "knees": one man was kin to another in the "third knee," "fourth knee," and so on. The number seems to count, not from a common ancestor, but from his children, — the point where the collaterals begin; so that the grandchildren, not the children, would stand "in the first knee." From the Anglo-Saxon *cnéow*, "knee," was formed the word for a family or clan: *cnéoris*. Other names were *mægð* and *cyn*, our "kin," whence "king" (*cyning*), or the "child of the tribe." It is on the basis of kin that we study Germanic institutions. A family, smaller or larger, held its members united by the strongest of bonds;

[1] See further von Amira in Paul's *Grundriss*,[2] p. 170.

they made common front against an enemy, and kept peace among themselves. The word *sib* means both "peace" and "relationship."[1] To give this little senate laws, to govern his immediate family and do his duty as member of the larger family, was chief business of the Germanic freeman aside from his vocation of warrior and his avocation of huntsman. Every member of the family was subordinate to its head, not simply under his control, but at his mercy: he could punish, sell, and, in primitive times, kill.[2] We must here as before clear our minds of modern sentiment, and keep in sight the rigid nature of household organization. We will begin at the foundation of the family, wedlock.

The German wife was not wooed; she was won, — and it is salutary to remember that "win" means first "to fight" and then "to get by fighting." In the time of Tacitus, a Germanic wife was probably bought with a price — not in our sense of buying wares, however — in a transaction between father and bridegroom, which marked a distinct advance from the earlier and universal practice of stealing one's wife. Of course, this earlier method of finding a helpmeet, did not cease utterly and at once. For Roman affairs

---

[1] "Gossip" has endured heavy fates. See also Old Saxon *sibbia* (Vilmar in *Altert.* p. 52); our words, *kind, gentle;* and Grimm, *R. A.* 288, where we are reminded that Old Norse *lid* meant both "help," "support," and "family."

[2] A little insight into this privilege and duty of a householder to punish — often by death — a guilty member of his family will set in clearer proportions the frequent domestic murders, as we should call them, of our old plays. Setting aside some obvious cases, we should thus understand the action of divers husbands and lovers, such as Philaster's act of "justice" in attempting to kill Arethusa, *Philaster*, Act IV.; Perigot's similar conduct towards Amoret, *Faithful Shepherdess*, Act III.; and, of course, Othello, and the rest.

we have the stock illustration of the Sabine women,
a fine concentration of immemorial custom into a
single act; and the Roman wedding kept a mock
abduction as one of its features. The winning of
Atalanta in the race is like those more strenuous
proofs of muscle [1] which Gunther found necessary to
win Brunhild in the Nibelungen Lay; while actual
survival is evident at peasant-weddings of the Continent, where there is often a mock fight for possession
of the bride, or a race between bride and bridegroom.
So, at Frisian weddings, a sword is borne before the
bride.[2] Actual traces — not by any means mere survivals — are found in Tacitean Germany. Arminius
is said to have stolen his uncle's daughter and made
her his wife. Perhaps the so-called indemnification
of the daughter of a murdered man, which consisted
in giving to her as husband one of the murderer's
family, is only a later way of explaining the old system of wife-robbing. In Norse mythology, when
the giant Thiassi is killed by a device of the gods,
one of these is given as husband to the daughter of
the victim. Severe laws were enacted against wife-
robbing, a proof of its popularity; and the substitution of a price for armed force in marriage is a step
in culture analogous to the composition of a murder
by payment made to the victim's family instead of the
primitive exposure to revenge, — the *wergild*. In fact,
Waitz identifies the woman's price in marriage with
her *wergild* itself.

Admirable as this arrangement must have seemed,

---

[1] Wrestling, hurling the stone, etc.
[2] Grimm, *R. A.* 167. For exogamy in England, see Grant Allen,
Anglo-Saxon Britain, p. 81 f.

immense as were its advantages over the raw and
brutal act of older times, even this peaceful bargain
may well have run counter here and there to the
stirrings of a young Germanic heart. In an Icelandic
saga, Helga takes with outward assent and obedience
the husband whom her father gives her; but her
heart remains constant to her lover, Gunnlaug Snake-
Tongue.[1] And we are led to ask the question, How
far was the sentiment of love a factor in the Germanic
marriage? Such material as Grimm accumulates [2] by
way of partial answer will not serve our purpose.
The passages are nearly all mediæval, and are rife
with the first riches of chivalry and the worship of
fair dames. We cannot possibly carry all that — a
song, for example, from the *Carmina Burana* — back
into Tacitean Germany. So that one is tempted to
claim for Germanic life in its full extent the remark
made by Grimm [3] in regard to Anglo-Saxon poetry, —
that nobody thought of portraying the love of woman.
Where men and women live in anything better than
savagery, some gleams of sentiment must flash out.
Moreover, it must be remembered that monks, who
wrote down our old literature, would be shy of
such material. The story of Walter and Hildegund
has all the external characteristics of a runaway
match, — if one were not constantly struggling with
the sensation that Hildegund and the treasure stolen
from Attila were somehow both of the same character
in the regard of the hero. The loves of Siegfried and
Kriemhilt are already touched slightly with the glitter

---

[1] *Gunnlaugssaga*, ed. Mogk.   [2] *D. M.* 330 f.; III. 113 f.

[3] Preface to his edition of *Andreas und Elene*, p. xxv: " An darstellung der frauenliebe hat uberhaupt auch kein andrer angelsäch-
sischer dichter gedacht."

of mediæval tournaments and mediæval chivalry. On
the other hand, the passion of Helgi and his Valkyria
Sigrûn — a Norse background puts the actual date in
some equality with far older Germanic material — is
not without the charm that we are wont to couple
with romantic love. But it is mixed with supernatural
traits; it is the old union of a peerless mortal warrior
with an immortal maiden. Helgi fights lion-like in
the heart of battle; down hastens Sigrûn, as the clash
of spears grows shriller, hovers protecting over her
warrior, and cries to him in joy of his victory. But
his answer is not a lover's. In the second lay of
Helgi, however, we meet the full wind of passion.[1]
"Hǫgni hight a king; his daughter was Sigrûn. She
was Valkyria and rode air and sea. . . . Sigrûn rode
to Helgi's ships." Then follows dialogue; then a
battle, after which Sigrûn, promised in royal assembly
to a certain king, seeks Helgi, greets him and kisses
him under helmet; then the hero is moved to love
the maiden. She says her father has promised her to
another man; now she has crossed his will, and woe
must follow. Helgi consoles her: "Fear not Hǫgni's
rage nor the hatred of his kinsmen. Thou shalt live
with me, maiden, for thou art of noble birth." In the
storm at sea, while Helgi is faring to battle, he looks
aloft, and lo, nine Valkyrias riding, and Sigrûn with
them: and the storm is laid. A battle takes place, and
all the kin of Sigrûn are slain, save only Dagr, and he
made his peace. And Sigrûn learns of all the slaughter
and weeps; but Helgi comforts her: "Weep not,

---

[1] See Neckel's *Edda*, pp. 147ff.; Bellows, pp. 313ff., Hollander,
pp. 225ff.. *C. P. B.*, I. 140ff.

Sigrûn, it was for thy sake. Kings cannot command
their destiny." And she [1] answers: " Fain would 1
give life to them that are dead, — but rest in thine
arms as well! " Then comes the tragedy. Dagr
obtains Odin's spear and revenges his father, and
Helgi falls, and Dagr rides to Sigrûn and tells her
what is done. First she launches her bitter curses
upon him for his falsehood and treachery; and then
she cries: [2] " Nevermore shall I sit happy at Sevafell,
nor have joy of my life at morn or eventide; for
nevermore shall I see the light flash on my lord's
company, nor the war-steed with its gold bit bearing
my king thither: nevermore shall I welcome the
king home. . . ." Then follows a fine bit of praise
of Helgi. The hero is buried, a hill heaped over
him; but the Viking-Paradise of Valhalla claims
him, and there is a characteristic touch of description
as he enters, spying his old enemy Hunding: " Hunding, do thou make ready a foot-bath and kindle a
fire for each of us (the company of the king), and
tie up the hounds and bait the horses. . . ." But in
the evening Sigrûn's maiden sees Helgi and a great
retinue riding to his barrow or mound. And Helgi
says, ghost-fashion, he is permitted to return to his
barrow, but must ride the paths of air again before
the dawn. And he calls on Sigrûn to come forth to
him. In vain the maid warns her, with Horatio's
arguments of harm, not to go forth. She goes, and
speaks: " I am as glad to meet thee as are the greedy
hawks of Woden when they scent the slain, their

[1] So Bellows, p. 320, st. 21, Hollander, p. 230, st. 22 *vs.* Neckel,
p. 151, st. 29.
[2] So *C. P. B.*, I, 141; cf. Bellows, 325, st. 35, Hollander, 233, st. 36,
Neckel, 153.

warm prey, or dew-spangled espy the brows of dawn.
I will kiss thee, my dead king, ere thou cast off thy
bloody mail-coat. Thy hair, my Helgi, is thick with
rime; thy whole body is drenched with gory dew;
thy hands are cold and dank. How shall I deliver
thee from this, my lord?" And Helgi answers: " It
is thine own doing, Sigrûn from Sevafell, that Helgi
is drenched with deadly dew. Thou weepest cruel
tears, thou gold-dight sun-bright lady of the south,
before thou goest to sleep: every one of them falls
bloody, dank, cold, chilly, fraught with sobs, upon
my breast. . . . " [1] Then the passion of their old life
gets hold upon them in the very tomb, and love is
stronger than death. " Let us drink costly draughts,"
cries Helgi, " though we have lost both love and land!
Let no man chant wailing dirges, though he see the
wounds on my breast! Now are maidens, royal
ladies, shut up in the barrow with us dead men."
Quoth Sigrûn: "I have made thee a bed here, Helgi.
. . . I shall sleep in thine arms, O king, as I should
if thou wert yet alive. . . ."

Aside from the fact that Bugge refers this story to a
Greek origin, and sees in Helgi and his Sigrûn a Norse
version of the loves of Meleager and Atalanta,[2] there
is too much of the Viking splendor in the whole setting for any primitive relations. True, the awe of
monkhood is not upon these wild verses, — perhaps
our English lovers sang as boldly, and made lays fit
to frighten the pious scribe, — but neither is the primitive simplicity of passion. It is a fierce, world-worn,

[1] A familiar touch, known to folk-lore and legend everywhere.
[2] Bugge, *Studien*, pp. (according to Norwegian ed.) 12 f., 166. See
W. Grimm, *Heldensage*,[2] p. 355.

martial love, with a Valkyria for Juliet, and a grim
warrior for Romeo. It is the glitter of the viking-
life, with its dash and spoil and glimpses of foreign
braveries in court and city ; and not even Helgi and
Sigrûn can give us the picture which we desire of
old Germanic love.

> Aus alten Märchen winkt es
> Hervor mit weisser Hand,
> Da singt es und da klingt es
> Von einem Zauberland, —

but the white hand beckons from a bower of romance,
and the enchanted country lies this side of German
forests. We must return to prose, and assume with
safety that there followed upon the custom of bride-
stealing the more peaceful marriage bargain, a step
in civilization; and that in course of time, by the
good offices of the church, women began to assert
their likes and dislikes, choice began, sentiment —
helped by what Dryasdusts call Mariolatry — un-
folded, and only the dowry and marriage-settlement
remained from the old conditions. For the first
transition, we have a most edifying document in the
shape of an edict issued by King Frotho of Denmark
to the conquered Ruthenians,[1] that in view of the
greater stability and safety of marriages made on the
basis of a definite bargain, people are not to wed

---

[1] Saxo Grammaticus, ed. Holder. p. 156, ll. 33—36: "*Ac nequis
uxorem nisi emptitiam duceret, venalia siquidem connubia plus stabi-
litatis habitura censebat, tutiorem matrimonii fidem existimans, quod
pretio firmarentur.*" One can fancy Polonius, a countryman of this
Frotho, saying to Laertes by way of further advice on the conduct of
life, "When thou shalt marry, take a receipt in full from thy father-
in-law."

unless they pay for the wife. These base respects of thrift are still common among the peasants of Europe. Tennyson's Northern Farmer probably has plenty of colleagues in actual life, and Weinhold quotes a peasant's saying, which is even more to the point: "It's not man that marries maid, but field marries field, — vineyard marries vineyard, — cattle marry cattle." [1] Only in old songs and legends, and rarely there, we hear of the maiden choosing her husband from a number of suitors; [2] and in one of these few cases it is a burlesque choice, a sort of raffle. Skathi, the giant-daughter, may choose one of the gods for husband, but is allowed to see nothing of them save their feet. [3] We are on safer ground when we find Hjǫrdis in the Volsungasaga choosing, at her father's bidding, between two kings, which she will marry. "Choose," says the father, "*for thou art a prudent woman.*" The transition to an unhampered choice was naturally slow. A cheerful milepost on the way is Cnut's law: [4] "Neither woman nor maid shall be forced to marry one that is disliked by her, nor shall she be sold for money, unless [the bridegroom] gives something of his own free will." But usually we find the notion of a bargain carried out quite aside from any fancies of the young woman. Another Anglo-Saxon law, [5] an old one, ordains: "If one buys a maiden, let her be bought with the price, if it is a fair bargain (*gif hit unfácne is*); but if there is deceit, let him take her home again and get back the price he paid." The

[1] *Deutsche Frauen,* [2] I. 319.   [2] *R. A.* 421, note.
[3] Prose Edda, in *Bragarøður.*
[4] Liebermann, I, 360, § 74.
[5] Of Æthelberht, Liebermann, I, 7. § 77.

nature of this bargain seems to have been slightly misunderstood by Tacitus; "the bride," he says,[1] "brings no dower to her husband, but the husband makes a gift to his wife." The price was not paid to her; but, at least in the oldest times, to her father or natural guardian; in later times the price was turned into a gift (like the famous Morning-Gift) or settlement for the bride herself. To sum up, and give an answer to the question about love or commodity in primitive Germanic marriages, it seems reasonable to exclude almost totally the workings of sentiment. Doubtless the ancestral German would have approved most cordially the sentence of Bacon's "Essay on Love": "They do best, who, if they cannot but admit love, yet make it keep quarter, and sever it wholly from their serious affairs and actions of life."[2]

All this concerns the marriage of free with free. If a free woman married below her rank, she came into a painful position, and must lose either her husband or her freedom. A curious custom of the Franks ordained that if a free woman was married against her will to an unfree man, she should go before the king and receive from him the offer of a sword or a spindle, — in this case, the signs of freeman and serf. If she chose the sword, she should then and there slay with it her unfree husband; if she chose the spindle, she went with him into unfreedom.[3] This was a mild case; in other laws there is less symbolic machinery and swifter, sharper justice.

[1] *Germ.* XVIII.
[2] Even the marriage of Joseph to the Virgin Mary is treated by the Old Saxon *Hêliand* as a formal bargain; he "buys" her. *Cf.* W. Wackernagel, *Kl. Schr.* I. 55, note.
[3] See Wackernagel, *Kl. Schr.* I. 5 f. and references.

Thus the Lombard killed a serf who ventured to marry a free woman, and sold her into slavery if her life was spared; West-Goths and Burgundians scourged and burnt them both; while the Saxons punished an unequal marriage of any sort with death of man and wife.[1]

Just as the husband bought his wife, so ancient custom permitted him to sell her   When the Frisians were forced by the officious severity of Olennius to pay a tribute laid upon them by the Romans, but hitherto exacted only in part, they gave "first their cattle, then their land, lastly their wives and children."[2]   The free Saxon had the right to sell wife and child;[3] and as late as the thirteenth century a German could do the same thing in time of famine and want. In Scandinavia the practice was common. Jacob Grimm,[4] explaining the Anglo-Saxon phrase *fœle freoðuwebbe* as applied to a wife, "the dear peace-weaver," shows that *fœle* meant originally "that which one may buy and sell," like German *feil;* then "property, what is valuable"; then "dear." We need not make such frantic protest of horror. The Germans are fond of citing, at every possible turn, the public sale of a wife in Manchester, England, in 1843;[5] while in the first decade of our century we find several cases on record. One wife "brought £1 4s. and a bowl of punch"; and another fetched

---

[1] Ibid. p. 6.

[2] *Ann.* IV. 72. Drusus had laid a light tax upon them, — tanned ox-hides for the use of the soldiers, — without specifying size or amount. Olennius required skins of the bison, — *terga urorum,* — or an equivalent.

[3] Weinhold, *D. F.* II. 12.

[4] *Andreas und Elene,* note, p. 143 (*El.* v. 88).

[5] Wackernagel, *Kl. Schr.* I. 10.

twenty guineas, being "delivered in a halter to a
person named Houseman."[1] By one of the oldest
Anglo-Saxon laws, whoever enticed away a man's
wife had to buy him another.[2] The thing sounds
very heathen; but a well-known path of British law
still leads an injured husband to much the same
result.[3]

Generally, however, a matrimonial purchase was
made for permanent investment. "Atli [Attila]
gave for Gudrun a mass of treasure, thirty men-
servants and seven handmaidens." Theodoric the
Great gave his niece Amalaberga to Hermanafrid,
king of the Thuringians, and received in payment
from the husband a number of "silver-white horses."[4]
Occasionally we find excessively high prices quoted,
as much as three hundred shillings among the Saxons, and among Alamannians and Lombards as high
as four hundred, — no mean price when we reflect
that one shilling represented the value of an ox at
sixteen months.[5] Moreover, it was all thrift, not
gallantry.

We will suppose the price paid down and the bride
ready to be brought into her new home. Not altogether empty-handed did she leave her father's
house.[6] According to Tacitus, she brought even
weapons to her husband; but the Roman's explana-

[1] Ashton, *Dawn of the Nineteenth Century in England*, II. 65 ff.

[2] Æthelberht, Liebermann, 1, 5, § 31: "If a freeman seduce the
wife of a freeman, let him pay his wergild and buy another wife with
his own money and bring her to the husband's home."

[3] See Thackeray's *Ballads of Policeman X.:* "Damages, Two Hundred Pound."

[4] Wackernagel, *Kl. Schr.* I. 7.

[5] Ibid. The modern Kaffir gives from six to thirty oxen for a wife.
Lippert, *Culturgesch.* II. 78.   [6] *R. A.* 429.

tion is wholly fanciful. Then came the betrothal
Symbolic ceremonies, we may be sure, were not
lacking; but they differed for different races. The
bride's hair was probably bound up, and it may be
that keys of the house were hung, in sign of office, at
her girdle.[1] A boy walked before her, bearing a
sword unsheathed, a custom which Müllenhoff refers
to the worship of Freyr.[2] The symbol of a ring, that
genuine *wed* or pledge, can be traced far back into
the middle ages, and was of course well known to the
Romans; but it cannot be proved to be of Germanic
origin. Grimm suspects foreign influence.[3] In the
north, Thor's hammer was used to consecrate the
bride, just as it consecrated the corpse for burial.[4]
Thrym, the giant bridegroom, eager for the nuptials,
cries out: —

> Bear in the hammer, bride to hallow,
> lay now Miǫllnir [5] on maiden's knee,
> hallow us twain in hands of troth ! [6]

In fact, this famous but frustrated ceremony is so
close a copy of old Scandinavian ways [7] that some
of the details may be given. Thor's hammer has
been stolen by Thrym, and cannot be had unless the
gods give the robber Freyja to wife. A trick is tried.
Thor himself is wrapt in the bride's veil of Freyja,
puts on the famous Brising necklace, has a bunch of
keys jingling at his girdle, has jewels on his breast,

---

[1] Wackernagel, work quoted, p. 7 f.
[2] *R. A.* 167.   [3] *R. A.* 432, 178.
[4] Mannhardt, a little too eagerly, insists on its phallic significance.
[5] Name of Thor's hammer.
[6] *Ꝺrymskv.*, 30, Neckel, p. 111, Bellows, p. 181, Hollander, p. 126.
[7] So say Vigfusson and Powell, *C. P. B.* II. 472.

and a hood wrapt about his head, and, with Loki as bridesmaid, fares to Giant-Land. " Up spake Thrym,[1] the Giant lord : ' Stand up my Giants all, and strew the benches; they are bringing me Freyja to wife.' . . . Early in the evening the guests gathered, and ale was served to the Giants. . . . In came the Giant's aged sister (mother?) begging boldly for a bridal fee: ' Take the red rings off thine arm if thou wouldst win my love, my love and all my heart besides.' . . ." Then Thrym calls for the hammer, Thor lays hold of it and slays the giants all.— Touches of burlesque are not unwelcome in this description, for the old-fashioned ways are evidently given with great care.

This actual marriage was surely an important ceremony. Waitz thinks [2] the affair was private and took place before the family alone. Tacitus does not commit himself; but Grimm insists that the ceremony was public, and collects later evidence in favor of his assertion.[3] The clan and kin system demand the active co-operation of relatives; and Anglo-Saxon laws show traces of this, even where the church has begun to regulate the whole affair.[4] Further ceremonies we may imagine. Thus, an oracle was doubtless consulted, and symbolic acts of cult were accomplished with reference to those divinities who presided over marriages, — Freyr and Freyja, one may guess. The good old ways were duly acknowledged by a mock fight, a race, or what not; and by the tears and lamenting of the bride's nearer

---

[1] Translation, *C. P. B.* I. 179 f.   [2] *Verfassunggesch.* I. 61.
[3] *R. A.* 433. Tacitus simply says: " *Intersunt parentes et propinqui.*"
Germ. XVIII.   [4] Liebermann, I, 442, 444.

relatives, o'ercrowed, however, by loud exultation from friends of the party of the first part. Songs and feasting could not have failed; rude jokes were perhaps in season, and the *gros rire* which lingered about the occasion down to comparatively modern times. So much of the Germanic function seems to have resembled the Roman ceremonies that we feel it a thousand pities to find no chronicler of the words spoken by the northern pair at their betrothal. What was the German equivalent of the Roman bride's simple declaration: "*Si tu Gaius, ego Gaia*"? — a piece of humility, by the by, which if generally known nowadays would distress honorable women not a few. It must be remembered that this formal engagement sufficed for the beginning of married life, and was so regarded long after Christianity had been introduced in Germanic lands. The actual ceremony in church took place later, and among the Anglo-Saxons was not allowed at all for the marriage of a widow.[1]

A few particulars from later practice may be added to our guesses about the earlier affair. The wooing, or rather the bargain, was probably begun by father or friend, who, mostly along with the wooer, went on his errand with a great crowd of relatives and backers.[2] During the negotiations, our young bridegroom-to-be sat silent, listened to the eloquent praise of his own excellent differences, and like Messrs. Dodson and Fogg under equally trying circumstances, "looked as virtuous as possible." It is well

[1] *R. A.* 435.

[2] Weinhold, *D. F.* I. 317, reminds us that even god Freyr sent a messenger (see *Skirnismal* in the *Edda*) to woo for him.

known that this vicarious wooing is still practised in
the very highest and in the very lowest classes of
European society — the two sets of conservatives,
princes and peasants. Again, the choice of a wife
was not so limited as now. There were hardly any
forbidden degrees of relationship. Mythology at
least countenances even the marriage of brother and
sister,[1] and in historical times one was at liberty
to marry a stepmother, as witness Eadbald of Kent
and Æthelbald of Wessex. The deceased wife's sister, the brother's widow, one's own niece, — any one
of these was a lawful mate. Only slowly and with
infinite pains could the church establish its salutary
discipline and the doctrine of forbidden degrees.

Early marriages, say both Cæsar and Tacitus,[2] were
rare among the Germans. Rare, too, were second
marriages, as we are told in the *Germania*.[3] As for
the first statement, we must remember what "early"
would mean in a Roman's mouth; for he was used to
seeing wives of eleven or twelve years of age.[4]
Again, in our oldest German and English chronicles
we find records of very early nuptials. This continued to modern times. Lord Herbert of Cherbury
married at fifteen a wife of twenty-one; in his Auto-
biography, all he finds worthy of comment in the
affair is "the disparity in years." However, Cæsar
and Tacitus were doubtless right in their general
statement; for it not only squares with our accounts
of Germanic chastity, but agrees with that doctrine

---

[1] See Weinholt, *D. F.*³, I, 325; *Lokasenna* in Bellows, pp. 162, 163,
st. 32, 36; Hollander, p. 113, st. 32. For further details see E. Young
in *Essays in Anglo-Saxon Law* (Boston 1876), pp. 126 ff.

[2] *B. G.* VI. 21; *Germ.* XX.   [3] Cap. XIX.

[4] Jung, *Leben und Sitten d. Römer*, I. 84 f.

of political economy which makes marriages scarce in proportion to the difficulty of supporting families. Such difficulty was no stranger to the German. As regards the second marriage, the old custom of widow-sacrifice would give a grimly sufficient reason for the female side. When this custom ceased, it left a strong sentiment against the second marriage. The widow laid her keys, emblem of household rule, upon the corpse of her husband, and they went with him into the grave.[1] So unusual, says Wackernagel, was the marriage of widows that it is used as tragical *motif*.

Death was not the only means of breaking the marriage bond; adultery — but, as was said, only on the side of the wife — destroyed the pact. The consequences of this crime have been in part defined;[2] but the punishments savor of a ruthlessness which must have corresponded to a great horror of the offence. To kill her was a clear privilege of the husband, but such a punishment as to be trodden and suffocated in mud or slime was prescribed for the Burgundian false one. The Frisian could hang, burn, kill with sword, or even flay his adulterous wife. The Anglo-Saxon punishment, already quoted, is much milder and falls on the seducer, who must pay his own[3] wergild and must buy the husband another wife. Perhaps the mildness is only accident of omission; for we are not told what became of the guilty wife. In later tradition we get some bloody and savage touches which may well preserve the

[1] *R. A.* 176, 453; Wackernagel, *Kl. Schr.* I. 31.   [2] See p. 139, above.
[3] See Liebermann, III, 9, § 31, 4.   But see Schmid.
p. 5, note.

practice of an older day. Thus, among other instances, the tragic ballads of *Old Robin of Portingale*
and *Little Musgrave and Lady Barnard* agree in
making the injured husband inflict a cruel mutilation
upon the wife.   In the first: —

> Hee cutt the papps beside her brest,
>   And bade her wish her will;
> And he cut the eares beside her head,
>   And bade her wish on still.

In the second: —

> He cut her paps from off her brest;
>   Great pity it was to see
> That some drops of this ladie's heart's blood
>   Ran trickling downe her knee. [1]

This agrees well enough with the scene in Tacitus,
an angry husband scourging the shorn and unclad
offender from his home; and it gives us by contrast
better ability to appreciate the infinite despair and
tenderness of Othello's words: —

> I that am cruel, am yet merciful;
> I would not have thee linger in thy pain.

[1] Child, Ballads,[2] III. 241, 245

CHAPTER VI

THE FAMILY

Hospitality and gifts — Responsibilities of the head of a family — Importance of kinship — Conflicting duties — Feud — *Wergild*, and other substitutes for feud — Paternal power — Exposure — Education of children — Names — Old age.

ESTABLISHED in their home, the young couple took up a life rude enough to our eyes, but not without its virtues and even its amenities. Hospitality was instinctive in the German. To be sure, the laws and customs of modern life, as they touch upon personal property, are far removed from the simple notions of our forefathers; and it is not to be denied that the idea of individual ownership has developed at the expense of that primitive generosity. So much may be granted; yet the effort to make this hospitality of the Germans a proof of their absolute savagery — one trait the more to support a parallel with modern Africans — is by no means to be allowed.[1] One is inclined to prefer the exaggerated praise of Tacitus.[2] While we may justly place much of this generosity to the credit of an almost communal system of property,

[1] Lippert's admirable book on *Culturgeschichte* goes too far in this direction. The author sees all things in Africa, after the Malebranche fashion of his school.

[2] *Germ.* XXI. See also Cæsar *B. G.* VI. 23.

enough of the pure virtue is left to deserve our
admiration. Savages do not pass laws to promote
the magnanimous treatment of guests; and the ordinances quoted by Grimm must rest on a very old
foundation.[1] Thus we find a penalty imposed on the
householder who may refuse shelter and fireside to
the traveller; "shelter, and room by the fire, and
water," — these were not to be denied under any
pretext.[2] Even if the guest had slain the brother of
his host, — no matter; he must come and go in
safety;[3] and what that meant in those days is evident from the song of the two mill-maids who are
grinding King Frodi's fortune, and in their description of a universal peace can find no climax better
than this: a time when "no man shall harm his neighbor . . . nor smite with whetted sword, yea, *not
though he find his brother's slayer bound before him.*"[4]
Similar phrases recur constantly in mediæval poetry
as type of the highest form of self-restraint and
noble toleration. This hospitality was limited, of
course, to transient guests; foreigners who came into
a country without friends and kin behind them, and
made mien to stay, were in danger of unfreedom: a
year and a day they might bide, and after that it
was often slavery.[5] But the wayfaring man who had
definite objects in view was welcome to this boundless hospitality. In later times we find the fixed
custom that a guest might tarry up to the third day;
and Grimm quotes an Anglo-Saxon law: "two nights
a guest, the third night one of the household."[6]

[1] *R. A.* 399 f.   [2] "Tectum et focum et aquam nemo deneget."
[3] *R. A.* 400.   [4] *C. P. B.* I. 185.   [5] *R. A.* 399.
[6] See also Liebermann, I, 330, § 28.

Interesting survivals of this doctrine of the three days' grace occur in popular sayings and customs. German doggerel, more vigorous than elegant, declares:—

> Den ersten Tag ein Gast,
> den zweiten eine Last,
> den dritten stinkt er fast,[1]—

which is astonishingly like Herrick:—

> Two dayes y'ave larded here; a third, yee know,
> Makes guests and fish smell strong;[2]—

and both are matched by a Latin effusion,[3] which is perhaps the original. But Herrick puts such growling rudeness into the mouth "of some rough groom"; and in conspicuous antithesis praises the fine old hospitalities of his friend in words that scent good cheer and spread the honest savors of an English kitchen. We may draw our conclusions of heredity, and fancy this knight with his "large ribbes of beef" an unmistakable descendant of Chaucer's franklin, whose

> . . . table dormant in his halle alway
> Stood redy covered al the longe day.

Further, we may think that this ruddy epicure himself, in whose house "hit snewed . . . of mete and drynke," did nothing more than keep green the laurels of Germanic hospitality. For let us listen to Tacitus:[4] "Banquets and hospitality find such favor

---

[1] Weinhold, *Altnord. Leben*, p. 447.

[2] "A Panegerick to Sir Lewis Pemberton," in the *Hesperides*.

[3] Printed by Wright, *Reliquiæ Antiquæ*, I. 91, and *Domestic Manners*, etc., p. 333.

[4] *Germ.* XXI. See Cæsar *B. G.* VI. 23, whose testimony is in the same strain.

in no other nation. To turn anybody, no matter
who he may be, from one's door, is held as a crime;
he is entertained according to the means of the host,
who provides his best. When that is gone, the host
becomes guide and companion to his guest, and together they seek the hospitality of some other board,
going uninvited into the first convenient house. Here
it is the same thing; they are received with like
friendliness. Neighbor and stranger are made equally
welcome. To the parting guest, so custom ordains,
is given whatever he happens to desire; and there is
equal freedom for the host to ask something of him."
It seems a little ungracious to ascribe all this to the
absence of any notions about individual property or
the value of things. The astonishing hospitality of
the Icelanders, who harbored absolute strangers an
entire winter, who kept a table always ready for
chance visitors whoever they might be, and whose
very dogs were glad to see a guest walk in,[1] — this
is certainly a point or two above the African standard, in kind as well as degree.

The guest, however, had certain forms with which
he must comply, if he would not run the risk of being cut down like a thief. He must keep to the
highway, and blow sufficiently upon his horn, that
no mistakes might be made.[2] "If a far-come man, or
a stranger, go out of the road through the forest, and
do not cry out nor blow his horn, he is to be held as
a thief." But if a man were lost, or could find no
house, he was at liberty to cut standing corn for his
horse, — one law says he may let the horse "tread

[1] Weinhold, *D. F.* II. 195.　　[2] Liebermann, I, 98, 99, § 64.

into the corn with his fore-feet, and so eat," — and
he might hew a little wood to mend his wagon.

Of course, it must not be forgotten, that along
with wider hospitality went narrower protection of
law. What law did not require was ordained by use
and tradition; and we may say of the Germanic
treatment of guests what Tacitus remarks about one
of the other virtues, — that "good custom avails more
with this people than good laws elsewhere." [1] Moreover, the family took the place of the state as regards
responsibility for a stranger's doings. "If," runs an
old Anglo-Saxon law, "if a man, in his own house,
harbors a stranger three nights, merchant or other
person, who has come over the mark (boundary), and
feeds him with his meat, and [the stranger] then
does evil to any one, let the host bring the guest to
reckoning, or do justice for him." [2] An insolent
guest might be promptly beaten by his host. [3]

The custom of giving some present to the parting
guest has been mentioned in the passage from Tacitus, and forms the subject of a monograph by Jacob
Grimm. [4] Of the articles which a German — prince
or freeman — was wont to bestow on vassal, friend,
or guest, Grimm names land, which was naturally
the favor of chieftain or king, then food and drink,
valuable animals, clothes, rings, and similar objects.
Even in the middle ages money was little used for
gifts; and we still shrink from such a present where
a definite object of equal value would arouse no scruple. The simplest gift was a glass of wine or mead; [5]

[1] *Germ.* XIX.   [2] Liebermann, I, 11, § 15.   [3] Grimm, *R. A.* 744
[4] *Ueber Schenken und Geben*, Kl. Schr. II. 173 ff.
[5] The double meaning of German *schenken*, "to pour out" and "to give," is thus explained by Grimm.

and often with the liquor, one gave the cup that held it. Of animals, horses were the favorite gift, as in our *Béowulf*, and we remember that the price of a certain Germanic bride was paid in white horses. An Anglo-Saxon alliterating formula was *mearas and maðmas*, " horses and treasure." Dress was often a gift, as in the Nibelungen Lay, where it is coupled with horses.[1] Golden arm-rings were the aristocratic present, — witness Hildebrand's last appeal for reconciliation with his son. Naturally, the course of conquest and settlement made land the gift which men prized the most; on the border of two epochs, and uniting the nomadic and the agricultural standard, may be mentioned the gift which Hygelac made to Eofor and Wulf when they had slain his enemy, "a hundred thousand in land and linked rings";[2] moreover, to Eofor he gave his own daughter. Generosity could go no farther.

These welcomes and gifts, these open doors and inviting tables of the old German, are not precisely in tune with that secret underground passage from the house to field or wood, which was provided for escape from the frequent raids and sieges of one's neighbors. The German's house was not only his castle, but it was very often a beleaguered castle, the refuge of his clan. For he was the protector and head of his house; all its quarrels were his quarrels; and when the family, or the meanest member of it, was wronged, he was its avenger. In the same way, he was responsible for wrongs done by his family; and thus all his relatives were bound with him in a

---

[1] *N. L.* 28 : " Den vremden und den kunden gab er ross und gewant."
[2] *Béow.* 2995 ff.

common bond of responsibility. To inherit the family privileges was to inherit its duties. A law of Cnut is very instructive as marking the passage of the Germanic mind out of the stern old logic into a temper of equity. "It was once the custom," says our wise king, "that the child which lay in cradle, even though it had tasted meat, was deemed by covetous men just as guilty as if it were possessed of its understanding (*gewittig*). But henceforth I earnestly forbid this, together with many other things which are loathsome to God."[1] A law of Ine had provided that if a man steal with the knowledge of his family, they should all go into bondage together.[2]

Thus the chief burden, as well as the chief glory, fell upon the head of the house. To be a father, or the eldest son of a widow, or the eldest of near kin in guardianship of minors, carried with the position responsibilities that now seem almost incredible. Such a person was executor of a code of vengeance which we do not know, simply because law and the administration of government have taken its place. "Revenge," said Bacon, "is a kind of wild justice"; but it is more exact to say that justice is tamed and ordered revenge. The law now stands in relation to the murderer where once stood the head of the murdered man's family, who has thus deputed the state to perform his ancient duty.[3] Despite a somewhat sophomoric note, this explanation agrees with the facts of the case. But it was a far intenser feeling

---

[1] Liebermann, I, 364, § 76, 2.   [2] *Ibid.*, p. 92, § 7, 1.

[3] *Lex Angl. et Wer.* VI. (and Uhland, *Kl. Schr.* I. 218) : "Ad quemcumque hereditas terræ pervenerit, ad illum vestis bellica, id est lorica, *et ultio proximi*, et solutio leudis, debet pertinere."

that then filled the avenger of blood, than any abstract
severities of our modern justice; for it knew no
extenuating circumstances, and did not sunder one
motive from another.[1] It had the tremendous sanctions of religion. By the old belief, by the cult of
family *manes*, an unappeased parent-soul hovered
about the very hearthstone, a perturbed spirit only to
be brought to rest by the grateful blood of the murderer offered by son or kinsman. So the sense of kin
took just precedence of all human bonds; and in the
swan-song of Germanic mythology, the *Vǫluspa*, our
sibyl can find no sign of impending doom so certain
and disastrous as the breaking up of family ties:
"Brother shall fight against brother, and they shall
turn to murderers; children of one parent shall bring
shame upon their race. . . . Adultery shall flourish."[2]

In this kindly soil of the family flourished such
growth of sentiment as that rough life brought forth.
Peace, good-will, the sense of honor, loyalty to friend
and kinsman, brotherly affection, all were plants that
found in the Germanic home that congenial warmth
they needed for their earliest stages of growth. The
double notion of blood-relationship and mutual peace
is shown by a passage in our oldest English poem,
Widsīð : —

> Hrothwulf and Hrothgar held the longest
> open concord, uncle and nephew,
> after they routed the race of Wicings,
> fell'd the pride of the power of Ingeld,
> hew'd down at Heorot the Heathobard's line.[3]

[1] See Stubbs. *Const Hist.* L 81
[2] Neckel, *Edda*, p. 10, st. 45. Metaphors C. P. B., II, 473 ff.
[3] vv. 45-49.

Pretty, moreover, is the old "kenning," or metaphor for "wife," — *the weaver* (or maker) *of peace;* whether with Grimm we explain it as referring to the household union,[1] or because a marriage brought together two families and tended to set aside feuds.[2] Situations akin to that of Rodrigue and Chimène in the *Cid* may well have burdened many Germanic lives, as witness an episode of the *Béowulf.*[3] Freawaru, daughter of the Danish Hrothgar, is married to Ingeld, son of a prince who has been slain in battle against Hrothgar's forces; and the marriage is meant to put aside the necessity of blood-revenge. For a while Ingeld forgets his wrongs; but an old warrior of his train[4] spurs him to vengeance, which is all the more easily suggested by the insolence of a young Danish noble, attendant upon his countrywoman and princess, who wears, in open sight of all, the sword once wielded by King Froda, the fallen father of Ingeld. Then oaths are broken, "the love of woman grows cooler in Ingeld after he has felt the waves of care," and blood must flow for blood.

Evidently it was a good thing to belong to some large clan, and an honorable thing to be its leader. Thus the power of King Hrothgar is described by the poet as based upon his increasing authority over kin and clan.[5]

> To Hrothgar was given such glory of war,
> such honor of combat, that all his kin
> obeyed him gladly till great grew his band
> of youthful comrades.

---

[1] *Andreas und Elene,* p. 144 f.

[2] See also such a name for a queen as *friðu-sibb folca,* "peace-kin of peoples," the relative who brings peace to clans. *Béow.* 2017.

[3] 2021 ff. See, for Danish parallels, Müllenhoff, *Beovulf,* p. 42 f.

[4] In Saxo (Holder, pp. 182 ff.) Starcatherus.   [5] *Béow.* 64 ff.

That is, he was head of the family, and his kin were glad to acknowledge it and serve him. The youths springing up in his service are partly kinsmen, partly the "retainers" or *comitatus*, a peculiar Germanic institution which we shall presently consider. The value set upon the ties of a family is shown by certain verses in the Old Saxon paraphrase of the gospels, the *Hêliand*. It is the passage of St. Matthew which makes it profitable for us that one of our members should perish, and not that the whole body should be cast into hell. As Vilmar points out,[1] the German laughed at scars, and found more sport than sorrow in the notion of mutilation. So the translator adds in explanation a far more terrible alternative, — separation from one's kin. "*Better to throw thy friend far from thee*, however close the *sibbia*, the kinship, may be," than to let him lead thee into sin.

The family tie engendered the earliest notions of duty, whether to the living or to the dead; and this sense of duty is the moral foundation of all Germanic history. Alive, the head of the house exacted obedience and respect, fostered order and justice; dead, he was the object of cult, grew mightier with lapse of time, and as a tribal god sanctioned wider and deeper laws of society. His fireplace was the primitive council chamber; his grave was the primitive altar. Originally the family or clan made a definite sphere or system of life; outside of it the homeless man felt indeed that chaos had come again. The heaviest punishment was expulsion from the family;[2] and banishment, the crown of sorrow for a German, is

---

[1] Work quoted, p. 57. *Hêliand*, ed. Heyne, 1492 ff.
[2] See Dahn, *Bausteine*, II. 79 ff., on Family and State.

a topic repeatedly touched upon in Anglo-Saxon poetry.[1]   The wretched victim of such a fate was cut off from all protection of law and order, and renounced the benefits of civilization.   Thus at the other extreme of fortune from the proud head of a proud and powerful clan stood the clanless man, the exile, the outlaw, who had no protecting relative, no strong kinsman, no "gold-friend and lord."   Those touching Anglo-Saxon lyrics, *The Wanderer* and *The Seafarer*, mourn such a fate.

The head of the narrower family in normal circumstances was the father.   The fatherhood of God appeals with peculiar force to the German.   Thus, as it would seem, when the poet of *Béowulf* tells of the murder of Abel and of the doom of Cain, he treats the punishment as an act of vengeance undertaken by God for one of his human children.[2]   Severe enough, too, seemed Cain's punishment.   He was "banished from his own kind," direst penalty short of death.   With such notions of the power and privilege of fathers, the Aryan horror of parricide can be understood.   Not without interest for mediæval sentiment on this theme is an account quoted by Kemble[3] from Barbazan's *Fabliaux et Contes*, as a parallel to Solomon's famous decision.   Two princes — brothers — quarrel about their inheritance.   The father's corpse is set before them, and it is announced that he who shall drive his spear furthest into the body is to be the heir.   "The elder strikes home; but the

---

[1] Lingering in words like ou.: "wretch," or German *Elend* (*Elland*).

[2] *Béow.* 107 ff.   The use of words like *gewræc* "wreaked, avenged," and *fæhðe*, "feud," as applied to the crime, surely upholds this notion.

[3] *Salomon and Saturn*, p. 106.   He thinks the source of the story is Cap. XLV. of the *Gesta Romanorum*.

younger, detesting the impiety, prefers losing all
share in the inheritance to mangling the corse: he is
in consequence, by consent of all the barons, put in
possession of the principality." In an age which
was full of murder and sudden death, which saw no
crime in the open killing of a man, this horror of
parricide is significant enough. Such a deed struck at
the very heart of social order and religious sanctions.

To the simple mind of those days it seemed a good
thing to rivet this family bond by gifts. If a young
prince, says the poet of *Béowulf*, will only give rich
gifts to his father's friends and kin, he may count in
his old age upon comrades glad to help him and stand
by him in stress of war.[1] For such pains and benefits
of kindred were not bandied about indiscriminately;
they were guarded with scrupulous care and kept at a
proper value. Hence, too, we find in all older dialects
a multiplicity of names to express relationship by
blood; and richer even than Germanic, are the Slavonic, Lithuanian, and Finnish, which, as Grimm has
noted,[2] longest kept up the primitive ways. When
this genuine relationship failed, the German could
enter upon an artificial one. It is true that adoption,
as a means of increasing one's family, was hardly a
Germanic custom;[3] but the so-called blood-brotherhood was a special device of our ancestors, and popular
enough. We know it best in its Scandinavian form.
Two youths, often foster-brothers, cut each the palm of

[1] *Béow* 20 ff   [2] *G. D. S.*[3] p. 92 f.
[3] A trace of adoption has been seen in *Beowulf* 946 ff., but "the
relationship entered into by Hrothgar and Beowulf does not signify
adoption in the strict legal sense, but implies fatherly friendship and
devoted helpfulness respectively, suggesting at any rate the bonds of
loyal retainership" (Klaeber, *Beowulf*, p. 162, note to vv. 946 ff.).

the hand and let the blood run from it into a hollow
in the ground; here their blood mingled while they
grasped hands and swore brotherhood for life.   More
solemn ceremony, with intricate symbolism, consisted
in their taking the oath as they kneeled under strips
of turf.[1] Thus their blood became one, they were kin,
and on each devolved the sacred duty of avenging the
other; such an artificial relative could even claim his
share of the *wergild*.   Sometimes the two held their
goods in common.   How vivid must have seemed to
the German that passage of Genesis where the blood of
a slain brother cries from the ground ! As usual, myth
has absorbed the human relation : Odin and Loki are
said once to have sworn brotherhood.   Loki, detected
mischief-maker, comes unbidden to a banquet of the
gods, where "not one speaks a good word for him."
The situation is dramatic.[2]

Loki. Thirsty, I, Loki, came to this hall . . . to beg the
Anses give me but one draught of the goodly mead. Why
sit ye so silent, ye moody gods, speaking no word ? . . .

Bragi. The Anses will never give thee seat or place at this
banquet. . . .

Loki. Dost thou remember, Odin, how we two in days of old
blended blood together ?   Thou sworest never to taste ale unless
we drank together.

Odin. Get up then, Widar, and let the Wolf's father [*sc.*
Loki] sit down to the banquet, that Loki may not make mock
of us here in Eager's hall.[3]

---

[1] See von Amira in Paul's *Grdr. d. germ. Philol.*[3] pp. 185, 186; Grimm,
G. D. S.[2] 96 f., and Weinhold, *Altnord. Leben*, p. 287 f.   The general custom was by no means specially Germanic, as Grimm's investigation
shows: examples, *R. A.* 192 f.

[2] Translation is from *C. P. B.*, I, 102; *Lokasenna*, st. 6 ff. (Neckel,
p. 94); Bellows, pp. 154 ff., Hollander, pp. 107 ff.

[3] Grimm (*G. D. S.*[2] 97) reminds us of the same relation between
Gunnar and Sigurd.

Blood-brotherhood is a very pretty word for our ears; but in the brave old days it was no metaphor. The soul was thought to abide chiefly in the warm blood, as well as in the breath and the eyes. "Heart and eyes" were the main thing, as can be learned from many a later folk-song. We need not discuss the question of survivals from an age of universal cannibalism;[1] there is no doubt that with our ancestors, as with Mephistopheles and his brethren, blood was "ein ganz besondrer Saft,"— though the signature in one's blood is only an academic fancy. The old notion was to acquire the courage and spirit of a slain enemy by drinking his blood; and vague survivals of this are rife in Scandinavian tradition. Blood is the abode and source of life. Blood brings a life glow into the cheeks of the dead, and loosens the tongue of Teiresias in prophetic speech, as Odysseus, in that unrivalled scene, stands by the trench filled with blood, and the pale shades flock about him, eager to drink. In the burning hall of Attila, Hagen and the Burgundian king ward off the effects of fearful heat by drinking the blood of the slain that lie about them,— here merely a touch of fantastic horror, quite forgetful of the original meaning. Blood mixed with honey we meet in Norse myth. Kvasir is the wisest of men. He is slain by the dwarfs Fialar and Galar, who mix his blood with honey; whoever drinks of this becomes a poet or a seer. Eating the heart is a tradition deep-rooted in Germanic mythology, and later it was a characteristic of witches, who fell heir to most of the earlier habits of Asgard. It

---

[1] *Cf.* Lippert, *Culturges.* I. 61 f. *Religion der europ. Culturvölker*, p. 48.

is needless to insist on modern survivals in proverb and tradition; " blood," we say, " will tell," or it " runs thicker than water."

The ties of blood being the most sacred known to the ancients, the one band of society, the beginning and chief sanction of religion, it was natural that any conflict of duty, any case of doubt which way the claim of blood should draw one, must have formed chief material for their tragedy. Known in some form all over the world, this tragic motive was developed among our forefathers with a simple grandeur which stands alone in history. Laius and Œdipus as tragic victims rank no whit higher for grandeur of conception than Hildebrand and Hathubrand, or Ruedegêr of Bechelâren in the Nibelungen Lay.[1] The episode of Ruedegêr outweighs a hundred tragedies. A vassal of the Hunnish king, he meets the Burgundian guests as they enter Attila's dominions, receives them in his own palace, and gives his daughter to the youngest of the brother-kings. When the great struggle in the burning hall grows almost hopeless for Kriemhild, she bids Ruedegêr, as her husband's sworn man and vassal, to go into the hall and slay or bind her own brethren, of whom young Giselhêr is the elected son-in-law of Ruedegêr. What shall he do? " God help me," he cries; " would that I were dead ! " Whatever he decides, his honor must be tainted, — to war against his own kin, or to desert his chieftain in his time of need; the agony of doubt was never

---

[1] Many other examples will occur to the student of tragedy, ancient or modern, — Orestes, Hamlet, Rodrigue, and many more. The sacred duty of revenging one's kindred or friends was the soul of feud, and fills Aryan literature from Achilles down to Hamlet.

painted with such naked force. Heavy-hearted, he obeys his lord, and goes to a brave though unwelcome combat and to a welcome death. Further, there is a little episode in *Béowulf*, — hardly an episode, one may say, but a mere hint, — where King Hrethel's oldest son, Herebeald, is killed by a purely accidental shot from the bow of the second son, Hæthcyn.[1] The old king pines away, not in our modern grief, but because of the relentless misery of irreconcilable relations with the second son, — the duty, as avenger, of killing him, and the paternal duty of protecting one's own offspring. For our forefathers, the tragedy of this situation needed no words: an allusion was enough. The famous saga of the Volsungs records still another case. Siggeir and Signy are man and wife; but Siggeir has killed Signy's father and all her brothers except Sigmund. Signy, as a duty to her kin, does all she can to help her brother accomplish his revenge against her husband. At last the hall of Siggeir is set in flames, and there is no hope for him. Then Signy, in spite of all appeals from her brother, kisses him farewell and goes into the burning hall to die, as befits a Germanic wife, at the side of her husband. Exaggerated, unnatural, void of all sweetness and light, this story is nevertheless full of a wild energy, like the times that brought it forth.

This wild energy, the provocations and opportunities of such a life, led, of course, to ceaseless feuds. Such a state of things became impossible; a race of men cannot go on forever cutting their own throats, and the race itself seems to make from time to time

[1] *Béow.* 2438 ff.

an almost individual effort at self-preservation, re-
form, and progress. So came the great step of civilization which compounded a murder by payment of a
definite price. Probably it began, as was only just,
with cases of accidental killing or maiming. This
wergild, or man-price, indicates system, organization,
and offers sure evidence of incipient political life. It
was already known in the time of Tacitus; and was
reckoned in terms of flocks and herds. The sum was
fixed according to the rank, birth, and office of the
person killed; and was paid to those whose duty
would otherwise compel them to take vengeance for
the deed. The *wergild* for women varied;[1] now it
was the same as that of a man, now only half as
much; but for a pregnant woman the price rose very
high.[2] Kings generally stood quite above any such
provisions, except in a few Anglo-Saxon laws. But
let us hear what Tacitus has to say about the whole
matter of revenge and composition for murder. "It
is a duty," he says, "to take up as an inheritance the
feuds of one's father or relatives. And yet these
feuds are not proof against all settlement (*nec im-
placabiles durant*); even murder is compounded with
the payment of a definite number of cattle or other
animals, and the whole family receives the price. . . ."[3]
We can see how eagerly kings would foster this check
on unlimited feud; and we are not surprised to note
the prominent place given to the *wergild* in all
systems of Germanic law. First of his secular laws
stands King Edmund's decree in regard to murder

---

[1] Of course these are mainly mediæval distinctions, but seem of
primitive origin.
[2] *R. A.* 404 f.   [3] *Germ.* XXI.

and the *wergild;* let the murderer, of whatever rank
(*sy swâ boren swâ he sŷ*), bear the vengeance that is
due unless he can pay the full price within twelve
months; and if any of his relatives harbor or help him,
they, too, are liable to the act of revenge.[1] Even where
a man has made himself hated far and wide by crimes
of every sort, his murder must be compounded.
Gregory of Tours tells this of one nicknamed Avus,
who after manifold sins was killed in a quarrel by a
servant of his adversary. The latter, however, was
forced to pay proper *wergild* to the sons of the dead
man.[2]

In course of time, fines were set not simply for
murder, but for every sort of wound; they were
assessed, much in the fashion of our modern " damages " for accident, in proportion to the importance
of the bodily loss, — eye, hand, limb, or what not.
The following law of Æthelberht marks progress
indeed: " If one man, with his fist, strikes another
upon the nose, [the fine is] three shillings."[3] As to
the price itself, there is great variation in different
places. From a hundred "shillings" up to very
large sums, the price was fixed according to the rank
of the slain, — freeman, noble, king's thane, and so
on. The church had part in the system, and ecclesi-
astics enjoyed a high *wergild*. But to define these
values would be a task almost as useless as hopeless.[4]

Feud, which this system was meant to lay aside,
seems to have been a wide word. It included the
strained relations between King Hrethel and his son,

---

[1] Liebermann, I, 186, § 1.   [2] Greg. Tur., VII. 13.
[3] Liebermann, I, 6, § 57.
[4] See Liebermann, II (Glossary) under *"wergild"*.

the murder of Abel, Grendel's direful raids upon the
hall "Heorot", and of course the hostility between two
families or clans, the private shedding of blood for
blood.   There was utmost need to curb this ferocity
of the Germanic temperament.   Maurer records a case
among the Norsemen, who kept longest and strongest
the old traditions, of children who would not play
with a companion until he had at least killed some
wild animal.[1]   The Scandinavian annals and legends
are full of such stories, in contrast to the records of
Slavonic races, who have always been averse to the
feud.   We open the *Egilssaga*,[2] and find that a certain
man has two sons, one of whom, Egil, "is said to have
begun to make verses in his third year, and in his
seventh year killed a boy who had affronted him at a
game of ball."   Another boy of nine could boast that
he had killed three men; and Olaf Tryggvason at the
same age took up a feud and avenged his foster-father.
Instructive is the dialogue, ascribed to Egil, between
the earl's daughter and the boy who is her partner at
table.[3]   She despises such a youthful gallant: "Thou
hast never given a warm meal to the wolf (*i.e.* slain
men in battle). . . ."   And the boy answers: "I have
walked with bloody brand and whistling spear, with
the wound-bird following me. . . ."   Such were the
credentials of good society.   To keep to the strict line
of the feud, we find Grettir coming back to Iceland,
after a long absence, to learn that his father is dead
and his brother slain.   "After he had visited his
mother, the first errand was to his brother's baneman

---

[1] *Bekehrung d. norweg. Stämme*, II. 172.
[2] See P. E. Müller, *Sagabibl.* I. 112.
[3] *C. P. B.* I. 373, whence the translation.

(murderer) whom he speedily killed."[1] So in Viga
Styr's saga, Styr boasts that he has killed thirty-three
men and never paid a penny of *wergild*. Later, he
meets death at the hand of a youth whose father he
had killed and to whom he contemptuously refused
the price of composition.[2] Earlier accounts, and from
a different country, record the same deep-rooted Germanic love of the feud, of bloodshed and revenge.
The Franks were so ferocious in their vengeance that
they even infected their Roman neighbors and subjects.[3] One story out of many may illustrate the
Frankish spirit. A queen, who in life had been a
monster of crime and oppression, lay on her death-bed.
Before she gave up the ghost, however, she demanded
companions in her death, "in order that at her funeral
others should be wept for besides herself." She called
the king, and complaining that the medicine which
had been given her by her physicians was the cause of
her death, made him swear that, as soon as she died,
these two doctors should be slain with the sword;
and it was done.[4] Sometimes the tragedy shades
down into comedy. A Scandinavian saga tells of a
man who was hit on the neck by an iron pan, thrown
in a quarrel, and was slightly injured. Some years
later, wooing a certain woman for his wife, he is rejected by her relatives because he has never taken
vengeance on him who hurled the pan.[5]

Sullenly and slowly feud yielded its rights to a
system of fines, — punishment would have been

---

[1] Müller, *Sagabibl.* I. 254. [2] Ibid. I. 37 ff.
[3] Loebell, *Gregor v. Tours*, p. 83.
[4] *Greg. Tur.* V. 35. See also Loebell, work quoted, pp. 38, 41 ff.
[5] Dahn, *Bausteine*, p. 104.

impossible, — and did not come to an end, so far as Germany was concerned, until the close of the fifteenth century.[1] Where the feud would not yield to the payment of a price, men turned to a quasi-process of law deftly hidden in the guise of warfare. At first sight, trial by battle as a legal remedy looks absurd enough; might is still right, as in the feud. We forget, however, that the old feud left no avenue open for any sort of justice, and made the innocent suffer in shoals for a wrong, — perhaps a right, — done by one man who happened to be of their kin. Blood was the test. The punishment was not only inherited, as in our commandment, but collateral. Kemble [2] quotes the indignant reproach of Wiglaf to the thanes who have deserted their prince: every member of their clan, every relative, he says, shall pay for the cowardice of these few men. For as the clan all shared in the *wergild*, so they were exposed to the feud: "recipit," says Tacitus of the former, "universa domus." [3] Accident, moreover, was no excuse; a mere bit of carelessness might lead to the death of a dozen innocent relatives of the innocent cause of feud. The famous myth of Balder shows this stern doctrine that accident, so far as the blood-feud is concerned, must be reckoned one with crime. Blind Hǫdhr is innocent, in our eyes, of his brother's death; [4] but the

---

[1] In the Diet of Worms, 1495. See Arnold, *Deutsche Urzeit*, p. 342. But the *Fehde* of German nobles in the middle ages was not the same thing as the older feud, the former being a sort of armed law-suit. For Anglo-Saxon feud and composition, see Kemble, *Saxons*, I. Chap. X.

[2] *Saxons*,[1] I. 235. *Béow.* 2884 ff.

[3] *Germ.* XXI.

[4] Loki puts in his hand the fatal mistletoe twig, and bids him cast it in sport at Balder.

avenger, Wali, by the usual Germanic vow,[1] neither
washes himself nor combs his hair till he has killed
Hǫdhr. Beda tells a story of an Anglo-Saxon warrior who was left for dead upon the battle-field, came
to life, and was captured by the enemy. Fearing
death if he made himself known, he said he was a
poor rustic; but when the "count" who held him
prisoner, amazed at certain miraculous circumstances,
asked him who he really was, and promised him his
life, the warrior confessed all. " Thou art worthy of
of death," answers the king, " *because all my brothers
and relatives fell in that battle;*[2] nevertheless, for my
vow's sake, I will not kill thee."

When this wide swath of injustice is considered,
the single case of a combatant in the trial by battle
seems justice itself, — though trial by battle is only a
circumscribed and legalized feud. Compare the Icelandic *holmgang*, or duel, with the wholesale murders
of a feud like that described in the *Nialssaga*. Similarly, the other forms of ordeal seem absurd; not,
however, if we regard them as the institution of men
who began to see that right was better than might,
and believed that God would defend the innocent
and confound the guilty. J. Grimm, in his account[3]
of the ordeal, assumes that only the nobler phase of
it, trial by battle, was a frequent form of justice for
the freeman; though both ordeal and duel strike their

---

[1] So (*Germ. XXXI.*) among the Chatti, where the custom of letting
beard and hair grow till one has killed his man, is not confined to
special feuds, but is universal. After a great victory over the Romans,
Civilis "laid aside his hair," — "*barbaro voto . . . propexum rutila-
tumque crinem . . . deposuit.*" Tac. *Hist.* IV. 61.

[2] See Bædæ *Hist. Ecc.*, ed. Holder, IV. 22. "Quia omnes fratres et
cognati mei in illa sunt pugna interemti." [3] *R. A.* 908–937.

roots deep into our heathen antiquity.   Divination and lots were also regarded as an ordeal, and expressed the will of the gods.

Trial by battle was known by the Germans of Tacitus, and was regarded as an appeal to higher powers.   He mentions [1] the strange custom of deciding the event of battle by a duel fought between some captive of the enemy and a representative of the home army; the result of this duel was accepted as an infallible sign of the greater issue.   Champions, too, might fight for their respective armies, — like the Horatii and Curiatii.   The Norse duel, mostly to decide a personal quarrel, was fought on a holm, or island, and hence called *hôlmgângr*.   The sagas tell of many a holmgang; that of Gunnlaug Snake-Tongue and Hrafn, which resulted in the death of both, caused the Icelanders to abolish such duels as judicial process.   An early case of combat for a lady's honor is mentioned by Paul the Deacon.[2]   Queen Gundiperga is accused of infidelity to her husband.   One of her own slaves, named Carellus, receives permission from the king to defend the honor of Gundiperga against her accuser.   The duel takes place before all the people, and the queen is vindicated.

Such were the slow steps of rationalism as it won inch by inch the territory of barbarous instinct and superstitions.   But the old customs died hard.   Nobler souls long looked on all these compromises and compositions as degrading, and held blood to be far better than gold.   " I will not carry my son in my purse! " says an old Norseman as he spurns the prof-

---

[1] *Germ.* X.   [2] IV. 47.

fered satisfaction. In the *Nialssaga*, old Nial is told that he too, as well as his wife, may leave the burning house where his sons have been surrounded by their enemies. "No," he answers, "I am an old man, unable to avenge my sons; and I will not live in disgrace."

As a feud involved the family, it is clear that something besides mere pride swelled the breast of a father who counted his row of stalwart sons : it was an assurance of present and future weal.[1] No feud could be lightly undertaken against a powerful and numerous family. Probably the average Germanic brood was no smaller than in barren Iceland; and there we read of such people as Hrut Herjolfson and his two wives, who had sixteen boys and ten girls. "When, in his old age, at the summer assembly of the people, he appeared surrounded by fourteen sturdy sons, he was the subject of numerous congratulations,"[2] — and no wonder. To lose one of these stalwart sons was a very serious thing for the Germanic father.

Over wife and child, and every member of his family, bond or free, the German had, in theory, an absolute control. But religion and custom, what Tacitus calls the *boni mores*, set up certain restrictions which gradually hardened from tradition into law. To sell wife and child was a last resort of the Frisians.[3] The Anglo-Saxon laws, and even the church, recognized a sort of right which parents had to sell their children into servitude, but endeavored

[1] "Quanto maior affinium numerus, tanto gratiosior senectus," *Germ.* XX.

[2] Weinhold, *Altnord. Leben*, 259.   [3] Tac. *Ann.* IV. 72.

to curb the practice.[1] To slay outright an able-bodied member of one's household may have been lawful, but, except in the case of punishment or defence, was doubtless rarely exercised. There would be a wholesome fear of the anger that the spirit of such a slain relative would feel towards the murderer and his kin. At last, individual freedom of every sort yielded to the waxing authority of the king, and his laws limited the power of husband and father; the state took up the old territory of kin and clan. All, however, was done by slow approaches.

According to old Jutland laws, a man was permitted to strike wife and child, provided he did it with a staff or a rod, *and broke no bones*.[2] Grimm reminds us of Siegfried's theory and practice: —

So women should be managed, said Siegfried, man of main,
That from pert and haughty sayings they ever should refrain;

and afterwards his wife bears testimony, as follows: —

Much have I rued my error, said Kriemhild furthermore,
Since for its sake my husband has beaten me full sore.[3]

Corporal chastisement, even of adult members of the household, was extremely common, lingered through the middle ages, and under the head of " Wife-Beating " is still a favorite topic with them that make or read the newspaper. " As late as the seventeenth century in France," says Kemble,[4] " it appears that it was usual to flog the valets, pages, and maids in noble houses." Mention is made of " a riot which arose in Paris from a woman's being whipped to death

---

[1] Kemble, *Saxons*, I. 199.   [2] *R. A.* 450.
[3] *N. L.* 805, 837.   [4] *Saxons*, I. 209.

by her mistress in August, 1651." Queen Elizabeth, we know, was wont to beat her maids of honor black and blue. Of course, the Germanic wife did not venture, any more than her children, to lift a hand against her husband. In Iceland, however, women achieved a remarkable degree of independence, and Weinhold gives an instance where a wife, openly declaring that her husband had dared to whip her, thereupon dissolved the partnership and left him, taking all her fortune with her.[1] On the part of the wife, direct and heavy insult aimed at her husband, — acute symptoms, we may say, of the common scold, — conspiracy against his life, and, above all, adultery, were just occasion for her immediate death; only the husband was obliged to kill her openly, and to announce his act immediately to his neighbors. It was mainly the efforts of the church which, little by little, secured to the wife rights of person, if not of property, nearly equal to those of her husband.

In general, it is safe to say that able-bodied persons were seldom killed through the exercise of paternal power. But there is no doubt whatever in regard to the custom of exposure,[2] applied to the very old and the very young. Life was hard in those days, and daily bread was often uncertain; strong hands must pay for well-fed bodies. The weak and sickly and old were more than superfluous; they were a burden. Remorseless logic pointed to a speedy relief. Particularly infants, whether by reason of some deformity, or, as in the case of girls, because they were not wanted in the family, — little

[1] Weinhold, *Altnord. Leben*, p. 250.
[2] "Exposition," Gibbon calls it.

Florence Dombeys, — were killed or exposed or, in milder act, sold into slavery. Even the mere fact that a new-born child was a girl often sealed its fate; male offspring counted so much more in the struggle for existence. Mild survival of this is the traditional law at Nestenbach, that the father of a new-born boy has the right to two wagon-loads of wood from the common forest, but only one load if the baby is a girl.[1] Legend and poetry often veiled the old and barbarous and cruelly practical custom, as in the case where some dream or warning causes the parents to expose the new-born infant, and so avert a calamity which it is fated to bring upon the race. The poetry of all nations is full of this. A rich Icelander, Thorstein, just before the birth of his child, dreams that he rears in his house a beautiful swan. Two eagles come and fight fiercely for the swan, and at last fall, both of them, dead to the ground, and the swan sits sorrowful and mourns. Then came yet another bird, and with him Thorstein's swan flew away. A Norwegian skipper interprets Thorstein's dream in the obvious fashion; and when the latter rides off to the assembly of the people, he tells his wife that if she gives birth to a girl, it is not to be reared, but exposed. The wife contrives that her little daughter shall find a home with one of her relatives; and Thorstein's caution proves, as usual, only a vain struggle against fate. His dream is fulfilled; for Hrafn and Gunnlaug, the eagles of the dream, fell in that holmgang already mentioned.[2] Thorstein, though a rich man and able to rear a dozen children, excited by his action no more sur-

---

[1] R. A. 403.   [2] *Gunnlaugssaga Ormstungu*, ed. Mogk.

prise than that which modern folk feel over some
unusual piece of economy on the part of a wealthy
neighbor.[1]

When a Germanic child was born,[2] it lay on the
floor (*barn er á gólfi*, "the bairn is on the floor," that
is, "is born") until the father decided whether it
should be acknowledged as a member of his family,
or whether it should be exposed. In the first case,
he *lifted it up*, or caused some one else[3] to lift it up;
it was sprinkled with water, had a bit of honey
smeared on its lips, and so became a human child, a
member of the family and clan, no longer — save in
such exceptional cases as a general famine — liable
to exposure. This act of lifting up is synonymous
with fatherhood itself; and Saxo Grammaticus,
speaking of a certain man's child, does not say
"whom he had begotten," but "whom he had taken
up," — *quem sustulerat*. Deformed children were
not taken up, but promptly exposed, — in oldest times
killed, — in the feeling that such lives were not worth
living, quite aside from the burden entailed upon
those who would support them. This exposing was
the business of the father, although, as Grimm points
out,[4] the legends soften down the barbarity of the act
by attributing it to those who have no direct author-

---

[1] It is needless to remind the reader, save in merest allusion, how
universal was this custom of exposure among all the nations of old.
Romulus and Remus, Œdipus, stories of the East, the flotsam and jetsam
of literature drifting down the centuries and still claiming our tears in
the sympathetic verse of Chaucer, — a book would be needed to name
them all.

[2] *R. A.* 455.

[3] The nurse; hence, says Wackernagel *Kl. Schr.* I. 12, the German
Hebamme. Kluge, *Etym. Dict.*, *s.v.* *Cf.* Danish *iordemoder*, "earth-
mother." [4] *R. A.* 456.

ity, like that family scapegoat, the stepmother.
Girls, as we saw, were often unwelcome guests; and
a curious superstition was often fatal to twins, for
these, men fabled, could not both be legitimate children. This superstition forms a basis for the mediæval legend of *Octavian*.[1] The exposure itself took
place mostly under a tree or in a rude boat that was
given to the waves.[2] There seems to have been a
vague notion that if the gods had any destiny in
store for the infant, they might see to its safety for
themselves ; or else, the child passed for a sort of
sacrifice. The feelings of the child were not considered at all. Grimm quotes a passage from *Gudrun*, where children are forbidden to cry and weep
aloud, on penalty of being drowned. It is a rough
shock to sentiment when we think that this old and
hopeless piece of barbarism lies at the foundation of
our most exquisite myths, — Lohengrin the swan-
knight, Arthur the forest-foundling, and that mystic
Scild who in the prelude of our national epic, *Béowulf*,
drifts in his boat, a child of destiny, to the shores of
a kingless land.

The right to expose a child ceased in ordinary
cases if food of any sort, especially milk or honey,[3]
had passed its lips. There is a legend of the mother
of St. Liudger, which shows the old Frisian custom.[4]
She was to have been drowned immediately after her
birth, because she was "only a girl." A neighbor
woman, coming by and taking pity on the infant, put

---

[1] See p. 63, note 4, above.
[2] *R. A.* 459.   [3] *R. A.* 457.
[4] Her name was Liafburg. The story is told in the *Vita Liudgeri*,
quoted at some length by Richthofen, *Friesische Rechtsgeschichte*,
II. 406 f.

some honey on the child's mouth. The honey was promptly swallowed, and in accordance with custom the baby was allowed to live. Tests were often practised in the case of boys to see whether there was promise of a vigorous life. Thus even for the water baptism, if we may so style it, Holtzmann [1] takes the very practical view that it was really a trial of hardiness. If the boy stood the shock of immersion, he had a strong constitution. The old Vikings thrust a spear toward the child as it lay on the floor, and if the little fist clutched at the weapon, good: the child should live and be a man of his hands. The same *motif* has crept into a legend of the Lombards, and is told in all seriousness by Paul the Deacon, in his history of that race.[2] Once upon a time, he tells us, a woman threw her seven little children into a pond, to let them drown there. It chanced that King Agelmund rode by the pond, and seeing to his astonishment the wretched infants, he stopped his horse and reached out towards them with his spear; one of them grasped it. Agelmund, moved with pity and wonder, said the child would one day be a powerful man, ordered him taken from the pond, had him carefully nursed and educated, and called him Lamissio.[3] When Agelmund died, Lamissio was made king of the Lombards. Somewhat different was the test of hardiness where a poor freedman died and left several children. They were put together in a pit — this is not precisely comfortable reading — and were suffered to starve one by one to death: he who held out long-

---

[1] *Germ. Alterth.* p. 212.   [2] I. 15.
[3] See p. 26, note 3, above.

est was taken up *in extremis* and allowed to live on
the score of his tough constitution.[1]

The cruel custom of exposure yielded but slowly
to the pressure of civilization and the teachings of
the church.   As helpful as anything was the instinct
of maternal pity and devotion and love, which
counted more and more as the position of women
was improved.   Grimm[2] quotes from a Danish
ballad, where a mother puts her baby in a chest,
lays with it consecrated salt and candles, and goes to
the water-side.

> Thither she goes along the strand
> And pushes the chest so far from land,
> Casts the chest so far from shore :
> " To Christ the Mighty I give thee o'er ;
> To the mighty Christ I surrender thee,
> For thou hast no longer a mother in me."

Imperial laws took the merciful side.   The Emperor
Valentinian issued an edict against what Gibbon
calls the " exposition of new-born infants."[3]   But
nothing clings to life like an old and once universal
custom.   When the popular assembly of Iceland
resolved to accept the Christian faith, the outvoted
minority submitted to be baptized on condition that
they might keep the right to expose their children,
as well as the privilege of eating horse-flesh.   Evidently the ceremony of naming a child, a sort of
baptism, had much importance in the heathen ritual ;
witness the sullen comment of Clovis, the Frank,
when his child died within a week after its baptism

---

[1] *R. A.* 461.   [2] *R. A.* 457, 459.
[3] *Decline and Fall*, Chap. XXV.

by Christian rites : " Had it been consecrated (*dictatus*) in the name of my gods, it would have lived ; but now because it was baptized in the name of your god, it could not live at all."

Elaborate was the ceremony of naming a Germanic infant; and with the naming went a gift. The young Norse hero wanders silent and nameless till he meets the Valkyria Svava, in the forest, and she hails him and calls him Helgi. Then Helgi answers: "What gift wilt thou give me with this name of Helgi? " Whereupon she tells him how he can find a wonderful sword.[2] Simrock says[3] that a present was demanded even when one in after life received a nickname. Woden unwittingly gives a sort of nickname to a tribe of men ("Langobardi"), — it is a Hera-like trick of his wife, Frea, — and so is forced to give them, along with the name, victory over their enemies. Another gift came by right. to the Scandinavian child when it cut its first tooth; and this custom also, thinks Jacob Grimm, rests upon old Germanic tradition.

The name itself was not so distinct and individual an affair as it is now; for the main thing then was to attach the new-born child to his proper clan and make him a member of that organization which meant so infinitely much for our ancestors. This name, which bound its owner to his family, was chosen with especial care. It will be remembered that the habit of fastening a general name on the descendants of one man, and then giving each individual a distin-

[1] Greg. Tur. II. 29, 31.
[2] Neckel, *Edda, Helgakv. Hv.* 7, 8, p. 138; Grimm, *G. D. S.*[2] 108.
[3] *Mythol.* p. 595.

guishing "Christian" name, was unknown to the
Germans, and indeed begins to be a settled custom
only with the twelfth century.[1] Not additions to
the family name, but variations of it, made the Germanic rule. Hildebrand names his son Hathubrand,
— that is one sort of variation. Somewhat different
are the cases where "the mother was called Ada, the
daughter Oda (Uota); the mother Adalhilt, the
daughter Uodalhilt; the mother Baba, the daughter
Buoba." Still another variation meets us in a rhyme
like Haukr and Gaukr.[2] We have already seen
the first of these systems of name-giving in the
Tacitean divisions of the Germanic race, — the
tribes Ingævones, Istævones, Irminones (for Herminones), descended from three brothers; in the
gods (W) Odin, Wili, Wê; and one could add a long
list, — Thusnelda and Thumelicus, Vannius and
Vangio,[3] and so on. Patronymic names in -ing are
of course very common in Anglo-Saxon. By their
aid, and with the ending -hâm or -tûn we trace back
many an English town to the head of a single
family.[4] For the deeper question about these names,
their meaning and purpose, Scherer[5] has made the
following general statement. The names that the
primitive German gave to his boy or girl "were for
the most part like the names of Catholic saints,
who are given to the children as patrons and protectors; these German names betokened patterns of
life, ideals, which must be followed and imitated."
Often the name was a compound of two members;

---

[1] Weinhold, *D. F.* 96.   [2] Ibid. 97.
[3] See for longer lists, Weinhold, *Altnord. Leben*, p. 265 ff.
[4] See Kemble's valuable lists, *Saxons*, I. 459 ff.   [5] *G. D. L.* 10 f.

and as in Aryan times, one of these members was often used alone as a pet or household name. Favorite compounds were such as *Gerhard*, the spear-bold man,[1] or *Gertrude* (*Gêr-drut*), "the spear-strong," applied to one of Woden's battle-maidens.[2] "In general," says Scherer, "the names of men in the Germanic period expressed the qualities which make for success in the great battle of life, — wisdom, strength, courage, readiness with weapons, power, leadership, passionate and determined purpose. All pointed to struggle or conquest." Among the names of women, however, Scherer sees two sharply sundered groups. One set of names had as basis the qualities of peaceful life, love, faithfulness, good cheer, beauty, grace, reminding us of nymph and dryad, of the light mist upon lake or meadow. The other group had names of battle and warfare, like Brünhild, "she who fights in armor." Whether the brilliant historian is right in assigning the respective origins of these groups to two distinct periods, one of which cherished peace as its ideal, the other delighting in war and bloodshed alone, is a question still open to debate. There can be no doubt, however, that at the time now under consideration the warlike principle prevailed in overwhelming degree. "She sat at home and span" was the coveted epitaph of the Roman matron; but the mother or wife of German warriors went with them to battle and once, perhaps, bore shield and weapon at their side.

Mythology, too, as Müllenhoff points out, played

---

[1] The Danes in *Béowulf* call themselves *Gârdene*, "Spear-Danes."

[2] For details, see reference above, and also Weinhold, *Deutsche Frauen*, p. 11 ff.

its part in Germanic names;[1] and not inactive was
the influence of heroic legend. Just as the patriot of
some decades ago named his son after one of the rev-
olutionary heroes, so a Germanic lad might receive
the name of a Siegfried, a Gunther, a Welant.[2]

The early life of the Germanic child was passed in
the narrow range of his paternal household; rich and
poor alike grew up together, unclad and dirty, an
ideal childhood.[3] So lived the son of the freeman
until the time when, in presence of the popular assembly, after judgment had been passed upon his fitness, he took spear and shield and became a member
of the state. A somewhat romantic tale of Paul the
Deacon, about Alboin (the Ælfwine of our own
poem, *Widsîd*) and his youthful bravery, asserts that
Alboin, while yet a prince, in battle with the Gepidæ,
killed their king's son in single combat. The warriors of Alboin thereupon begged his father, the king,
that he would admit the youthful hero to the royal
table. "No," answered the king; "you know our
custom that a king's son may not sit at meat with his
father till he has received gifts of arms from some
other king."[4] This gift of arms, whether so intricate
a ceremony as here, or the everyday occurrence of a
German community, was the all-important moment of
the freeman's life. For arms were the sign of his
freedom. "They go about no business," declares
Tacitus of his Germans, "either public or private,

---

[1] *Zur Runenlehre.* p. 44 ff.

[2] Symons in Paul's *Grundriss,*[2] III, 625, 626.

[3] "Nudi ac sordidi," Tac. *Germ.* XX.

[4] *Paul. Diac.* I. 23. What follows (24) is a strained account of Germanic hospitality. Young Alboin goes as guest to the king whose son
he has slain, and asks the latter's arms as gift.

unless armed. But no one is allowed to take arms to himself until the state (*civitas*) is satisfied that he knows how to use them. Then in the public assembly, either one of the princes, or the father, or a relative, adorns him with shield and spear. That is with them the *toga* and the first honor of youth; until this occasion he is reckoned of the household, but not of the state."[1] Later law and custom ordain that at seven years of age a boy is taken from the control of the women and begins his education among men. At eight, with many tribes, he had a *wergild*. To prove his fitness, says tradition, an apple and a bit of money were placed before him: if he grasped at the apple, he was not worth reckoning; if at the money, he was worth half the *wergild* of a man.[2] At ten years an Anglo-Saxon youth seems, under two codes of law, to have become free of his guardian,[3] so far as the latter's hold on the former's property was concerned; and among the West-Goths a youth of ten, if he fell sick, could dispose of his estate.[4] Other Anglo-Saxon laws fix twelve years for such responsibilities; and this is legal age in other places. At fifteen, others were thought ready to bear weapons, — an age which agrees better with our notions of fitness; and eighteen, and even twenty-one, have judicial sanction.

From such a time till old age reduced his strength, the freeman was active member of the state, bore arms, took part in council, had the duties of fighting and the privileges of idleness, and was thus distinguished from the unfree. In education, says Tacitus,

---

[1] Tac. *Germ*. XIII. [2] *R. A.* 411.
[3] *Ibid.*, 413; Liebermann, I, 10, § 6. [4] *R. A.* 414.

there was no distinction. A playmate in boyhood could be the slave of riper years. Weinhold thinks that. boys were often sent to other households for purposes of general education, — mostly to a relative;[1] but this is only a guess. Certainly there was nothing in the nature of our modern schooling with book and pen; a robust contempt for this business of monks and women held strong throughout the middle ages, and was doubtless based on a genuine old Germanic sentiment, — latent, of course, in the absence of an alphabet. But it was otherwise with the education of muscle, agility, courage. Look, for example, at the accomplishments of our Jarl in the *Rígs Þula*.[2] Gymnastics of some sort our forefathers undoubtedly practised; witness their sword-dance. This was education and sport, task and theatre, combined.[3] The young men of free rank carried out the dance and had charge of it; they were clad as in battle, naked to the waist, with sword, or *framea*,[4] in the hand. Then they leaped or threw themselves about, among or under the quivering, flashing swords. Müllenhoff assumes[5] that this was done to a musical accompaniment; "from the start, Germans knew fife, horn, and probably a sort of drum." Something of the same sort, though performed in full armor, was the Pyrrhic dance of the Greeks, in which all motions and postures of combat were imitated, and the whole

[1] *Deutsche Frauen*, I. 105.

[2] See above, p. 62. Wackernagel (*Kl. Schr.* I. 14) refers to. Seneca *Epist.* 37.

[3] Tac. *Germ.* XXIV. It is the subject of an admirable monograph by Müllenhoff, printed in the *Festgaben für G. Homeyer*, Berlin, 1871, p. 111 ff.

[4] A sort of spear, the national weapon. See below, p. 250.

[5] p. 117.

affair was made into a training-school for actual warfare. There was a similar Italian dance. Our Germanic tongue made little difference between "play"
or "dance," and "fight"; both were expressed by the
word *lâc*, of which our discredited "lark" or "larking"
is lineal descendant. Among the many "kennings"
for "battle," derivations of this *lâc* are beloved metaphors: "sword-lark," "warriors'-lark," "shield-lark";
or else the compound is with *plega*, "play": "spear-
play," "sword-play," "linden-play" (*sc.* of the shield),
and many more.

Such an education might well lead up to a vigorous manhood and, by our reckoning, to a green old
age. But the second childhood of a German had
all the risks of his first; exposure was as common a
fate for the graybeard as for the infant. "Old age,"
cries Lear bitterly enough, "is unnecessary"; but
the ancients came to this conclusion without any
such cruel tuition as his. "The young tree," says
the hero of a legend told by Saxo Grammaticus,
"is to be nourished; the old tree should be hewn
down";[1] and the phrase is characteristic. For not
as a gentle messenger, an "angel," not as the softly
approaching genius with inverted torch, beckoning
the soul, or "standing pensively, his hand lifted to
his cheek," did death come to the German;[2] it
charged full upon him, a relentless warrior. The
Germanic conception of death was neither the comely
youth, twin-brother of sleep and son of night, as
the Greeks represented him,[3] nor yet the repulsive

---

[1] *Arbor alenda recens; vetus excidenda.*   [2] Grimm, *D. M.* 709.
[3] Lessing, *Wie die Alten den Tod gebildet*, Berlin, 1769, p. 5 f. Death
carved to resemble an Amor, see p. 10 f.

skeleton of our mediæval traditions;[1] death, mostly
personified by the Germans as "Battle," or the like,
seized each man and bore him away. "If Hild
(Battle) shall *take* me," says Béowulf, thinking of
his possible death. Germanic life was all struggle,
stress, battle; and death was only the hardest out of
many buffets. All races, says Victor Hehn, in a
certain stage of the development of reflection come
to the notion that death is no great evil;[2] and he
quotes the famous story told by Herodotus about a
Thracian tribe who wept when a man was born and
rejoiced at the death which set him free from reach
of human ills. Probably we pity those gray-haired
victims of exposure more than they pitied themselves;
and they could have echoed in all simplicity, so far
as old age was concerned, the words of the Preacher
who praised the dead that were already dead more
than the living which were yet alive.[3] We must be
careful, however, not to slip any poetry into the other
side of the account. The German did not philos-
ophize very much; the stolid fashion of a peasant,
face to face with death, gives us a better hint. It
was not a sentiment that old and tired should die; it
was a custom. Still, a rough sentiment often moulds
our habit, and those weary veterans of life may well
have said with the Greek poet that old age is intoler-
able and hated even by the gods; while they were
not modern enough to join Lear in his magnificent
appeal for sympathy: " O heavens, *if you do love old
men,* . . . *if yourselves are old,* . . . send down and
take my part!"

[1] J. E. Wessely (*Die Gestalt des Todes und des Teufels in der dar-
stellenden Kunst,* Leipzig, 1876) gives abundant details.

[2] *Kulturpfl.*[3], pp. 537, 538.   [3] *Ecclesiastes,* IV. 2.

The prime and best of life, so reckoned the ancients, lay for men in the period from twenty to fifty, and for women from fifteen to forty, — of course, a rough average. These particular figures apply to the West-Goths,[1] but would doubtless hit the Germanic notion as a whole. Sign of one's abiding manhood was the power to mount and back a horse, swing sword, and walk without staff or other help.[2] Three-score-and-ten is the biblical limit of strength; but as among the Romans, sixty years were enough to bow the Germanic frame.

Now while these years of strength endured, it was good for the German to live; he had no doubts about that. Life was sweet to him who had all powers of mind and body, and a fair share of good fortune. The primitive and irresistible logic of it is charmingly expressed in one of Chaucer's happiest bits of humor, where Arcite is thrown from his horse and mortally hurt just after the tournament in which he has won his peerless bride: —

> " Why woldestow [3] be deed," thise wommen crye,
> "*And haddest gold ynowgh, and Emelye?*"

But when the senses were dulled, strength waning, disease and pain getting upper hand, there came to the German, not our modern weariness of life, which is often found in very strapping young gentlemen, but a willingness to leave the useless abode, to pass into the next world, to try one's chances in that region

---

[1] *R. A.* 416.

[2] Ibid. The German laws required that one could walk in the common highway " ungehabt und ungestabt." *R. A.* 96. Later, a woman's test of general ability was her power to walk to church.

[3] *Cant. Tales,* A. 2835—36.

of spirits whose existence no one seriously doubted. Let us hear the conclusion of the whole matter of Germanic life from one of the older Scandinavians:[1] "I have slain this Tusk-gnasher, first of the fourth ten (*i.e.* he is the thirty-first I have slain). . . . I have cut down thirty-five men as quarry for the black-feathered raven. I have got me a name for manslaying. May the fiends take me when I am no longer able to wield my sword! Let men bear me into my barrow then; the sooner the better." Another sings of old age: " I grope in blindness round the fire. There is a cloud on my eyes. This is the ill that sits upon the white fields of my brows. My gait is tottering. . . . The forest of my head is falling; desire has failed me, and my hearing is dried up."[2] Such a life had no redeeming features; it was no hard matter to leave it. Moreover, we know the Germanic wish to die in some violent way, not to pine and dwindle into one's grave, — a wish that flames out in the wild " Death Song " of Faust, and hails him happiest who dies in the midst of victory or love: —

> O selig Der, dem er im Siegesglanze
> Die blut'gen Lorbeern um die Schläfe windet,
> Den er nach rasch durchrastem Tanze,
> In eines Mädchens Armen findet !

Warriors in Scandinavia gashed themselves with Odin's spear, and so avoided that dreaded " death in the straw."[3] The *Gautrekssaga* tells of a lofty rock

---

[1] It is of the heathen period. Translation from Vigfusson and Powell's *C. P. B.* II. 70.   [2] *C. P. B.* II. 73.

[3] Of course, a common barbaric trait. See Ammian. Marc. 31, II. 22, for the sentiment of the Alans; those who lived to old age, or died of sickness, were treated with contempt.

whence those who were weary of life were wont to
cast themselves down ; a case is mentioned where
father and mother, led by their children to the cliff,
leaped "glad and joyful to Odin." [1] On the other
hand, there was plenty of involuntary faring to Odin,
— or to the mistress of the cheerless world. Says Ari
the Icelander: "There was a great winter of famine
in Iceland in the heathen days, at the time that King
Harold Grayfell fell, when Earl Hakon took the rule
in Norway. It was the worst of famines in Iceland.
Men ate ravens and foxes, and much that was not
meet for food was eaten, and some slew old folks and
paupers, hurling them over the cliffs into the sea. . . ." [2]
It is related that a formal motion was made and carried
in the Icelandic assembly, that on account of the
famine and cold, all the old, the sick, and the infirm
should be abandoned to starvation. [3] The ancient
Prussians and Lithuanians killed their useless old
people without scruple ; while worn-out servants,
sickly children, beggars not "sturdy," and such persons, shared a similar fate. Certain tribes of the
Gothic race killed their old and sick, — this in the
sixth century. [4] Beda, in telling about the conversion of Sussex, mentions the poverty of the place,
and the ignorance and superstition of the inhabitants,
who in time of famine would flock to the shore of the
sea, and, forty or fifty together, *junctis misere manibus*,
leap into the waves. [5] Survivals abound. Grimm

---

[1] *R. A.*486.   [2] Vigfusson-Powell, *C. P. B.* II. 35.   [3] *R. A.* 487.

[4] Grimm, *Kl. Schr.* II. 241; Procop. *d. bell. Goth.* II. 14. It is worth
noting that "though relatives kindled the funeral-pile, a stranger was
employed to give the death-wound."

[5] Bæd. *Hist. Ecc. Gent. Angl.* IV. 13. The custom is well established
for the ancient Hindus, as well as for a host of modern barbarians; it
was doubtless a general Aryan habit.

quotes an old English tradition of "the holy mawle, which they fancy hung behind the church door, which, when the father was seaventie, the son might fetch to knock the father in the head as effete and of no more use." Long after the "mawle" ceased to be used, the tradition remained.[1] In poetry and legend we find the same sort of survival. A single example, perhaps a little strained and rhetorical, may be taken from the German *Wunderhorn*.[2] A boy carries part of an old horse-blanket to his aged grandfather, who is kept in abject misery, shivering and starving in an outhouse. "Why the blanket?" asks the father, meeting the boy. Then the boy answers: —

> I take the half, he said,
> Unto thy father's bed.
>
> The other half I keep
> For thee, when thou shalt lie
> Where now thy aged father
> Is thrust away to die.

Against this treatment of the aged seems to stand in sharpest contradiction the well-known reverence for gray hairs and the wisdom that they brought, the piety and veneration for old age, which we find in all the writers of antiquity. Not only Nestor of the Homeric poems, but the sentiment lying behind words like *presbyter*, or the Anglo-Saxon *ealdormonn*, or our epic phrase *frôd and gôd*, a sort of hendiadys expressing the fortitude and experience of mature years, — these are good witnesses. But there is no great contradiction. The latter sentiment applied originally

---

[1] Grimm, *Kl. Schr.* VII. 175, quoting W. J. Thoms in a work edited for the Camden Society, 1839.   [2] *Das vierte Gebot.*

to a healthy, vigorous old age, the wisdom of saga-
cious counsel still fortified by a sound body. Whatever, on the other hand, bore the visible mark of
death, the palsied frame, the sightless face, was ab-
horrent and unclean; and this was what the heathen
hastened to put out of sight. As the feeling of
respect for old age in and for itself gained ground,
the early prejudice grew weaker; in this, Sir Henry
Maine [1] sees one of the chief signs of advancing
civilization.

[1] *Early Law and Custom,* p. 23.

CHAPTER VII

TRADE AND COMMERCE

Household industries — The smith — Commerce — Exports — Amber — Myths relating to commerce and seafaring — Ships — Love of the sea — Money and bargains.

ASKING the free-born primitive German what trades he had, we feel sure that if he could "speak back," it would be with a choice array of primitive German abuse. He was a soldier, he. His women and his slaves carried on nearly all of his industries. Among these, weaving would take a prominent place; for the Germans had known the art and practised it long before they came in contact with the south.[1] That "white cloth" of divination, mentioned in the *Germania*, upon which the priest cast the kevils and read the runes — if runes they were — was doubtless of home manufacture. Their linen they exported, and it fetched a good price; while the dresses of German women were preferably of the same material.[2] "Linen as popular garb," says Hehn, "is of northern (*i.e.* not Roman or oriental) origin."[3] In the Scan-

[1] Evidence of the making of woollen cloth is found in graves of the early bronze period in Scandinavia; and towards the close (several hundred years before our era) of that age, linen makes its appearance. Kalund in Paul's *Grundriss*,[2] III, 409, 410.

[2] Tac. *Germ.* XVII.   [3] Work quoted, p. 149.

dinavian lands, linen served in the place of money.
Of industries which are somewhat allied to weaving,
and supply the family needs, we may mention soap-
making, another old Germanic art. Leather tanned
with the aid of bark gave shoes; while the sinews
of cattle and the fibre of the linden tree furnished
cords and ropes. All this was household work, and
so remained far into the middle ages. That reproach
still clings to the trades of the tailor and the shoe-
maker, and is due to the old association with
labor done only by women or slaves. Earthenware
must have been made,[1] and came under the same
category.

But there was a craft well worthy of the freeman
and one that lay close to the heart of Germanic life,
— the craft of the smith, a noble art, held high by
all warrior races. "Smith," of course, is the same as
Latin *faber;* and we remember that in *Rigsþula,*
one of the sons of Karl, the freeman, is named Smith,
the artisan. "Smith" is the masculine pendant to
webbe, the woman who weaves, later *webster.* Just
as in Anglo-Saxon, a wife, by the kenning already
quoted, was called weaver-of-peace, so the word
"smith" was used to form compounds in the sense
of "one who causes or makes." Thus we have "lore-
smith" (*lârsmið*) for learned men, "laughter-smith"
for him who makes laughter or fun, and "war-smith"
(*wîgsmið*) for the warrior.[2] This general meaning of
faber or artisan was slightly broadened in Scandinavian, and narrowed in Anglo-Saxon. In Old Norse,
as Grimm reminds us,[3] it meant not so much "work-

---

[1] Tac. *Germ.* V.   [2] Bode, *Kenningar i. d. ags. Dicht.* p. 48.
[3] *D. M.* 453.

man," as one skilled in the arts generally, particularly
the master-builder. In Anglo-Saxon it refers to the
worker in metals, while the still common "wright"
(*wyrhta*) was he who wrought in wood of all sorts,
ship or wagon or house.[1]

Like Vulcan of old, the Germanic smith found his
way into mythology and cult. In England we know
him as Wayland the Smith;[2] and our oldest English
lyric, the song of the minstrel Deor, introduces him
in its first verse. His legend or myth was a great
Germanic favorite; in the north it is elaborated into
one of the most striking poems,[3] and allusions to it
are frequent even in the scanty wreckage from the
literature of our forefathers. Various accounts made
Wêland grandson of a king and a mermaid, and son
of a giant, — by no means a born thrall; and his
deeds are deeds of a god. The legends of Wêland
seem to have begun in Low German territory; and
when both Béowulf and Waldere, in our early epic,
call their swords "Wayland's work," we know that
this is praise indeed.[4] A later version of the Siegfried legend makes that splendid hero, the Germanic
Achilles, learn the art of a smith.[5]

Manifold, even in that simple life, were the products of this craft. Tools, to begin with, must be

[1] In Wright-Wülker, *Glossaries*, Col. 272, the heading "Incipit de
metallis" covers *smið* = faber, *smiððe* = officina; while in Col. 112 there
is a list of wrights. However, "Latomus" is *stanwyrhta*.

[2] His cave is pointed out in Berkshire. Scott's treatment of Wayland in *Kenilworth* is hardly fair, though that other smith, Henry Gow
in *The Fair Maid of Perth*, has a more heroic role.

[3] Charmingly told in the translation of the Grimms (Berlin, 1815,
1885), or in Vigfusson-Powell, *C. P. B.* I. 169.

[4] See Klaeber's note to *Beowulf* 455, and B. Dickins, *Runic and
Heroic Poems* (Cambridge, Eng., 1915), pp. 37 ff.

[5] Wackernagel, *Kl. Schr.* I. 47.

made; and with these tools were fashioned the rough instruments of farming life, the houses and their scant furniture, the wagon — such as that of the goddess Nerthus, — and above all the ornaments, the drinking-horns, and the weapons.[1] Of course with the passage from age of bronze to age of iron, the smith's art increased in its variety if not in its importance, and with iron, brass, silver, lead, and glass came into consideration.[2] Probably, as is so often the case with conquering tribes, the Germans learned the finer shades of this craft from captives of a more civilized but less warlike race. The Celts are the most obvious teachers of manual training for the Germans, though Roman examples must be reckoned with. Warriors often made their own weapons;[3] and as in modern days, some leader doubtless saw from time to time the chance to improve his warriors' weapons, and so introduced reforms. A recent African instance may be quoted; the chieftain of a certain tribe made a considerable change in the character and use of his people's favorite arm, and in consequence subjugated a number of neighbor tribes who depended on the older weapon. The forging of iron weapons became general for Germany in the times of the wandering; but tradition and fair evidence[4] would seem to make the beginnings of the industry far older than contact with Rome. Nomadic tribes have often been good weapon-smiths. In later times, the Vandals and the Lombards had high repu-

[1] Wackernagel, *Kl. Schr.* I. 44 f.   [2] Montelius, work quoted, p. 89.
[3] Ibid. p. 172.
[4] Tac. *Germ.* VI.: "Even iron is not abundant (he has mentioned the scarcity of gold and silver), as may be gathered from the character of their weapons. Few use swords. . . ."

tations in this art. A Vandal king elevated to the
rank of noble a smith who had especially distinguished himself.[1] The sharp spear-heads of the men
who fought so bravely against Drusus and Germanicus, and put Roman military skill to all its shifts,
must have made plenty of work for the weapon-
smith. The sword is the darling weapon of Germanic song, though it was seldom seen in the hands
of the ordinary warrior. It is not the early national
weapon, like the short lance; but what a wealth of
affection is showered upon it by the later heroic
poetry! It is called " the work of giants," " Wayland's work," " the heirloom "; runes were cut upon
it; it had will and passion; mystery was about it.
It had its pedigree of owners; its fate seemed almost
human. What, then, as time went on, and Germanic
life came to be all warfare, — what of its maker?
Was he not as well paid and as highly held as the
Armstrongs or the Krupps of to-day?

Ornaments being so dear to the primitive German,
the goldsmith was counted among the " noble " craftsmen. Of great interest to us is the so-called golden
horn of Gallehus (Denmark), filched, alas, long ago
from the Copenhagen museum, but represented there
by an accurate copy in gilded silver. It dates from
the fifth century; and the runic inscription upon it
shows linguistic forms (in early Norse) older than
the Gothic. This inscription, the mark of the Germanic craftsman, runs as follows: "I, Hlégestr
from Holt (i. e. Holstein), made the horn."[2] Sev-

---

[1] Wackernagel, *Kl. Schr.* I. 47.

[2] "*Ek hlewagastiR. holtija R. horna. tawiðo*", A. Noreen, *Altisl. u.
altnorweg. Gramm.* (4th ed., 1923), p. 379, No. 25.

eral other products of the goldsmith's industry have
been found in Denmark with inscriptions of the same
date as that of the golden horn. They surely justify
our assumption that even the early Germans not
only stole ornaments, but made them. The skill of
Wêland in making the most artistic ornaments, such
as are detailed in his story, leads us to the same
inference.[1]

Passing to the general esteem in which our early
Germans held the smith, we find that when such a
trade was plied by an unfree person, his *wergild* rose
very high, the goldsmith's highest of all.[2] In Anglo-
Saxon laws the king's smith is mentioned as an important person.[3] When a *gesithcund man*, that is,
one of the great persons of the kingdom, moves his
residence, the laws of Ine allow him to take with him
his reeves (*geréfan,* — *socios suos*), his smith, and his
child's nurse.[4] We hear in another place of a special
punishment for injury done to the hand "of the
harper, the goldsmith, and the embroideress."[5]

Trade, which has so often opened new countries to
the civilized world, found early its way into Germany. True, the account of Cæsar shows little of
what we now call commerce; traders, he says, are

[1] The splendid arms of the Cimbrians in Italy, and especially the
brazen bull which they carried about with them (Plutarch's *Marius*),
are hardly in point. There had been too many opportunities for plunder and trade during their long migrations. But those "images of wild
animals taken from the sacred groves," which Tacitus mentions (*Hist.*
IV. 22), are better evidence.

[2] *Cf.* T. Wright, *Celt, Roman, and Saxon*, p. 486, with references.

[3] Liebermann, I, 3, § 7.   [4] *Ibid.*, I, 118, § 63.

[5] *Lex Anglor. et Werinor.* tit. V. 20; see Thorpe's Lappenberg, *Anglo-
Saxon Kings*, I. 120, Bohn's ed. "Music and the smith's craft," says
Wackernagel, *Kl. Schr.* I. 49, with reference to Jubal and Tubal Cain,
"are the oldest industries."

admitted among the Germans, but it is mainly that the spoils of war may be disposed of rather than for any lust after imported articles. Especially is the importing of wine forbidden, because the Germans think they are made too soft and effeminate by its use.[1] Moreover, the products of the spinning-wheel soon found their way into a profitable market.

On the whole, however, such commerce as the German knew must have been of a fitful and fragmentary kind. Holtzmann says roundly that a band of robbers has no trade. Again, we know that the German hated cities; and these are of course the result and prop of trade, the local fixing of a market. Still, traders went about among the German tribes; and Baumstark reminds us[2] of the Germanic hospitality as likely to cover even these isolated merchants. They were probably half-breeds or freedmen. No freeborn German, we may conclude, ever stooped to trade; he fought for his living, although there was much incidental plunder. Tacitus tells us that when no war was near at hand, the adventurous young man took up distant and doubtful quarrels and found fight where he could, — a sort of speculation *à fonds perdus*. Even the plunder of these ceaseless wars made a merchant desirable, and a sense of advantage prompted the German to accord certain rights to a foreign trader.[3] Wine, — when not forbidden, as by

[1] Cæs. *B. G.* IV. 2. This is said of the Suevians. The Ubii, another German tribe, who lived close to the Rhine, admitted traders freely. IV. 3. Roman traders among the Germans are mentioned, *e.g.* Tac. *Hist.* IV. 15.

[2] *Germ.* p. 300.

[3] In later times, of course, the king protected merchants. See Liebermann, I, 68, § 34, and below p. 288.

Cæsar's Suevi, — ornaments of that flashy character, doubtless, which have always attracted primitive races, and such matters, were coveted property; and it was occasionally good to procure them without fatiguing preliminaries with the legions. Baumstark breaks a lance, in his usual impetuous fashion, for the native German trader, apart from the warriors; and insists that such home merchants bought of the Roman and sold to their remoter countrymen. Tacitus expressly tells us that the interior tribes carry on commerce by barter;[1] while the others use Roman money. We may feel sure that there was considerable trade in salt, the oldest commodity traded from tribe to tribe.[2]

Germanic exports were slaves, amber, skins, woven stuffs, chiefly linen, soap, goose-feathers, and probably many other articles which had become essential to Roman luxury. The imports were not of a very solid character, for each Germanic household provided its own necessities; in early times iron and its finished products, chiefly weapons, may have made an exception, but a law of the empire wisely forbade the exporting of iron in any shape from Rome into Germany. With no cities to collect and divide labor, the German did considerable part of his own domestic trading at the religious festivals, when scattered members of a clan or confederation of tribes came together to worship a common deity. The fair or *Messe* of to-day represents the old combination of cult and trade, though the latter element alone survives.

[1] "Permutatione mercium utantur." *Germ.* V. See Baumstark, p. 197.

[2] See Hehn's monograph, quoted above (*Das Salz*).

For the trade with Rome, carried on by that class
of half-breeds and nondescripts always found on the
border between civilized and uncivilized lands, we
may safely assume amber as the oldest and most important staple.[1] The export of amber led to the first
communications recorded between the shores of the
Baltic and the civilized world about the Mediterranean ;[2] Greeks, Syrians, and Egyptians knew its use.
To the Romans amber was first known as a product
of the Baltic coast about the time that Drusus made
his great campaign, a few years before the beginning
of our era ;[3] and it soon became a very popular article in the Roman market. Used by rich and poor,[4] it
was employed not only for charms and amulets, but
was recommended by physicians as a potent remedy
for disease. Indeed, cheap or "imitation" jewelry
was made of it, and it furnished a good counterfeit
of certain precious stones, like the topaz. In the
time of Nero a Roman knight went to the source of
supply, and brought back enough to cover the nets
which surrounded the circus, — an enormous freight,
with one piece weighing thirteen pounds alone.[5]

The Germans themselves were not blind to the
merits of their chief export. Graves of scattered
races dotted about the continent, often far from the
bit of territory which produced the whole supply,
testify to the love of our forefathers for ornaments
and charms of amber. Tacitus, it is true, says that
the people who gather what in their own tongue they

---

[1] Wackernagel, *Kl. Schr.* I. 72.   [2] See above, p. 11.

[3] Müllenhoff, *Deutsche Alterthumskunde*, II. 31.

[4] Dahn, *Bausteine*, I. 20 f.

[5] Plin. *Nat. Hist.* XXXVII. 11, 2, quoted by Wackernagel, I. 76.

call *glesum*, a word evidently connected with "glass," do not use it, but export it in the raw state.[1] This, however, does not exclude the use of it by neighboring Germanic tribes. Valuable as this export seemed, there was one article which the Romans sent in exchange to Germany, a shrewd bargain for the north, and worth a wilderness of amber, — the alphabet. The so-called runic alphabet, about which theories of the wildest possible nature have been advocated, is now generally admitted to have been introduced among German tribes about the end of the second century after Christ, and is simply the Roman system of letters, modified by the needs of cutting in stone or wood, and by the inevitable variation of imperfect and distant copies.[2]

The Germans further exported an unsightly, but tough little breed of horses, not, of course, the wild race referred to above as a part of Germanic food, but such as were trained to the saddle, — that is to say, to military work; "for nothing is held so shameful and effeminate among them as to use the saddle."[3] Moreover, a few articles were exported for the Roman table; such were the beets and turnips of which Tiberius was so fond.[4]

All this trading, or nearly all of it, was naturally overland; for from time immemorial there had been a trade-route from the Baltic to the south. Of traf-

---

[1] *Germ.* XLV. For the old paths of commerce from Germany to the south, see Wackernagel, *Kl. Schr.* I. 75 f.

[2] See p. 468, below; and the standard work of L. F. A. Wimmer, *Die Runenschrift*, German trans. by Holthausen, 1887; also Sievers in Paul's *Grundriss*,[2] I. 248—262.

[3] Cæsar *B. G.* IV. 2.

[4] Plin. *Nat. Hist.* XIX. 28, and Wackernagel, *Kl. Schr.* I. 62.

fic by water there is not so clear a record,[1] but it
reaches back into the realm of myth; and as the
smith's art should properly begin with a Germanic
Vulcan, so we look for our earliest seafarers to the
myths of Scéaf, of Wade, and of Hilde. Leaving
aside for the present all myth for myth's sake, we may
point to the venerable form of Scéaf as representative
of the seafaring instinct in our oldest ancestors, the
people who lived along the German Ocean, and on
both sides of the Cimbrian peninsula.[2] Connected
with this purely mythical and shadowy but enticing
figure are the clearer-outlined forms of Scandinavian
Freyr and that earlier Nerthus, goddess of plenty,
whom Tacitus has drawn for us. Peace and plenty
go with trade; and we are sure enough that Freyr
was the merchant-sailor's god, and gave him favoring
winds. Of Ing, the founder of our Ingævonic race,
we have vague hints of a seafaring proclivity; and
the famous swimming-match of Beowulf and Breca,
translated above,[3] is thought by Müllenhoff to be a
myth of the northward progress of culture and trade
in the figure of the cult-hero or god making his way
through the frozen and unfriendly seas. But these
are no new things; the tradition of them reaches
back into a dim antiquity. Likewise of primitive Germanic origin, thinks Symons,[4] is the widespread myth
or legend of Hilde, full of the plunge of ocean billows; it found special welcome and cultivation in
the Netherlands,[5] and is the basis of the beautiful
German epic *Kudrun*. Again, Wade,[6] that is "the

---

[1] Ibid. p. 78 ff.   [2] See above, p. 49.   [3] p. 114.

[4] Paul's *Grdr.*[2] III. 711 ff.; Fr. Panzer, *Hilde-Gudrun* (Halle, 1901).

[5] There is allusion to one of its characters in our oldest English
lyric, *Deor*.   [6] Symons, as above, pp. 718, 719.

wader," originally doubtless a sea-monster of some sort, is the father of our smith Wayland, and is mentioned, along with his boat, by Chaucer.[1] So thoroughly are all these myths and legends mingled with the sights and sounds of ocean, that we are justified in thinking of the Ingævones as a race of seafarers from the most primitive times. One strong proof of this seafaring instinct is found in the burial of Germans in ship-like tombs, or in real boats, and in the universal belief in a spirit-land whither souls are ferried in some ghostly ship.[2]

Let us now turn from myth to history. As usual, the exaggeration of the former is offset by a most melancholy depreciation in the latter. Pliny and Tacitus tell us of the awkward canoes and the hollowed tree-trunks used along the northern coast of Germany.[3] There is a dash of the picturesque in the following story of an eye-witness, the historian Vellejus Paterculus, who served with Tiberius in the German campaigns. The Roman army was encamped upon the Elbe in the very heart of Germany. On one side rose the camp of Rome; the opposite bank glittered with hostile arms, until the imperial ships

---

[1] *Canterbury Tales*, E. 1424, in the "Merchant's Tale": "*Wades bote* (boat)". See Skeat's note *ad. loc.*, also A. Heusler's excellent article in Hoops' *Reallexikon* under "Wate" (Wade).

[2] See below, p. 326.

[3] Holding, we must remember, thirty men or more apiece, and making head against the fleet of Rome. Germans also used captured Roman ships. Back, moreover, of all Roman influences, we find in the rock-pictures of the Scandinavian bronze-age, representations of boats, high in bow and stern, and meant for rowing. In the early iron age boats were built of admirable lines, and calculated for some thirty oars; we should prefer to trust a Northman's judgment of good boats rather than the opinion of Pliny. See Kålund in Paul's *Grundriss*[2], III, 464 ff.

arrived. About this time an elderly German of fine appearance and, to judge from his arms, of high rank, took boat — a trough-like affair of hollowed wood — and rowed to the middle of the river, asking that he might be permitted to land and gaze upon the Cæsar in all his state. Then follows a wealth of compliment for Tiberius; but as Vellejus was himself present, and as the scene must have been near the mouth of the Elbe, we may without great danger behold in the curious barbarian one of our own forefathers, or a near relative of them, and accept the picture as one among the very few authentic ancestral portraits from that time of which we can boast ownership.[1] From such a boat to the exquisite lines of the Viking ship now preserved at Christiania, and said to be over a thousand years old, is no leap of a decade or so. Still, we may be sure that these Germans of the coast knew in their way as much about boats as the Romans did; and their rough canoes may have been seaworthy enough. The Chauci actually used them on plundering expeditions to the coasts of Gaul. In the third century our Saxons[2] suddenly appear as accomplished sailors, and their swift keels measure the ways of ocean in all directions, — witness the Saxon shore of Britain, and the long line of fortified points to guard the colony against a tireless foe. These Saxons are said to have learned the art of shipbuilding by the treachery of Carausius. Hehn, too, insists that it was only when they had borrowed from neighboring

[1] Vell. II. 107.
[2] Also tribes from the Baltic, like the Heruli. Müllenhoff, *Beovulf*, p. 19.

people the idea and use of sails that the Saxons were able to play their pirate parts; but not quite so rapidly are sailors made. In the *Germania*,[1] Tacitus describes the Norsemen as ignorant of sails; their boats are two-prowed, and are not arranged with permanent rows of oars. But as oars still remained a prominent feature of the Viking ships, so we are fain to think that even the sailless craft of our Saxon forefathers were at home on the high sea itself, and dared many a bit of piracy with nothing but stout hands to propel as well as man the boat. As time passes, these Saxons achieve a great reputation for their skill and ferocity upon the water. Sidonius Apollinaris describes them in a letter, as well as in one of his poems;[2] they are perfectly at home upon the stormy sea, and govern their boats in a fashion evidently puzzling to the poet.[3]

The booty won by these raids can hardly be called merchandise, but it made occasion, and even need, of later traffic. We know that the Scandinavian trade with Ireland began in and even before the Viking period; the influence of Irish art is plainly seen in Norse ornamental work.[4] Even the Viking raids, that organized system of plunder pure and simple which attained its height about the tenth century, opened, like the crusades, a way for commerce. And let us particularly remember that this Viking instinct lay in the race; its great success came with its great opportunity. The beginnings of it, however, are to be sought in those rudest possible forerunners of

---

[1] XLIV.   [2] Both extracts in Zeuss, p. 490.

[3] "Hostis est omni hoste truculentior. Improvisus aggreditur, prævisus elabitur. . . . Si sequatur, intercepit; si fugiat, evadit."

[4] Montelius, work quoted, p. 136.

modern Red Rovers, — the wretched boats burnt or otherwise hollowed from a tree-trunk, in which the indomitable Chauci faced a Roman fleet (whether these naked desperadoes were any more *prædones*, — it is Pliny's word, — than the imperial visitors themselves, is not at all certain), or the *lintres*, the light canoes assigned to the same neighborhood by Tacitus.[1]

Trade, as may be seen, ran fairly abreast of all this plundering, even on the unsatisfactory footing of stolen goods.[2] There were profits large enough to tempt the daring trader; and does not commerce nearly always begin with its wares in one hand and a sword in the other? It must have been a nice art in those old days to tell a pirate from a peaceful trader or visitor; and the duty of the "strandward" at Hrothgar's chief harbor could have been no sinecure. Striking is the picture of this coast-guard who rides along the headlands to watch the stretch of sea, and spying the boat of Béowulf, gallops down to meet him at the strand, shakes the long spear, and asks what has brought him and his vassals hither, peace or war:—

> "Who are ye, then, ye arméd men,
> mailéd folk, that yon mighty vessel
> have urged thus over the ocean ways,
> here o'er the waters ?"[3]

With the art of oar and sail went the knowledge of the pilot. Such a person guides Béowulf and his

---

[1] *Ann.* XI. 18.

[2] When in *Béow.* 57, certain treasures are called *of feorwegum*, "fetched from far," are we to infer a peaceful importation or mere plunder?   [3] *Béow.* 237 ff.

men upon their journey over the sea, and is called a *lagucræftig mon*, " one who knows the waters." With the opening of history we find our forefathers possessed by a passion for voyage and ocean-adventure ; it fills their descendants of to-day ; and we reasonably infer it in those older ancestors of whom history is silent, and whose deeds waver doubtfully in the mist of legend and tradition. *Die Nordsee ist eine Mordsee ;* its first Germanic victim, " long-headed blond " or what not, has had no lack of followers.[1]

Lastly, we turn to those figures in which Germanic poetry has expressed its love of the sea, of ship and storm and life upon the waves. As we read the early pages of Grein's collection of Anglo-Saxon poetry, how the monotony is broken when once the fiery singer of " Exodus " fairly comes in sight of the Red Sea ; and what wealth of image and trope to describe the triumph of that " hoary warrior," ocean, over the hosts of Pharaoh ! No more sympathetic picture has been drawn by an Anglo-Saxon poet than where the wanderer [2] in exile falls asleep at his oar and dreams again of his dead lord and the old hall and revelry and joy and gifts, — then wakes to look once more upon the waste of ocean, snow and hail falling all around him, and sea-birds dipping in the spray : —

> Him seems at soul that he sees his master,
> clips him and kisses and lays on his knee
> head and hand (as erewhile he used
> in days that are gone), of the gift-throne fain.

[1] Wackernagel (*Kl. Schr.* 185) remarks that practically all technical terms used by sailors are of Germanic origin, and that marine activity, even when shown by Celtic races, is due to Germanic beginnings.

[2] Poem of same name, Grein-Wülker, *Bibl.* I. 285, 37 ff.

> Then once more wakens the weary outlaw,
> sees before him fallow waves,
> plunge of sea-birds, spreading plumage,
> hoarfrost and snow with hail commingled. . . .

So fares the man fated " to stir with hands the rime-cold sea." Yet another picture of the same sort greets us in the *Seafarer*.[1] These are descriptions; let us look a moment at the poetical figures themselves, the kennings for sea, ship, and sailor. For " sea " Bode counts twenty "literal " terms in Anglo-Saxon, and could add more. Of figurative terms we have such kennings as : the home of the whale, the realm of monsters, the sea-fowl's bath, the pathway of the whale, the swan-road, the sail-street, the beaker of the waves, the realm of billows, the water-fortress, the wave-roll, the salt-stream, — and that difficult word, *gârsecg*. The frozen sea is called " waves' fetters." For " ship " we have the wave-stallion (we still say a ship rides at anchor), sea-horse, sea-swimmer, wave-walker, surf-wood, the tarred board, the wave house, the curved prow, the ringéd prow (on account of the ornaments of the bow). A sailor is called sea-rider, or guest of the waves, in addition to a number of literal terms.[2] These are Anglo-Saxon, but the life of the Scandinavian Vikings developed such simpler kennings into an ingenuity and obscurity which belong more to puzzles than to ordinary verse.[3]

Commerce nowadays implies an exchangeable medium and interest on capital. The latter, says Tacitus, was unknown to our Germans; and out of

---

[1] Wülker-Grein, I. 290 ff.

[2] See Bode's dissertation on *Kenningar in d. Ags. Dichtung*, 1886.

[3] Examples in Vigfusson-Powell, *C. P. B.* II. 457 ff.

this fact he makes great trumpetings for their virtue. The currency, he says, was in terms of flocks and herds;[1] and we infer that a definite kind of animal — in Scandinavia it was the milch-cow — made a unit of value.[2] Three one-year calves are there worth one cow, while a seven-year bull is worth two cows, and a stallion from four to ten years old equals one cow. "Three times eighty" pounds of sheep's wool were also worth one cow. So ran Scandinavian computation, though cloth or linen was often reckoned as standard of value. Milk and cheese have here and there passed for money.[3] The Anglo-Saxon values of flocks are set forth in the laws;[4] as "a sheep with its lamb is worth one shilling until fourteen days after Easter," or "the horn of an ox is worth ten pennies (pœninga)." In the seventh century, horses were used as standard of value, and fines levied in corresponding terms.[5] But actual money in the shape of Roman coins was known even among the Germans of Tacitus. Probably to prevent the use of counterfeit coin in their trade,[6] Germans, as Tacitus narrates, preferred old Roman coins of the Republic, many of which had serrated edges and could not be clipped; silver, moreover, they preferred to gold. All this is evidence of bargain and sale, as well as mere exchange. Among the more important commercial transactions, we may safely reckon the sale of real estate, a species of trade which, in whatever form and

---

[1] *Germ.* XXI.   [2] Von Amira in *Grundriss*², p. 199.

[3] Rochholz, *Deutscher Glaube und Brauch*, I. 12.

[4] Liebermann, I, 114, 116.

[5] Otto I. "condemnavit Everhardum centum talentis aestimatione equorum." *R. A.* 586 f.

[6] Wackernagel, *Kl. Schr.* I. 64; *Germ.* V.

frequency, must have been familiar to the ancient Germans. This we may fairly infer from the symbolism in later transactions of the sort. A stick or branch from the growing timber, a piece of the actual turf or sod, a blade of grass, were handed in presence of witnesses to the new possessor.[1] The cleverness and presence of mind of William the Conqueror are nowhere better seen than in the jest with which he rose from his fall on touching English ground, with a handful of earth as symbol that he took possession of the realm. This appealed to the men whose Scandinavian blood still flowed in comparative purity.

Of regular Germanic professions there can be even less record than of trade. The healing art was largely bound up with religious rites, as the charms and incantations testify;[2] but there was the beginning of a science in the selection of herbs and simples. The confusion of both methods may be seen in such a collection as the Rev. Mr. Cockayne's *Leechdoms, Wortcunning, and Starcraft of Early England.*[3] Women had much to do with these things; and the sibyl was no doubt invoked for aid in case of disease or hurt. It is curious enough that painful attacks of gout or rheumatism were attributed to the arrows of the "hags," the mighty women who course the sky, and send their shafts at the unwary mortal.[4] This for the matter of ordinary medicine ; but so far as surgery was concerned, Weinhold[5] is of opinion that an age of constant warfare and battles would attain considerable

---

[1] *R. A.* 112 ff.   [2] See below, p. 423.
[3] Master of the Rolls Series, London, 1864–1866.
[4] See below, p. 372. The Germans still call such a twinge *Hexenschuss.*   [5] *Altnord. Leben,* 387.

skill in the treatment of wounds, the art of amputation, and kindred matters.   As for other professions, the schoolmaster was emphatically "abroad," and the lawyer was chieftain or priest.[1]

[1] For the monopoly of legal lore by the Indian priests, see Sir H. Maine, *Early Law and Custom*, p. 46.

CHAPTER VIII

THE WARRIOR

Military service of two kinds — War the chief business of Germanic life — Courage — Types of the warrior — Cowardice — Germanic weapons — Armor — Cavalry — Importance of the infantry — Tactics of the army — The onset — Second kind of military service — The *comitatus* — Its meaning in Germanic life and history — Age at which the German took up arms.

UNQUESTIONED and absolute lord of his household, the free German had well-defined duties towards the state. These duties were military and civil; and, as we may well imagine, the military were of chief importance. In Anglo-Saxon times, both varieties are represented by the three obligations laid upon every free citizen (thane): to repair the burg or fortified place, to mend the bridges, and to serve in the militia.[1] Military service, obligatory upon every Germanic citizen, called him in time of need to take his place in the general army, which was simply "the folk in arms."[2] A second sort of military service was voluntary; the free man fought abroad under foreign princes or wherever war could be found. But service in the main army was a very frequent matter, calling for and developing the supreme Germanic virtue, —

[1] See, among other cases, Liebermann, I, 242, § 26, 1.
[2] Waitz, I. 402.

a virtue that was born in the freeman, and made
strong in him by every possible device of example
and training. In fact, the whole education of a
Germanic youth was a lesson *de contemnenda morte*.[1]
Now Rome was a military state and was founded
upon the idea of a folk in arms; but the desperate
courage of the German warrior made an almost
uncanny impression upon the legions. As for the
Germans, they had no false modesty about their
merits. During the reign of Nero, certain Frisian
ambassadors came.to Rome and in the course of their
entertainment were brought into the theatre. Here
they quietly and uninvited took the seats of honor,
remarking that no people in the world surpassed the
Germans in courage. As we have repeatedly noticed,
they always went about armed, no matter how peaceful their business of the moment;[2] and a man unarmed
was no better than a slave. They took their weapons
to bed with them, as we may read in the account of
Béowulf's watch in the hall on the night when he
expects a visit from the monster Grendel.[3] There
are some very curious regulations in the Anglo-Saxon
laws with regard to the degree of blame and the fine
attaching to a man who carries his spear so carelessly
over his shoulder as to injure other people;[4] and
we may see the earliest advances of law over license
in the edicts against drawing a weapon in the hall

[1] Müllenhoff's fine summary may be quoted: "Etenim majoribus
nostris fortitudo non modo summa sed prope divina virtus ac sola
pugna esse videbatur, qua simul et omnis viri virtus et suprema omnium fatalis vis cerneretur." *De antiq. Germ. poesi*, p. 12.

[2] *Germ.* XIII. J. Grimm, *R. A.* 287.

[3] See also Lehman, in the *Germania*, Vol. XXI. p. 494.

[4] Liebermann, I, 68, 70.

or presence of the king.[1] Spear and shield are an easy metonymy for warrior, and warrior is synonymous with man; hence the legal phrase of "spear-side" for the male line of descent, in contrast to the "spindle" of the female side. We still hear occasionally this phrase of "relatives on the spindle side" used for maternal kin. King Alfred's will speaks of the *spere-healfe* and the *spinl-healfe*.[2]

When the German was not fighting, he loved to feast in his hall and hear good songs and tales of war. "To hear of battle and conquest was the German's delight;"[3] and long after his conversion to Christianity, it is the deeds of valor which most attract him in the Bible and the legends of the church. The poet of the *Hêliand*, with his evident partiality for "valorous Earl Peter," and the revel of battle-metaphors which describe the attack upon Malchus, shows what he would do if only the quiet gospel narrative afforded him an opportunity. Coming back to the Anglo-Saxons, we find the subject of Judith offering unusual attractions to one of our old but nameless poets; the resolute widow smiting off the head of drunken Holofernes, the ensuing fight, the rout of the heathen, are all close to the Germanic heart, and it responds in a fiery piece of epic, perhaps our finest fragment of the oldest period. From their scraps and shards of poetry alone we could

---

[1] Alfred's Laws, Liebermann, I, 52, 54, § 7.

[2] Quoted from Thorpe's *Diplomatorium*, p. 491, in Wright's *Womankind in Western Europe*, p. 59. "Das nechste blut vom schwert [here taking place of spear] geboren erbet, und da kein schwert vorhanden, erbet die spille." *R. A.* 163, 171.

[3] Grimm, *Andreas und Elene*, XXIV.; Ten Brink, *Geschichte d. engl. Lit.* p. 56 f.

tell why Tacitus calls the Germans "a race that thirsts for dangers."[1] The passion began with infancy. Tacitus, speaking of the Tencteri, a Low German tribe which excelled in horsemanship, says: "Not greater among the Chatti is the renown of the foot-soldier than the fame of the horseman among the Tencteri. So the ancestors established it, and so the offspring imitate. It makes the sport of children, the rivalry of youth, the habit of age."[2] What Tacitus means by sport of children is evidently their early skill in sitting and managing a horse; but a certain commentator looks deeper. Evidently, he says, the Tencterian children begin their chivalrous career "on wooden rocking-horses."[3] Cæsar, too, bears testimony to this training of the German youth. "All their life is spent in hunting and in military exercise."[4] Seneca speaks of their "tender children," who early learn to "brandish the spear."[5] A host of later Roman witnesses could be called, when the almost generous admiration of great captains like Cæsar, and statesmen like Tacitus, changes into the tone of fear. When Salvianus speaks of the Saxons as "ferocious [efferi]," we have a whole commentary on the changed attitude of Rome towards Germany. True, there is no lack of justification for the phrase. Whenever we wish to see any Germanic trait in its most exaggerated form, we look to Scan-

---

[1] "Gentes periculorum avidas." *Hist.* V. 19.

[2] *Germ.* XXXII.

[3] We quite agree with Schweizer-Sidler that this view is "*fast lächerlich.*"

[4] *B. G.* VI. 21.

[5] *Epist.* 36. 7. Other references of the kind will be found in Müllenhoff's article on the Sword-Dance, cited above, p. 112.

dinavia.　Of course, the "Bearsarks," the *Berserker*,[1] are the stock illustration of the old Norse ferocity and lust for battle; yet according to Vigfusson and Powell,[2] this matter of the Bearsark rage and frenzy has been vastly exaggerated. "Bearsarks were really *chosen champions;*" and they doubtless made great clamor when they went into the fight, with "their war-whoop, and the rattling of sword and spear against shield," which only agrees with the Tacitean account of the noise made by a German line of battle at the first wild onset. Bearsark, says our authority, means simply the fur coat of the nobler henchmen. We may remember that the Germans of Tacitus wore skins. That these men were gentle, is not asserted; but they were not crazy. The Germanic temperament was savage, uncertain, and gloomy; pent up in the narrow Norwegian valleys,[3] increased by seclusion and intermarriage, these characteristics took an acute form. Even in recent times, the Norwegian's knife flashed out on very slight provocation. Battle would naturally fan their fury to its height; but it was all in the way of natural, not artificial ferocity. The Bearsarks were not professional lunatics.

The prime quality of barbaric courage is a fine contempt for death. Of this we shall have more to say under the head of Germanic belief in immortality; here we may consider it as it affects the warrior. High over all suspicion of rhetoric rises the

---

[1] Maurer, *Bekehrung der Norweg. Stämme*, II. 408, makes it thus, and refers the name to the same idea as that of werewolves. Others insist on *baresarks*, because they went into fight without armor.

[2] *C. P. B.* I. 425, 530.　　　　[3] Ibid. p. 426.

death-cry of Ragnar Lodbrok, as he lies in the pit full of serpents: —

Lapséd is life's hour; laughing I die.[1]

It was the Germanic virtue to take death with this "frolic welcome." The *Atlakviða* or *Old Lay of Atli* (Attila) gives us an excellent illustration, drawn in sharper lines than the corresponding scene of the Nibelungen Lay. The translation is by Vigfusson and Powell:[2] —

" They asked the brave king of the Goths[3] if he would buy his life with gold. [Then said Gunnar,] 'Hogni's bleeding heart must be laid in my hand, carved with the keen-cutting knife out of the breast of the good knight.' They carved the heart of Hialli (the thrall) from out his breast and laid it bleeding on a charger and bore it to Gunnar.

" Then spake Gunnar, king of men : ' Here I have the heart of Hialli the coward, unlike to the heart of Hogni the brave. It quakes greatly as it lies on the charger, but it quaked twice as much when it lay in his breast.'

" Hogni laughed when they cut out the quick heart of that crested hero, he had little thought of whimpering. They laid it bleeding on the charger, and bore it before Gunnar.

" Then spake Gunnar. . . . ' Here have I the heart of Hogni the brave, unlike the heart of Hialli the coward. It quakes very little as it lies on the charger, but it quaked far less when lay in his breast.'

---

[1] " Lifs ero liðnar stundir, læjandi skal-ek deyja." See *C. P. B.* II. 341 ff. Grimm, *G. D. S.* 89 f.

[2] *C. P. B.*, I, 48 f.; Hollander, p. 337, § 22 f.; Bellows, p. 490 f.

[3] Gunnar.

" . . . The band of warriors put the king alive into the pit that was crawling with serpents. But Gunnar, alone there, in his wrath smote the harp with his hands; the strings rang out."

When the German could no longer " drink delight of battle with his peers " in that " game of swords," as his most popular kenning termed the battle, he found nothing left to live for, and was fain to die. So died by their own hand those noble Sigambri, " men of mark " in their clan, whom, though ambassadors, Augustus treacherously disarmed and distributed among various cities: " out of very shame they put themselves to death." [1]

Indeed, wherever we look,—at the boys who learn to back a steed and send spears home to the mark, at the warlike names of man or woman, at the actual combat, and if, perhaps, we include the fight which late Scandinavian myths insist shall end the world, — everywhere the evidence presses upon us that our ancestors were " fond o' fechtin' " to a degree rarely met with in history. The very metre of their poetry is the clash of battle, and knows scarcely any other note. This passion of bravery, not uncommon in barbarians of a mounting race, was further strengthened in the German by his belief in another world. The belief itself we shall consider later, but its fruits we may briefly notice in this place. In the *Pharsalia* of Lucan,[2] the connection of Germanic courage with Germanic faith is strongly asserted; and the native records themselves are full of the same testimony. The song of Ragnar Lodbrok, from which a quotation was just made, contains a passage which shows how bravery

---

[1] Dio Cass. 55. VI., and *Deutsche Vorzeit*, p. 304.   [2] I. 458 ff.

and faith went hand in hand. " The fearless man," says Ragnar, " does not quail before death. *I shall not come into Withri's* [Woden's] *hall with a word of fear.*" Not, we can almost say, not as a tired actor going off the scenes did a German die; but rather as the actor, fresh from his rehearsal, waiting for the word that sends him on the stage before an audience of warriors and kings. What better entrance than in the thick of fight, with a song of defiance and a laugh? This passion of ferocity, tutored by centuries, results at last in the calmer and nobler but still cheerful courage of Harry the Fifth at Agincourt, or of his father's antagonist in the lists at Coventry: —

> As gentle and as jocund as to jest
> Go I to fight: truth hath a quiet breast.

Sometimes the consolations of death are based entirely on the bravery which has dared it, on the source of it, and on what we may call its artistic setting and merit. Fine are the dying words of Wolfhart in the Nibelungen Lay.[1] He and the youngest of the Burgundian kings have given each other mortal wounds.

> And if my kin be minded to weep that I am dead,
> Go tell the best and dearest that this is what I said:
> They must not wail and mourn me, there is no reason why;
> A king's right hand hath slain me, a lordly death I die.

This has a fine ring, and lacks not for a late echo in the words of Hotspur before Shrewsbury field: —

> An if we live, we live to tread on kings;
> If die, brave death when princes die with us.[2]

[1] *N. L.* 2239.   [2] *I. Hen. IV.* V. 2.

But we are overwhelmed with material of this sort; take, for example, that highly dramatic scene of the Nibelungen Lay,[1] where Dancwart cuts his way through the Huns, and bursting into the banquet hall, where sit Etzel and Kriemhild with their royal guests, cries out to his brother Hagen that all the Burgundian retainers have been massacred in their quarters; and grim Hagen asks:—

"But who has done it, then?"
"That has fair Master Bloedel and with him all his men!
Yet dearly has he paid us, let this at least be said,
For with these hands of mine, I've stricken off his head."

"That is no weeping matter," made answer Hagen bold;
"If only of a warrior such story may be told,
That hero's hand hath slain him in free and open fight:—
For such a death fair women should make their mourning light."

The thought lapses from this grave old setting into the lighter frame of a modern commonplace; we find it, for example, in Herrick, who if a "pagan," as critics will call him, was as English a pagan as ever loved beef and ale.

To conquer'd men some comfort 'tis to fall
By th' hand of him who is the generall.[2]

On the other side of the picture, we find terrible disgrace in the death of a hero or warrior by the hand of woman. This is the very climax of tragedy in our Nibelungen Lay. All are slain save the arch-murderer, Hagen, and the arch-avenger, Kriemhild, the too faithful vassal and the too faithful wife. Kriemhild takes her dead husband's sword and kills

[1] Avent. XXXIII.   [2] "Some Comfort in Calamity."

with it the murderer, who is bound and helpless before her; in some ways, we are ready to concede, a just retribution. But the sentiment of Kriemhild's own living husband and ally in vengeance cannot applaud the act.

> " Alas," bewailed the monarch, " Alas, and now is slain,
> All at a woman's hands, the best and noblest thane
> That ever led in battle and ever lifted spear!
> And though he was my foeman, his fall shall cost me dear."

> Out spake old Hildebrand : " No comfort shall she know
> Because she dared to slay him ! "

And the gray-headed warrior springs to the woman and kills her, and no one holds him back or blames him for his deed.

But this sense of fitness and unfitness, the consolations of an honorable death and the horrors of slaughter at unworthy hands, are less intense than the religious and fatalistic sanctions. It is instructive, so far as fatalism is concerned in the matter, to see how the opposite notion of individual freedom, personal responsibility, that tendency to trust in one's manhood and in nothing else, keeps alternating in Germanic hearts with the sense of an inevitable, inexorable fate. The Germanic creed is undoubtedly expressed by King Gernot:[1] —

> Dâ sterbent wan die veigen, —
> Only the doomed ones die, —

which is nothing more than Hamlet's, " If it be now, 'tis not to come; if it be not to come, it will be now . . . the readiness is all."[2] But the impetuous sense

[1] *N. L.* 149.   [2] *Ham.* V. 2.

of individual manhood, the anticipation (if we must find a modern instance) of Fletcher's nobler astrology, — "man is his own star," — rebelled against this helpless note of acquiescence, and tacked a fiery rider to the wonted phrase. Fate, says Béowulf, as he tells of his battle with the sea-monsters,[1] fate often saves a man *if he have plenty of courage.*

> For Wyrd oft saveth
> earl undoomed if he doughty be!

The same idea and the same phrase, with very slight change, passed into the Christian poetry of our ancestors, and have since become a commonplace. In the Anglo-Saxon *Andreas* we read:[2] —

> Therefore sooth will I say to you; —
> never leaveth the living God
> earl to his doom, *if he doughty be.*

"Wyrd," the fate-goddess, has been changed to suit the new faith; but the essentials of the old epic phrase are there. In one passage of the *Béowulf* we have a characteristic[3] blending of the two religions. Grendel the monster would have devoured many more warriors of the Danish court, —

> Had not wisest God their Wyrd averted,
> and the man's bold mood, —

that is, had not Béowulf slain the demon.[4] We may

---

[1] *Béow.* 572. *Fæge* is the same word as *veigen* above, like Scotch *fey.*
[2] 459 ff.

[3] Characteristic, because the *Béowulf* is a heath n epic put together by a Christian monk.

[4] *Béow.* 1057 f. The idea is of course evident enough; the original sentiment, however, is not a commonplace, but an ethical theory, a

add one example from Scandinavian poetry. In the
Skírnismál, where Skirnir is to ride to giant-land and
win for the god Freyr that maiden Gerthr, whose
fair white arms "shed a light through all the sky and
sea," Freyr gives to the messenger both steed and
sword : "a horse will I give thee that shall bear thee
through the murky waver-flame,[1] and a sword *which
will brandish itself and fight, if he is brave that holds
it.*"[2] This rises quite above the commonplace, even
of the old epic; a sword of self-respect evidently,
that will not move to its miraculous calling, if it be
held in ignoble hands. What were thought to be
noble hands in such a case would be easy to prove
from even random selections of Germanic poetry.
Let us take a single example. It is that fine old
Saxon ballad of the *Fight at Maldon* where "Alderman" Byrhtnoth, with a hastily gathered array of
the local militia, opposes a party of Danish pirates.
These offer him peace in return for tribute, a bargain
too often struck in the degenerate days of Æthelred. But the Saxon answer has a ring ancestral
at once and prophetic of the later English hardihood.

part of the most intimate Germanic life. It is always instructive to see
these epic forms and phrases passing into burlesque, which loves to
catch popular sentiment. Thus our fine old personal equation of the
providence of Wyrd finds echo in Chaucer's *Sir Thopas*. That gallant
knight is hard put to it in combat with a giant, Sir Olifaunt by name :—

> Sire Thopas drow abak ful faste;
> The geant at hym stones caste
>   Out of a fel staf slynge,
> But faire escapeth sire Thopas;
> *And al it was thurgh Goddes gras,*
>   *And thurgh his fair berynge.*

[1] The girdle of fire about the maiden's hall.
[2] *For Skírnis*, 9; Neckel, p. 68, Bellows, p. 110, Hollander, p. 77.

> Byrhtnoth spake, his shield uplifting,
> waving light spear, with words replied,
> angry and resolute, answered back : —
> " Hear'st thou, seaman, what say this folk ?
> They will pay you tribute in trusty spears,
> venom'd darts and dear-held swords,
> war-gear that steads you the worse in battle!
> Herald of pirates, hear our answer!
> Say to thy people no pleasant message : —
> Here stands, not unhonor'd, an earl with his band,
> who is fain to defend these fields ye see,
> Æthelred's land, my lord and master,
> the folk and the ground. . . ." [1]

The fight begins, and Byrhtnoth struggles gallantly, but he is sorely pressed by the foeman and at last wounded with a spear. He —

> pushed with his shield that the shaft broke off,
> and burst the spear that back it sprang;
> fierce grew the thane, and he thrust his lance
> in the wicing proud who had wounded him.
> Sage was the chieftain, sent his lance
> through the pirate's neck with knowing hand,
> till he reached the heart of the heathen foe.
> Straightway a second spear he drove
> that the corselet burst; the breast was wounded
> through ringéd mail, in the midst of the heart
> stood the poisoned edge: the earl was blither,
> the bold one laughed, and his Lord he thanked
> for this good day's work that God had sent him . . . [2]

Then he is himself killed, but dies fighting to the last, shouting courage to his men, and with a song of proud thanksgiving on his lips : —

> I praise and thank thee, Prince of nations,
> for all my delights while I lived on earth, —

[1] *Maldon*, 42 ff. [2] 136 ff.

and expires with a prayer for his soul's welfare. So fought and so died a true Saxon, true to the spirit of his ancestors who nearly a thousand years before had defied the legions. For Byrhtnoth, with his splendid achievement, stands just midway between our time and the times of Cæsar and Tacitus.

If such was the Germanic estimate of courage, it is easy to guess what would be for them the vice of vices and the crime of crimes. Disgrace was stamped indelibly upon the man who left his shield behind him in the battle. He was shut out from tribal worship, entered no fane, took part in no council, and — if this is not the flourish of Tacitean rhetoric[1] — often ended his infamy by a self-inflicted and ignominious death. Direct cowardice, desertion, and similar crimes found no mercy whatever.[2] Such offenders, where treachery was suspected, were promptly hanged; while the mere coward and the fugitive, like the doer of nameless crimes, were sunk wretchedly in a swamp with a wicker-hurdle pressed over them, the punishment of women : —

> Cowards who were in sloughs interred alive;
> And round them still the wattled hurdles hung
> Wherewith they stamp'd them down, and trod them deep,
> To hide their shameful memory from men.[3]

Crimes, says Tacitus, should be punished openly: but scandals stifled in darkness and silence. Both of these modes of execution survived in the middle ages.

We have mentioned hanging as in some degree a soldier's death. To hang a convicted man to the

---

[1] *Germ.* VI.   [2] *Germ.* XII.   [3] Matthew Arnold, *Balder Dead.*

nearest good tree was the sentence of the Westphalian *Vehmgericht*.[1] Our old friend of the ballad,
Johnie Armstrong, with many others of the "most
noble thieves," — that is, marauders of the Scottish
marches, — were all, by the king's command, "hanged
upon growing trees."[2] These were gentlemen born.
The punishment of the gallows was widely used by
our earliest ancestors, and finds a varied expression
in the older literature, — chiefly in Scandinavian
poetry.[3] It was by no means so ignoble an exit from
life as it is now, and indicated no absolute disgrace
like the vile indignities of the hurdle and the swamp.
The gallows did not mutilate a body, and its victim
had moreover a fine chance to join the Wild Huntsman as he swept by, and so to storm the heights of
heaven and Valhalla.[4] Nay, Odin himself, as he
tells us in the *Hávamál*, "hung nine nights on the
windy tree," that is upon the gallows;[5] and whether
or not this be a Norse version of the Crucifixion, the
honorable association remains. Oddly enough, some
distorted mediæval legend proclaimed that Crœsus of
old ended his days in this fashion, as had been foretold him in a dream; and in defence of popular faith
in visions he is cited by the hero of the *Nonne Prestes
Tale* in Chaucer.[6] --

> Lo, Cresus, which that was of Lyde kyng,
> Mette he nat that he sat upon a tree —
> Which signifieth he sholde anhanged bee?

[1] See a popular but accurate account in *Vehmgerichte und Hexen-
processe*, by Dr. Oskar Wächter, in the "Collection Spemann."
[2] See Child's Ballads,[2] VI. 365.　　[3] Grimm, *R. A.* 682 ff.
[4] Rochholz, *Deutscher Glaube und Brauch*, I. 273.
[5] Bugge, *Studier*, 292.　　[6] *Canterbury Tales*, B. 4328—30.'

Since hanging had these associations, ingenuity was quickened to put some disgrace into the fact; and a fashion often employed was the device of hanging wolves or dogs along with the culprit, who was also placed head downwards, — one of the numerous compliments which mediæval law paid to the Jews.[1] Even under the more ignoble circumstances, hanging was a penalty reserved for males; women were burnt, drowned, or stoned to death. " Den dieb soll man henken und die hur ertränken." [2] Later it was the prerogative of nobles to be beheaded, while common men were hanged; but the poet of *Béowulf* seems to indicate that if the old king, Hrêthel, had punished Hæthcyn in the way of blood-feud for the innocent murder of the elder brother Herebeald, it would have been by the gallows. The monarch cannot bring himself to it: —

> Too awful it is for an agéd man
> to bide and bear, that his bairn so young
> rides[3] on the gallows[4].

We may conclude that a gallows-destiny, while not yearned for, and far less noble than death by sword or spear, did not acquire its peculiar disgrace until the middle ages. In the time of Tacitus, men who, certainly at some bodily risk, deserted their own cause and betrayed it to the enemy,[5] were hanged to trees — probably, says Grimm, dead and leafless trees. The victims were thus a sacrifice to

---

[1] *R. A.* 685.   [2] Ibid. 687.   [3] " Ride " is the technical term.
[4] *Béow.* 2444. In the Sacred Grove at Upsala in Sweden, says Adam of Bremen, could be seen many corpses of men and beasts hung upon the trees.   [5] *"Proditores et transfugas"*, *Germ.* XII.

tribal gods. But no god cared for the coward who fled in sheer physical terror, nor for the worker of abominations in ordinary life: these were stamped and buried out of sight, in slime and mud.[1]

It is evident that cowardice was the unpardonable Germanic sin, and courage the cardinal virtue of a Germanic warrior. Let us now glance at these warriors in their array. The make-up of the army was not very intricate; discipline, system, the strategic conduct of a campaign, were hardly known at all. An Arminius, trained as he was to Roman discipline, might for a while animate the army with single plan and spirit; but he could not organize his troops for permanent work nor establish a regular system. Leadership consisted not so much in direction and organization as in example of valor. The individual warrior was the one supreme element, his personal strength and his courage; and he was, moreover, decidedly better than his weapons. These were poor enough. With some allowance for the purpose of the speech, the description given by Germanicus in his address to the legions[2] furnishes our best idea of the German soldier and his arms. "Not only the open field," said Germanicus, "was a good battle-ground for the Roman soldier, but also, if one acted in a rational way, the forests and thickets. For the huge shields and the long spears of the barbarians could not be managed among the tree-trunks and low bushes so easily as the javelin, the sword, and close-fitting coverings. The main thing for the Romans was to rain their sword-strokes upon the faces of the

---

[1] Kemble, in his *Salomon and Saturn*, p. 89, gives some further illustrative passages.　　　[2] Tac. *Ann.* II. 14.

enemy; the Germans had neither armor nor helmet;
not even their shields were made of iron or leather,
but were simply a sort of plaited willow-work with thin
painted boards. The foremost line of battle might be
fairly well supplied with spears; the rest had darts,
short, or else with points hardened in the fire."[1] This
is not a very good showing for the Germanic arsenal;
but we must not forget the occasion. Moreover, we
have the testimony of the graves and other finds.
If the bronze age is reckoned from about 1500 to
500 B.C., we must count bronze swords, of which
Denmark's soil has surrendered such numerous and
exquisite specimens, among the possible acquisitions
of a sturdy German warrior.[2] Perhaps such are the
enta geweorc, the work of giants, of which we hear so
often; and there is good reason to think that these
are meant when, in Saxon or Scandinavian poetry,
reference is made to the "fallow" sword.[3] True,
Germanicus does not mention the sword in his list of
the barbarian arms; and we may well infer that it
was not the universal weapon. Metals were rare in
Germany; and iron, though familiar, does not seem
to have been mined and worked.[4] Swords were,
nevertheless, known and valued by the Germans; and
nothing is so often mentioned in their traditions. On
the column of Marcus Aurelius the Germans are represented with short, crooked swords; and swords are

---

[1] The account of Cimbrian arms given by Plutarch speaks of swords,
armor, and so on, but they are evidently booty taken from the enemy.
What forges were there in the German forests to turn out such work?

[2] See Montelius, *passim*.

[3] See Vigfusson-Powell in *C. P. B.* II. 481.

[4] *Germ.* VI.: " *Ne ferrum quidem superest* "; that is, not even iron
abounds. But in the early days it was imported.

mentioned among the Germanic tribes which, notably
under Ariovistus, made front against Cæsar.   A
sword was undoubtedly expensive and highly valued;
for as late as the sixth century, among the Franks,
sword and scabbard are reckoned at the worth of
seven cows, while shield and lance together only
equal two cows.[1] The antiquity of the sword as Germanic weapon can be inferred from another consideration — the name of the Saxons, which is supposed to
be derived from the short sword or *seahs* (our oldest
English form of the word) carried by warriors of
that race.[2] To be sure, the name of Saxons is not
known to Strabo, Pliny, or Tacitus, and is first mentioned by Ptolemy in the middle of the second century as belonging to a small tribe on the Cimbrian
peninsula.   For all that, however, the name is far
older than the mention of it, and was doubtless
applied to themselves by all the minor tribes along the
Elbe and the Weser.   By the fourth century, Saxons
and Franks are the chief Germanic races.   Saxnot is
one of the abjured divinities in the famous renunciation; and in the genealogy of the kings of Essex,
Saxnéat is the son of Woden.   Saxons, then, must
mean "the men with short swords," and Saxnéat
"the sword-companion."   Grimm quotes the well-
known account of Nennius,[3] where Hengist tells his
men: "When I cry out to you and say '*en Saxones,
nimith eure Saxas*,'[4] seize your knives and rush upon

---

[1] Arnold, *Deutsche Urzeit*, p. 279.

[2] Zeuss and Grimm uphold, Kemble opposes, the etymology. See
Kemble's *Saxons*, I, 41; Grimm, *G. D. S.*², p. 424; *New English Dictionary, s. v.* 'sax'; also the article "Sachsen", § 11, in Hoops' *Reallexikon* for a summary of etymological views.

[3] *Hist. Brit.* Cap. 46.   [4] That is, "Saxons, take your swords."

the foe." Continental Saxons of a later date were
wont to bring their knives when they came to court,
and thrust them in the ground as they declared themselves guilty or innocent of a given charge;[1] and
this, Jacob Grimm thinks, is a survival of the Germanic habit of going armed to all popular assemblies.
Other names that may be connected with the sword
are the Cherusci,[2] the clan of Arminius, and the tribe
which our Widsith calls the "Swordsmen"; for personal names a good example is the father of Béowulf,
Ecgtheow, — that is, "Sword-servant."

Short swords of this pattern were carried by the
Rugii, as Tacitus especially notes.[3] But the Cimbrians in Italy had longer swords; and the description
of their weapons by Plutarch points, as was hinted
above, at a long career of plunder on the part of
these invaders who had made their way through
Gaul, and had met repeatedly troops of good equipment. Plutarch describes their cavalry as furnished
with "breastplates of iron and white glittering
shields; and for their offensive arms every one had
two darts, and when they came hand to hand, they
used large and heavy swords."[4] Kemble[5] speaks
of the "long, heavy Celtic or German sword," as
contrasted with the short weapon of the Roman.
These long swords were often two-edged. — and are
found in German graves.[6] In the Waltharius Lay,
the hero carries two swords, one short and with
single edge, on his right side, the other long and

---

[1] R. A. 772.   [2] Grimm, G. D. S. 426.   [3] Germ. XLIV.
[4] Plutarch, Marius, Dryden-Clough translation.
[5] Horæ Ferales, p. 63.
[6] Holtzmann, Germanische Alterthümer, 141 f.

double-edged, on his left. It is often assumed that all
these swords were of iron; but Grimm in his list of
weapon-names [1] says under *seax* "ursprünglich wohl
eine steinwaffe," and Baumstark [2] reminds us not
only of the stone swords found along the Baltic, but
also of the great number of swords made from bronze.
Swords found in those German graves which are
known to belong to the period of tribal movement
are mostly of iron; by that time the iron sword and
(among the Franks of the sixth century) the battle-
axe were chief weapons of the German foot-soldier.
When Tacitus says that "few Germans use swords," [3]
he is stating for the first century what still held true,
to a large degree, in the ninth or tenth. In Cnut's
time shield and spear, bow and arrow, were weapons
for the rank and file; and a sword is in our own
day mark of the officer as distinguished from the
common soldier. Anglo-Saxon law made a "ceorl"
"siðcund," that is, raised his rank, when he had
helmet, coat-of-mail, and gilded sword, no matter
whether he owned land or not. [4] The importance of
the sword is proved not only by the traditions and
survivals to which we have alluded, but by the number of names for it in literal statement; [5] by the
poetical names or kennings for it, like the Norse *gun-
nlogi*, or battle-flame, and the corresponding Anglo-
Saxon *beadoléoma;* [6] by the personifications of it and
name-giving, like Nægling and Hrunting, where we
note the humanizing force of the suffix; and finally

---

[1] *Deutsche Grammatik*, III. 440.   [2] *Germ.* p. 308 f.   [3] *Germ.* VI.
[4] *Cf.* Schmid, *Einl.* LXVI., and Lehmann, *Waffen im Béow.* "Germania," 31. 486 ff.   [5] Grimm, *Grammatik*, III. 440, gives a list.
[6] See Bode, *Kenningar*, p. 55 f.

by the actual worship of it. How our forefathers would have felt the force of the dialogue in the fine Danish ballad *Hævnersværdet*,[1] where the hero takes counsel with his sword, or where by naming its name he restrains its thirst for blood![2] Sometimes we find a sort of pact or league between warrior and sword, and when both keep the promise there is great glory won. So of the hero and his good brand in *Béowulf*:[3] —

> Neither softened his soul, nor the sire's bequest
> weakened in war.

When a sword is about to kill some one, it gives forth a noise;[4] in the Anglo-Saxon *Finnsburg* fragment, besides the usual battle-omens of screaming birds, the coat-of-mail "yells" or clangs, the warwood (spear) dins, and "shield answers shaft."[5] When Béowulf is going to seek and slay the monster mother of Grendel in her own ocean fastness, he borrows a sword; its name, the poet tells us, is Hrunting, and it is the noblest of ancient treasures, an heirloom; its edge is iron, stained with poisondrops and hardened with blood of battle; in fight it never yet had played false to the man who brandished it, whenever he dared the ways of warfare, the meeting-place of foes; this was not the first time that it was fated to do brave deeds. Noting, now, this seeming independence and individuality, we are not surprised at the expression which the poet uses when

---

[1] Grundtvig, *Danmarks Gamle Folkeviser*, I. 350, stanzas 16 ff., 35.
[2] See also Child, Ballads,[2] I. 96.   [3] 2628 f.
[4] Maurer, *Bekehrung d. norweg. Stämme*, II. 123.   [5] *Finns.* 5 ff.

he records a failure in the fight with the monster.
Béowulf then found —

> that the Light-of-Battle was loath to bite, —

and so it failed to work his will upon the foe.   As for
the speaking of swords, their word and wish, we are
reminded of Wordsworth's personification; for, as Mr.
E B. Tylor has somewhere remarked, Wordsworth's
power in this respect almost seems to revive the force
of òld mythology: — ·

> Armor rusting in his Halls
> On the blood of Clifford calls ;
> " Quell the Scot," exclaims the Lance ;
> " Bear me to the heart of France," —
> Is the longing of the Shield.[1]

Swords are full of supernatural traits, and often
give out a magic light; one "conquering blade," an
"old sword of giants," sheds such radiance, —

> as when from the sky there shines unclouded
> heaven's candle.[2]

and thus illuminates the uncanny hall of the monsters
with a light that reaches from the depths to the surface of the sea.[3]   A host of legends, gathered in
recent times, but rooted in our oldest heathen superstitions, tell of charmed weapons which are now carried by the living, and now buried with the dead, but
are always endowed with miraculous power, often
gleaming far off through the night.

> His sword well burnisht, shineth yet,
> And over the barrow beam the hilts.[4]

---

[1] *Song at the Feast of Brougham Castle.*
[2] *Béow.* 1558 ff. " Heaven's candle " is, of course, the sun.
[3] See Heyne's *Halle Heorot*, p. 46, note [4].   [4] See p. 312, below.

To swear by one's sword — coming to the last category — was common down to modern times, not simply as some commentators on *Hamlet* assert, because the hilt formed a cross, but for traditional reasons. Indeed, we have evidence that the sword was worshipped. The princes of the Quadi, making submission A.D. 358 to an imperial army, draw their swords, "which they worship as deities," and swear to keep faith. So writes Ammianus Marcellinus;[1] and in another place, after an elaborate description of the Alani, a Scythian tribe, he says that their only notion of religious ceremonies is to thrust a sword into the ground and worship it "as Mars," — this, of course, simply an *interpretatio Romana*.[2]

It was the fashion to write runes on the sword. Often, as on the spearhead of Kovel described by Wimmer,[3] the owner's name was graven upon the blade. The spearhead in question is probably from the fourth century,[4] and bears the Gothic name *Tilariðs*, or "bold rider." But incantations and spells, taking the place of our modern mottoes, were frequently carved; and these mysterious runes could be of good or of evil omen. When Freyr's zealous henchman is wooing Gerthr for his master, and the maiden refuses his gold, he begins to threaten her: "Look on this blade, maid, slender, marked with characters, that I hold in my hand; I will hew off thy head. . . ."[5] Then he goes on to praise the terrible potency of the weapon, due in part to the mysterious working of the runes. In like manner, a sword could

---

[1] Bk. 17, Chap. XII. [2] Bk. 31, Chap. II.
[3] *Die Runenschrift*, p. 57. [4] Ibid. p. 71.
[5] *C. P. B.*, I, 114; Neckel, p. 71, st. 25; Hollander, pp. 81—83; Bellows, p. 114 f.

be made useless by incantations, and Saxo tells of a
certain Gunholm, who was wont to dull and lame
(*obtundere*) the hostile blade by his runic charms
(*carminibus*).   In *Salomon and Saturn*[1] we are told
that evil spirits

> write on his weapon woe-marks an heap,
> baleful bookstaves;[2] the bill[3] they bewitch,
> the pride of the sword.

Against this evil, one's remedy consisted in singing a
pater-noster as one drew the sword out of its scabbard,
and the blade was then fit to do its work.   Of course
this pater-noster takes the place of some ancient and
heathen "backward mutter of dissevering power."

Scarcity of iron made a relative scarcity not only
of swords, but also of the longer lances, those "huge
spears" mentioned several times by Tacitus.   The
common weapons of a German warrior were the *framea* for attack and the shield for defence; in the
public assemblies assent was shown by clashing these
weapons together.   Concerning the nature of the *framea*, much has been said; and a close investigation by
Müllenhoff,[4] based mainly on philological data, concludes that although later Christian literature uses
framea for sword (*gladius*),[5] nevertheless we are to
hold to Tacitus, who distinctly says it is a small
lance or spear (*hasta*) with short and scanty iron.

---

[1] Ed. Kemble, p. 144 f.   [2] *Buchstaben*, letters.   [3] Sword, blade.

[4] In his far too sharp and contemptuous review of Lindenschmidt's
Handbuch d. deutschen Alterthumskunde, "Haupt's Ztst." Anzeiger,
VII. 209–229.

[5] Müllenhoff notes that Juvenal uses *framea* for the lance of Mars,
and Gellius names *frameæ* as missiles.

As for the word, it must be Germanic; in Müllenhoff's opinion it is a derivative of *fram*, and means
"toward the front," — a projectile for close quarters
or long range, precisely as Tacitus describes it. Jähns
thinks that the so-called "celts" of stone or bronze,
found so plentifully in ethnological museums, were
fastened on a straight shaft and so formed the *framea*.[1] In later times, and with the greater abundance
of iron, the better wrought *gêr*, Anglo-Saxon *gâr*, or
spear, took the place of the missile, which thenceforth disappears from history. This change increased
the efficiency of Germanic soldiers, precisely as in the
case of the African chief mentioned above,[2] who converted the missile lance into a long, stout spear meant
for thrusting alone.

The shields of German soldiers were not elaborate.
Otherwise they had little armor, if we except certain
leather or possibly iron helmets used by eastern
tribes.[3] Holtzmann is rash when he says they went
without armor, not only because they had no iron,
but "because they loved defiance and gladly sought
scars," — an argument that appeals, perhaps, to a
German student, but hardly covers the ground. The
huge shield left them in a measure independent of
other armor; and indeed we find them scarcely clad
at all, fighting naked to the waist, like the older
Gauls. We are told that the German cohorts in the
army of Vitellius fought "with bodies naked, after
the fashion of their country." In this guise appear
the barbarian figures on Trajan's column; and Cæsar
so describes the warriors of Ariovistus.[4] Paul the

[1] See Hoops under "Framea".   [2] See p. 209.
[3] Baumstark, *Germ.* p. 328.   [4] Cass. Dio, 38. 45.

Deacon testifies of the Heruli, that they fought naked
save for a cloth about the loins.   Who does not
remember that picture in Plutarch's *Marius*, where
the barbarians in sheer defiance let the snow fall upon
their naked bodies, and setting themselves on their
broad shields go sliding down the Alps?   These
immense shields covered a great portion of the body;
Waitz says, all of it.[1]   They were flat, made of wood
or wicker-work, had often a metal boss, and were frequently colored.   Like "ash" as name for spear,
"linden" or the like is often used for shield, — the
material for the weapon itself.   Naturally, such
shields cost but little, and were subject to very rough
usage in battle.   At the end of the fragmentary Hildebrand Lay, we read of flying splinters from the rapid
sword-strokes of the combatants; and elsewhere we
are told of a shieldbearer who in the heat of battle
reaches a fresh shield to his warrior.   With regard to
the color, white shields, as in the case of Hildebrand
and Hathubrand, as well of the Cimbrians in Italy,
are often mentioned.   The shields of the Harii[2] were
black; those of the old Frisians were brown or
white; the Saxons preferred red.   For the Franks in
the fifth century, Sidonius Apollinaris describes the
shields as snow-white in the circle, tawny in the
boss.[3]   Holtzmann thinks these colors were a rude
heraldry, a means of distinguishing tribe from tribe,
and even clans and families.   Perhaps a symbol
of some sort was painted on the shields.   The Cimbrians wore forms of animals on their helmets, like

---

[1] *Verfassungsges.* I. 44.   [2] *Germ.* XLIII.

[3] "Lux in orbibus nivea, fulva in umbonibus."   See Weinhold,
Altnord. Leben, 207.

the carven boar of Anglo-Saxon times;[1] and we hear in other places of the "emblems" of the Germanic shield.

How useful the shield was — and became — can be seen from the "board-wall" (*bordweall*) or wall of shields[2] which Anglo-Saxon warriors made, and which would have held the field at Senlac if Harold's orders had been carried out,[3] and his men had kept their ranks. So in the ballad of *Maldon* we have allusion to this shield-wall; and the poem gives us a spirited picture of the doughty "Alderman" arranging the line of battle and exhorting his warriors to play their parts like men. In *The Battle of Brunanburh*,[4] another ballad of Anglo-Saxon heroism, we hear the cry of delight that warriors have hewn their way through this shield-wall; for "cleaving the shield-hedge" was as much as routing the enemy.

Armor, except of the rudest kind, was introduced among Germanic tribes during the great migration. In *Béowulf* there is frequent mention of the coat-of-mail and the "ring-net," — the latter a corselet woven out of small rings, — as well as of the boar-guarded helmet. We remember, too,[5] that Béowulf expressed solicitude about his noblest war-weed, warding the breast, and desired that in the event of his death, this "work of Wayland" should be sent home.

Other weapons were doubtless familiar to the Ger-

---

[1] Seen also on Scandinavian helmets. See Montelius, work quoted, p. 162. For painted shields among the old Norsemen, see Weinhold, *Altnord. Leben*, p. 428.

[2] Also called the shield-hedge, *bordhaga*.

[3] See Mr. Freeman's fine description, *Norman Conquest*, III.[2] 468 ff.

[4] v. 5 f.   [5] See p. 111, above.

man. The hammer, weapon of old Thor, must have had its warlike as well as peaceful functions; [1] the battle-axe, which made the later Franks such a dreaded foe, found some use among their ancestors. The silence of Tacitus in regard to these weapons, just as with the bow and arrow, is not proof that the Germans did not have them; indeed, bows and arrows are mentioned by the *Germania*[2] as in use among the Finns. Gothic archers were afterwards in high repute; bows are mentioned at Maldon; at Senlac, among the English, bows and arrows were exceptional.[3]

Infantry, if we may use so technical a term, was the favorite Germanic array of battle; but cavalry was also known, and in the earliest times. Cæsar testifies to the tactics of the German horsemen. In the Commentaries we are told that before a general engagement, the cavalry of Ariovistus made constant attacks upon the Roman encampment, after this fashion: Six thousand horsemen were accompanied by as many warriors on foot, picked men, who formed a support and rallying-point whenever the cavalry retreated. When it was necessary to dash swiftly forward in long attack, or fall back rapidly to the rear, the foot-soldiers kept pace with the cavalry, holding often to the manes of the horses.[4] In another place, speaking of the Suevians, Cæsar mentions the poor breed but toughness and exact training of the horses, which, when the rider dismounted to fight on foot, were sure to stand on the same spot till needed.

---

[1] Grimm, *Deutsche Mythol.*[4], p. 151; *Rechtsaltertümer*, p. 64; Schultz in Paul's *Grundriss*[2]. III. 223 ff.

[2] Cap. XLVI. [3] *Norman Conquest*, III. 472. [4] B. G. I. 48.

Moreover, it was deemed disgraceful to use the saddle.[1] Tacitus tells about horses and men much the same story as Cæsar gives us, though the great general is far more clear and definite.[2] Some tribes must have leaned more to cavalry combats, — we may instance the Tencteri and the Batavians; but in general, and this is the statement of Tacitus, the chief reliance of the German was upon his foot-soldiers, a taste that prevailed down to the middle ages. It is curious to find English warriors, in the time of King Æthelred, riding up to the fight at Maldon, dismounting, and driving their horses off the field : —

> he [3] bade each soldier forsake his horse,
> drive it afar, and fare along,
> have mind on his hands and a manful battle![4]

At the same fight, another warrior —

> let from his hands his hawk so lief
> fly to the forest, and fight-ward strode.[5]

So, at Senlac, every man in the Saxon army fought on foot : —

> *Omnes descendunt et equos post terga relinqunt.*[6]

Ammianus Marcellinus gives us a much older instance, with an exquisite reason. The Alamannian infantry,

[1] IV. 2.
[2] *Germ.* VI. This mode of fighting with horse and foot mixed together is not peculiar to the Germans. For other examples see Hehn, work quoted, 45–47. It is to be noted that German auxiliaries serving in the Roman army are at first mostly mounted men, and once Cæsar actually took horses from Roman soldiers and gave the mount to Germans.
[3] Byrhtnoth.   [4] *Maldon*, 2 ff.   [5] Ibid. 7 f.
[6] Freeman, *Norman Conquest*, III. 472.

about to begin battle, make a great outcry because
the princes do not descend from their steeds; for if
the battle were lost, these gentry might ride off and
leave their humbler brethren in the lurch.[1]

Regarding the army as a whole, we find that it
moved to attack — a supremely important moment [2] —
in the shape of a wedge; the Frankish historian,
Richer, says that as late as the ninth century this
wedge-shaped column was still the order of battle
among his countrymen. Strange, moreover, is the
statement of Saxo Grammaticus that Odin [3] taught
Hadingus to form his army in such fashion that two
should stand in the first row, four in the second,
eight in the third, and so on; while on the side
should stand (a foreign touch?) the archers and
slingers. This formation Scandinavians called *the
boar's head*. The same thing and the same name
appear in the laws of Manu, and were not unknown
to the Greeks. Scherer hence concludes an Indo-
European origin.[4] Holtzmann, relying on another
place in Tacitus, where we are told that the Germans
fought in loose order, and were arranged by families,
essays the parlous etymology that *cuneus* (wedge) is

---

[1] Amm. Mar. XVI. 12. 34.

[2] Religious rites, revel, and feasting often marked the whole night
before a battle (*Ann.* I. 65; II. 12; *Hist.* IV. 14; V. 15); after favorable
auguries, and with high pomp and ceremony, the tribe went into the
fight. Says Müllenhoff in his essay *de antiq. Ger. poesi*, p. 13, "Nulla
enim erat major neque sanctior apud Germanos pompa, quam ubi ordi-
nata acie universus populus ad prc lium ibat."

[3] Müllenhoff shows that this is important for Odin worship. He was
held as "auctor aciei corniculatæ et ordinandi agminis disciplinæ
omnisque denique bellicæ artis ac scientiæ traditor (*i.e.* magister) ac
repertor et animi bellici creator moderatorque sapientissimus esse cred-
ebatur." Müllenhoff, *de Chor.* p. 15.

[4] *Haupt's Zeit.*, Anzeiger, IV. 97.

Roman misunderstanding of *kuni*, "kin," family or tribe. Probably the Germans dashed into battle as a wild, surging mass (*vagis incursibus*),[1] but with coherence and order according to families, and with the general shape of a wedge. A few men of valor in the van, the vast mob of ordinary warriors would naturally spread out behind the leaders.

Leaders we call them, for generals, in our sense of the word, hardly existed; though there was doubtless a rude system by which a number of officers were graded up to a supreme commander. Tacitus tells us[2] that the duty of such a leader was to set example rather than to issue commands. We may assume that high rank was helpful to his authority, and that election was necessary. Such an election of a general is mentioned by Tacitus,[3] who says that the Canninefates, a Low German tribe, chose for their leader a man named Brinno, who was thereupon raised upon a shield, after the ancestral custom, and so rocked about (*vibratus*) upon the shoulders of those who carried him. It is probable that this sort of leader was elected for a considerable period,[4] that he carried special weapons and adornments, and that he had, in common with the method of his election,[5] much of the authority of a king. Like a king he received gifts.[6] We are at some loss to set forth the true functions of a German leader, especially of the first in command. We may gather from Tacitus that he did not plan campaigns or direct tactics after the Roman fashion; and yet Ariovistus, and particularly Arminius, were not mere barbarian champions. They

[1] Tac. *Ann.* II. 15.   [2] *Germ.* VII.   [3] *Hist.* IV. 15.
[4] Waitz, I. 271.   [5] *R. A.* 234.   [6] Ibid. 245 ff.   *Germ.* XV.

certainly planned and calculated and directed large movements of their respective forces. In regard to the subordinate leaders there is no difficulty; they were leaders in the literal sense, and set examples of prowess to their men. Indeed, the king or supreme chieftain himself had to show this quality, just as long afterwards William the Conqueror was foremost warrior of his army; and Hagen tells us what Germans expected of their monarch: [1] —

' Twere fitting, spake out Hagen, for such a folk's delight [2]
As chief and lord to battle the foremost in the fight, —
Right so as these my masters [3] have here united stood,
And hewn thro' helm and harness till swords were bathed in
    blood.

It argues a lower state of military science, or else a great jealousy of aristocratic privileges, that in some parts of Germany the leaders were chosen by lot. This is mentioned by Beda as customary among the Saxons,[4] and is found elsewhere, as among the Goths. However, the uniformity of tactics lessened the need of a general; for the main system of battle was to attack the foe with tumultuous energy, bearing down all opposition by sheer force of valor and strength. Like our modern opening battery, as sign of battle begun, so in Germanic warfare a spear hurled over the enemy gave signal for attack.[5] Plu-

[1] *N. L.* 2074.
[2] "Kenning" for king; literally, "comfort of the people."
[3] The three Burgundian kings.
[4] *Hist. Ecc.* V. 10. When the Germans served as Roman auxiliaries, they were allowed to have their own officers.
[5] The hostile army was thus dedicated as sacrifice to the gods. In the *Voluspa* Odin hurls a spear into the host, and so arises "the first war."

tarch, in his account of the Cimbrian attack, says that the Germanic infantry came upon the Romans like a tossed and roaring ocean. As they rushed into the fray, the warriors were wont to raise a wild chant, probably ending in a mere din of thunderous volume, for they used the shields to make echo and increase the volume of sound, holding them close to the mouth;[1] while women and children, near to the line of battle, lifted up a great noise of wailing, which was meant to remind the warrior of his stake in the combat and so to spur him to utmost achievement,[2] — a rough anticipation of Tennyson's picture : —

> A moment while the trumpets blow
> He sees his brood about thy knee,
> The next like fire he meets the foe
> And strikes him dead for thine and thee.

These songs, thinks Müllenhoff, which warriors sang as they rushed into battle — who does not remember Senlac and the brawny minstrel of the *Chanson de Roland?* — ended in "hoarse and strident sounds . . . where, one may conjecture, the *r* and the *u* particularly prevailed."[3] Early in the historical period — perhaps before — musical instruments were in use; drum, horn, and trumpet.[4] A fair idea of such a Germanic onslaught, with accompanying battle-cry and song, is given by Ammianus[5] when he describes

---

[1] *Germ.* III.

[2] Ibid. VII. and Müllenhoff, *de antiq. Germ. poesi*, p. 11 : "Liberique a tergo positi ululatum sustulerunt; viri autem cantum." See also his references, *Ann.* IV. 47 and *Hist.* II. 22.

[3] Müllenhoff, *de antiq. Germ. poesi*, p. 20: "Stridores sonosque raucos . . . inter quos *r* et *u* prævaluisse conjici licet."

[4] Schultz in Paul's *Grundriss²*, III, 223.

[5] XVI. 12. 43. Bohn's translation is used.

the fight at Strasburg, in the year 357 of our era. Certain of the combatants, "frightening even by their gestures, shouted their battle-cry, and the uproar through the heat of the conflict, rising up from a gentle murmur and becoming gradually louder and louder, grew fierce as that of waves dashing against the rocks." Such was the Germanic onset.

Tactics of actual combat, so far as any are mentioned, seem to have been of a trivial nature, — like the feigned retreat. Hehn makes the admirable comment that German war-tactics were borrowed from those of hunting. The German fought men as he fought wild beasts, "by cunning, ambush, and surprise."[1]

To the terror of this wild attack the Romans opposed discipline and system. German success depended on an overwhelming onset and rush; checked, flung back on itself, the "wedge" became a helpless and irregular mass, without order or direction, unable to cope with organized assault. It was Marius who saw this, and placed reserves behind his line of battle.

We have considered the first and more important branch of military service, obligatory upon every citizen. The second was voluntary. Aside from enlistment in the Roman army, — a custom which indeed took larger and larger proportions as time went on, but was regarded by the nobler Germanic sentiment as treason, — the young men were wont to enter the retinue of some powerful native chieftain. Cæsar[2] gives us our earliest information on the subject. Raids for plunder, he says, are not regarded as

---

[1] Hehn, p. 16.   [2] *B. G.* VI. 23.

wrong, but as a useful occasion to give practice and
discipline to the younger warriors. If a prince[1] in
the popular assembly offers himself as leader and
calls on those who will follow him, all who approve
the affair and the man rise, and amid the shouts of
the multitude signify their assent. If then any one
of these volunteers refuses to go, he is held as traitor
and deserter. So far Cæsar. Very probably such
raids as these passed into permanent expeditions;
and we know that such an enlistment in the prince's
service was frequently for life. Volunteers of this
sort combined the attributes of a mediæval free-lance
and a Swiss guardsman. It is the difference between
these two types that may guide us in comparing the
account of Cæsar with the description which Tacitus
gives of the *comitatus* or retinue; the *comitatus*, as
we shall presently see, has a firmer basis and a better
organization than the earlier system of volunteering.

The *comitatus* was evidently one of the great moral
factors in Germanic life and achievement. Inter-
woven with the sense and pride of kindred, and pat-
terned after the family compact itself, the system
fostered a definite obligation and inspired mutual
devotion of prince and warrior. Here, perhaps, is the
key to Germanic success and the secret of Germanic
supremacy. In war, indeed, of whatever kind the
Germanic virtue of courage came to the front; but
in the *comitatus* courage was no more prominent than
fidelity, loyalty, and truth. The sense of duty, the
sense of standing and enduring for a principle, has

[1] Who was this prince? Waitz, I. 246 f., says it was not any given
noble, but one of the *principes* elected by the people; while Arnold
holds a very different view. See the latter's *Deutsche Urzeit*, 336–357.

always been the mainspring of Germanic success;[1] and here the sense of duty went hand in hand with affection and gratitude. Where the relation was entered into for life, all these elements were invested with supreme ethical importance. Tacitus tells us[2] that young men of the best blood attach themselves to a leader and serve in his train. They struggle for the nearest place to the chieftain; and he in turn strives to keep the most numerous and effective retinue. It is his pride to be surrounded by such a band, his honor in peace and his defence in war. In this way his name and influence are carried beyond his own country, and bring him return in renown and gifts; sometimes his reputation alone is enough to put down a war. In actual battle, the chieftain must not be surpassed in prowess, and the followers must not fail to emulate him. Shame without end befalls the man who deserts the chieftain, and his retainers must stand by him in his captivity and even in his death. After the battle of Strasburg, where Julian defeated the Alamanni, a German chief surrenders himself to the Romans, whereupon "his companions, two hundred in number, and his three most intimate friends, thinking it would be a crime in them to survive their king, or not to die for him if occasion required, gave themselves up also as prisoners."[3] In short, as Tacitus says, the chieftain fights for victory, the followers fight for the chieftain.[4]

For our own early history, both the epic *Béowulf*

---

[1] On the Continent this *Pflichttreue* has become collective and monarchical; with Anglo-Saxons it is individual, as in the case of little Tom Brown half frozen on the roof of the stagecoach, with his "consciousness of silent endurance, so dear to every Englishman, — of standing out against something and not giving in." [2] *Germ.* XIII.
[3] Amm. Marc. XVI. 12. 60, trans. of Yonge. [4] *Germ.* XIV.

and the spirited ballad of *Maldon* are very helpful in
showing how strong a hold this system kept on national life long after the days of Tacitus. In *Béowulf*
we see both of those phases to which we have just
referred. In the first part of the epic, Béowulf, a
kinsman and "battle-thane" of Hygelac, lives at the
latter's court. He hears of the troubles heaped upon
the head of a neighbor king, Hrothgar the Dane;
and, in nobler mood than that of the booty-seeking
chieftains chronicled by Cæsar, chooses fourteen companions and sets off to free the monarch from his foe.
Here is a *comitatus*, but it is for a specified time, an
enlistment, as we used to say, for the war; whereas
the Danish retainers who were destroyed by Grendel
are the permanent followers and dependents of their
king. Says Hrothgar: —

> Sore is my soul to say to any
> of the race of man what ruth for me
> in Heorot Grendel with hate hath wrought,
> what sudden harryings. *Hall-folk fail me,*
> *my warriors wane;* for Wyrd hath swept them
> into Grendel's grasp.[1]

To lose this *comitatus* is evidently the direst of ills;
to increase it and strengthen it is the supreme good.
Thus, in his happier days —

> To Hrothgar was given such glory of war,
> such honor of combat, that all his kin
> obeyed him gladly till great grew his band
> of youthful comrades[2]

that is, his success and honor drew young men to his
side, and swelled his *comitatus* to stately proportions.
And so Hrothgar determines to build a splendid hall,

---

[1] *Béow.* 473 ff.   [2] Ibid. 64 ff.

the "Heorot" described above, where he may divide his treasure with these warriors and give them feast and revel.

Generosity and the foremost place in valor are the duty of the prince; absolute fidelity and devotion mark the clansman. "Once in battle, it is a disgrace for the prince to yield to any one in bravery, a disgrace for the clansman not to match the valor of his chief. Shame and utter ruin of all reputation are his who leaves a battle-field alive after his prince has fallen." So runs the eloquent tribute of Tacitus;[1] and it is instructive to see how faithfully our early poetry bears out his testimony. We may take an example of the minor sort of fidelity, an incident in *Béowulf*, not without its homely pathos. The hero has gone deep into the waters to fight against the mother of Grendel in her ocean fastness. On the bank sit his vassals, with the clansmen of Hrothgar; but when, after weary hours, blood begins to rise to the surface of the water and stain all the floods, men fear the worst for Béowulf; and the Danes, giving up all hope, leave the place. But the clansmen of Béowulf still hold their mournful watch upon the shore, and when at last their chief returns triumphant, he finds them where he left them, hopeless but constant. On the other hand, the paternal solicitude of Béowulf for his retainers in case he should not survive his perilous undertaking causes him to remind King Hrothgar of a former promise : —

> thou wouldst loyal bide
> to me, though fallen, in father's place!
> Be guardian thou, to this group of my Thanes,
> my warrior-friends, if War should seize me ![2]

[1] *Germ.* XIV.   [2] *Béow.* 1479 ff.

A still better note sounds in the final scene of our epic. Béowulf goes out to fight the dragon, and, scorning to use an army,[1] he takes with him only a few of his best retainers, — eleven picked men.[2] But at sight of the monster, belching flame and poison, the clansmen beat an inglorious retreat and leave their master to his fate, — all but one. Wiglaf, ashamed of the cowardly flight, sees from his covert how the old hero bears the stress of battle against overwhelming odds, and thinking of all the gifts and bounties his lord has heaped upon him, a nobler passion seizes him. He thinks of his own boastings in hall:[3] —

> "I remember the time, when mead we took
> what promise we made to this prince of ours
> in the banquet-hall, to our breaker-of-rings,
> for gear of combat to give him requital,
> for hard-sword and helmet, if hap should bring
> stress of this sort![4]

and he urges the others to go to the help of Béowulf : —

> I am far more fain the fire should seize
> along with my lord these limbs of mine!
> Unsuiting it seems our shields to bear
> homeward hence, save here we essay
> to fell the foe and defend the life
> of the Weders' lord[5].

Alone he springs through smoke and flame to the side of his prince, speaks to him a few words of cheer, and then fights manfully against the dragon. When all is over, and Béowulf lies dead along with

---

[1] Ibid. 2345 ff., 2401.   [2] 2638 f.
[3] For these boastings in hall, see some later instances in Child's Ballads,[2] II. 277.
[4] 2633 ff.   [5] 2651 ff.

the foe, the ten come where Wiglaf, sprinkling water on the face of his lord, is vainly endeavoring to win him back to life. Out breaks the young hero's reproach, which closes with this prophecy of denunciation: —

> Now gift of treasure and girding of sword,
> joy of the house and home-delight
> shall fail your folk; his freehold-land
> every clansman within your kin
> shall lose and leave, when lords highborn
> hear afar of that flight of yours,
> a fameless deed. Yea, death is better
> for liegemen all than a life of shame!"[1]

It is a dull pulse, to be sure, that does not beat the quicker for these words; but in *Maldon* the tone is even more intimate and direct. What passionate scorn is poured out upon the heads of those cowardly thanes who flee from the battle-ground and leave their lord dead among his enemies! *Maldon*, with this superb energy of patriotism, waited in vain for a rival until the *Agincourt* of Drayton; while modern poetry has essayed the note only to end in a sad, unreal chatter, saving always that passage in which Sir Walter's big heart throbbed to the fates of Flodden Field, — Scott himself no unworthy son of the old clansmen who put fidelity to one's chieftain at the head of all virtues, and his verses no unworthy echo of the early song: —

> The English shafts in volleys hailed,
> In headlong charge their horse assailed,
> Front, flank, and rear, the squadrons sweep
> To break the Scottish circle deep
> That fought about their king.

[1] *Béow.* 2884 ff.

But yet, though thick the shafts as snow,
Though charging knights like whirlwinds go,
Though billmen ply the ghastly blow,
   Unbroken was the ring;
The stubborn spearmen still made good
Their dark impenetrable wood,
Each stepping where his comrade stood
   The instant that he fell.
No thought was there of dastard flight;
Linked in the serried phalanx tight,
Groom fought like noble, squire like knight,
   As fearlessly and well.

Fidelity to chieftain and king redeems and raises Hagen of the Nibelungen Lay from a mere assassin at the outset to a splendid hero at the end. The character of Ruedeger in the same lay shows us a situation as acute as any Greek tragedy can produce. Not even Orestes, with filial duty dragging him in opposite directions, is so completely tragical a figure as this Germanic warrior halting in agony between disobedience to his lord and battle with his guests and son-in-law; it is instructive to note that in this struggle between kin-duty and vassal-duty, the latter conquers. Finally, we may mark that when missionaries came into the Germanic lands to preach Christ and his twelve apostles, nothing appealed more actively to the native than the resemblance of this bond between master and disciple to his own system of chieftain and clansmen. Christ died for his beloved, and they endured martyrdom for him. What simpler theology?

Of the various names for the clansmen, the Latin *comes* seems to have been the outcome and survivor. When Tacitus talks of the "clients" of Segestes, it

is by a very evident *interpretatio Romana. Comes,*
perhaps from *cum* and *eo,* would thus correspond
exactly to Anglo-Saxon *gesíð* — one who goes with
you on a journey. More vivid are the other words
of our old speech, *eaxlgestealla,* "shoulder-comrade,"
or he whose place is at the shoulder of his lord; and
heorðgenéat, "hearth-comrade." Another word, often
used in Anglo-Saxon law, is *ðegen* or "thane," with
the prevailing notion of service, — such service as
a freeman might, without loss of dignity, render to a
powerful nobleman or prince.[1]

Mediæval survivals and new creations are often
inextricably entangled, and it is not safe to trace the
simple *comitatus* of German forests amid the varying
phases of the feudal system. Confining ourselves to
the earlier compact, we may assume it to have been
sometimes temporary, but often permanent. We need
not idealize it too highly; the arrangement was obviously good for both parties to the bargain, and
there were substantial presents, swords, horses, jewels,
land, for the ambitious clansman to keep before his
eyes.[2]

The age at which a warrior, whether in the militia
or in the *comitatus,* began his career differed, it would
seem, for different Germanic tribes. Holtzmann[3] collects the evidence, which fixes twenty years among

---

[1] See Schmid, *Ags. Ges.* Glossary, *s.v.* and the well-known anecdote of Lilla, the dearest thane of Edwin, king of Northumbria; an
assassin aims his dagger at the king; the thane leaps before his master
and receives the blow. Bede, *Eccl. Hist.* ii, 9.

[2] See Grimm in his already quoted essay on *Schenken und Geben;*
Vilmar, *Altert. im Hêliand,* p. 51; and for general subject of *comitatus*
among the Norsemen, Vigfusson-Powell, II. 477 f.

[3] *Germ. Alter.* p. 196.

the West-Goths, eighteen for the Lombards, and —
if one can believe it — twelve for the Anglo-Saxons
and Franks.   For later times and customs, we have
a vivid picture of the military coming of age given
us in the Nibelungen Lay, where the festival is
described which Siegfried's parents give in his honor
for such an occasion; but here the old simplicity has
been succeeded by a number of feudal and chivalric
elements.

CHAPTER IX

SOCIAL ORDER

The king originally a creation of the race — His authority and duties — Inheritance and election — Ideals — The queen — Nobles by birth and by office — The Germanic freeman — The freedman and the slave — The alien.

AT the head of the family we found, of course, the father; and at the head of the state we naturally look for the king. The word "king" means the child or son of the tribe, its representative or even creation;[1] man of race, man of rank. Gradually the king ceases to be regarded as a creation of his race; his ancestry is pushed back to the gods, and his right is quite above all sanctions of popular choice or approval. The early Germanic king was still a creation of his race; true, as Tacitus tells us, he was chosen on account of his noble birth, — but he was chosen. A number of Germanic tribes can be named which have no king in their earliest historical period; such were

---

[1] "He who belongs to the race," explains Waitz, *Verfassungsgesch.* I. 326; and so interpret Curtius and Scherer. Arnold seems to take the same view: *Deutsche Urzeit,* p. 333. Grimm, *R. A.* 230, will not derive *king* from *kin.* For details of Germanic kingship, see Rosenstein, *über das altgermanische Königthum* in the Zschst. *f. Völkerpsych. und Sprachw.* VII. 113–188; and Dahn, *Die Könige der Germanen.*

Marcomanni, Franks, Lombards, and Anglo-Saxons.[1]
The great movement of tribes which begins German
national history, lays the foundation of saga and epic,
and crystallizes a mass of myths into a system, was
also the chief factor in the development of early Germanic royalty.   A constant struggle demands constant leadership; and the republican elements of our
old constitution disappeared rapidly in the presence
of perennial warfare.   Out of a mass of small democ-
racies or elective monarchies, arose at last the great
nations of the Franks, the Bavarians, the Alamannians.   The popular assembly became impossible,
except in compact England, which built up a representative system.[2]   Monarchy of some sort, it is true,
was probably inherent in the earliest Germanic constitution; but it sat lightly on the state, and in the
time of Tacitus there seems to be a distinction in the
Roman mind between the German tribes that had
kings and those that had none.[3]   The kings who,
according to Tacitus, were chosen on account of their
nobility of birth, and the leaders (*duces*) who were
chosen for their valor, were alike of the best blood of
the race.   Where a single monarch did not reign,
princes or chieftains (*principes*) of the foremost

---

[1] See von Amira in Paul's *Grundriss d. germ. Philol.*², p. 150; cf.
Tacitus' *Germania* VII.

[2] Rosenstein, work quoted, p. 163.

[3] Waitz, *Verfass.* I. 295.   Gregory of Tours speaks (II. 9) of long-
haired kings (*reges crinitos*) chosen from the noblest families; and
Beda, in a famous passage (*Hist. Eccl.* V. 10), about the continental
Saxons, says that "they have no king, but several lords that rule their
nation; and when any war happens, they cast lots indifferently, and
on whomsoever the lot falls, him they follow and obey during the war;
but as soon as the war is ended, all these lords are again equal in
power."—Transl. of Giles.

clans made up a sort of oligarchy; and we hear of a
king with associated or inferior kings ruling over one
people.[1] In time of war, out of several such chieftains (*principes*) might be chosen a leader (*dux*), as
in the case of Arminius. Indeed, the Germans seem
to have been fond of two leaders even in war; Waitz
cites the case of Hrothgar and Hrothulf.[2] Moreover,
we must note that Tacitus uses the expression "take"
or "choose":[3] "they [4] take to themselves" kings or
leaders, as the case may be. Jacob Grimm describes
this elective monarchy as one where inheritance was
modified by the necessity of confirmation, and election
was modified by restriction of choice to the royal
family.[5] Thus the Cherusci sent to Rome for a
person of kingly lineage who happened to be the sole
survivor of his race; for the nobility, says Tacitus,
were destroyed by civil strife.[6] The Anglo-Saxon
genealogies, mounting always to demi-gods and gods,
show the stress laid upon kingly descent; though we
must in this case allow for the abnormal conditions of
ceaseless raids, and a considerable concentration and
increase in royal authority.

The newly elected king was lifted upon a shield
and thrice borne about the assembly. He made as
soon as possible a formal progress through his domin-

[1] A passage in *Béowulf* (vv. 2152 ff.) tells us that after the hero's
liberal presents to King Hygelac and his queen, the monarch presented
his kinsman Béowulf with a splendid sword, and also gave him "seven
thousand, a house (home) and ruler-seat (*i.e.* dominion, royal power)."
The "seven thousand" may refer to hides of land, an area equivalent
to the whole of Mercia! (cf. Klaeber, *Beowulf*, p.197, note to v. 2195).

[2] Waitz, *Verfass.* 322.   *Béow.* 1191.   [3] *Sumunt.*
[4] The popular assembly.   [5] *R. A.* 231.
[6] *Ann.* XI. 16: "amissis per interna bella nobilibus, et uno reliquo
stirpis regiæ."

ions, that he might be seen and known of all his folk. His external tokens of royalty were originally meagre, and the flowing locks he shared with all freemen. Crown and such insignia are later matters imitated from the Romans; but a military standard of some sort was doubtless borne before the German king. In peace his functions must have been judicial, and often sacred or priestly; though this was not always the case. In historic times the priestly function was a royal duty for Scandinavia, but not for Burgundian and other German monarchs. Many a race made a god of its departed ruler; particularly when he had won wide lands or brought new culture and social order into his dominions, deification was likely to follow his death.[1] But in war was the chief strength of a Germanic king; to his personal conduct of a campaign was due success or failure, and as he was to keep peace within his own borders, so he was expected to spread desolation or conquest beyond them. Failure was fatal. As he had been elected, so he could be deposed. The centre of ancient Germanic states was the popular assembly; and a king was its creature, to be deposed if he were not equal to his task, but doubtless to hold authority amid comparative awe and silence so long as he was successful. In times of peace he had no authority whatever to issue decrees, make laws, or initiate any sort of legislation; he was executor of popular law and popular will. Progress in kingly power is marked by the oath of fidelity; and with the anarchy of war and conquest, kings must have acquired, little by little,

---

[1] See also von Amira in Paul's *Grundriss*[2], pp. 150, 166.

that sense of proprietorship and absolute right which distinguished mediæval royalty. The church lent her authority to make personal and individual that doctrine of divine right which before had been distributed over a whole family, and the elective kingship of old Germanic days was lost beyond recovery for feudal Europe. One land alone held fast, if not to the old form, at least to the old principle; and it was England which by incessant struggles on the soil of two continents sustained, despite all reactions, the genius of Germanic freedom side by side with the derived reverence for law and discipline. The constitutional history of England properly treats these matters; suffice for our purpose a single sentence from the close of the introduction to Alfred's laws for his people: "Now I, Alfred, king of the West-Saxons, have showed these to all my Witan, and they have told me that it liked them all that everything should be kept." The Witan, as everybody knows, were the legal councillors or advisers of the king, and in a measure representatives of the people; thus we need assume no great change, except in circumstances, from the Germanic king and the Germanic assembly.

Of this Germanic king, prince, or leader, we have many descriptions in praise and in blame. At the opening of *Béowulf* we are told what was for those days a good king: —

> for he waxed under welkin, in wealth he throve,
> till before him the folk, both far and near,
> who house by the whale-path,[1] heard his mandate,
> gave him gifts: a good king he![2]

[1] Sea.   [2] *Béow.* 8 ff.

The secret of prosperity — so, at least, the singers
have all said — lay in liberality to the royal retainers; and so our *Béowulf* goes on with its ideal
picture : —

> So becomes it a youth to quit him well
> with his father's friends, by fee and gift,
> that to aid him, aged, in after days,
> come warriors willing, should war draw nigh
> liegemen loyal :[1]

The free-handed monarch is praised by Widsith in
our oldest English poem: —

> Likewise with Ælfwine in Italy was I:
> of all mankind I ken, he cherished
> heart most ungrudging in gift of rings,
> sheeny treasure, the son of Eadwine.[2]

The ideal king at home was the "ring-breaker,"
who sat upon his "gift-seat" or throne, and dealt
out treasure from an inexhaustible store, while
tribute flowed in from countless subject tribes, and
hostility was paralyzed by the memory of his former
deeds.   To this conception belong those epithets
for royalty which emphasize the bond between the
ruler and his folk, those "kennings" which call
him, if a Hrothgar, "friend of the Scyldings," *wine
Scyldinga*, or "refuge for earls," *eorla hléo;* and
which often combine the virtues of friendship and
generosity, as in "gold-friend of men," *goldwine gu-
mena*, a kenning which occurs in Béowulf's petition
to Hrothgar that the latter may remember his promise and be a father to his guest: —

> . . . of what we two spake,
> gold-friend of men, be mindful now.[3]

[1] *Béow.* 20 ff.   [2] *Widsið*, 70 ff.   [3] *Béow.* 1474 ff.

Other kennings [1] of this peaceful connotation are:
treasure-lord, treasure-herdsman (guardian), gold-
giver, hoard-ward, wish-giver, ward (guardian *par
excellence*), folk's-ward, warriors' ward, folk's-herds-
man, helmet, people's protector, caretaker of folk,
friend (*par excellence*), lord-friend, folk's owner, lord
of men, judge, lord and judge, first in the land. Of a
warlike origin are : helmet of armies, leader of squad-
rons, leader of the people, first in deeds, "the first
spear (*frumgár*)," first in battle, battle-ward of men,
army-leader.[2] It is from names like these, most of
them old poetic forms, like the Homeric epithet, that
we may best make up our conception of the Germanic
king.

The queen was naturally a prominent figure; but
the kennings for her are rare. "Weaver of peace"
is of course applied to her; but "lady," *hlœfdige*, if
like "lord" it comes from the notion of loaf-sharing,
is a wider term. That women now and then exercised royal functions, we learn not only from the
famous Lady of the Mercians, but from the older
case of the Gothic queen Amalasuntha. Offices of
gracious hospitality we have already noticed in the
queen of Hrothgar;[3] nor, as representative woman
of the race, could she have failed to enjoy a rich
measure of that reverence which the Germans paid
to her sex.

Besides the king and the leaders of the people, we
must allow for an order of nobles, men whose birth

---

[1] I draw liberally upon Wilhelm Bode's *Die Kenningar in der Ags.
Dichtung,* Darmstadt und Leipzig, 1886.

[2] Similar Scandinavian kennings in Vigfusson-Powell, *C. P. B.* II.
479 f.   [3] Above, pp. 117, 134.

and alliance with princely houses raised them above
the rank of ordinary freemen. The name of this
noble quality is preserved in the German *Adel*, and
in the Anglo-Saxon *œðeling*, with the general notion
of "race," "descent." The *wergild* was based chiefly
on birth and rank ; although age, sex, office, and connection with the king were also criteria.[1] The honor
of birth was not the honor of office, but was rather
an inherent, one might say passive, distinction. If
there were duties as well as privileges connected
with it, the former doubtless lay in priestly and judicial responsibilities. By old custom, the head of a
house was its priest as well as judge and ruler. Nobility, we may assume, entitled men to a prominent
place in war ;[2] and in time of peace, forms and ceremonies of the state religion would call for officials
from the families to whom tradition gave divine or
high heroic origin. Indeed, the theory that priesthood was an avocation and not a regular caste or calling is strengthened by the remarkably small part it
played in opposition to Christianity; it is Coifi, the
Northumbrian priest, who leads in the attack upon
the altar of his gods.[3]

The Germanic nobles were thus the oldest and
most venerable families. We hear of them in Tacitus,
who pays them an enemy's generous tribute in an account of battles among the Batavians.[4] Whereas in

[1] Waitz, *Verfass.* I. 195 f. The Angli and Werini had for the noble a
wergild thrice as great as for the ordinary freeman.

[2] Waitz, p. 280.

[3] Waitz, ibid. See also Beda, *Hist. Ecc.* II. 13: "Cumque a . . .
pontifice [*sc.* Coifi] sacrorum suorum quæreret [*sc.* the Christian bishop],
quis aras et fana idolorum cum septis, quibus erant circumdata, primus
profanare deberet; ille respondit: Ego. . . ." [4] *Ann.* II. 11.

historical Anglo-Saxon, the word *æðeling* always means a member of the royal house,[1] in older times, notably in our epic *Béowulf*, as also in many proper names familiar to all of us, it had a wider signification, and meant a man of noble blood, a man of "descent." Again, even before Danish influences made our old word *eorl* denote a special title of nobility like the Scandinavian *jarl* (Hakon Jarl),[2] there must have dwelt a certain odor of eminence in the term, as opposed to *ceorl*, "man" of any sort. Nobles were of better clay than common freemen; and the founder of their race being deified, his home worship, at first the regular manes-cult, would pass into symbolic rites and then into poetical traditions. To men of this stamp the minstrel sang about the deeds of their forebears, livine now, and now heroic. "We have heard," begins the singer of *Béowulf*, "how in days of yore the æthelings did valiant deeds." Similarly, the nobles of the middle ages found chief delight in a lay which celebrated their ancestors; and such legendary songs were as indispensable to a genuine noble as the family pictures to the gentleman of to-day, and often as open to suspicion.

In course of time, and by reason of the ceaseless wars of the wandering, this old nobility of the Germanic clans died out; its place was taken by the *comitatus* and the official nobility springing up about powerful kings, until the new order became, in its turn, hereditary. Of the great English officials, chief place belongs to the so-called "alderman," who was representative of the king for a given shire or other

---

[1] Liebermann, II, s. v. æ/.eling; cf. Stubbs, *Const. Hist.*, I, 151.
[2] See von Amira in Paul's *Grundriss*[3], pp. 128, 129.

-division of land. Such an alderman is the high-hearted Byrhtnoth;[1] he collects and leads the royal troops against all enemies of the king, maintains order in his district, and occasionally presides at court. The alderman seems to have been a creature of the king, but with consent of the *witan*.[2] Later, the Danish "earl" took the Saxon *ealdorman's* place and privileges; but the word had acquired a general connotation of superior rank.[3] "He came to the town-reeve, who was his alderman," quotes Schmid from Beda; and we find a curious passage in the Leechdoms (Herbarium), where mention is made of *Achilles þe ealdorman*.[4] Other examples of this domestic rendering of foreign rank may be found in an Anglo-Saxon homily, where Christ is called an *æðeling*, Moses a *heretoga* or leader, the saints *þegnas*, thanes or warriors, and the Jews in Egypt, — foreigners, of course, — *Wealhas*, "Welsh."[5]

Ownership of land was ultimately the test of gentry; but it could not have made so prominent a part of the Germanic noble's credentials.[6] Still, such traditions best flourish on the soil which produced them, and the connection of tracts of land with a given noble family must have been an early factor in

---

[1] See p. 237.   [2] Liebermann, II. s. v. *"ealdormann"*.
[3] It was probably unknown to continental Saxons, though used by the Frisians. *Cf.* Waitz, p. 215.

[4] Cockayne, *Leechdoms*, etc., I. 308. The "satraps" (*satrapæ*) or governors, whom Beda (see above, p. 271) mentions among the Old Saxons, are rendered by *ealdorman* in Alfred's translation. See Stubbs, I. 42.

[5] Another classification of ranks, found in the homilies, is 1) *oratores* (clergy) ; 2) *bellatores* (warriors) ; 3) *laboratores*.

[6] Historians disagree. *Cf.* Waitz, I. 167 f., and Stubbs, *Const. Hist.* I. 155.

the pomp and pride of nobility. The amount of land held by a person determined in Anglo-Saxon law the amount of his *wergild*. Blood was the origin of rank; it meant more than property, and far more than any station or command. Certainly, for the earliest times at least, we must not think that office and nobility were convertible terms.[1]

The unit of Germanic public life was the freeman, the son of a free father and a free mother. True, old and vague traditions made the mother alone responsible, and, based on that original maternal system to which reference has been made above, founded the maxim of "free mother, free child"; but a later custom caused the offspring of free and unfree to "follow the worse hand," whether maternal or paternal.[2] Further, the freeman might be created from an unfree man by course of legal ceremony, or as in older times, by adoption. If our old word "earl" rightfully convey, even before the Danish influence, an echo of nobility, it is no fault of the ancient German freeman that the name "churl" stares at us moderns with such a stupid and ungracious air. This is a commentary on the havoc wrought by wars and conquests upon the old Germanic constitution. The free man of the Norse *RigsÞula* is named "Karl"; and an old Holstein form of administering the oath, to freemen of course, reads: "Step up, ye *Kerls.* . . ."[3] Grimm finds the name not only in Carloman, but in the word for king (*kral*), used by Slavs and Lithuanians, and derived from the founder of the

---

[1] Waitz, p. 243. Loebell, *Gregory v. Tours*, pp. 87, 392 ff.
[2] Scandinavian law gave benefit of the "better hand." See von Amira in Paul's *Grundriss*[2], pp. 126, 127.

German empire.[1] So the Anglo-Saxon form *ceorl* seems to have meant "man"; that is, of course, the normal man, the freeman. Significant is the dignity of the word in our *Béowulf*. When the hero is planning his errand of mercy to help King Hrothgar, "wise men" praise his purpose and encourage him, — *snotere ceorlas*.[2] The word is applied to the warriors and courtiers of the Danish king; and twice, with the epithet "old," it is used of royalty itself.[3] This is for the heroic age : in the laws *ceorl* drops to the two meanings "husband" (among animals we find *carl* as a prefix indicating the male of a given species) and "countryman" or "peasant."[4] In one old law, however, it is used in the ancient sense of "freeman." A more descriptive name is preserved in an account of the heathen Saxons (continental) written by Hucbald in the tenth century,[5] who in turn partially quotes Nithard, the grandson of Charles the Great, whose material was close at hand. It is noted that the Saxons had no kings, but were divided into three classes, called in their own tongue *edlingi, frilingi, lassi*. The *friling* is our freeman.

The freeman (*capillatus*) was distinguished by his long, flowing hair, and by his arms, the so-called folk-weapons.[6] The Salic Law ordains severe penalties against any one who shall cut or shave the hair from a *puer crinitus* without the consent of the latter's parents ; and on the other hand, for people to let a slave's hair grow long was criminal offence. The freeman had the right of waging private feud, so far

---

[1] Ibid. 282. [2] *Béow.* 202, 416.
[3] *Béow.* 1591, 2444, 2972. [4] Liebermann, II, s. v. "*ceorl*
[5] Life of St. Lebuin. See Stubbs, I. 42 ff. [6] *R. A.* 283 ff.

as the increasing severity of legislation did not bar his way. He was member of his village and district assemblies, as of the larger council of his tribe; among people like the Saxons this meant self-government. As long as the freeman was mainstay of the state, Germanic freedom kept its vigor; with his decline, we pass into the tyrannies of feudal Europe, where nobility and serfdom, spreading out their borders, left scant space between them for the honest *friling*.

We need here delay no longer with the freeman, for it is about his life that all our task revolves, and whatever has been said without explicit limitation, belongs to his account. We turn, therefore, to that class which, being neither bond nor free, offers considerable trouble to the exact student of our constitutional history. Manumission from slavery gave rise to the so-called freedmen. These, if we may venture a broad assertion, seem to have been without the tasks of slavery or the privileges of citizenship. Among Anglo-Saxons, a lance and a sword, emblems of the freeman's rank, were handed in symbolical ceremony to the person thus released; but he did not thereby become peer of the freeman, and even his descendants remained in a class by themselves, between the freeman and the slave.[1] Such a subordinate rank, moreover, was doubtless held by men who submitted in a body to some conquering tribe and were allowed to keep land and liberty; their seeming freedom was a concession, not a right. On the same

---

[1] The wergild followed the shades of unfreedom down to the actual slave, who had none at all. See also von Amira in Paul's *Grundriss d. germ. Philol.*², p. 137 f.

footing were foreigners, whom our ancestors everywhere called " Welshmen." The specific name for
this class of freedmen among Low Germans was in
Latin form *litus*, in Frisian *let*, and in our own Kentish dialect, *læt*.[1]

There must have been a wide range of privileges
among this class, scanty enough in some instances
and little better than a slave's "seven hundred and
twenty loaves of bread a year," but running up to
very solid benefits. The freeman who for bread and
clothes, or, in those old times, for a gambling debt,
went into voluntary subjection to another man would
be in any event better treated than the outright
slave.[2] The church, working as a rule on lines of
humanity, interfered in many ways to help the bond-
man and make his lot more tolerable. Private agreement between superior and inferior would further
complicate the once simple conditions and create new
degrees of servitude,[3] with a general drift towards
fixed limits of work for corresponding wages. As
the Germanic freeman ceased to be the most prominent factor of national life, the freedman, especially
when a creature of the king or of some high official,
became more and more important and could rise, like
the Roman freedman, to exalted office. The old
noble, the old freeman, had seen their day; kings
and the tools of kings began their long career.

From this stage of the freedman let us look back

[1] Found in a single law of Æthelberht, which fixes a læt's *wergild*.
Liebermann, I, 4, § 26.
[2] Tacitus, with a touch of rhetoric, says that shame compelled the
winner to send the loser into a distant place, as he could ill rejoice in
such a gain. *Germ.* XXIV.   [3] *R. A.* 335, 337.

at his predecessor in the days of Tacitus.[1] "The freedmen (*liberti*)," he tells us, "stand but little above the slaves; they are seldom of any consequence in the house, and never in the state, if we except those races which are under the rule of kings,[2] for there the freedmen are superior to noble and freeborn alike. With the other races, however, the low standing of the freedmen is a proof of liberty." The freedman, in this sense, is probably of common Germanic origin; at least he is found in historical times among all Germanic races save the Gothic and Scandinavian.[3]

Lowest of all was the slave, a chattel, with no "man-worth" at all, no *wergild*. The murder of a slave was paid for as one now pays for damages inflicted on a neighbor's horses or cattle. Yet we may be sure that slaves were no worse off in barbarian Germany than in civilized Rome, where the punishments inflicted on that wretched class were elaborately cruel. German slaves had no such artistic and systematic ill-treatment; they might be killed in a sudden fury of the master, but escaped the harder persecution of joyless years.[4] It is remotely possible — though this flight needs all the wings of romantic fondness — that a love of freedom, the intense passion for absolute liberty of the individual, may have held back many a freeborn German from subjecting his slaves

[1] *Germ.* XXIV. By *liberti* Tacitus probably means those who have acquired freedom in whatever way, hardly a regular class of the community.

[2] "Gentibus quæ regnantur."   [3] Waitz, I. 154.

[4] Anglo-Saxon ordinances of the church fixed a penance for the man who slew his serf without judicial authority. Kemble, *Saxons*, I. 209.

to scourge and torture.[1]   Again, the Germanic slave
had some solid privileges which were denied to his
Roman brother.   The slave lived in his own house,
and paid his owner a stated rent in corn or cattle or
woven garments;[2] and there is a note of domesticity
in the Roman's statement that a German serf has his
own household gods, and rules over his own fireside,
— *suos penates regit.*   Then follows the remark that
a German seldom beats his slaves, or puts them in
chains; a sudden tempest of anger will make him
kill his serf, but slow punishment he ignores.   The
simple conditions of German life required no army
of slaves, no elaborate divisions of labor, as at Rome.
Where it was possible, Germans sold their slaves to
more civilized masters, as the Goths sold their own
conquered kinsmen.   These northern giants were
sought as slaves in Rome; and we all know Beda's
account of Gregory and the fair-haired Anglian
youths in the Roman slave-market.   Slavery, one
may say, was only an accident, an external thing,
in the Germanic state; the freeman was the state,
and a widely ramified system of slavery would have
sapped the foundations of that barbaric strength.
Splendid is the tribute which Tacitus pays to this
Germanic prowess and this Germanic freedom.[3]   "Not
Samnites nor Carthaginians, not Spain nor Gaul, not
even the Parthians, have given us sharper warnings.
For mightier than the Parthian throne is the freedom
of the Germans."

[1] Anglo-Saxon slaves were cruelly treated.   See Wright, *Domestic
Manners and Sentiments,* p. 56 f.
[2] Tac. *Germ.* XXV.   Later duties of the slave, *cf.* Grimm, *R.A.* 350 ff.
[3] *Germ.* XXXVII.

The chief origin of slavery must be looked for, as Grimm remarks, in the captivity of a conquered tribe. The whole race of Germans may have subdued an indigenous population at the settlement of the country; those "blond long-heads," as Huxley calls them, may have conquered "brunet broadheads" or what not, and so have laid the foundations of their slave system; but this can be neither proved nor disproved.[1] In historical times, the more capable and intelligent prisoners of war were used or sold as slaves, after a definite number had been sacrificed to the gods. Years after the victory of Arminius over Varus and the legions, Romans taken at the battle were found serving as slaves among their German captors. Children of such captives would naturally form a class of serfs; and even in cases where one of them married a freeborn person, the offspring, as we have seen above, would in most cases count as slaves.[2] Indeed, to marry an unfree person often led to slavery. Again, we may add to these causes of serfdom the too common cases where hunger and destitution forced a man to give up his freedom. Kemble quotes a case where an Anglo-Saxon lady in her will frees all those who had been forced into slavery through poverty and hunger — "all who in the evil days had bent their heads for food."[3] Hopeless debt made many a slave; and the descent from freedom into thraldom was facile enough. The church and the laws, while they enjoin forbearance and

---

[1] See also Waitz, I. 158.   [2] R. A. 324.

[3] *Saxons*, I. 196. For other causes *cf.* R. A. 330 f. For legendary accounts of the origin of slavery, see, of course, *Rigsmál* and references of Elze, *Englische Philologie*, p. 212.

mercy as far as possible, make no question of the fact itself. A law of Æthelred, repeated by Cnut, runs as follows in Cnut's version: "And we command that one shall not all too easily sell Christian men out of the country, certainly not send them among the heathen; but let it be seen to that the souls which Christ has redeemed with his own life be not brought to destruction."[1]

The sign of the slave was his close-cut hair, and, often, the marks of mutilation in his face, "A slit nose is the mark of a thrall," says Scandinavian law.[2] Slaves were maimed or lamed for the sake of security, though this precaution must have been sporadic among the Germans; the capture of a whole army, for instance, may have made necessary something of the sort. We may be sure that no sentiment would have forbidden it. The slave had no family name. He wore short, scanty garments, with dull colors and rough material. He bore no weapons; had no right to go away from his master's land; and naturally took no part in the popular assembly, whether to vote as a citizen, or to prosecute as an accuser in process of the rude civil law. He could marry only with the consent of his lord, and in that case even was obliged to pay a marriage-tax. It is perhaps well to note that recent investigation has exploded several venerable legal fictions about the Germanic slave; for example, that bit of historical horse-play, the theory of a *jus primæ noctis*.[3]

---

[1] Liebermann, I, 310, § 3 and p. 250, § 9 (Æthelred, with the proviso "unless the person have duly forfeited his liberty"). [2] *R. A.* 339.
[3] See Kemble's *Saxons*, chap. VIII, and on merchet see K. Schmidt, *Jus Primæ Noctis* (1881), pp. 83 ff.

A peculiar position was that of the stranger or
visitor in a Germanic community. He is called "the
far-comer," or simply "comer," "stranger," "he who
has come over the mark"; one name for him, "guest,"
is the same word as Latin *hostis*, which so easily passed
from "stranger" into "enemy." German *elender* and
English "wretch" have acquired their present meaning from the connotation of the older words which
meant nothing more than an "outlandish" man, an
exile. Originally such a stranger had no legal protection whatever; he was dependent on individual
hospitality,[1] and otherwise was subject to maltreat-
ment and eventual slavery. In some cases the old
laws enjoin hospitality as a part of private if not public morals; and the binding law of three nights' entertainment we have already noticed.[2] It is a proof
of the artistic design of Tacitus that he sets the hospitality of the old Germans so sharply and immediately in contrast with their family feuds.

Little by little, as commerce increased, and the
stranger was oftener seen in Germanic lands, stability
and development of trade made it necessary to protect him. This right, or duty, fell upon the king;
royal protection was extended to the foreigner and
laws were passed in his favor. The king was thus
the guardian of all wayfaring men from other lands;
he was their *mundbora*, and therefore had a right to
their estates, later to a part of their personal property. With the settled international life of mediæval
Europe, the stranger becomes in every nation a permanent object of legal protection.

[1] *R. A.* 396ff.; Liebermann, II, s. v. *l c. "fremde"*.
[2] Above, p. 163.

CHAPTER X

GOVERNMENT AND LAW

Gifts, not taxes — Organization of government — Elements of
monarchy and of democracy — Popular councils and assemblies —
The town-meeting — Legal system — The function of priests in
civil administration — Punishments for crime — Forms of law —
Ordeal and trial by battle.

IN Germany and certain other European states,
where every sound man must learn to use weapons
and fight at need for his fatherland, military duty
would perhaps stand first in a list of the good citizen's
obligations to his country. But we may be very sure
that the second duty would be to pay one's taxes.
This the early German did not do,[1] but instead he
made presents to his chieftain, sending him goodly
gifts in corn or cattle. We know how long the excellent memory of monarchs treasured up this custom;
Queen Elizabeth, we are told, took care that what
she received on a New Year's day should always
largely exceed her own benefactions.[2] Yet these gifts
of the early German were presents pure and simple,
no taxes, no prerogative of the prince. Even of
booty and plunder in war the king might take no
more than his share as a warrior, and the division

---

[1] *Germ.* XV.   [2] Brand, *Antiquities*, " New Year's Day."

was not one of choice: all was left to the lots. It is
on the margin between the old dispensation and the
new rule of kings that we meet that famous vase of
Soissons. A bishop asks the mighty leader of the
Franks for a vase of extraordinary beauty which had
been taken with other plunder from the church. The
king promises it to the bishop if it fall to the royal
lot — no very near chance; however, he goes to his
warriors and begs the vase as a favor to royalty, not
at all as a right. The warriors assent; but one man,
striking the vase with his battle-axe, cries out, "Claim
nothing but thy lot!" The king takes no steps
against this gross defiance, but contents himself with
sending the vase to the bishop; until, at the next
great assembly of the nation, and before the whole
army, he fells the objector to the earth, crying,
"That for thy blow upon the vase at Soissons!"
No one dared a word or act of protest.[1]

Conquered land was at first shared in this fashion;[2]
but later, as among the Anglo-Saxons, the king took
a special part for himself. The old maxim, however, held the freeman exempt from all taxation:
frei mann, it said, *frei gut*.[3] What was not exacted
by direct law came, nevertheless, to be demanded
by custom as well as by the growing importance of
the king. In addition to yearly gifts, there was
imposed upon freemen the necessity to entertain
and harbor the sovereign with his retinue, to aid
him in war, and to contribute horses and wagons
for the royal need. Little by little, custom hardened into law and recognized the definite nature
of taxes; among the earliest of these direct burdens

[1] Gregor. Tur. II. 27. [2] *R. A.* 246 f. [3] Ibid. 297.

on land, Grimm counts the church tithes.[1] Nor was this taxation, even in its milder form, altogether without the consent of the taxpayer. He was represented, or else took a direct part, in the councils of his nation. Every freeman was member of this General Court.[2] Whether these popular assemblies counted for more or for less than the royal authority, is a perplexing question, and historians have had no difficulty in seeing now a monarchy and now a republic in the old Germanic communities. We do not know how far judicial and executive organization had made progress, nor how many elements of the modern state were present. Probably, when Tacitus wrote, there was a fairly organized government, — if such a name may be applied to a community so loosely united, — since it often took three days for the popular assembly to come together at the season of new or full moon, and it is reasonable to suppose with Holtzmann that this could not have been the case with members of a single canton. Wider groups indicate firmer organization;[3] probably we are not far out of the way when we assume that the early Germanic state inclined to democracy in peace and to a monarchy in war. The continental Saxon village had a sort of governor who ruled over his own district while peace was maintained; when war broke out, these governors, or, as Beda calls them, satraps,

---

[1] R. A. 300.

[2] For the later decline of the Germanic freeman, especially the Anglo-Saxon, see Stubbs, earlier pages; and also Green, *Short History*, p. 90.

[3] See Stubbs, *Const. Hist.* I. 26 ff.; Waitz, *Verfassungsgesch.* I. 201 ff.; and such works as Seebohm's *Village Communities*; G. L. Gomme's *Primitive Folk Moots*; and the valuable studies of Professor E. A. Freeman in books and essays.

chose by lot one of their own number for the supreme command, which lasted until the close of hostilities.[1]

Popular government was clearly recognized even by the later kings, who went through the form of appealing to the great council for sanction of the royal deeds. In *Béowulf* we read of the Danish king sitting with his council in anxious deliberation how they may resist the attacks of Grendel.[2] Alfred tells us that he drew up his code of laws with the advice of his *Witan*.[3] Among the Saxons and Frisians, where Roman influence was never strong, and where we may find the origin of our own institutions, "local self-government" seems to have been the rule whenever the nation was at peace. The northwestern districts of Germany have always shown more or less republican spirit; though an irresistible current swept them — with what difficulty, Charlemagne could tell — into the grasp of monarchy. This change and concentration of government is very marked. Dahn notes that at the great battle in 357, Alamannians had twelve so-called "kings," evidently mere local leaders; whereas in the fight against the Franks in 496 there was only one king of the Alamannians.

In the time of Tacitus, general government rested in the assembly or moot (Anglo-Saxon, *gemôt*) of larger and smaller districts. The exact nature of these districts — canton, hundred, mark, community, what not — has been the subject of much discussion; but it seems clear enough that representative bodies carried on such government, local or general, as ex-

---

[1] See the whole passage, Beda, *Hist. Ecc.* V. 10, and above, p. 271.
[2] *Béow.* 171 f.   [3] Liebermann, I, 46, § 49, 10.

isted outside of the conduct of war. The folk-moot was the central fact of public life and public interests;[1] and the *Campus Martius* of the Carlovingians, the shire-moot, the town-meeting, are continued and different forms of the same old institution. The privilege of belonging to this primitive body was rated high; the right of attendance was withdrawn from no freemen whatever save only those who had been guilty of the crime of crimes and had left their shields upon the field of battle.[2] The meetings of the tribes were held at full or new moon;[3] but for the larger assemblies, where a whole race convened, two meetings in the year were probably sufficient, and naturally coincided with the times of the great heathen feasts.[4] Daytime — "holy is the day" — was the legal limit of session. The summons for an extraordinary assembly may have been, as in later times, a stick, an arrow, or the like; perhaps even a hammer for the court.[5] The place of meeting was under the open sky, high and prominent; and was at or near some place sacred to the gods — mountain, meadow, fountain, tree. Even the high-road was a favorite place. Local assemblies in England and elsewhere were held by preference under sacred and memorial trees, of which the chief are linden, oak, and ash.[6]

---

[1] Waitz, I. 338.   [2] *Præcipuum flagitium;* Tac. *Germ.* VI.

[3] The A. S. hundred may have met monthly; see H. M. Chadwick, *Studies* pp. 240, 244, 248, and Hoops under "Hundertschaft".

[4] Lippert thinks the origin of the general council was the nomadic spring meeting of tribes before the herds were driven out to pasture. *Christentum, Volksbrauch u. Volksglaube,* p. 583 ff.

[5] Waitz, I. 345; Kemble, *Saxons,* 1. 55.

[6] G. L. Gomme, *Primitive Folk Moots.*

What was done at these assemblies? Naturally, business varied with the size and character of the gathering. Tacitus tells us of an embassy sent by one German tribe to another, and received in full assembly, where proposals were considered regarding a combined and systematic opposition to Roman rule.[1] Further, we are told in the *Germania* that important matters were discussed by the people, minor affairs by the chieftains; and as in modern times, so then, we may be sure that influential men knew how to guide the sentiment of the meeting. Executive or presiding officers were few and of vague functions; there was little need for such men when individual freedom was so great and the execution of law so limited. Of ancient origin, we may assume, was the town-reeve,[2] for he is mentioned among the old Saxons as the *villicus*,[3] which is the same as Alfred's *tûngerêfa*. He was probably elected by the smaller community, and presided over its councils: over the larger assembly presided a high official — prince or even king.

The assembly was under the protection of the tribal gods, and was opened by a command of silence from the priests, who thus imposed conditions of peace upon the gathering. At the beginning of the Old Norse *Voluspa*, "The Sibyl's Prophecy," we find this solemn call for silence on the part of all peace-loving mortals: "Be silent, all men, high and low." Moreover, the priests, as executives of divine command, had power to punish such as might defy their authority, and through their persons insult the majesty of the patron gods. The session thus opened,

---

[1] *Hist.* IV. 64.   [2] Waitz, I. 136.   [3] Beda, *Hist. Ecc.* V. 10.

distinguished men of the tribe are heard in behalf of whatever proposition is before the meeting. If the people approve a man's speech or recommendation, they clash their weapons lustily together; if they disapprove and dissent, there is an ominous murmur.[1]

Religious ceremonies were doubtless abundant at such a meeting. The custom of casting lots, described by Tacitus,[2] is under the charge of the state-priest "if it is upon a public occasion." An example of the use of such lots in deciding a public question is quoted by Waitz[3] from the *Vita Anskarii*. A king of Sweden consults the gods by lots to see whether or not he shall allow Anskar to bring forward his plea for Christianity. The judgment is favorable, and the king submits to his people the question of a new religion. Many other ceremonies of divination and enchantment even were doubtless common at such an assembly, but are more properly considered under the head of religious rites.

Aside from religion and diplomacy, the business of these meetings must have partaken largely of a legal character.[4] With the exception of small villages, every district made a court out of its general assembly;[5] and it is Grimm's opinion[6] that the whole assembly of freemen heard and judged such causes as came before them, — questions of public interest, transfer of land, settlement of personal disputes over property, the enfranchisement of slaves, the award of *wergild*, the ceremony of a free youth's admittance to the privi-

---

[1] Tac. *Ger*. XI.   [2] Ibid. X.   [3] I. 350.

[4] Sir H. Maine says that the court of the Hundred is the oldést of the organized Germanic courts. *Early Law and Custom*, p. 169.

[5] Waitz, I. 339.   [6] *R. A.* 745.

leges of citizenship, and similar affairs. Something
of this same sort was the Icelandic *Thing*. An officer
presided over the Germanic court, a sort of judge,
whose token of office was a staff, mostly white in
color,[1] and who often sat upon a conspicuous seat
hewn out of stone. Some curious old laws enforce
upon a popular judge that he shall sit with one leg
over the other; and other laws, not so curious, insist
that he shall keep himself clear of drunkenness. In
such courts of the historical period, the judge faced
the east; on his right was the plaintiff, and on his
left the defendant, who thus had to take the north, a
quarter of bad omen.[2] True, these are late customs,
but their roots not improbably strike well into the
most ancient judicial practice. Doubtless, too, many
old ceremonies were retained by the famous *Vehmgericht* of Westphalia, to which we have already
referred, — that Vigilance Committee in the grand
style which served as almost the only curb upon a
lawless age; which, like its prototype, the old Germanic assembly, held court under free sky, had
no secret chambers, no tortures, and executed its
decrees with unerring certainty by hanging the convicted offender to the nearest living tree.[3] Nor are
the collections of Germanic law so very recent in
date. The earliest codes were probably poetical
(alliterative) in character so as to be more readily
retained by the memory. The Goths had their
system of laws; but the earliest Germanic code preserved to us is the Salic Law, about which so much

---

[1] *R. A.* 761.   [2] *R. A.* 808.
[3] For a salutary rebuke of the nonsense written about *Vehmgerichte*,
see Dr. Wächter's little book already cited, p. 63 f.

misunderstanding has been spread abroad: it dates from the fifth century.

Although Tacitus is authority for the statement that priests were charged with the execution of decrees, as well as with ordinary punishments, a recent writer is very decided in his assertion that common law as administered by these courts was a matter of tradition and the direct affair of each voting and deliberating freeman. Much of the sacredness attaching to law, he says, has been the result of Christianity and was foreign to our heathen system. Nor was there, he adds, any hieratic monopoly of law; it was not kept, recorded, and interpreted by priests.[1] Nevertheless, we know on the authority of Tacitus that the priests were its executors. A pretty Frisian legend records the sacred sanction of law. King Karl orders twelve men to be chosen from Frisian land in order that they may determine what is law in Frisia. Unable to do as he bids, these twelve men beg a respite, but after a week are still in doubt. Then Karl declares them doomed to death, but allows them to be set in a boat without sail or oar, and exposed to the sea. They beg God for help and ask him to send a thirteenth man to them (as Christ was to the disciples) to teach them what they need to know. Suddenly this thirteenth one is sitting among them. He rows them to land with a bit of wood, strikes the ground and causes a spring of water to gush forth, and proceeds to teach them all the law. This, thinks Richthofen, points to the old heathen customs, when a priest set forth the law.[2] Similar

[1] Von Amira in Paul's *Grundriss*[3], pp. 10—12.
[2] Richthofen, *Friesische Rechtsgeschichte*, II. 456, 459, 488.

conclusions may be drawn in regard to Iceland.
This Asega, Judex, Sapiens, — by all these names
the Frisian interpreter of law is called, — seems to
have a genuine heathen pedigree ; he was the local
magistrate of old.[1]

Cases of public punishment are given by Tacitus
and have been mentioned here under the head of
cowardice in war.[2] The offender could be declared
an outlaw, " *vogelfrei*," as in the case when a murderer
refused to give satisfaction of any sort. Moreover,
there remain in modern collections traces of older
laws which prescribe frightful forms of death ; these
horrors are nevertheless traditional and do not seem
to have been enforced in historical times.[3] But
certain modes of execution, terrible enough, may be
followed far back in Germanic records ; such were
death on the wheel, decapitation, stoning, trampling
to death by wild horses, burial alive, flinging from a
rock, drowning, burning, exposure to wild animals,
and, for coast-dwellers, sending to sea in a leaking
boat. In the north, a barbarous custom called " carv-
ing the eagle " — that is, on the back of the victim —
finds frequent mention. Milder punishments were
known, and records of the early middle ages tell of
cutting off a victim's hair, which thus deprived him
of his external sign of freedom ; whipping, — a pen-

[1] Richthofen, *Friesische Rechtsgeschichte*, 482.   [2] *Germ.* XII.

[3] *R. A.* 682. Enforced, however, were the elaborate punishments for
him who profaned a temple of the gods. In Frisian law such a criminal
"ducitur ad mare, et in sabulo, quod accessus maris operire solet, fin-
duntur aures ejus et castratur, et immolatur diis quorum templa violavit." Richthofen, *Fries. Rechtsges.* II. 507. Compare *Tempest*, I. 1 : —

> would thou mightst lie drowning,
> The washing of ten tides.

alty reserved for slaves; flaying; cutting off hand
and foot, nose, ears, or lips; blinding; cutting out
the tongue; breaking out the teeth; branding, and
other less violent forms, down to a mere reproof
by the proper authorities.[1] The Anglo-Saxon laws
are very explicit in the definition and gradation
of crimes; but while many penalties of mutilation
occur, most of the punishments are in terms of
money paid as fine and *wergild*. Adjustment of the
wergild must have taken up much of the time in
these assembly-courts. Fines were assessed — about
collection we cannot feel so sure — upon criminals of
every grade; and great complication arose from the
difference made in the amount according to the rank
of the injured party. Even verbal injuries and attacks
upon honor or reputation were punished by fine, and
this in some of the early Anglo-Saxon codes; to call
a man a perjurer, for example, or to heap abuse upon
him in the house of another, is punished by a fine of
one shilling to the owner of the house, six shillings to
the insulted person, and twelve shillings to the king.[2]
Should royalty be even remotely concerned, the fine
is increased. "If the king drink at a man's house
and any one shall commit wrong there, this one is to
pay double fine." — "If a freeman steal from the king,
let him pay ninefold." [3] This is, of course, no crite-
rion for primitive relations; but we are distinctly told
by Tacitus that the Germans of his day had a system
of fines which were assessed in terms of cattle.[4] For
less serious offences than those for which death was
imposed, he says, there is a scale of punishments

[1] For details. *R. A.* 680 ff.
[3] *Ibid.*, p. 3, §§ 3, 4.
[2] Liebermann, 1, 10, 12.
[4] *Germ.* XII.

graded according to the crime, with fines in horses or
cattle ; a part of these fines is paid to the king or to
the community, a part to the injured person or his
relatives.   Thus we see a state of affairs distinctly
analogous to the system of Anglo-Saxon codes.   It
is an Aryan tendency to distinguish carefully between
crime and crime and to shade the punishment in heavier or lighter fashion.   Even among the Franks, Salic
law interposes to protect woman from insult, and lays
fines upon the man who may take liberties with her
person : according as he grasps her forearm or upper
arm or touches her breast, he pays 1200, 1400, and
1800 *denarii*, and if he knocks off her head-dress, the
fine is fifteen *solidi*.[1]   Moreover, apart from the fine
or " damages," which make restitution to the sufferer,
there was something like our modern fine, the *wíte* of
Anglo-Saxon law, which had to be paid to the state.[2]

The freeman, the citizen, was the person who
made the laws and for whose sake they existed; but
there was a class of people outside the protection of
law.   Such were abandoned criminals in the first
instance, and then those people who followed any
despised occupation, the professional fighter or champion, wandering minstrels and mountebanks, beggars, tramps; later, illegitimate children ; and latest
(towards the end of the middle ages), the hangman.[3]

Allusion has been made already to the shy advances
undertaken by law upon the domain of feud and pri-

---

[1] *Lex. Sal.* c. 75.   The late Thomas Wright quotes this and more in
his *Womankind in Western Europe*, p. 38.

[2] The relative amount of respect paid to law by the different Germanic tribes is not easy to fix.   For general lawlessness the Franks
must claim precedence.   See Von Locbell, *Gregor v. Tours*, pp. 35-57.

[3] Von Amira in Paul's *Grundriss*², p. 146.

vate warfare. Among such advances we must count
the duel and trial by battle; these were in all probability carried on before the full assembly of the people.
Tacitus tells us of a case where combat between two
champions — a captive from one army, a soldier from
the other — was thought to foreshadow the event of
war, a sort of divination.[1] Oaths, too, must have been
taken, along with an appeal to heaven, when the combat was of a judicial nature. In Scandinavia, the
accused as well as the accuser grasped the holy ring
stained with sacrificial blood, and made oath; while
a late survival caused the same persons to swear
upon the boar's head.

Another ceremony which was probably carried out
before one of these general assemblies was the ordeal.[2]
Jacob Grimm thinks that the ordeal, which concerns
itself with past or present, just as the oracle is busied
with the future, was of remote heathen origin;[3] and
Mr. E. B. Tylor approves Jamieson's derivation of
our phrase "to haul over the coals" from the time-
honored rite of passing through the fire.[4] The grave
injustice of the ordeal, falling heavily upon accused
persons, who were dependent on a miracle for the
establishment of their innocence, has led Grimm to
the conclusion that the early middle ages seldom
applied this test in the case of freemen. A freeman
took oath of innocence; while the slave and the
dependent were driven to the terrors of the ordeal.
Precisely so, in later days, it was the witches, mostly

---

[1] *Germ.* X.

[2] See Dahn, *Bausteine*, II. 1-75, "Studien zur Geschichte der german. Gottesurtheile."

[3] *R. A.* 909   [4] *Primitive Culture*, I. 85.

from the poorest classes of the population, who were compelled to undergo the ordeal by water or by fire. In the old heathen times, however, it must have been prescribed for all classes of society. A queen herself submits to it in what has been called "the best and earliest description of a heathen ordeal." It is Gudrun purging herself from the charge of adultery. In sight of the court, — "seven hundred men came into the hall to see the king's wife deal with the cauldron," — she dips her hand to the bottom of the boiling water, and unhurt takes out the stones. Then the accuser is forced to undergo the trial, and is badly scalded.[1] The ordeal was so strongly founded upon popular approval that the church was forced to recognize it along with many another suspicious ceremony.[2]

Of the different kinds of ordeal, we may note the thrusting of one's hand directly into the fire, walking through the flames, seizing a red-hot iron with naked hand; fetching with bared arm a stone or ring from the bottom of a kettle filled with boiling water; being flung into pond or river, with the condition that floating means guilt and sinking innocence, — an alternative mocked in certain verses of *Hudibras;* and passing before the corpse of a murdered man, with the expectation that the body will begin to bleed at the approach of the murderer, — as in the Nibelungen

---

[1] *C. P. B.*, I, 322f., 561; Hollander, pp. 321, 322; Bellows, p. 468.

[2] A Frisian legend makes the "good" King Karl and the heathen King Redbad enter upon an ordeal to decide ownership of Frisian territory: who can longer remain still shall conquer. Twelve hours long they stand motionless. Then Karl drops his glove; Redbad picks it up, and loses, as Karl exclaims, "Thou art my 'man'!" See Richthofen. *Fries. Rechtsges.* II. 418.

Lay, where Siegfried lies upon the bier, and the kings,
and Hagen his murderer, enter the church : —

And all denied the murder ; but Kriemhilt cried in teen, —
"Whoso would prove him guiltless may let it now be seen.
In presence of the people let him approach the bier,
And stand before the murdered man, and truth shall then be
    clear."

That is a mickle wonder, whene'er before the dead
(Ye see it yet full often) the murderer is led,
Again the wounds gin bleeding : and so it happened here.
The guilt of Hagen on this wise right plainly did appear.

The wounds they fell a-bleeding, as they had done before. . . .[1]

The Anglo-Saxon laws show the ordeal purely as
an appeal to God's judgment, and prescribe various
religious preparations in addition to the judicial pro-
cedure.[2] The most remarkable of these Old English
ordeals was the so-called *corsnœd*, where a piece of
bread or cheese — later it was the consecrated bread
of the church — was swallowed by the accused, with
the idea that a guilty person must choke in the
attempt. It was noted whether the swallower trembled
and turned pale in his attempt ; and a prayer was
often put up that if he was guilty, his throat and
digestive organs might fail to perform their office.[3]

The foregoing tests require but one person : the
trial by battle brought both parties into action.

---

[1] *N. L.* 984. See also *R. A.* 930 f. Familiar, too, is the scene in
Shakspere's *Richard III.*, I. 2, where King Henry's corpse bleeds at
the approach of his murderer.

[2] Schmid, *s.v. ordâl*, and references, especially pp. 144 and 416 ff.
For the Greek use of this ceremony, see the well-known passage of the
Antigone, 264 ff.

[3] "Fac eum, domine, in visceribus angustari, ejus guttur conclude,"
etc.

Grimm records a form of duel where physical endurance decided the cause. In heathen times this was probably a test to see which of two persons could longer sustain the hands and arms aloft. In Christian practice, this was changed to the custom of standing with uplifted hands by a cross, the *judicium crucis*. We have noted above Karl's contest with Redbad, where the test was to stand motionless as long as possible.

CHAPTER XI

THE FUNERAL

The weapon-death — Burning and burial — The former a primitive Germanic habit — The mound or barrow — Its position — What was burnt or buried with the dead — Sacrifice of the living — Ship-burials — The land of souls — Germanic horror of the grave — The elegiac mood in our poetry — Games and feasts at the funeral — Ceremonies at the burial of Attila and of Béowulf.

DEATH, we have already seen, came to the German upon the battle-field, in the feud, and at sea; but nowhere so dreaded as where it found him in his bed, — the "straw-death," as he called it. Men who die thus inglorious are doomed to tread wet and chill and dusky ways to the land of Hel. Old warriors of the Viking age, when caught by illness, gashed themselves with Odin's spear, and so bought "Valhalla" with their blood.[1] Of the various paths to death, old age had the worst adjectives. A passage in *Béowulf* preserves some of the primitive sentiment, though the note of sermonizing has slipped in and given a modern tone to the whole: —

[1] The earlier belief gave all dead to Hel, and later to Thor. Odin is the Viking god. See Schullerus in P. B. *Beit.* XII. 246, and Petersen, *Om Nordboernes Gudedyrkelse og Gudetro i Hedenold*, p. 90 ff. For another notion, which worked against mutilated bodies, see Tylor, *Primitive Culture*, II. 87.

> but erelong it shall be
> that sickness or sword thy strength shall minish,
> or fang of fire, or flooding billow,
> or bite of blade, or brandished spear,
> or odious age; or the eyes' clear beam
> wax dull and darken . . .[1]

A famous passage of the poetic Edda[2] mentions the different deaths which men may die. "I counsel thee ninthly," says Sigrdrífa to Sigurd, "that thou give the dead man burial no matter where thou shalt find him, *be he sick-dead, or sea-dead or weapon-dead.* . . ." The sea-death came often enough to these northern pirates, and was by no means without honor. But it is the weapon-dead who fare straightway to Odin; unwasted by sickness, in the full strength of manhood, they leap mailed and armed into the new life. This feeling about the compensations of a warrior's death is still abroad, and is not yet a mere sentiment. The Horatian maxim was certainly more than sentiment, — it was Roman faith and Roman pride; and there is even for us something full-blooded about those adjectives *dulce et decorum.* The warrior in Germanic times had the stateliest funeral; his arms, and often his wife and slaves, gave him fitting escort to the other world. A violent death of almost any kind was the only aristocratic way to leave life in Scandinavia. Suicide was honorable when undertaken from motives which men then deemed proper, and is a matter of frequent occurrence in Old Norse annals.

As regards the funeral rites of the German, we are

---

[1] *Béow.* 1763 ff.   [2] *Sigdrífomál,* 33, ed. Neckel, p. 191.

not without fairly copious sources of information.[1]
Burial and burning of the corpse alternate in history,
and are conditioned by the circumstances of a given
tribe. "The soberest nations," says Sir Thomas
Browne in his *Hydriotaphia*, "have rested in two
ways, of simple inhumation and burning," while he
asserts that "carnal interment . . . was of the elder
date." It is curious, by the way, to compare the
fantastic reasons given by Sir Thomas for these practices, with the poetical explanation of the German
scholar and romanticist, Jacob Grimm. "Some being
of the opinion of Thales, that water was the original
of all things, thought it most equal to submit unto
the principle of putrefaction, and conclude in a moist
relentment. Others conceived it most natural to end
in fire, as due unto the master principle in the composition . . . and therefore heaped up large piles, more
actively to waft them toward that element. . . ."
Grimm, too, regards burial as the primitive custom,
and gives it a poetic motive, — the body sinks to the
mother of all things, earth; whereas by fire the soul
soars in flame to the father, to Jupiter.[2] Burning, he
therefore concludes, shows a higher stage of culture;
and he connects with this custom the formation of a
belief in the end of the world through fire. On the
other hand, burial would often be a necessity, — after
a battle, or in a country destitute of wood. Where
the two customs existed side by side, burning was for

[1] The best summary is J. Grimm, *über das Verbrennen der Leichen*,
an admirable paper, read before the Berlin Academy in 1849. *Kl. Schr.*
II. 211 ff.

[2] Work quoted, p. 214 f. One involuntarily recalls Goethe's sympathetic ballad, *Der Gott und die Bajadere*, with its fine ending; and
Grimm quotes the conclusion of the same poet's *Braut von Corinth*.

the rich and burial for the poor. A nomadic folk
tends to burn, an agricultural folk to bury. The
stone age probably buried,[1] thinks Grimm, the bronze
age burnt, while the age of iron returned to burial. In
broader generalization, the heathen races have mostly
preferred to burn their dead, while Christians incline
to burial. The importance of some sort of funeral
rites was conceded by primitive man; only the
roughest tribes have left the bodies of their dead to
dogs and birds of prey, — a fearful fate reserved for
conquered warriors, and familiar in the Iliad and in
our Anglo-Saxon poetry. The old Persians, however, treated their dead in this way, and some Mon-
golians still keep up the practice; but for these latter
there are explanations in the theories of soul-cult,
advanced by modern anthropology. One thing is
quite certain : our Germanic ancestors burned their
dead.[2]

To Tacitus, the Germanic funeral ceremonies
seemed simple in the extreme. But there was
probably more meant and more carried out than met
his ear; and we must remember the extraordinary
pomp and circumstance of funerals at Rome. Cæsar
testifies[3] that Gallic funerals were very sumptuous; but
the only peculiar custom which Tacitus finds worthy
of notice in Germanic rites is the use of certain kinds
of wood for the funeral-pile of illustrious men. No
costly coverings, he says, are used, no spices; but the

[1] Certainly did, says Montelius, *Civilization of Sweden in Ancient
Times*, trans. Woods, p. 35.
[2] Swedish graves of the early iron age show both burnt and unburnt
bodies. In the boat-burials bodies were now burnt, now unburnt. Montelius, pp. 122–139.
[3] *B. G.* VI. 19, "funera ... magnifica et sumptuosa."

arms, and often the horse, of the warrior are given
with him to the flames. The grave is then marked
by a mound of turf.[1] While the funeral was less
splendid than those sung in some of our early epics,
— as in *Béowulf*, — there is no doubt that it was of
the highest importance; for in another place,[2] Tacitus
tells us that even amid the most desperate battles Germans were wont to carry away (to the rear) the bodies
of their dead. That the Germans burnt their dead was
natural enough for people shut in among such cre-
mating races as the Gauls, Romans, Greeks, Thracians,
Lithuanians, and Slavonic tribes.[3] Christianity cleaves
to burial, not only because Christ's stay in the sepulchre hallowed it, but from Old Testament pre-
cedents. In the third century burning of the dead
had ceased in Rome, and in the fourth century it was
there spoken of as a matter of antiquity. Charlemagne, in an edict for the Saxons, made burning of
corpses a capital offence, and Boniface worked against
it, as against the eating of horse-flesh, — pagan practices both.[4] Certain names of places in England
preserve traces of the old custom; such are *Adeshâm*,
in Kent, — now Adisham, — where *Ad* certainly
means funeral pile; and *Bœlesbeorh* in Gloucester-
shire.[5] Kemble quotes the *Orvar-Odds Saga*, where
the hero gives direction for his funeral. Men are to
make a stone trough and take it to the wood: " There,

---

[1] Tac. *Germ.* XXVII. The rest is rhetoric.   [2] Ibid. VI.

[3] J. Grimm, work quoted, p. 241.

[4] " Jubemus," says Charlemagne, " ut corpora Christianorum Sax-
onorum ad cimeteria ecclesiæ deferantur, et non *ad tumulos Paga-
norum.*"

[5] Given by Kemble in his *Horæ Ferales*, p. 119 f. in an essay on
" Burial and Cremation."

when I am dead, I am to lie in fire and burn up
entirely." Oddr, we must remember, was a convert
to Christianity. For a long time converts used a
certain amount of fire in funeral rites, as if insuring
themselves the advantages of both systems. Moreover, when the custom of burial had superseded the
heathen funeral pile, choice and nature of the grave-
mound remained for a long time under control of
private persons. Not, thinks Kemble,[1] till the clergy
saw decided power and profit involved in the super-
intendence of funeral ceremonies — say about the end
of the ninth century — were regular churchyards
established in England. The Anglo-Saxon loved to
be buried in a chosen place — by a stream, or on some
headland that looked out far over the ocean.[2] Grimm,
in another interesting paper,[3] notes the antiquity of
such choice of burial-sites. In days when corpses were
burned, the ashes were committed to a huge mound
or barrow, sometimes by the great military highway,
or by the ford of the river, if inland, or else on the
shore of the sea. Greek, Roman, and Saxon examples
show a common trait. In the Odyssey, we have a
description of the burial of Achilles.[4] "So thou wert
burned in the garments of the gods, and in much
unguents and in sweet honey, and many heroes of the
Achæans *moved mail-clad around the pyre where thou
wast burning*, both foot-men and horse, and great was
the noise that arose. But when the flame of Hephæs-
tus had utterly abolished thee, lo, in the morning we

---

[1] Work quoted, p. 109.
[2] For these lofty burial sites in Scandinavia, see Weinhold, *Altnord.
Leben*, p. 498, note, and Montelius, p. 85.   [3] *Kl. Schr.* VII. 406 ff.
[4] Bk. 24; the translation is that of Butcher and Lang.

gathered together thy white bones, Achilles, and be-
stowed them in unmixed wine and in unguents. Thy
mother gave a twy-handled golden urn. . . . Therein
lie thy white bones. . . . Then over them did we
pile a great and goodly tomb, . . . *high on a jutting
headland over wide Hellespont*, that it might be far
seen from off the sea by men that now are and by
those that shall be hereafter." In the same way
Elpenor asks Odysseus to burn him with his armor,
and "pile him a barrow on the shore of the gray sea
. . . that even men unborn may hear his story"; and
Æneas buries the ashes of his friend Misenus in a
huge mound [1] on a headland of the sea. Such burial-
sites are often mentioned in the Norwegian, Swedish,
and Icelandic sagas. Grimm finds "hohe Poesie" in
the account of Yngwar's burial-place. " The Baltic
sings a joyous wave-song to lull the Swedish hero ;
the sleeper in the hill hears the billows breaking
near him, and their murmur cheers his loneliness."
Burial in such conspicuous places is easily proved for
Anglo-Saxon times. Taking first the antiquary's
evidence, we may note the " fine Saxon barrow," " on
a bold conical hill overlooking Folkestone in Kent." [2]
Further, " the hill of Osengal, overlooking Pegwell
Bay near Ramsgate, and furnishing a magnificent
view of the Channel, . . . is perforated like a honey-
comb with the graves of an immense Saxon cemetery." [3]
Finally, we have the testimony of our old epos. Says
the dying Béowulf to his young kinsman Wiglaf : [4] —

---

[1] " Ingenti mole." See *Odyssey*, XI. 56 ff., Verg. *Æn.* VI. 232, and
Grimm, work quoted.

[2] T. Wright, *Celt, Roman, and Saxon*, p. 469.

[3] Ibid. 470. [4] 2802 ff.

"A barrow bid ye the battle-famed raise
for mv ashes. 'Twill shine by the shore of the flood,
to folk of mine memorial fair
on Hronës Headland[1] high uplifted,
that ocean-wanderers oft may hail
Beowulf's Barrow, as back from far
they drive their keels o'er the darkling wave."

Kemble remarks[2] that the inland tumuli or barrows are often used in old charters as the boundaries of Anglo-Saxon estates. These ancient documents either couple with the mention of the mound the adjective "heathen," or else give a name of the person who lies in the tomb, and probably, as Kemble argues, was a Christian. Ordinarily, we have either simply "the heathen barrow," or else "Hoce's barrow"; but in a charter of the year 976, we read: "Thence to the heathen 'burial' (tomb); thence westward to the boundary where Ælfstán lies in heathen barrow." This, Kemble takes to signify the burial of a Christian in the midst of old heathen graves. Poetry easily laid hold of these places, and gave them that needful touch of the mystic and uncanny. In a remarkable passage of *Salomon and Saturn*,[3] there is something of the later romantic shudder, as well as a good movement of the verse: —

His sword well-burnisht shineth yet.
and over the barrow beam the hilts.[4]

The study of primitive culture leads us to the conclusion that burials, whether of the body or of

---

[1] *I.e.* after the funeral pile is burnt.   [2] Work quoted, p. 110.
[3] Kemble's ed. p. 156. See p. 248, above.
[4] Of course souls often appear over their graves in the shape of flame. So Angantyr and his brothers in the *Hervararsaga*. See Mogk, in Paul's *Grundriss*[2], III, 260.

the ashes left from the funeral-pile, began in or near
the home itself. Survivals and traditions point this
way, even if we neglect the study of savage customs.
Thus Alboin was buried in Italy under the steps of a
palace, and with him were his arms and ornaments.[1]
Primitive races have buried their dead under the
threshold, with a general feeling that the spirit will
protect its former home. Here, however, we note a
curious conflict between two ideas, — the desire to
keep a spirit near one's home and so enjoy the benefits
of its protection, and the fear of evil influences pro-
ceeding from such hovering souls. A half-way dualism prompts us to call for aid upon the shades of our
fathers, and yet at other times to conjure into peace
the perturbed spirit, and bid it cease to haunt us.
Men placed for these spirits the little offering of
meat or wine; and even yet a prevalent superstition
forbids the carrying out of a corpse through door or
window: there must be a hole cut for it through the
wall, or it must at least take some unwonted way of
egress.[2] It was once common with German peasants
to bury the dead man in the house where he had
lived;[3] it is still custom in many places to open doors
and windows of the sick-room where one has just died,
— let the soul fly off and rid the survivors of an unwelcome presence. The tomb reared over a grave is
itself originally nothing more nor less than a house,
and the home of the dead was like the home of the

[1] Paul. Diac. II. 28.

[2] Weinhold's (*Altnord. Leben*, p. 476) facts are true, but his theory is
false. Not because the corpse is "unclean" is this exit chosen; it is
to keep the spirit from finding its way back.

[3] Henning, *das deutsche Haus* (Quellen und Forschungen, No. 47),
p. 37.

living. The Egyptians carried this idea to its most
elaborate conclusion. So arose the temple, say some,
in Greece; it was the house built over the grave of a
hero. Lippert even asserts that the whole doctrine
of an under-world originated with graves, the subterranean homes of the dead.[1] Trees were planted
about such a grave, and the sacred grove grew up
about the resting-place of powerful ancestors, or of
the deified founder of the race itself. Such groves
are mentioned in Bugge's text of the *Harbardslióð:* [2]
" When didst thou learn these things?" asks Thor;
and Harbard (= Odin) answers: " From the old folk
I took them, the people who live in the woods."
Graves were sometimes used as treasure houses
which the ancestral spirit could guard; or else they
served as a meeting-place,[3] and the folk met there
for councils, courts, and the like. Kemble[4] says that
Cwichelmes Hlǽw, one of the most commanding
barrows in England, was in the eleventh century *seat
of the shire-court.* Tradition, moreover, told of former
pagan rites at Enta Hlǽw and Scuccan Hlǽw, the
Giants' Barrow and the Devil's Barrow. There were
no regular council-halls for Germanic chieftains until
the time of Charlemagne; but a bit of enclosed land,
the shade of a tree, an ancient sepulchre, were favorite
places. In the same way, this notion of the grave
acted upon its own inner arrangement; for a tomb
was found in Bavaria with five skeletons "seated

---

[1] *Religion der europäischen Culturstämme,* p. 10.

[2] So Neckel, p. 82, st. 44; but Hollander, p. 94, and Bellows, p. 134,
rendering *haugum* instead of *skógum,* translate "hows" (hills).

[3] Weinhold, *Altnord. Leben,* p. 499.

[4] *Horæ Ferales,* p. 116. We noted the love of Germans for *high or
conspicuous sites* for their courts and councils.

about a vessel, by the side of which lay two long iron knives." [1]

There can be no doubt that the heathen Anglo-Saxons first burnt, and then buried, their dead. Grimm collects the evidence of our old poetry, and the results of antiquarian research only confirm us in our belief. That the thanes of Béowulf are ordered to bring from far the "balewood," supports the statement of Tacitus, that distinguished men were burnt on a funeral-pile made of certain kinds of wood. Moreover, we have an epic formula in Anglo-Saxon used as a variant or "kenning," for the simple notion of dying. Instead of "dies" a man "chooses the funeral-pile," — seeks it, goes to it.[2] Two such burnings are described in *Béowulf*, — that of the hero, and that of Hnæf the Dane.

We learn from these descriptions how familiar and necessary seemed to the Anglo-Saxons the burning of their dead. We see how the funeral-pile was hung with weapons and shields; and how when the mound had been raised, it was surrounded with a wall, and furnished like a mortal's own house, with rings and treasure and whatsoever gladdens the heart of men as they sit secure in their hall. Ornaments, weapons, horse, slave, spouse, — all these were needed by the warrior in his life, and a simple logic concluded his need of them in what was literally the other world. All this is strange to modern notions, or at best exists in shadowy survival. Till late in the middle ages a knight's best steed was killed when its owner died; nowadays, we lead the favorite war-horse in the fune-

---

[1] Lippert, *Rel. d. eur. Cult.* p. 148.
[2] *Cf. Béow.* 2818, "ær he bæl cure."

ral procession. In some places of Germany, only a
few years ago, the custom prevailed of putting comb,
razor, and soap, into a man's coffin.[1] Suggestive is
the lingering habit of giving the dead man a pair of
stout shoes; for the way that led to the land of
spirits might well be rough. In Scandinavia, it was
the custom for a near relative to fasten these shoes
firmly to the feet of the corpse.[2] Often a staff was
added; and in the great majority of cases food and
drink were provided, ghostly *viaticum*, found in countless graves. Corn, fruit, and the like are favorites;
and Kemble [3] mentions the Saxon fondness for hazel-
nuts. In modern Sweden, they give the dead man his
tobacco-pipe, pen-knife, and a flask of brandy;[4] while
even in ancient Sweden it was considered proper to
give him draughts and dice to beguile the weariness
of his journey.[5] But kings. and men of might must
not be left to walk; and the horse plays a great part
in legends which have to do with graves. Such is the
Danish *Helhest*. Says Thiele:[6] " In the old times,
they used to bury in every churchyard, before any human body was interred, *a living horse*." This horse,
which, of course, haunts the place as a terror to evil-
doers, is often headless, or three-legged, or what not;
now it is white, now black. In Germany the *Schim-
mel* or white horse plays a similar rôle; and he is

---

[1] Kuhn and Schwartz, *Nordd. Sagen*, p. 435. Visitors to the famous
Museum of Northern Antiquities in Copenhagen remember the pathetic
sight of that body from the moor, so well preserved, and the little
wooden comb withal. But it is a fine head of hair, and deserves the
vanity.

[2] Weinhold, *A. L.* 494.   [3] *Horæ Ferales*, p. 69.

[4] Weinhold, *A. L.* p. 493.   [5] Montelius, p. 122, in earlier iron age.

[6] *Danmarks Folkesagn*, II. 293.

known even in far Arabia. In another tale,[1] Thiele
mentions the belief that great store of treasure can
be raised from a grave where a " gold-horse," or " *a
gold-prince on horseback*," lies buried. Some workmen
once saw a grave open — it was known to contain a
mass of treasure — " and a large man on horseback,
with glittering buttons in his coat, rode out of the
portal of the mound." The prosaic theory of Lippert,
that most of the dragon stories are due to the old
habit of burying treasure with the dead, and to the
natural desire to frighten off plunderers, is, to be
sure, wholly inadequate as a solution of the dragon-
and-treasure problem, but has none the less its probable features. The legends of buried treasure, of
ghosts who must " walk," because they have up-
hoarded in their life " extorted treasure in the womb
of earth," have surely some relation to these old burials. It seems fair to suppose that the angry spirit-
tenant of the mound might well have his share,
though not the sole proprietorship, in the manufacture of dragon-myths. There is no doubt that
graves were often rifled; we can see how the Viking
ship at Christiania has been broken and plundered.
Often, too, the grave was opened by a member of the
family, or even by the state, and a loan or contribu-
tion was forced from the dead capitalist. Kemble,
in the interesting work above quoted, speaking of
the barrows often named as boundary-marks in the
old charters, points out an interesting phrase: " tó
þam brocenan beorge," *to the broken barrow*. Another
is, " westward of the barrow that has been dug into."
Horse and treasure do not exhaust the possibilities,

[1] I. 348.

and sometimes a chariot was added, that the spirit might make his way to Valhalla in still greater state. Grimm[1] instances the burial of King Harald, after the great battle of Bravalla.[2] Conquered and slain in battle, he was sumptuously buried by the victorious King Hring. Harald's body was washed, clad in armor, laid upon the chariot of King Hring, and so driven into the mound. The horse was killed, and the conqueror laid beside it his own saddle, and cried to the dead king: "Now thou canst ride to Valhalla, or drive there, as thou wilt!" Before the mound was closed, all the warriors threw in rings and costly weapons. Another account of the same occurrence says that the body was first burned, and this would be the oldest version; but even when the burning of the corpse was forgotten, men clung to the accessories of horse and chariot. Besides horses, we often hear of the burning or slaying of dogs and falcons. *Le roi s'amuse.*

Above all other possessions which must go with the dead warrior, stood his weapons, and of his weapons, the sword. We see nothing out of the way when a general or a military monarch is buried with sword at his side. Thus armed, the French soldier in Heine's well-known poem was fain to lie in his grave and wait till his emperor came back again. The legends and sagas show us how stubbornly the dead hand of a German warrior was clasped about his sword. Thiele[3] gives the Danish legend of King Hiarne who was buried on an island with his thirty thanes about him. By accident his sword was dug up, and a man named Niels Østergaard carried it

[1] Work quoted, p. 271.   [2] About 790 A.D.   [3] Work quoted, I. 13.

home. But from that time Niels had no luck, and all went wrong in his house. At last he carried back the sword, and buried it; and since then no one has disturbed King Hiarne's tomb. Still more demonstration was made by the robbed sword of the great Holger Danske, which took twelve horses to drag it away, and in the house where it was laid caused such terrible commotion and shaking of walls, that people were fain to haul back the sword to its place; and this time it needed only two horses.[1] There are many similar legends. It is needless to dwell on the survivals of this custom of giving precious possessions along with the dead. Instead of burying or burning treasure, the Chinese burn paper which represents it. Among the Western nations we have the penny put in the mouth of a dead man. Modern instances would not be far to seek, though entirely confined to ornament.

The darker side of this picture is familiar enough. Not only tool or ornament or weapon, — the living went down with the dead. This sharing of a husband's or a master's death might be voluntary or involuntary. Often the wife esteemed it her privilege as well as her duty to die upon the funeral-pile of her lord; and in the famous legend which impressed so strongly the imagination of our Germanic race and gave it its one great epos, when Brynhild's jealousy has slain Sigurd, her love for him prompts her to share his grave. The story of her fate is told in the verse of the *Sigurðarkviða*,[2] and in the prose of the *Volsungasaga*.[3] The

---

[1] Thiele, I. 20.   [2] *Edda*, Hollander, p. 306.

[3] Chap. 31. A translation of the poetical version, with attempted restoration of the missing words, will be found in Vigfusson and Powell's *Corpus*, I. 302 f.

latter is given here because free from the gaps of the older version: "Now I beg thee, Gunnar, one thing, and it is the last I shall beg of thee," — it is Brynhild who addresses her husband. "Make a great funeral-pyre for all of us upon the mound, for me and Sigurd and all that are slain along with him. Cover it with human blood, and burn me there by the side of the Hunnish king; and on his other side my men, — two at his head, two at his feet, and two hawks. . . . The doors [1] shall not fall upon his heels where I follow him; and our retinue is no sorry one when five handmaidens and eight serving-men, whom my father gave me, follow him, and they too are burnt who are slain along with Sigurd. . . . Now was Sigurd's corse cared for in the ancient fashion, and a huge funeral-pile was built. And when that towered so high that it could be seen from far, they laid upon it the bodies of Sigurd and his three-year-old son, whom Brynhild had caused to be slain, and also the corpse of Guthorm, who had murdered Sigurd And when the flames were hot, went forth Brynhild. She said to her handmaidens they might take her gold, and she died, and she was burnt there along with Sigurd, and so her life was done." Less passionate, but full of quiet devotion, are the words of the wife of old Nial: "Young I was married to Nial, and I have promised him that one fate should take us both." She refuses to leave the burning house, and dies with her husband. Wherever we turn in ancient history, examples of this custom press upon us. The modern school of criticism is not inclined to lean on poetry or sentiment in its explanations of these

[1] Of Hel's domain.

sombre rites ; and even a philologist like Hehn finds Grimm's treatment far too romantic.[1] Through these rifts in the fabric of our old culture we catch glimpses of the sheer brutality and indifference to human life which marked the earliest stages of primitive religious systems. Hehn collects a mass of examples. We remember that Achilles offered to the shade of Patroclus not only horses and dogs, but twelve young Trojans whom he had captured for the purpose; and on his own grave, in after days, Polyxena was burned. In some countries the wife was expected to hang herself at the grave of her husband. Most cruel, perhaps, was the Scythian custom.[2] When the king dies, one of his wives is strangled and buried with him, likewise a number of servants and horses. On the anniversary of his death, fifty slaves, whom he had chosen for the purpose, and fifty choice horses are treated in the same manner. The burial of Alaric the Goth is familiar to readers of Gibbon. Boniface, in a letter to the king of Mercia, about 745 A.D., describes the custom among the Wends: the wife is buried with her husband. As regards the sacrificial side of this custom, we shall have more to say in the consideration of Germanic religion.

Whatever is sanctioned by religion and dateless custom comes to be regarded as a virtue, and finds willing devotees. Possibly some of the more important ceremonies and duties of modern life will one day be counted in the list of painful superstitions; but, however that may be, the voluntary death of a wife at her husband's funeral was reckoned among the conspicuous virtues of the Germanic woman. Hakon

[1] Hehn*, p. 540.　　[2] Hehn*, p. 540, and Herodotus, iv, 71ff.

Jarl was refused in his old age by Gunnhild because she would in all probability have early occasion to die with him. Nor was the tie of husband and wife the only one which called for such a sacrifice. Sons, as in the case of Sigurd, or brothers, were chosen as the victims; and the bonds of friendship and love were often hallowed by a sense of similar obligation. Cases can be found where two men agree that should either die, the other will straightway follow. True lovers, in countless tales and ballads of a later time, die at the selfsame moment; instead of the old mingling ashes, they are buried side by side, and two rose trees spring through the turf and twine lovingly together.

On the general subject of burial, there is little to say. To cover the corpse, even of one's bitterest foe, was a custom in Iceland whose breach might lead to banishment.[1] No pious Scandinavian passed a corpse without tossing a bit of turf or a stone upon it by way of covering; and since this corresponds so closely to the well-known classical traditions, it seems reasonable to infer for the whole Germanic race a general sense of the immense importance of funeral-rites. We have no reason to suppose that women and children were refused the ceremonies which are told of kings and warriors and peasants. Cases of the funeral-rites of women are on record; and skeletons of children have been found in circumstances that abundantly justify the conclusion.[2]

Full of a weird interest are the ship-burials of our sea-loving ancestors. Let us first hear how the white god Balder was burnt Viking-wise upon his ship.

---

[1] Weinhold, *Altnord. Leben*, p. 474.   [2] Ibid. p. 482.

"Then the Æsir took Balder's corpse and bore it to the sea. The name of Balder's ship was *Hringhorni;* it was the greatest of all ships. The gods were fain to push it from shore and make thereon Balder's balefire, but the ship would not move. Then they sent to Jotunheim after the giantess who is called Hyrrokin; when she came, she rode a wolf and had a snake for its bridle; when she leaped from the steed, Odin called up four Berserkers and bade them hold it, but they could do this only by felling it to the ground. Then Hyrrokin stept to the bow of the boat, and with her first thrust she pushed it so that fire flashed from the rollers and all lands trembled. That made Thor angry, and he grasped his hammer and would have shattered her head, had not all the gods asked peace for her. Then Balder's corpse was borne out to the ship, and when his wife, Nanna, daughter of Nep, saw that, she burst for grief and died. Then she was carried to the funeral-pile, and it was kindled. Thor came up and consecrated it with his hammer, and before his feet ran a dwarf called Litr, and Thor lifted his foot and thrust the dwarf into the fire, where he was burned. . . . Odin laid upon the pile a ring. . . . Balder's horse and all the trappings were likewise laid upon the pile. . . ." [1] Relics of such naval sepulchres have been discovered; such is the famous Viking ship, now in the possession of the university of Christiania, and recently dug up from its resting-place of a thousand years.

Famous is the so-called "Passing of Scyld"; [2] we find, however, no mention of burning the corpse, and

[1] *Glyfaginning*, XLIX., Prose Edda, ed. Wilken, p. 75 f.   [2] *Béow.* 26 ff.

a too hasty inference of Sarrazin[1] makes this fact prove that an Anglo-Saxon editor or translator of the Scandinavian original (such is Sarrazin's nigh impossible theory) allowed his own ideas of burial to predominate in the description.

> Forth he fared at the fated moment,
> sturdy Scyld to the shelter of God.
> They they bore him over to ocean's billow,
> loving clansmen, as late he charged them,
> while wielded words the winsome Scyld,[2]
> the leader belovéd who long had ruled .... —
> In the roadstead rocked a ring-dight vessel,
> ice-flecked, outbound, atheling's barge:
> there laid they down their darling lord
> on the breast of the boat, the breaker-of-rings,
> by the mast the mighty one. Many a treasure
> fetched from far was freighted with him
> No ship have I known so nobly dight
> with weapons of war and weeds of battle,
> with breastplate and blade: on his bosom lay
> a heapéd hoard that hence should go
> far o'er the flood with him floating away.
> No less these loaded the lordly gifts,
> thanes' huge treasure, than those had done
> who in former time forth had sent him
> sole on the seas, a suckling child.
> High o'er his head they hoist the standard,
> a gold-wove banner; let billows take him
> gave him to ocean. Grave were their spirits,
> mournful their mood. No man is able
> to say in sooth, no son of the halls,
> no hero 'neath heaven, — who harbored that freight!

This charming myth is found in many places, the story of infants who come mysteriously floating to

---

[1] *Béowulf-Studien*, p. 39. [2] "Friend of the Scyldings."

the shore in a boat with gorgeous trappings, evidently
a gift of heaven to the kingless realm.   There they
rule wisely and well, win lands, fame, vassals, and
at last, dying, order their funeral in the same boat
that bore them to their adopted country.   Of kindred
spirit are the Celtic myths about King Arthur, and
those Germanic legends which have found their most
popular type in the story of Lohengrin.[1]   Romance is
less obvious in the custom of South-Sea Islanders,
who put their dead into old disabled boats, and so
send them off to sea; and not only the dead, but
those also who are mortally sick.[2]   In the *Nialssaga*,[3]
old Flosi is weary of life, takes a bad boat, and sails
on his last voyage: "Folk said his boat was wretched,
but Flosi said it was good enough for one who was
old and 'fey.'   He took in cargo, and put to sea; but
nothing has ever been heard of the ship since then."
In the old English ballad of *Edward* we have such an
allusion :[4] —

> " What death dost thou desire to die,
>   Son Davie, son Davie?"

> " I'll set my foot in a bottomless ship,
>   Mother lady, mother lady;
> I'll set my foot in a bottomless ship,
>   And ye'll never see mair o' me."

Ship-burial seems in most places to have been a prerogative of kings and princes and heroes of great
fame.   Saxo tells us that King Frotho[5] made the law

---

[1] References, *D. M.* 693.   [2] Lippert, *Seelencult*, pp. 6, 13.   [3] C. 160.
[4] Child, Ballads,[2] I. 169.   See also ballad *Lizie Wan*, A, stanza ii.
Vol. II. 448.
[5] Saxo, ed. Holder, p. 156; Grimm, *Kl. Schr.*, II, 272; Holzmann,
Deutsche Myth., p. 123.

that a chief (*satrapa*) shall be burned with one ship;
but for ordinary persons, ten shall be burned with
each ship. Such a vessel — *an œtheling's barge*, the
poet of *Béowulf* calls it — filled with treasure and
wrapt in flames, drifting slowly out to sea, watched
by a great throng upon the shore, must have made a
royal funeral indeed. This custom of ship-burial
continued in the case of kings and heroes after it
had become usual for the masses to be buried in
mounds or common graves.√ A curious combination,
or else survival, was the custom best known in
Scandinavia, of burying people first in actual ships,
then in coffins made to represent a ship, and lastly in
an ordinary grave with stones piled about it in the
shape of a ship.[1] "Doubtless," says Grimm, "men
were buried in a boat so that when in the underworld they came to bodies of water they might have
their boat at hand." For just as burial in the earth
brought about belief in that shadowy land, the
"under-world," so perhaps these old boat-burials made
men think of a spirit-world oversea. As with the
Greek, Germanic superstition made this an island;
and even Hel's mansion is surrounded by water.
The classical Charon is not without his relatives in
our own Germanic legend. To a fisherman at Speier
on the Rhine came one night a person dressed like a
monk and asked to be ferried over the stream; this
done, the fisherman returned and found five others
waiting for him.[2] The legend is incomplete; but its
origin and tendency are evident enough. Many old
skeletons have been found in Germany with a *coin* of

[1] Grimm, work quoted, p. 274; *D. M.* 692.
[2] Grimm, *Deutsche Sagen*, No. 276; *cf.* also *D. M.*[4] 694.

some sort still remaining in the mouth.[1] Moreover,
just as the mysterious western ocean held for Greek
superstition those Fortunate Islands, the mystic
Atlantis, the Gardens of the Hesperides, the abode
of the blessed dead, — so there lay for Germanic
belief a world of souls in the waters toward the setting sun. Procopius [2] relates a legend of the island
"Brittia," whither the souls of the dead were ferried from the mainland; on the shores of the latter
dwelt fishermen and others who were free of all
taxes and similar burdens of state, on condition that
they held themselves ready to row the dead across.
"Before midnight they hear a knocking at their
doors, and then the voice of an invisible person who
calls them to their work. Immediately they get up,
and, following a certain undefined impulse, go to the
shore. There they find boats ready for the journey,
but quite empty, — not their own boats, moreover,
but foreign vessels. They go into these boats and
take the oars, whereupon they notice that such a
crowd of passengers is on board that the craft sinks
to the level of the deck, but no one is to be seen. In
an hour they reach Britain, whereas with their own
boats they can scarcely row the same distance in a
night and a day. Then the boats are emptied, and
they row back: the vessels are so light that only the
keel is on the water." Meanwhile no one whatever
has been seen, although a voice is heard calling out
the name of each person who arrives; women are
not named directly, but are called by the name of
those to whom they have belonged in life. Kemble
queries whether this silent land may not be the place

[1] Grimm, *D. M.*[4] III. 248.   [2] *De bello Goth.* IV. 20.

about which is asked a question in the *Salomon and Saturn* : —

Tell me of the land
where none of the folk with foot can walk.[1]

Brittia, of course, is England, whither our earliest ancestors, destitute of sails, could scarcely come save by accident or great stress of need. Hence the mystery and the myths. Mannhardt tells of the widespread belief that souls of children are fetched from " Engelland " ; the name was applied to Britain, but taken to mean " the place where angels live." Wackernagel quotes an old story which calls Britain "Seelenland," soul-land.[2] We have another description of this ghostly ferry given by Claudian, who wrote early in the fifth century. On the Gallic shore, he says, the same place where Odysseus poured his libation and spoke with the shades, "there may be heard weeping and lamentation and the low rustle of flying souls ; and folk who dwell there see pallid phantoms, and watch the shapes of dead men pass by. . . ."

Est locus, extremum qua pandit Gallia littus,
oceani prætentus aquis, ubi fertur Ulixes
sanguine libato populum movisse silentem.
illic umbrarum tenui stridore volantum
flebilis auditur questus.   Simulacra coloni
pallida, defunctasque vident migrare figuras.[3]

But these infinite projections of the old boat-burial concern rather the realm of myth and of religious

[1] *Sal. and Sat.* p. 177, note.
[2] See Mannhardt, *Germ. Mythen*, p. 326 f., 370, 405. Procopius seems to mean that the souls are taken to an island near " Brittia," — Ireland, says Wackernagel. See *Haupt's Ztst.* VII. 191.
[3] Claudian *in Rufinum*, I. 123 ff.

belief. Actual burial was for the great majority of
our race connected with inland places, and where
water played a part it was the water of sacred wells
and streams. Legends tell of streams or fountains
that spring from old heathen tombs, and there are
magical properties in the water. Thus the Danish
tradition of a certain mound " in which, in old times,
men say there was a heathen burial-place. Near the
foot of it wells out a spring, about which there is a
prophecy of the sibyl, that it shall one day save
(the neighboring town) from great danger." [1] Church-
yards inherited all this wealth of heathen shudders
and superstition; and the folk-lore of every nation is
filled with these tales. Our Saxon temperament
seems especially inclined to a certain solemn enjoy-
ment of funereal matters. How much has not the
subject contributed to make Gray's *Elegy in a
Country Churchyard* the most widely read English
poem! The *Poema Morale*, a middle-English didac-
tic piece in the septenarius or ballad metre, was
enormously popular: it is full of the sepulchre. Even
our most imaginative poetry takes a strange energy
from the contemplation of death; let Beaumont's
fine verses " On the Tombs in Westminster Abbey "
bear witness: —

> Here be sands, ignoble things,
> Dropt from the ruin'd sides of kings.

Add the emphatic testimony of Jacob Grimm: [2]
" No race, to my knowledge, was ever more strongly
impressed by the horror of the dark and narrow grave

[1] Thiele, *Danmarks Folkesagn*, II. 35.
[2] *Verbrennen d. Leichen*, Kl. Schr. II. 308.

than were the old Saxons and Frisians when they
turned from burning to burying." Müllenhoff[1] says
that "the Frisian legends, especially those of the
islands, show a certain melancholy "; and all of their
witch stories and superstitions were more terrible
and demonic than those of the mainland. Long-
fellow rendered into English some Anglo-Saxon
verses which he called *The Grave ;* and made special
mention[2] of the " Debate between the Soul and the
Body," of which he translated a few lines.[3] Persons
familiar with our old poetry — such as that fine fragment called *The Ruin,* or *The Wanderer,* — will
recall a dozen elegiac passages all more or less
based on the contemplation of death and decay. The
somewhat obscure passage in *Béowulf,* which seems
to describe a sort of self-burial, is in point.[4] An old
man, the last of his race, fashions or finds a burial-
place in a cave among the rocks, and carries into it
all the treasure which once delighted his kinsmen.
Then he chants his farewell to the splendors of
life : —

"Now hold thou, earth, since heroes may not,
what earls have owned! Lo, erst from thee
brave men brought it! But battle-death seized
and cruel killing my clansmen all,
robbed them of life and a liegeman's joys.
None have I left to lift the sword,
or to cleanse the carven cup of price,
beaker bright. My brave are gone.

[1] Introduction to *Sagen . . . von Schleswig-Holstein,* etc. p. liii.
[2] In his *Poets and Poetry of Europe.*
[3] Wülker, *Grundriss d. ags. Lit.* p. 74.
[4] See Bugge in P. B. *Beit.* 12. 370. *Béow.* 2233 ff.

And the helmet hard, all haughty with gold,
shall part from its plating. Polishers sleep
who could brighten and burnish the battle-mask;
and those weeds of war that were wont to brave
over bicker of shields the bite of steel
rust with their bearer. The ringéd mail
fares not far with famous chieftain,
at side of hero! No harp's delight,
no glee-wood's gladness! No good hawk now
flies through the hall! Nor horses fleet
stamp in the burgstead! Battle and death
the flower of my race have reft away."

So the last of his clan. This elegiac mood has been
attributed by a German critic,[1] not to the tendency
of the race itself, but rather to the softening influences of Christianity. This seems to be a surface-
criticism; melancholy of some sort is inherent in the
Germanic temperament, and a sheer ferocity of the
Viking or even Berserker type is not enough to offset
the countless examples of the elegiac and pathetic
in our oldest literature. Thus the "dying with a
laugh" of Scandinavian heroes is not necessarily
opposed to a melancholy habit of mind. There are
laughs and laughs.

The funeral-ceremony was accompanied by games,
feasting, and sacrifices; and these might well be continued for some time. The act of taking formal possession of one's patrimony was probably connected with
these rites; and Sir Henry Maine[2] speaks of that
"close relation between succession to property after
death and the performance of some sort of sacrificial
rites in honor of the deceased." At the Scandina-

[1] Heinzel, *über den Stil. d. altgerm. Poesie*, Strasburg, 1875.
[2] *Early Law and Custom*, p. 78. *Cf.* also his *Ancient Law*, p. 191.

viar funeral-feast, the heir sat on a bench near the
high-seat[1] until the Bragi-beaker was brought to him.
Then he rose, drank, made certain vows, and thereupon took his father's seat, by this act entering on his
inheritance and becoming head of his family. Games
at the funeral are of very ancient record; their funda-
mental purpose was a common amusement for the
spirit of the dead man and his living kinsmen, since
he was thought to eat, drink, and make merry with
the survivors. Feats of horsemanship are favorite
forms of this merry-making. A sailor, Wulfstan,
told King Alfred of some odd customs which the
Esthonians of his time observed at funerals. They
feast a long time in the dead man's home, burn his
body finally, and then carry all his property from the
house and arrange it in several heaps along a considerable distance, the largest heap being farthest from
the house. Then all the men ride as swiftly as possible towards the different heaps; the fastest rider
naturally gets the largest amount. This must have
added terrors to death for all the kinsfolk, and certainly rendered superfluous any ceremonies of entering on the inheritance.[2] We hear of games at the
grave of Attila, and Jordanes describes them briefly.[3]
In the midst of the plain and under silken tents they
placed Attila's body, and celebrated certain remarkable games (*spectaculum*). The best horsemen chosen
from the entire race of the Huns rode, after the
fashion of the circus, about the place where he lay in

[1] *Cf.* above, p. 106.

[2] Voyages of Ohthere and Wulfstan, inserted in Alfred's *Orosius.*

[3] "Pauca de multis dicere." See Jord. *de orig. act. Getarum,* ed.
Holder, c. 49.

state, and glorified his deeds in a funeral-song, somewhat like the following: "Attila, mighty king of Huns, son of Mundzuccas, lord of the bravest races, who hath ruled alone with power unheard before the realms of Scythia and Germany, and with taking of states and cities hath terrified both the empires! Then lest everything should fall a prey to the enemy, was he moved by prayer to accept a yearly tribute. When finally he had happily done all these things, it was not the wound of a foe, not the treachery of a kinsman, but joyful in the joy of his people, and without a pang, that he fell in death. Who, then, could call that a decease,[1] which no one thinks of avenging?"

Compare with this the account of Béowulf's funeral: —[2]

> Then the bairn of Weohstan bade command,
> hardy chief, to heroes many
> that owned their homesteads, hither to bring
> firewood from far — o'er the folk they ruled —
> for the famed-one's funeral. "Fire shall devour
> and wan flames feed on the fearless warrior
> who oft stood stout in the iron-shower,
> when, sped from the string, a storm of arrows
> shot o'er the shield-wall: the shaft held firm,
> featly feathered, followed the barb."
>
> *   *   *   *   *   *
>
> Then the woven gold on a wain was laden —
> countless quite! — and the king was borne,
> hoary hero, to Hron ës-Ness.[3]
> Then fashioned for him the folk of Geats
> firm on the earth a funeral-pile,
> and hung it with helmets and harness of war
> and breastplates bright, as the boon he asked;

---

[1] *Exitum.*   [2] 3110 ff.   [3] *Hron* = whale.

and they laid amid it the mighty chieftain,
heroes mourning their master dear.
Then on the hill that hugest of balefires
the warriors wakened.[1] Wood-smoke rose
black over the blaze, and blent was the roar
of flame with weeping (the wind was still),[2]
till the fire had broken the frame of bones,
hot at the heart. In heavy mood
their misery moaned they, their master's death.
Wailing her woe, the widow old . . .[3]

    *   *   *   *   *   *

The folk of the Weders fashioned there
on the headland a barrow broad and high,
by ocean-farers far descried:
in ten days' time their toil had raised it,
the battle-brave's beacon. Round brands of the pyre
a wall they built, the worthiest ever
that wit could prompt in their wisest men.
They placed in the barrow that precious booty,
the rounds and the rings they had reft erewhile,
hardy heroes, from hoard in cave, —
trusting the ground with treasure of earls,
gold in the earth, where ever it lies
useless to men as of yore it was.
Then about that barrow the battle-keen rode,
atheling-born, a band of twelve,
lament to make, to mourn their king,
chant their dirge, and their chieftain honor.
They praised his earlship, his acts of prowess
worthily witnessed; and well it is
that men their master-friend mightily laud,
heartily love, when hence he goes
from life in the body forlorn away.

[1] A favorite trope in A.-S.; here = "kindle," "fan into flame."
[2] Another reading: —

> roaring played,
> mingled with weeping of winds, the flame.

[3] The text is very difficult here, on account of defects in the Ms.

Thus made their mourning the men of Geatland,
for their hero's passing his hearth-companions:
quoth that of all the kings of earth,
of men he was mildest and most belovéd,
to his kin the kindest, keenest for praise.

No one can fail to see the likeness between this burial of Béowulf and the ceremonies at the funeral of Attila.

The whole logic of the primitive funeral was based on a supposition that the spirit sundered from the body lived after death. The grave is a house, — eorðhûs. "Immortality," if we may use such an expression, was assumed without question and lies fossil-like in ancient speech. Phrases like "faring to another light," found plentifully in Anglo-Saxon and Old Norse, are of heathen origin, and must not be referred to theology of later times.[1] Gudrun says she is fain to go to another light;[2] and in Béowulf, one "gave up the joyous life of men, he chose God's light." The phrase is here lightly touched with the new theology, but is of far older origin. Even the Hêliand clings to ancient expression and the simpler form: sôkian lioht ôðar, to seek the other light. Other kennings for death are significant, as "to go" — from world, body, house, hall, "to go" forth or hence, "to seek the joyless place," "to part soul and body." Of a certain prince we are told, "his father had gone elsewhere." Death is called "the journey," "the miserable journey," or "the parting of the soul." Sometimes the body is

[1] For lists, see Bode, Kenningar; and Vilmar, Altert. im Hêliand, p. 20, note 2.

[2] Atlamâl, 87, 4 (ed. Neckel, p. 254); Bellows, p. 529, st. 82.

regarded as a garment which man doffs at death.[1] The
summons to depart comes "at the hour of fate"; then
it was that old Scyld fared forth. The Viking heroes
of Scandinavia expected the fixed moment of Odin's
choosing; and the word "fey," still known in Scotland, was once the commonest of Germanic words.
"There die," says a character in the Nibelungen
Lay, "only the doomed ones," — *ez sterbent wan die
veigen.* "Danger (a pit, abyss) is everywhere for
the doomed one," is a Norse parallel.[2] This combination of the sense of fatalism with implicit belief
in a future life leads, we all know, to the highest
conditions of bravery and contempt for death; and,
indeed, it takes us quite away from the realm of
daily Germanic custom. Across the border-land of
the funeral, we come into the wide domain of religion.

[1] Here we may compare the swan-raiment of wise women and the
belief in werewolves. See Mannhardt, *Germ. Mythen,* p. 692.

[2] *Fafnismál,* 11 (ed. Neckel, p. 178); Bellows, p. 375.

CHAPTER XII

THE WORSHIP OF THE DEAD

Germanic religion in general — Cult and creed — Heathen scepticism — Agreement of old and new faiths — Cult of ancestors, and superstitions about the dead — Survivals — All Souls — Swiss customs — Heathen rites made Christian — The patron-saint and the *fylgja*.

RELIGION in general has two sides, the cult and the creed. Primarily, the cult is a series of ceremonial acts, rather than a system of what we should call worship; and the creed is not so much a logical statement of belief as a record or tradition, which, nowhere definitely set down, finds expression in a number of more or less coherent tales about supernatural persons and supernatural experiences. Or, we may put the dualism in a different fashion. Religion rests upon ethics and emotion. In its primitive stages the ethical phase is entirely occupied by a sense of duty to demonic powers, — a slavish sense of duty as to a master who must be obeyed in fear and trembling; and the emotion is wholly a sense of wonder at inexplicable facts and processes, mainly of the physical universe, which spur the fancy to express the superhuman in terms of the human, and in the shape which we call a myth. That is, myths are

a series of compromises between the tendency to pro-
ject personality into all operations of nature, and the
tendency to seek such a cause for these operations as
shall be wholly free from observed human impotence.
The history of cult and ceremonial religion traces the
development of an ethical sense, from physical offering and sacrifice through symbolical rites up to the
notion of duty to one's fellows as the outcome of
duty to one's God. The history of religious emotion,
on the other hand, is for all early stages a part of the
history of poetry,[1] and must chronicle the attempts
of the human mind to set in order and realize its
sense of wonder at the supernatural. The realization
of this sense of wonder is expressed in the myth,
and a series of myths may foster a primitive creed.[2]
From both of these great religious factors, the ceremony and the myth, constantly there slips and escapes the living faith which gives them being. But,
notwithstanding this loss of vitality, myth and rite
remain firm, and form a part of traditional religion.
Long after the living sense for a myth, or the tangi-
ble belief in a divinity, has lapsed from people's mind,
the cult and creed survive, and men go through form
after form, careless of the reason, but tenacious of
the ancient rite. It is evident, however, that the
work of destruction or indifference is far more swift
with creed than with ceremony. Creed is a garment
which one may hold more or less dear, but not refuse to discard; cult is the habitual round of one's

---

[1] *Quellen u. Forschungen*, No. 51, Müllenhoff's preface to Mannhardt's *Mythol. Forsch.* p. viii. f.

[2] Rationalistic elements enter very early into the making of myths,
as where a story is told to explain what has hitherto passed as inexplicable.

life which one easily identifies with life itself. It follows, therefore, that in an early stage of the decline of a great religious system we should find the creed uncertain and easily uprooted, the cult still vigorous and tenacious of its place.

Precisely in such a condition we find the heathenism of the Germanic race at the time of its early contact with Rome and Christianity; and precisely for these causes we can understand the ease with which Christian doctrines, allied with the new culture and the new lore which so dazzled our forefathers, battered down what ought to have been stubborn barriers of inherited Germanic belief. With admirable discretion, the early missionaries made their main assault on the belief, and left the custom and ceremony to be undermined by slow siege, or driven away by strategy.[1] Pope Gregory laid down this admirable system in his advice to certain preachers of the new faith in heathen England; and urged in all possible cases a toleration of old rites or else a gentle wresting of them into Christian uses.[2] If the heathen have been sacrificing oxen to their idols and holding feasts, let the oxen still be slaughtered, the

[1] This policy was not always adopted. The missionaries who, in the eighth century, sought to convert the Frisians and Saxons, were extremely violent in their methods, and began their work by abrupt attack upon the dearest heathen sanctities. See von Richthofen, *Friesische Rechtsgesch.* II. 411 ff. He contrasts all this with the mild conversion of Iceland.

[2] Beda, *Hist. Ecc.* I. 30 (ed. Holder). This chapter is of great importance for the subject. See specially the passage: "... fana idolorum destrui ... minime debeant; sed ipsa, quæ in eis sunt, idola destruantur; aqua benedicta fiat, in eisdem fanis aspergatur, altaria construantur, reliquiæ ponantur." As a result, the new church bore in many cases close resemblance to the heathen temple. For Scandinavia, see Henry Petersen, *Om Nordboernes Gudedyrkelse og Gudetro i Hedenold*, p. 22.

feasts still be held, *nec diabolo . . . sed ad laudem dei.* " Concentrate your attack," said, in effect, the wise pope, " upon the false gods[1] and the false belief: deal tenderly with immemorial customs. Destroy the idols, but spare the altars and the temple." Precisely in this strain, Remigius laid his famous command upon the just converted king of the Franks: " Adore what thou hast burnt! Burn what thou hast adored!"

The attack upon heathen divinities was made yet easier by a certain spirit of doubt which had begun to affect the Germanic mind itself. Thoughtful souls were reaching after something better than the worn-out tales of a rude mythology, and daring souls had flung all faith aside. Our best view of a race on this border between an old and a new religion is in Scandinavia. Many a hard-headed Norseman mocked at the old-wives' tales of the Edda, and snapped his huge Viking fingers at an Odin or a Thor. At Throndhjem in the days of Hakon Jarl, Svend, a worshipper of Thor, pleaded with his son Finn, who had insulted the ancestral god. Thor, urged Svend, had crushed the rocks and fared through the mountains; Odin gave victory. " It is no great matter," answered Finn, " to break up stones or to conquer by witchcraft. He is the mighty god who has first of all created hill and sky and sea."[2] The Icelander

---

[1] The debate between Frankish Cloyis and his Christian wife hinges on the true or false nature of the heathen gods (where the tirade against Jupiter and the others is, of course, mere monkish invention). And very significant is the king's remark about the Christian deity: " He is not even of our race of gods!" See *Greg. Tur.* II. 29, and Rettberg, *Kirchengeschichte Deutschlands*, I. 273.

[2] P. E. Müller, *Sagabibliothek*, III. 322.

Thorkell, as his end drew near, commended his soul
"to him that created the sun."[1]   Men turned in
disgust from the rout of weak or knavish gods.   In
the saga of Hrolf Kraki, we are told that King Hrolf
and his men honored no gods, but trusted in their
own might.[2] "Not Odin," cries another, "but chance
rules over the life of man."   "I am an old man,"
urged Ketil; "see how long I have lived, and yet
I have never honored Odin."   Down at Byzantium,
a sturdy heathen Icelander was asked by the Greek
emperor in whom, then, he believed. "In myself,"
was the reply.   Hrafnkel says, "I hold it folly to believe in gods."   Among Anglo-Saxons, the very min-
isters of the old faith stood ready to welcome the
new. We all know Beda's two stories, one of Coifi,
the high-priest, who rode spear in hand to shatter the
temple of his own gods; the other, of that old Northumbrian counsellor who told his king that since life
was but as a bird's flight through their own warm and
lighted hall, in from the darkness and out into the
darkness, — since their own faith had nothing to say
of that outer dark, let them welcome the new faith
which could.   Energy of fresh and high belief overwhelmed half-hearted followers of custom.   When
Christian and heathen were contending in Iceland
what religion the whole nation should adopt, the
heathens proposed to sacrifice eight men to the gods.
The Christians answered by calling on the same number of men to take the vows of a pure life, — a pro-
posal accepted at once by the adherents of the new

[1] W. Müller, *Geschichte u. System d. altdeutschen Religion* (henceforth *System*), p. 100.

[2] See Dahn, *Bausteine*, I. 133–135, where many examples are given.

faith, while on the heathen side no volunteers whatever could be found.[1]

Christian dogma had an easy victory. It was a
compact and logical system elaborated by the subtlest
intellects of the time, and it swept the loose array
of myths and traditions from the field. But the old
rites, the old ceremonies, and even the shadowy forms
of old gods and goddesses, so far as they had been
connected with cult, lived on. The rout of spirits
and demons, with a slight change by way of adapta-
tion to the new creed, were undisturbed, and held
their old places in fireside tradition and fireside cult.
On certain homely occasions even the great divinities
of heathendom could be invoked. Says J. Grimm:[2]
"People who held in strictness all the Christian
creed and were ready to persecute and damn the
doubter about trinitarian dogmas or the sinner who
broke a fast, had no scruples in time of bodily disease, even if only a finger was hurt, to recite incantations in which the old gods were called upon for
help." Even in the seventeenth century, a Scandinavian toothache was best banned by a direct appeal,
and even a sort of sacrifice, to Thor. Moreover,
there were many instances where men endeavored to
serve at once the old gods and the new faith; such
was the case with Æthelbert of Kent, who allowed
images of heathen deities to stand by the Christian
altars.[3] In Frankish Germany, during the eighth
century, we hear of priests who sacrifice to Wuotan
(Woden), attend the heathen feasts, and yet profess

[1] Vigfusson-Powell, *C. P. B.* I. 140, and references.
[2] *Ueber Marcellus Burdigalensis*, Kl. Schr. II. 115.
[3] Grimm, *D. M.*[4] III. 7.

themselves Christians and administer the rite of baptism.[1] Again, the new religion had yet another ally in addition to the waning belief of heathendom. There were articles of faith in the old creed which substantially agreed with important tenets of the new.[2] The church assured and defined that vague but insistent belief in personal immortality which is common to half-civilized men the world over; it emphasized the sense of horror, felt as strongly by the barbarian as by Milton,[3] at the thought of a human soul going out like a candle-flame in the dark. The soldiers of Ariovistus fought with such desperate courage, explained the Roman historian, because they knew death to be a mere transition to another life. This, of course, is no Germanic peculiarity. The Celtic druids held so strongly to the notion of immortality that they actually contracted debts which were to be paid in the next world.[4] Often at a Celtic banquet, when the mirth grew dull, some accommodating young warrior would kill himself in novel or artistic fashion to divert the guests; it was only a step into another group, where with old comrades he could wait — in those days, not very long — for the rest of

---

[1] See Rettberg, I. 326.

[2] Rettberg, I. 247 f., remarks that ethical tendencies of our heathendom, the high value set on chastity and certain forms of justice, would welcome analogous tendencies, more sharply outlined, of the new religion.

[3] *Paradise Lost*, II. 146:

> To be no more: sad cure; for who would lose,
> Though full of pain, this intellectual being,
> Those thoughts that wander through eternity,
> To perish rather, swallowed up and lost
> In the wide womb of uncreated night,
> Devoid of sense and motion ?

[4] Cæsar *B. G.* VI. 14, and Holtzmann, *Deutsche Mythol.* p. 196.

the company. These same Celts sold themselves to
be killed, for a sum of money, or even for a few
casks of wine.[1] This is crude fatalism; and we must
admit that the church vigorously opposed such a
phase of the belief in immortality: our own English
Ælfric, for example, is eloquent against it. But the
more general notion of immortality was fixed in the
heathen mind; the new religion individualized, en-
nobled, and confirmed the faith. To put it briefly,
Christianity forbade that a man's future should be
merged, after the heathen fashion, in the future of
his family or clan; it treated him as an individual
and mediated directly between him and God. This
personal religion began by slow degrees to take its
place in the midst of collective and ceremonial religion; and thus arose that great modern fact which
we call sentiment. Contrast the ceremonial worship
of a heathen clan with the personal sentiment of a
mediæval hymn! Contrast the chorus, the feast,
the wide pagan publicity of worship (and the church
took care to preserve a plenty of this element) with
the direct and piercing individualism of the monk
who in his solitary fervor poured out such words as
these: —

> O Deus, ego amo te! . . .
> Tu, tu, mi Jesu, totum me
> Amplexus es in cruce,
> Tulisti . . .
> Innumeros dolores,
> Sudores et angores,
> Et mortem et hæc propter me,
> Ah! pro me peccatore!

State and family religion, with the head of state

[1] See Mommsen, *Rome*, Dickson's transl. p. 277.

or family as priest, yielded ground to the personal
expression of awe, of reverence, of love; the mere
sense of conduct, modern writers would say, became the sense of conduct touched by emotion.
From our notion of primitive religion, and especially
of Germanic heathendom, we must take pains to
clear away this element of emotion which we are
so apt to regard as the chief part of religion itself.
Where to seek the beginnings of sentiment as a
factor in domestic, social, or religious life, is a difficult problem; but recent writers agree that it is
foreign to primitive races, and even that it is a result,
not a cause of culture. Certainly the church did
much to spread it over rough mediæval life; everywhere we find her ritual touching ancient custom
with this new grace of emotion. The old perfunc-
tory service to the dead, the journey to a burial-place,
and the food or treasure heaped upon an ancestor's
grave, became a memorial service and a wreath of
flowers; the act, once all in all, became a symbol,
for modern worship places or professes to place
more weight on the spirit than on the act. "The
kingdom of God is within you." It is therefore
necessary to put aside our modern notion of worship when we come to examine the religion of
the early Germans. We have seen that a certain
scepticism about the tales of their mythology, a certain familiarity with prominent parts of the new
doctrine, made them comparatively docile converts
to a new faith; but what we most need to consider
is the nature of their actual cult. the observance of
their practical religion, as compared with the pomp
and ritual of Rome. How much of this pomp was

forced upon the church in place of the earlier simplicity of apostolic times, is an open question. Not only the ceremonies incident to a state religion brought about the change; the barbaric races, soon to be the great props of the church, were incapable of any worship which scorned external helps and which needed only the fervor of the heart. Hence the accommodation to heathen custom, the feasts, the saints'-days; hence all the external attractions, and the subsequent enlisting of every art from music to the drama.

It is evident from the foregoing considerations that the one religious element which entered into the life of our forefathers was the round of ceremonies and observances, the cult. Myths belong elsewhere, and are a part of Germanic literature, of Germanic poetry. In these pages we are concerned with the cult, and shall appeal to mythology only so far as it throws light upon the history of Germanic ceremony and superstition.

A form of worship found in all low grades of culture, and existing everywhere in more or less obvious survival, is the worship of the dead.[1]   A favorite with writers on anthropology, this territory has been heretofore greatly neglected by the mythologists. At present, however, it is getting more and more attention, and must be recognized as one of the most important divisions in the study of religious develop-

---

[1] For the sources of our information about Germanic worship, see Grimm, *D. M.*,[4] *Vorrede*, Bd. II., especially pp. x. ff.; and E. Mogk in Paul's *Grundriss*[2], III, 233 ff., and the same article, pp. 249 ff., for the special subject of this chapter and references.

ment.[1] We may in the main accept for Germanic
people generally the statement of Vigfusson and
Powell, with regard to Scandinavian antiquity, that
" the habitual and household worship of ancestors "
was " the main cult of the older religion." [2]

This worship of the dead we shall assume as a definite fact in primitive culture, and shall make little
inquiry in regard to its origin.[3] The dead were
thought to lead as spirits an existence which closely
resembled actual life; as head of a family, the dead
man exacted tribute from his surviving children and
grandchildren; they continued to obey his supposed
demands, and perhaps ascribed petty but mysterious
ailments to his anger at neglected duty. At least,
we have the well-known modern instance of an African
chief who suddenly took leave of his white guest, saying that since his head ached violently, he knew that
his dead father was scolding him, and he must hasten
to offer something to the angry spirit. A regular cult

[1] E. H. Meyer formally incorporates it in his system of mythology
(*Indogermanische Mythen*, I. 1883; II. 1887). Holtzmann recognized
it, cautiously enough, saying that a material part of the old heathen
religion was worship and service of ancestors. Perhaps, he adds, " it
was harder for the church to suppress this sort of worship than the
worship of the gods " (*Deutsche Myth.* p. 202). He had leaned to the
same opinion in his *Germanische Alterthümer*. Vigfusson and Powell
assert the fondness of Scandinavians for this manes-cult, and cite the
testimony of Jordanes for its popularity among the Goths; ancestors
of the royal Gothic house were *Anses*, — " not men, but demigods," —
who were worshipped by their descendants. J. Grimm himself collects
abundant material in regard to the survivals and traditions of such
worship. See especially Chap. XXXI. of the *Mythology*.

[2] *C. P. B.* I. 413.

[3] Ample material in Spencer, *Sociology*; Tylor, *Primitive Culture*
and *Early History of Mankind*; Lippert, *Culturgeschichte*, etc. For
an opposing theory, see the introduction (by J. S. Stuart-Glennie, M.A.)
to Lucy M. Garnett's *The Women of Turkey and Their Folk-Lore:
The Christian Women*, London and New York, 1890.

of the dead is one of the stubbornest facts of human history, and in the refined form of "Spiritualism" counts thousands and thousands of votaries to-day. In its grosser manifestations, it was contrary to the teachings of Christianity, and hence our best information in regard to a Germanic spirit-cult is to be found in the various edicts and regulations of the early church. The canons of Eadgar [1] forbid swearing or bewitching *by means of the dead; licwȋgelung* is evidently the same as necromancy; and proof that this ban was needed may be found in an old interpretation of dreams, — taken, of course, from the Latin, but current and approved in Anglo-Saxon popular lore, — which tells us that it is a token of good fortune to talk with the dead.[2] "If [one] dreams that he kisses a dead man, that is good and long life." [3] That the neighborhood of sepulchres hallowed a place and made it likely to prosper, was a widespread belief. An Anglo-Saxon charm or incantation, one of several for the use of women in pregnancy, opens with the following directions: "The woman who cannot bring forth her child should go to a dead man's grave (*birgenne*), and step thrice over the grave and speak then these words. . . ." And further on in the same charm (v. 15), we have the efficacy of the "barrow" or sepulchre more directly attested.[4] So, too, there seems to have been at Anglo-Saxon funerals more or less heathen ceremony which pointed directly to the wor-

[1] Thorpe, *Ancient Laws and Institutes*, p. 397.
[2] " Mid déadum spellian [sprecan] gestrion hit getácnað." Cockayne, *Leechdoms*, III. 202; twice on the page.
[3] Ibid. III. 174, 208.
[4] *Journ. Amer. Folk-Lore*, XXII (1909), 207 (E. 1).

ship of the dead. Ælfric tells [1] the priests of his time
not to go to funerals unless invited, a praiseworthy
but commonplace piece of advice; then, however,
adds that if they do go, they are to forbid "the
heathen songs of the laity (*lœwedra*) and their loud
laughter," and not to eat nor drink where the corpse
is lying; this he commands in order that good church-
men shall not imitate heathen ways. Further,[2] the
Indiculus Superstitionum et Paganiarum, referring to
the continental Saxons and dating from the year 743,
speaks first of all *de sacrilegio ad sepulchra mortuorum*
and *de sacrilegio super defunctos, id est,* "dadsisas," —
of sacrilege at the graves of the dead, and of sacrilege
over dead persons; that is, *dadsisas*. This last word
is explained by Grimm [3] as a " song of lament for the
dead "; and that it was not a mere funeral-song as
we understand the phrase, but rather belonged with
offerings and sacrificial rites to the dead, is made
probable by the urgent opposition of the church. In
the Anglo-Saxon Confessional of Ecgberht it is provided that "whosoever in the place where a man lies
dead shall burn corn for the good of living persons
and in his house,[4] shall fast five winters." The corn
was burnt for the benefit of the dead man, who would
for this reason look with favor upon the survivors.
Again and again the church forbids these offerings
and songs and other ceremonies in connection with

[1] Thorpe, *Ancient Laws and Institutes*, p. 448. Most of the older
literature on this subject was collected by Bouterwek in the introduction to his *Cædmon*.

[2] See *D. M.*[4] III. 403 ff.; also p. 406 f., extract from Burchard of
Worms, 10. 10; 10. 34; etc.   [3] Grimm, *D. M.*[4] I. 1027.

[4] As Bouterwek (*Cædmon*, p. lxxxvii.) notes, the Latin text reads
"pro sanitate viventium *et domus*."

the dead;[1] and there can be no doubt that it was a matter of worship rather than of ordinary grief. The Anglo-Saxon barrow-song or lyke-song[2] was no mere threnody. People prayed by night, standing at the ancient places of burial; originally the prayers were to the dead, but, no doubt, in course of time were directed to gods or demigods of tradition, for whom the grave-stone served as an altar.

Popular faith had little to do with abstractions; and when the dead were addressed in prayer, they were thought to be personally involved in a palpable and questionable shape. Hence the many spells or incantations to raise the dead and bid them open mysteries of the present or the future. Hence the Old Norse *valgaldr*, a charm or incantation meant to awaken the sleeper from his heavy death-slumber; in particular, it is a spell by which Odin forces the sibyl to rise from her grave and foretell the fate of Balder.[3] "On Woden rode . . . till he came to the lofty hall of Hell, then Woden rode to its eastern gate where he knew the sibyl's barrow stood. He fell to chanting the mighty spells that move the dead (*valgaldr*), till she rose all unwilling and her corpse spake." Schullerus[4] cites a similar case in Saxo Grammaticus, where Hadingus wishes to ascertain particulars of his own fate, and compels a dead man to give the required information; bits of wood are

[1] Christian priests took part in them, to the great scandal of the church. Rettberg, I. 326.

[2] *Byrgensang; licsang.* See also *D. M.*[4] I. 1027 f.

[3] *Vegtamskviða,* called by Vigfusson and Powell *Balder's Doom, C. P. B.* I. 182. The translation, used here, always gives the English form of the names, as Woden for Odin. [4] P.-B. *Beit.* XII. 236, note.

laid under his tongue, a device which reminds us somewhat of the miracle told in Chaucer's *Prioresses Tale*, and the corpse thereupon begins to speak. Of course, *dira carmina*, runes and incantations. are written on these fragments. In another Old Norse poem,[1] the disguised Odin says that he learned his sharp words from the old people who live "*in the home-graves.*"[2] Everywhere in the old Scandinavian life we find traces of this direct worship of the dead; sacrifices were made to them in order to insure good crops, and the ceremony was conducted by the head of the family among the ancestral graves.[3] Authr was a rich woman who had embraced the new faith; but when she was dead and buried in a certain mountain, her descendants, who kept their heathendom, made an altar there and brought sacrifice, and believed that all of Authr's kin would gather after death within this mountain.[4] It is easy, as many scholars have pointed out, to see the connection between this worship of ancestral dead near the cave or hill in which they are buried, and the countless myths and legends which tell of a prince or chieftain who "'sleeps" in a mountain, and will one day ride forth to conquest.[5] The sacrificial feast at an ancestral grave lingered long in survival. In the Prologue to the *Canterbury Tales*,[6] we are told that certain craftsmen had so prospered in the world that they were fit to be aldermen; and

---

[1] *Harbarðslj.* 44.

[2] Reading *haugum* with Hollander and Bellows vs. *skógum* with Neckel; see p. 314, note 2, above.

[3] *C. P. B.* I. 413 ff.　　　　[4] *Landnáma Isl.* S. I.

[5] Mogk's protest (Paul's *Grundriss*[2], III, 257) against the custom of regarding all these legends as so many Woden myths is surely well founded.　　　　[6] v. 375 ff.

to this dignity their wives would surely make no objection, for —

> It is ful fair to been ycleped *Madame*,
> And goon to vigilies al bifore,
> And have a mantel roialliche ybore.

Precedence, a matter of old tradition evidently, obtained at the *vigilies*, that is, the meetings of the parishioners "in their church-houses or church-yards, where they were wont to have a drinking-fit for the time," and where "they used to end many quarrels between neighbor and neighbor." In 1638, "one of the Suffolk articles of inquiry was: 'Have any *Playes, Feasts, Banquets, Suppers, Church Ales, Drinkings, Temporal Courts* or *Leets, Lay Juries, Musters, Exercise of Dancing, Stoole ball, Foot ball*, or the like, or any other profane usage been suffered to be kept in your Church, Chappell or Church Yard?'"[1] It is easy to see the connection with ancient rites. Dancing in graveyards gave frequent scandal in England; and we shall presently see the same survival in the rites of burial.

Recurring to the actual worship of the dead, we find testimony in Beda,[2] who, speaking of the several months, says that February, called *solmonath*, is the "month of *cakes*," which at this time were offered by the heathen to their gods;[3] whereupon Holtzmann remarks that for "gods" we should probably read "spirits" — *manibus*.[4] These offerings were made

---

[1] Brand, "Churchyards."   [2] *De temp. rat.* c. 15.

[3] "Solmonath dici potest mensis placentarum quas in eo dis suis offerebant." See also Grimm, *G. D. S.* p. 77, who approves Beda's etymology.

[4] *D. M.* (Holtzmann) p. 202. "Die Götter sind die Vorfahren."

at the graves, which then as now were marked by stones; church edicts keep forbidding laymen to make sacrifice "at stones." *Kristnisaga* tells of a bishop who sang Christian spells over a stone where the "family spirit" was thought to dwell; at last the piety of the prelate had its reward, and the stone burst asunder.[1]

The dead were supposed to abide either in the immediate tomb or else in that vast realm which is only the infinite projection of the tomb, the so-called underworld or domain of hell. So that the inmate, when conjured to appear, may make immediate appearance, or else come as from a long journey. When Odin's strong charm conjures up the sibyl, she complains: "What mortal is it . . . that hath put me to this weary journey? I have been snowed on with the snow, I have been beaten with the rain, I have been drenched with the dew, long have I been dead."[2] Similarly, Helgi's appearance is described by Sigrun, when she meets him at the barrow. We are justified in assuming with Schullerus that the grave is in the closest connection with Hel's cold and dreary dominions.[3] Mostly, however, the dead are conceived to be close at hand, resting in the narrow cell or invisibly haunting the scenes of their active life.[4] Significant perhaps in this regard is the saying of Tacitus about Germanic sepulchres,[5] that no monuments are raised above them because such would be too heavy for the departed;[6] it may be, however, only a piece of Tacitean

---

[1] *C. P. B.* I. 416.
[2] *Balder's Dream*, *C.P.B.*, I, 182; Hollander, p. 137, Bellows, p. 197.
[3] *Zur Kritik d. Valhollglaubens*, P.-B. *Beit.* XII. 238.
[4] Material for Scandinavian belief, *C. P. B.* I. 415 f.
[5] *Germ.* XXVII.   [6] Ut gravem defunctis.

rhetoric, with chief application to the pomp of Roman burial. Certainly the dead were thought to continue their existence in the tomb, and hence we find the earliest barrow built in the shape of a house, where the body or even the ashes of the old freeman could still find a home. The Viking who lived on the sea was fain to have a ship-tomb. If we may believe many writers on sociology, the temple of worship is merely a development of the house built over the dead, where the altar represents the sepulchre itself.

The custom of carrying food to graves and of eating near them, is a survival of the greater banquets and sacrificial ceremonies at the tomb, where the dead and the living were supposed to share the feast. Drinking with the dead became drinking to the dead; hence the Roman libation and our modern silent toast, known in olden times as the Minne Drink. "At the burial of a [Scandinavian] king, a beaker was presented which was called Bragafull; every one present arose, made a solemn vow and emptied it. . . . This custom was not given up at the conversion, but one drank the *minne* of Christ or of Mary or of one of the saints."[1] *Minne* is "loving memory." The *erfi* or wake in Old Norse times was a most important affair, and we read of guests to the number of fourteen hundred; while in England the *arval* or *arvil* was kept up until comparatively modern times, with such outlay for food and drink that "it cost less to portion off a daughter than to bury a dead wife."[2] Jordanes tells of the endless feasting and drinking of the Huns at the burial of Attila, a ceremony which was called

[1] Grimm, *D. M.*[4] 48 f. See also Tylor, *Primitive Culture*, I. 96, and references.   [2] Brand, "Funeral Entertainments."

strava.[1] Moreover, the games which were celebrated
at the funeral of an important personage seemed to
have been meant in the earliest times as an affair in
which the dead man took actual part. For some reason these feasts and games were specially forbidden
by clerical authorities; but an easy compensation
was offered in a custom which amounted to little less
than actual worship of the dead, — the saints'-days
celebrated by the church. " All Souls " is a significant name. A general feast, which we may take to
have been in honor of the dead, was held by the
ancient Germans, and is mentioned by Widukind,
abbot of the monastery at Corvey on the Weser, who
about 980 wrote a history of the (continental) Saxons.
" Thereupon [2] for three days they held their feast of
victory, shared the booty, paid the wonted military
honors to their slain companions, and praised unmeas-
uredly the courage of their general. . . . Now all
this happened, as runs the tradition of our forefathers,
on the first of October, and these heathen festivals
have been changed by the consecration of pious men,
into fasting and prayer and offerings for all departed
Christian souls." [3] There can be no doubt that Widukind's story deals with no isolated event, but with an
immemorial Germanic rite.

This time-honored and doubtless precious ceremony
of Germanic heathendom the church accepted with
but slight modification. It was called the feast of
All Souls, and was placed, not far from its old date,
on the second day of November; autumn is the

[1] Jordan. XLIX.

[2] After a great victory over the Thuringians in the sixth century.

[3] Widukind (in *Geschichtschreiber d. deutsch. Vorzeit*) I. 12. *Cf.*
also W. Müller, *System*, p. 74.

proper season for any *memento mori*, and with the
equinoctial storms, the fall of leaf, the frost, the roar
of winds when Woden and his train of spirits sweep
the sky, man easily blends the universal picture of
decay and the remembrance of parted souls.[1] The
meaning of this All-Souls festival lingered long among
the peasants of modern Europe, and does not lack
analogy in older systems. Grimm[2] sees connection
between this feast, when people visit graveyards
and lay garlands on the tomb, and the three festal
days in Roman custom, when the underworld was
thought to open and the spirits to revisit upper air.
On the night of the second of November, the Esthonians set out food for the spirits; and near Dorpat,
souls of the departed are then received in the bath-
room and, one after the other, bathed. That the
church has so purged away the grosser elements of
this festival and made it a memorial service, does
infinite credit to those who brought about the change;
and it reflects little honor on the Protestants to have
abolished it.[3]

Such universal worship of the dead reflected the
private and particular custom. Every hearthstone
was an altar, and the father of the family was its
priest. Wherever settled abodes were known, this
altar was hallowed, and in many cases the fire burned
there without intermission throughout the year. Here
lingered the ancestral spirits, protecting and helpful;
and here the head of the family offered to them food
and drink, asked their help, cast lots, and sang the

---

[1] See Pfannenschmidt, *Erntefeste*, p. 128, 165.   [2] *D. M.*[4] 761, note 1.
[3] It has been restored in the reformed church of Prussia and Saxony.
Pfannenschmidt, *Erntefeste*, p. 168.

incantation.   The great memorial feasts of the people
which Widukind describes were matched by the
private feasts of the different families.   The funeral
itself was only the first of a series of feasts; the
dead man took his place among the ancestral spirits,
and the survivors shared with him and his new asso-
ciates the food, the drink, the song, and the dance.
In the eighth century, popes were forced to forbid
the too outspoken heathen character of a popular
funeral, the "profana sacrilegia mortuorum." [1]   We
have seen Ælfric's advice to the priests of England
that they should not frequent funerals of this sort.
But the church was far too wise to undertake any
sweeping measure.   The old rites were forbidden so
far as the grosser heathen characteristics of them
were concerned, or were changed, when it was prac-
ticable, into petty ceremonies, or, finally, were permitted to endure in a lingering and for the most part
dwindling survival.   For English customs, the collection of Brand [2] gives ample material; and the
survivals of southern Germany and Switzerland have
been carefully studied by Rochholz. [3]   Whoever, in
Switzerland, has the duty of watching with a corpse,
must have unlimited supply of brandy and wine.
Prodigality and reckless expenditure prevail among
this otherwise economical and thrifty race so soon as
a funeral is concerned; they believe that any mean-
ness displayed at this time on the part of the heirs
will rob the dead man of his rest in the grave.   It is

---

[1] *Cf.* Pfannenschmidt, *Erntefeste*, p. 166; the pope is **Gregory III.** in
739.

[2] *Antiquities*, "Watching with the Dead."

[3] *Deutscher Glaube u. Brauch im Spiegel d. heidnischen Vorzeit*, I.
194 ff., 299 ff.

not hard to summon a host of parallel cases, from the
funeral of an Irish Romanist to-day, back to the peculiar ceremonies among the Finnish tribes described
to King Alfred by the sailor Wulfstan. During one
of these peasant funerals in Switzerland the bake-
oven in the house of death must not become cold for
the space of three days between decease and burial;
bread and cheese are free to all comers. Food of
this sort, thinks the peasant, gives far more strength
than does one's daily bread: an ounce goes as far
now as two pounds eaten at another time![1] A person known as the *Leidfrau* or mourning-woman is
charged with the main ceremonies; and cases[2] are
on record where a part of her duty was to offer bread,
salt, and wine to the spirits of the house, the ancestral
souls. Before the coffin is closed — we are still with
Rochholz's Swiss peasants — each member of the
family grasps in farewell the hand of the deceased.
During the actual bearing of the body to its last
resting-place, bread and wine are distributed. The
burial over, — and the corpse of the Christian peasant
like that of his heathen ancestor must be buried fac-
ing east, — there are thirty days of mourning; the
third, the seventh, and the thirtieth of these are celebrated by certain rites in the church. Every morning, however, the *Leidfrau* goes to mass; says thirty
pater-nosters at the grave on the first, and one less
each day during the month; and has numerous other
duties to perform, in return for which she has prescribed allowance of food and drink, a new garment,
and, above all, place at the funeral-feasts. These, as
Rochholz says, make the chief article of the Swiss

---

[1] Rochholz, p. 195.   [2] As late as 1860 in Servia.

peasant's luxury in life. Peasants of to-day still think
the more they eat and drink at a funeral, " the better
it is for the dead." Church and state have been trying
for a thousand years to reduce the size and cost of
these banquets; and here we see again the ethical
character of Christianity face to face with the merely
ceremonial nature of heathendom. The church could
not brook singing, revel, and actual dancing at this
solemn ceremony, and held up the duty of genuine
sorrow for the dead. Repeated decrees insisted on
the "diabolical" character, "contrary to human nature," of such customs; and forbade as far as possible
the rude revelry and noise. Such remains of the old
habit as were tolerated by the authorities became in
due time the theme of attack by reforming opponents
of the church; and as late as our own century there
are cases of actual dancing in honor of the dead,
preceded of course by a sort of memorial service, in
mourning garb, within the church.[1] Add to these
grosser survivals the minor superstitions of peasants
everywhere in Europe, the bit of food flung into
the fire, thrown out of the window, or set upon
the roof "for the poor spirits," the lore of house-
goblins, and the little observances of the same
sort practised by the laborer in the field, — all
these things point to the once universal cult of the
dead.[2]

Where survival seemed dangerous, and where
actual uprooting was unwise, the church turned a
heathen ceremony into a special Christian rite. The

[1] Rochholz, p. 317.
[2] For feasts with the dead, see further Tylor, *Primitive Culture*,
Chaps. XI., XII., and particularly Vol. II. 30 ff.

offerings to the dead[1] were converted into gifts for
the parish poor; and we even find the two objects
recognized for the same act. Thus Rochholz quotes
from the Confessions of St. Augustine an account
of the practice of eating and drinking among the
graves, and giving a share to the poor, — a custom
of certain Christians in which the pious mother of
the saint had shared. But in more modern times the
feeding of the poor has excluded older rites. Poor
and sick folk took the place of the dead; and the
gifts of corn and wine were often fixed for certain
days, especially when the benefaction assumed the
form of a legacy or a gift of the dead man's heirs.
As regards the original purpose of offerings to the
spirit, it is needless to point out how closely the practice of buying masses for the dead would fit ancestral
notions. Tylor[2] quotes the invective of a Manichæan
who charges the Christians with keeping the heathen
ceremonial under a new name: "Their sacrifices
indeed ye have turned into love-feasts, their idols
into martyrs, whom with like vows ye worship; ye
appease the shades of the dead with wine and meals, ye
celebrate the Gentiles' solemn days with them. . . ."[3]
Thus the church, true to its general theory that sorrow
of a practical character should take the place of mere
revel and a crass notion of the dead man's participation,
instituted the solemn ceremony of masses for the dead,
an infinite gain over older and ruder rites. With

[1] An allusion to this among other races is found in Tobit, iv. 17.
"Pour out thy bread on the burial of the just, but give nothing to the
wicked."

[2] *P. C.* II. 34 f. *Cf.* also Hampson, *Medii Ævi Kalendarium*, 53 f.

[3] Tylor (p. 35) gives a number of survivals, coming down to modern
times.

the steady growth of the doctrines concerning purgatory, masses for the dead assumed an overwhelming importance. Moreover, the church encouraged the worship of patron-saints, and in this way kept up a venerable institution of heathendom. For the patron-saint seems to be legitimate successor of the "guardian angel," the "genius," and that attendant spirit in which the old Germans believed. Germanic belief gave to every man a protecting spirit or follower; we find the best information on the matter in Scandinavian records.[1] In the later development of Norse mythology, the Valkyrias seem often to take this part; they follow and protect a chosen hero, and at his death conduct him to Valhalla. In the legends of later Europe, many a wood-fay, white lady, or fairy, may still become in this way the protecting spirit of some hero and share his mortal love. We have seen Svava waiting on her Helgi, and Sigrun protecting Helgi Hundingsbani; Sigrdrifa, who is really Brynhild, loves Sigurd.[2] But men believed in a more prosaic spirit, — a far older belief than this offspring of the Viking age, — the *fylgja*, an invisible guardian, only to be seen when one was nigh unto death. We remember how Drusus, just before his fatal accident, saw a sort of *fylgja;* it was in the shape of a barbarian woman, gigantic in form, who told him he dare go no further. So Alexander Severus saw a similar figure that prophesied misfortune; and even Attila was confronted by a rune-maiden who warned him thrice: "Back, Attila!" In the *Nialssaga,*[3] a heathen Icelander is converted under the condition

[1] Survivals collected by Rochholz, I. 92-130.   [2] Grimm, *D. M.*[4] 351.
[3] Chap. 96, transl. G. W. Dasent (Everyman's Library).

that he may have the Archangel Michael for his
"following angel," *fylgja engill;* and Grimm[1] notes
that Michael was the Christian receiver of souls.   To
see this following-spirit meant death; sometimes one
saw it in shape of beast or bird.   Bjarki saw his as a
bear; raven, and later, swan, perform a similar office.[2]
An English name for this *fylgja* is the *fetch*, familiar
enough in popular superstition; while its highest type
is the conception of a general "following-spirit," fate
itself, to which our ancestors gave the name of
Wyrd,—

> The Wirdes, that we clepen Destinée

as Chaucer[3] puts it.   This conception of overmastering
and irrevocable fate makes dark background in our
oldest epic, existing side by side with Christian influences.   "Wyrd wove me this," says the Anglo-Saxon;
and approaching death is stated in similar terms:
"thy Wyrd stands near thee."   The weird sisters
survive in Macbeth, and are to be considered more
particularly in another chapter.   "I thought I saw
dead women, poorly clad, come in here to-night;
they wished to choose thee, . . ." says one who will
prophesy to Gunnar his approaching death.[4]

The "familiar spirit" is not far off from this
fylgja; and both of course belong to spirit-cult.
Moreover, very old expressions of our language show
this notion of a spirit not under our absolute control
—its precise relation to the ego was hardly matter of

---

[1] *D. M.* 730.   The festivals of St. Michael, says Hampson, are obviously purposed " to give countenance to the worship of angels."   *Medii
Ævi Kalendarium*, II. 140.   They are also connected with the doctrine
of tutelar spirits.   See Brand, *Antiquities*, under " Michaelmas."

[2] *D. M.*[4] III. 266.   [3] *Legend of Good Women*, 2580.

[4] *C. P. B.*, I, 335 (*Atlamál*); Hollander, p. 350, st. 25; Bellows,
p. 508, 509.

Germanic speculation — abiding within us and moving us without our wish or will. "It ran into his mind" is our "occur"; but what was the "it"? Men believed that during dream or trance, the soul in visible shape, — a mouse or a snake, for example, — could desert the body; and they seem also to have believed that something not oneself spoke within one's own bosom. When a man begins to talk, he "unlocks the word-hoard"; when he will be silent, he bolts and bars his breast. Instead of "he spake," the poet of *Béowulf* says: "the point of the word brake through the breast-hoard"; and in another place, "he let the word fare out."[1] Indeed, it was no metaphor for our Germans when they said that the spirit of his ancestors spake from the breast of the son. On this inner voice, however, we must not lay too much emphasis; for the *fylgja* was mostly conceived as outside of one, a comrade and follower. The conception could widen from an individual's *fylgja* to the good genius of family, clan, or race. In the church, St. Michael took these old functions upon himself; and Michaelmas is set apart, as Bourne suggests, for the election of municipal officers, "the civil guardians of the peace of men, perhaps . . . because the feast of angels naturally enough brings to our minds the old opinion of tutelar spirits, who have, or are thought to have, the particular charge of certain bodies of men or districts of country, as also that every man has his guardian angel who attends him from the cradle to the grave."[2]

In many other ways the church perpetuated certain forms of this cult of the dead. Conspicuous martyrs,

---

[1] *Béow.* 2792. See Bode, *Kenningar*, p. 43.   [2] Brand, "Michaelmas."

prelates. and others were canonized and practically worshipped, so that the strongly rooted custom might bear its fruit on consecrated ground of clerical ceremonies. We may sum up the whole matter in the words of Mr. E. B. Tylor: "It is plain that in our time the dead still receive worship from far the larger half of mankind, and it may have been much the same ever since the remote periods of primitive culture in which the religion of the manes probably took its rise." [1] Where we are not concerned with actual worship, as soon as we leave creed and ceremony and take up superstition, then we enter the great realm of ghosts; here the old beliefs have found their haven of refuge. The dead still visit the glimpses of the moon, rise to demand blood for their own murder, come to warn or protect or scare, — what not: and all these faded superstitions have their roots in the ancient manes-cult. Precisely the same origin must be assigned to the famous *nightmare* [2] and all its relatives. The "mare," a word which Kuhn connected with Latin *mori*, is evidently in its original form a spirit, a dead person, who tramples or rides its victim to death. Thence the conception passes into that of a living person who has assumed this shape; and so through all the grades of superstitious belief. Similar origin must be assigned to the *werewolf*, a person "clad" in a wolf,[3] and evidently another offspring of the belief in spirits. But these various manifestations belong rather to Germanic mythology than to our present subject.

---

[1] *Primitive Culture*, II. 123.   [2] Mogk, *Grundriss*[2]. III, 267.

[3] So Kögel in Mogk, *art. cit.*, p. 272 n.; but see *NED.* s. v.

The place where one meets the spirits, can summon them and appease them, is by preference the burial place; but they are also fond of crossways. The time is, of course, night; and chiefly in the season of Christmas and New Year, when the nights are longest. A host of superstitions and popular observances connected with this time of the year have their roots in the primitive customs of manes-worship. On St. Thomas's day, December 21st, in an English village it was till lately the custom to deposit five shillings in a hole in a certain tombstone in the churchyard; this done, the lord of the manor could take no tithe of hay that year.[1]

---

[1] Hampson, *Medii Ævi Kalendarium*, I. 83.

CHAPTER XIII

THE WORSHIP OF NATURE

Dualism in worship — Spirits of the natural world — House-spirits — Spirits of the air — The Mighty Women — Charms — The Wild Hunt — Spirits of the earth — Wood-spirits — Tree-worship — Water-spirits and well-worship — The Swan-maidens — Giants — Worship of the elements — Water, air, and fire — Mother Earth — Sun, moon, and stars — Day, night, and the seasons.

IT is not our province to discuss problems of mythology, but a question must be asked in regard to the objects of Germanic worship. We have learned that the primitive German worshipped his ancestral spirits. Starting with this fact, many writers on anthropology endeavor to develop the whole system of Germanic deities from ancestor-worship alone. This we cannot admit. One often hears a remark quoted from Immanuel Kant to the effect that two things filled him with wonder and awe, — the starry heavens above him and the sense of moral responsibility within him. Now for primitive man we may assume an analogous dualism, corresponding of course to the undeveloped condition of his intellect. The world of dreams and of consciousness gave him the conception of spirits and the impulse to worship them. On the other hand, from the start he must have felt a not-himself

— a *not-like-himself* — in the nature that surrounded him. We assume this dualism from the outset: a cult of ancestral spirits, which chiefly haunted the tomb and the underworld; and a cult of natural forces dimly felt to be instinct with life and volition. In other words, primitive man did not delay his worship of natural forces until remote ancestors had become in some way identified with these forces. Storms might gather in the neighborhood of mountain graves, and might be attributed to ancestors, for wind and air belong to the spirits; but the bolt of lightning had no analogy in any human act and was surely never regarded as the work of an ancestor. There must have been a gigantic storm-god from the beginning of human thought; for if there was intellect enough to infer ancestral acts, there was fancy enough to imagine a superhuman power.[1]

Between the worship of ancestors, known and acknowledged as such, and the cult of great divinities like Woden, lay a border-land which is not to be rashly annexed to either kingdom. We prefer to treat this worship independently; it dealt with spirits of the stream, the cave, the air, and the forest. Doubtless much of this worship once belonged to ancestors, but it soon ceased to be regarded as such. Spirits were supposed to haunt the secret places of nature, and were in many cases thought to be souls of departed men; but from the start man must have felt that the water or the cloud or the cave had a population not entirely dependent on emigration from

[1] This is counter not only to the anthropological view, but also to the system of the philologist, E. H. Meyer, who assumes (*Indogerm. Mythen*, I. 87. 210 f.) that the Pandemonium came first and out of it grew the Pantheon.

the living world of men: he must have recognized at the outset a *natura naturans*. Ancestral spirits would belong to a general locality, and would have at heart the interests of family, clan, or race. Thus we find a curious law in Iceland about the precaution to be observed by shipmasters whose boats rode at anchor in the harbors. If these boats had figure-heads, — dragon, snake, or what not, — the prow was to be turned away from the shore so that the land-spirits should not be terrified.[1] These are undoubtedly the kindly spirits of the race, guardians and protectors of their old home. But spirits assigned to some particular element have not this intimate and ancestral quality; and it was these latter spirits which became in our Christian era the object of bans and curses.

> From haunted spring and dale,
> Edged with poplar pale,
> The parting genius was with sighing sent.

To "lay" spirits was business of the priest; the sign of the cross reminded them of a lost empire and sent them in confusion to yet remoter haunts. Thence, however, they can still be invoked, as Wagner reminds Faust, by the presumptuous and reckless man who does not shrink from dealings with them. To ban spirits and to invoke them are arts not so widely sundered as might be supposed; and the old spirit-cult lent itself readily to the new ceremonies of the church. The carpenter in Chaucer's *Miller's Tale*, avails himself of such a form when he wishes to cure the clerk of his pretended trance: —

[1] Maurer, *Bek. d. norweg. Stämme*, II. 231; *Landnáma*, IV. 7.

"Awake, and thenk on Cristes passioun:
I crouche thee from elves and fro wightes!"
Ther-with the night-spel seyde he anon-rightes
On foure halves of the hous aboute
And on the threshfold of the dore with-oute: —
'Iesu Crist, and seynt Benedight,
Blesse this hous from every wikked wight,
For nightes verye, the white *pater-noster*
Where wentestow, seynt Petres soster ?"

This passage [2] Tyrwhitt suspects "to be an interpolation"; but a good old English charm it is most undoubtedly, whether Chaucer's insertion or not.

One class of spirits to be noticed at the outset have nothing to do with natural forces, and evidently belong entirely to the ancestral division. These are the house-spirits. Robin Goodfellow is a well-known English representative of the class. They dwell in cellar, garret, stall, corncrib, and closet; they are mostly invisible, but often appear as little men in grotesque raiment, pointed hat, and boots. Another sort of home-spirits remain invisible, and it is to avoid pinching or hurting these that one is admonished not to slam doors, throw knives about, and so forth. The cult of these spirits exists to this day in some shape. Food is given to them, and in reward they do all sorts of household work;[3] our literature abounds in references to their ministrations.

With spirits of the air[4] we enter upon a field where the mystery of natural forces is joined to the

---

[1] Make the sign of the cross.

[2] *Cant. Tales*, A. 3478 ff.; passage no longer regarded as suspect.

[3] *D. M.*[4] 422 f.

[4] St. Augustine divides "in deos, ,homines, dæmones. . . . Nam deorum sedes in cælo, hominum in terra, in ære dæmonum." *C. D.* VIII. 14, quoted *D. M.*[4] III. 122.

worship of the dead. The air is of course full of spirits, for the very name of "spirit" shows this affinity; and we must try to sunder two elements in the cult of these mysterious beings. The old custom of "feeding the wind" at the approach of a storm is a case in point. The rising wind is connected with ancestral spirits; we know that when, for example, a man is hanged, or meets an equally violent death, there always arises a sudden gust of wind. The food, therefore, is partly meant for these unfortunate spirits, who seem to murmur ominously in the rising gale. But besides the souls, there is something superhuman in the storm itself, an indefinite animating presence which the worshipper desires to propitiate: and hence a part of the offering goes to this mysterious power. Thus the beings who haunt the air are doubtless to be referred in part to the worship of ancestors; but with them is connected the mystery of the element itself. As the spirits retire further and further from their ghostly character, they acquire more and more of the terrible and the overwhelming.

Let us take, first of all, the *dís* of Scandinavian superstition, a word which Grimm connects with the Anglo-Saxon *ides* (woman), and which is found as final syllable in many Norse names. The guardian angel is often a *dís*; or the word may stretch far enough to include the notion of a "goddess." We read of a temple of the *dísir* in Scandinavian worship, of sacrifice to them (*dísablót*), and of a scald or poet who sang in their honor.[1] "One harvest," — we note the season of year, — "there was made a great

[1] Cleasby-Vigfusson, *Icelandic Dict. s.v.*

sacrifice to the woman-spirits (*dísablót*) at King Alf's, and Alfhild performed the sacrifice . . . and in the night, as she was reddening the high-place, Starkad carried her away.[1]" These woman-spirits are sometimes friendly, sometimes hostile, and on the whole seem to be the sublimated wise-woman whom the German reverenced in life for her prophetic and sacred nature, a "magnified and non-natural" Veleda of the unseen world. Such *dísir* are said to have made away with mortals,[2] and it is good to propitiate them with the *dísablót*. They are distinctly connected with graves and spirits of the dead, as Grimm points out from the use of such a phrase as *blóta kumla dísir*, "to sacrifice to the women of the tombs." As active in human affairs, they journey about doing help or harm; but unlike their elder sister, the implacable Wyrd, these mighty women may be pacified or cajoled with a gift. It seems to be a very old notion that mystic and supernatural women attend the birth of children and have abiding influence on the destiny of those who are born under their auspices. They are to be treated liberally, — the uninvited fairy of our story-books as a warning! Since all unseen ills come from unseen persons, as even death in battle by a visible weapon must be referred to a mysterious personality, — "if War shall take me off," says Béowulf in no abstract, modern way, — so the old German felt an impulse to propitiate or baffle the powers that did him secret harm. Anglo-Saxon literature contains some striking survivals of this cult of the mighty women. In the strange mixture of pedantry and superstition known

---

[1] *Herv. Saga,* apud *C. P. B.* I. 405.   [2] *D. M.*[4] 333.

as *Salomon and Saturn*,[1] our Hebrew monarch describes the nature of Wyrd or fate, and gives some features which undoubtedly belonged to all the race of *dísir*. As befits a fallen deity, Wyrd has in Salomon's description pronounced diabolical traits : —

> Wyrd is wrathful, she rushes upon us,
> she waketh weeping, with woe she loads us,
> she shoots the spirit, a spear she bears.

The last line, a sort of prolepsis for "she carries a spear and hurls it at the spirit," is especially interesting to us on account of an Anglo-Saxon charm against rheumatism or a sudden "stitch" in the side. Hovering and mysterious woman-spirits, invisible often, and horsed upon sightless couriers of the air, send little spears or javelins at the unwary mortal, just as in nobler office the Valkyrias, concealed by the swan-raiment, flew above the clash of battle and protected a favorite warrior. With the advent of Christianity they all came into equal disrepute; witness a suggestive gloss of the eighth century, — "*Eurynis*, walcyrge. *Eumenides*, hæhtisse." That is, the Furies, by *interpretatio Saxonica*, are Valkyrias; and the Eumenides are *hægtessan*, or witches. Now the charm against rheumatism distinctly names the *hægtessan* as authors of the trouble in question, and is here given in full translation:[2] —

"Against sudden-stitch [take] feverfew, and red nettle which grows through the house, and dock ("waybroad"): boil in butter [and say] : —

---

[1] Ed. J. M. Kemble.

[2] See F. Grendon, *Journ. Amer. Folk-Lore*, XXII (1909), 165, 167 (text, transl.), pp. 214, 215 (notes).

Loud were they, loud, o'er the law[1] as they rode,
wrathful they were as they rode o'er the land :
shield thee now, that thou mayst 'scape from the danger.
Out, little spear, if in here thou be !

I stood under linden, 'neath light shield,
where the Mighty Women their main[2] prepared,
when they sent their screaming spears abroad.
I will send in answer another spear,
flying arrow forth against them.
Out, little spear, if it in here be !

Sat smith, forged little knife,
[angriest of iron, wondrous strong].[3]
Out, little spear, if it in here be !

Six smiths sat, war-spears wrought.
Out, spear ! be not in, spear !

If herewithin be aught of iron,
work of witches,[4] it shall melt !
Wert thou shot in the fell, or wert shot in the flesh,
or wert shot in the blood, [or wert shot in the bone][5]
or wert shot in the limb : be thy life never harmed ![6]

---

[1] "Hill" : Scottish " law."

[2] Strength.

[3] Rieger's emendation. The original has simply "ïserna wund swiðe." Sweet reads this as "wounded with iron" ; *i.e.* beaten with an iron hammer.

[4] *Hægtessan.* See above. Our "hag" is the same word, probably from " hedge," as these baneful women may lurk behind hedges and copses. Compare for the English use of the word Herrick's spirited poem " The Hag."

> The hag is astride,
> This night for to ride,
> The devile and shee together,
> Through thick and through thin,
> Now out and now in,
> Though ne'er so foule be the weather.

[5] Verse so completed by J. Grimm.

[6] "Teased" ; *i.e.* plucked, tormented.

Were it shot of the gods,[1] or shot of the elves,[2]
or were't shot of the hag, — I will help thee now.
This to heal shot of gods : this to heal shot of elves:
this to heal shot of hag : now I will help thee.
   Flee to the mountain-head![3]
   Whole be thou ! help thee God !
   Take then the knife, throw it into water.

The mythological importance of this charm is very
evident. Its use in Anglo-Saxon times, with the
faint touch of orthodoxy added to the last verse,

---

[1] *Esa.* The same root is preserved in the first syllable of Oswald,
etc. The word occurring here is of great value, and shows the genuine
heathendom of the charm. *Ós*, the singular, is the name of one of the
runes, and has the general meaning " god."

[2] Etymology is here important. The word " ælf " is familiar enough
in itself and as first syllable of proper names like Alfred. Another
form is " oaf": see Shakspere's " ouphes " in *Merry Wives,* IV. 4.
For the facts, we have the interesting word " elf-arrow," applied in
Scotland to certain stones, such as pieces of flint; also " elfbolt."
These are believed to be actual missiles, such as our charm describes.
Sick cattle in Norway are said to be " æliskudt," elf-shot. This term
is also Scottish; see Grimm, *D. M.*[4] 381. Brand says that in England
as well as in Scotland those relics of the stone age — arrow-heads of
flint — are popularly called elf-shots, and even the *ignis-fatuus* was
called elf-fire. Cattle suffer from them, and, as Brand reminds us,
Collins says in his Ode : —

> Then every herd by sad experience knows
> How wing'd with Fate, their elf-shot arrows fly,
> When the sick ewe her summer food foregoes,
> Or stretch'd on earth the heart-smit heifers lie.

Several diseases were named after elves: — water-elf disease. elf-hic-
cough, and so on. Cockayne, *Leechdoms,* I. xlvii.

[3] This is Sweet's reading, in Anglo-Saxon Reader,[6] p. 123, and the
simplest. Grimm reads " Flee to the mountains [she that sent the
bolt]. Be thou whole in head! " In the above translation " flee " must
refer to the little spear which caused the trouble ; a sequel to the command " Out! " is the command " Flee! " We might of course read
" fléoð " and refer to the Mighty Women. See Wülker, *Grundr. d.
ags. Lit.* p. 350.

points to an older ceremonial and a more exalted
station. When its temple was ruined, this rite
sought shelter in the cottage, nor was it confined
to England; for references to these evil-working
hags are found in Scandinavian literature. In
the *Hávamál* Woden tells us the tenth item of
his wisdom: "If I see hedge-riders dancing in
the air, I prevail so that they go astray and cannot find their own skins and their own haunts."[1]
They are elsewhere called "night-riders" and "mirk-
riders"; one of them is seen to ride a wolf at
twilight.[2]

While these fashions of the mighty women bring us
close to modern witchcraft, we may also look at them
in their more warlike functions. Those stern old
German women whom we saw among the Cimbrians
and Teutons in Italy, or who, according to Tacitus,
were wont in their own borders to rally a wavering
line of battle, are only mortal models for the invisible beings who hover over a battle-field, help their
favorites, and hinder the enemy. Such are the supernatural women mentioned in an old German spell,
found by Waitz in a manuscript of the cathedral library
at Merseburg, and presented with comment and translation by Jacob Grimm to the Berlin Academy of
Sciences.[3] The handwriting is of the early tenth
century. As usual with charms and spells, — for example, the Anglo-Saxon spell just given, — we have
an epic opening, three verses of description, and then
the application, or spell proper, in the fourth line.

---

[1] *C. P. B.*, I, 27; Hollander, p. 45, st. 156.   [2] *C. P. B.*, I, 95, 146.
[3] 1842. See Grimm's *Kl. Schr.* II. 1 ff.

"Once sat Women, sat hither and thither.
Some bound bonds: some hindered the host:[1]
some unfastened the fetters.[2]
'Spring from fetters: fly from the foe!'"[3]

Not so grandly supernatural as these shadowy goddesses of battle are the "balewise women" against whom the Scandinavian warrior was warned. "The sons of men need an eye of foresight wherever the fray rages, for balewise[4] women often stand near the way, blunting swords and mind." This blunting of weapons by witchcraft was common enough in old Germanic times. Certain runes on the blade could do it, and such a weapon was *forscrifen;* a work attributed in *Salomon and Saturn* to the agency of the devil. "On the [doomed man's] weapon the devil writeth a mass of fatal signs, baleful letters; he 'forscribeth' the blade, the glory of the sword."[5]

In this place may be mentioned the agency of "witches" in raising storms. This has become in later times a function of witchcraft and a prerogative of Laplanders; but in the old days it was an affair of greater dignity, and belonged doubtless to these same supernatural women of the night, as well as to the god of storm and wind himself. Spells were uttered

[1] Those who bind bonds are helping the victors, and make fetters for the prisoners; those who hinder the host are actively embarrassing the enemy.

[2] That is, the fetters of those warriors of the favored army who had been captured. Thus the first group of women are in rear of the favorite army, the second at the line of battle, the third behind the hostile army. (Scherer.)

[3] This is what the women say to the prisoners, and is the efficacious word in any similar situation.

[4] Horrible, detestable, devilish.   [5] *S. and S.* 162 f.

against hailstorms ;[1] strange beings were appealed to
for protection, and in course of time these became
Christian saints.

Lastly, we come to the thinly disguised worship of
ancestral spirits, which we find in the customs and
myths connected with the so-called "wild hunt."
Woden, the god of wind and storm, is their leader;
but the hunt itself, the rout of spirits that howl along
the wintry sky, are undoubtedly the souls of the dead.
The myth is universal in Germanic traditions,[2] and
abounds in all collections of legendary and popular
lore; but the characteristic features of a hunt, the
bark of dog and crack of whip, have all been added
to what was originally a mere clamor of passing souls.
A definite cult is hardly to be discovered; the subject
lies wholly in the province of myth and legend. We
may note, however, the custom of feeding the wind, to
which we have made reference above. In Carinthia,
about the time of Christmas, this custom is very generally observed.[3] "In Swabia, Tyrol, and the Upper
Palatinate, when the storm rages, they will fling a
spoonful or a handful of meal in the face of the gale,
with this formula in the last-named district, 'Da Wind,
hast du Mehl für dein Kind, aber aufhören musst
du!'"[4] It was not simply the spirits who were to be
appeased; the shadowy dread itself, the storm-god,
was an object of cult as early — we are persuaded —
as the ancestral souls themselves.

---

[1] *D. M.*⁴ 529; III. 493, 499 f.,

[2] Liebrecht, *Otia Imperialia of Gervas. Tilb.* 173 ff. See also *D. M.*⁴
765ff.; Mogk in Paul's *Grundriss²*, III, 255.

[3] *Mythen aus Kärnthen,* by Pogatschnigg in Pfeiffer's *Germania,*
II. 75.

[4] Tylor, *P. C.* II. 269, 407, from Wuttke, *Volksabergl.* p. 86.

In passing from the cult of these spirits of the air, and taking up the scanty remains of such ceremonies as may have been meant for spirits of the earth, we are reminded how difficult it is to show the necessary relation between modern superstitions and an ancient worship. In the majority of cases we must content ourselves with a probability. Creatures of the underworld, who live in cave or hillside, are particularly plentiful in Norse traditions; they belong mainly to the province of mythology, but here and there we have a glimpse of systematic worship and ceremonies. Burial would naturally bring the lore of elves and dwarfs of the hillside into close connection with the traditions of the family dead. The *Kormakssaga*[1] testifies to Scandinavian worship of these dwarfs and elves. A bull was killed, its blood was sprinkled *on the hill of the elves*, and with its flesh a sacrificial feast was made in their honor. Here we are evidently not far from the funeral-mound, and the offerings set out upon ancestral graves. Grimm notes that in the Netherlands people call such hills as happen to contain burial-urns *alfenbergen*. Graves were marked by stones, and we hear a great deal in decrees of the church concerning worship at sacred stones;[2] offerings were brought to these places long after the notion of direct ancestor-worship had faded away. Often there was an enclosure, as well as a stone. Anglo-Saxon laws provided a penalty for any one who should deliberately lay out such an enclosure — for purposes of the cult — "about stone or tree or well."[3] The Scandinavians sacrificed at home to

[1] See *D.M.*[4] 370.
[2] For stones as sacred in themselves, see Pfannenschmid, *Erntefeste*, p. 21 ff.   [3] Liebermann, I, 383, § 54; III, 225.

these creatures. "The surly housewife," says a Norse poet, "that turned me away like a wolf, said that they were holding a Sacrifice to the Elves within her homestead."[1] This household cult of the elves was, of course, frowned upon by the church; hence the antipathy felt by all the elvish race for church-bells, holy-water, and similar belongings of a worship which was stamping out their own cult.[2] The elves of modern folk-lore invariably lament the good old times; people, they wail, have now begun "to count the loaves in the oven," "to make marks on the loaf," and what not. Of Elfland, the elf-queen, and all the myths of faery, we find ample account; as to the cult itself, we must be content with a general conclusion gathered from the host of more or less evident survivals. The "good people," whether elves of "mount" or "dune," are ready to help men in return for the trifling but necessary payment; their best work is that of the forge, the loom, or the oven. Weapons they will make of the best; in all sorts of household labor, such as spinning and weaving, they excel; and it is notorious that their bread and cake are unsurpassed. Moreover, they know and impart the secrets of medicinal herbs and stones of virtue. In return they often demand the aid of human beings, and particularly in three cases.[3] Elf-women in travail desire the aid of a mortal nurse; when elf-men divide treasure, or fall into dispute, they often call in a wise mortal to assist them; and they often borrow a room in some man's dwelling where they may hold an elfin wedding-feast. In all these cases they give rich compensation to the mortal

[1] *C. P. B.* II. 131.   [2] *D. M.*[4] 380, 401.   [3] Ibid. 378.

in question, but instances of their mischievous and harmful nature are plentiful enough. In all probability these traditions arose with the spread of Christianity and the consequent discredit thrown upon elvish ways. Evil of their sending fell upon men and cattle; the elf-shot, as we have just seen, was justly dreaded; and spells and charms which once perhaps invoked their aid were turned against them, and intended to put them under ban. Analogous with the mass of mediæval stories which tell how men cheated the devil out of a bargain for soul or service, are the legends of troll or dwarf defrauded in similar fashion. The favorite bargain was for "heart and eyes" of a mortal if he failed to keep his pact; but if the mortal could call the troll by name, the obligation was forthwith cancelled. Such is the legend which Whittier has put into verse in his "Kallundborg Church." The oldest race of elves, however, were surely friends of man; in evidence, we may call upon those fossil-like witnesses of a vanished worship, the names of places and persons. The widespread cult of elves has left its trace in local compounds like *Ælfestûn* [1] or the more familiar personal names of *Ælfred*, *Ælfgifu* ("elf-gift"), and the like. Mingled Germanic and Celtic traditions meet us in the story of Arthur's mystic birth, as told by English Layamon. Elves take him at his birth, sing charms over him, and give him many blessings; for one of his battles an elf-smith makes him a noble coat of mail.[2]

---

[1] Leo, *Rectitud. Singul. Person.* p. 5.

[2] Layamon's *Brut*, ed. Madden, II. 384, 463, and Ten Brink, *Eng. Lit.* p. 238.

The dwarf-cult is not entirely a matter of ancestor-worship. In some cases a conquered race, often inferior in size to the conquerors, has been thrust into remote and desert regions, into the hills and wilds, and has thus passed into tradition as a race of dwarfs. Such a race is naturally feeble and despised in any comparisons of outright valor; but in a sort of revenge, the reputation of witchcraft and secret power of doing harm attaches to them and makes them feared. Hence the reputation of the Lapps, whom the Scandinavian Aryans conquered.[1]

It was an evident piece of reasoning for the ancient world to connect the mysteries of vegetation with the benefactions of those spirits who housed below the earth. A mass of material has been collected by Wilhelm Mannhardt illustrating the ceremonies observed by European peasants in connection with seed-time and harvest.[2] These customs are mainly indicative of older ceremonies which had in view a helpful spirit, to whom offering was made, and a harmful demonic being which is still exorcised in varying fashion. Myths may be guessed behind many a modern legend, and find parallel in the records of Greek and Roman mythology. We shall presently find occasion to trace certain Germanic rites in their relation to the goddess of fertility and vegetation, as well as to the spirits which were more directly identified with the kindly elements themselves.

---

[1] Tylor, *P. C.* I. 386.
[2] Mannhardt, *Die Korndæmonen; Antike Wald- u. Feldkulte*, Bd. II.; *Roggenwolf u. Roggenhund;* and *Mythologische Forschungen*, a posthumous book, being No. 51 of the *Quellen u. Forschungen.*

Spirits haunted the Germanic forest, and the mysterious whisper of its foliage was their evident murmur and message to the man who could rede it.[1]

Feld hath eyen, and the wood hath eres,

says Chaucer; but to older men the wood had also a tongue. Germans were children of the woods, and sacred trees abounded in their tradition. As Grimm pointed out,[2] and as everybody now repeats, even the Gothic cathedral has imitated in its plan the climbing and arching branches of a German forest; while the endless variety of detail easily suggests the labyrinth of twig and foliage. In speaking of the spirits of this forest, we feel sure that emigration from the human world is not to account for all of them or for their entire nature; something of the mystery and personified activity of the forest itself was in them from the beginning. The doctrine [3] that trees were simply habitation of the gods, — that is to say, a sort of fetish, — is one extreme; the other is Grimm's belief that it was the actual tree which our forefathers worshipped.[4]

We have to do at present not with the sacred grove and the forest sanctuary, which are to be considered in connection with the heathen temple, but rather with the spirits of the wood. In an Anglo-Saxon glossary of the tenth or the eleventh century,[5] " Dryades " has the gloss *wuduelfen*, wood-elves, while

---

[1] Again we are indebted to Mannhardt for an excellent collection of material in his *Baumkultus*, the first volume of the *Antike Wald- u. Feldkulte*.

[2] *D. M.*[4] 56.   [3] Held, for example, by Lippert.   [4] *D. M.* 60.

[5] Wright-Wülker, *A.-S. and O.-E. Vocabularies*, col. 189.

" Hamadryades " are *wylde elfen*, and " Castalides "
dûnelfen, dune or hill elves. " Satyrii vel Fauni "
are glossed as *unfœle men*, unclean men; but, as
Wright remarks, this is probably transposed from
another place, and the gloss should be *wuduwasan;*
indeed, *woodwose* is given as the definition of Satyrs
in a dictionary of the year 1608. Very interesting
is the gloss [1] for Echo, *wudumœr*, wood-mare, the
being which answers folk out of the wood and has
the same deceptive nature as its more violent relative, the nightmare. In all these names and glosses
we see a certain similarity between classical and
mediæval wood-lore; in fact, we must be on our
guard when learned men of the middle ages catalogue contemporary heathen practices. A just decision is often difficult. Thus in the list taken by
Grimm [2] from Burchard of Worms, mention is made
of certain "agrestes feminæ quas *silvaticas* vocant," [3]
women of the wood who appear and vanish and oft
times accept a mortal lover. Here classical parent-
age seems an easy inference; yet we must bear in
mind what a store of similar notions inform later
and even modern folk-lore. From our oldest myths
down to these peasant stories of to-day, the wood is
peopled with mystic beings, mainly women. Classification of these belongs of course elsewhere; [4] here
it is our task to trace their cult. Not very much
importance may be put upon the " weird lady of the
woods " whom Grimm mentions [5] as named in a poem
— he gives no title — in Percy's *Reliques*. It is
" The Birth of St. George," where the weird lady

---

[1] W.-W. col. 391.   [2] *D. M.*[4] III. 404 ff.   [3] Ibid. 409.
[4] Ibid. 357 ff.   [5] Ibid. 337.

from her cave, which is described as a most uncanny place, prophesies the future of Lord Albert's unborn child; she is sought for advice, is able to foretell the future, and is in touch with a deal of supernatural machinery. Like the water-women, the ladies of the wood have the old sibyl nature; and Grimm reminds us that Veleda herself dwelt amid the forest. So we approach ancestor-worship, and are made to think of the "women of the tomb"; indeed, one reading of a passage already quoted,[1] makes disguised Odin learn his wisdom from the "old people who live in the *forests*," where other texts read "graves." Related, in like manner, to ancestor-worship is the household cult of a spirit who dwells in some tree near the family dwelling and feels a peculiar interest in the welfare of the race. By Swedish folk-lore, one must not only abstain from cutting or breaking the tree itself, — on penalty of the spirit's departure, and with him all luck of the house, — but also there must be no hacking or spinning on a Thursday evening, for this is offensive to the dweller in the tree.[2]

Definite worship of trees is still to be found in survival, and was distinctly forbidden in decrees of the church. It is one of the points of "heathenship," as defined in the laws of King Cnut: "Heathenship is where one worships idols, that is, where one worships heathen gods and sun or moon, fire or flood, water-wells or stones, *or any sort of tree*."[3] The Anglo-Saxon homilies repeatedly condemn the practice of people "who are so foolish" as to bring offer-

---

[1] Above, p. 351.
[2] *D. M.*[4] 421. The "family-tree" has with us another meaning, out the metaphor is suggestive. See *D. M.*[4] III [3] Liebermann, I. 312, § 5.

ings to a mere stone, a well, a tree. Wells, stones, and trees were holy places; water-spirits, earth-spirits, and tree-spirits had prescribed and traditional rites which the church found hard to destroy. In the list quoted by Grimm, from Burchard, we find specific mention of these practices, — bringing votive offerings to tree or fount or stone, bringing a *candle* thither, or any such gift, " as if there were a divinity (*numen*) there which could do good or harm." Again, bishops and their assistants are to make every exertion that "such *trees as are consecrated to demons* and worshipped by the people, to such an extent that no one dares to cut off branch or twig, should be hewn down and burned." Mention is further made of auguries and the casting of lots, which are undertaken under the shade of a sacred tree.[1] A modern instance of offerings made at or to a tree is quoted by Mr. Tylor,[2] from a Scandinavian authority, who says that to this day on outlying Swedish farms is observed the sacrificial rite of pouring milk and beer over the roots of trees. Tylor collects ample evidence of similar tree-cult among savage tribes.[3] Mannhardt has a volume devoted to the Germanic phases of the subject. Anglo-Saxon leanings towards utility are plain enough, along with traces of absolute worship, in the custom of "youling" trees which are to bear fruit and so benefit the worshipper directly; the tree is often whipped, or, again, has cider, beer, or the like, poured upon its roots.

The sacred character of trees is shown by their use in the naming of places such as *Lindentûn, Thorntûn,*

---

[1] *D. M.*[4] III. 404, 406.   [2] *P. C.* II. 228.
[3] II. 215, 221 ff. See his references.

and many similar names.[1] Moreover, sacred trees
were used as boundary marks for an estate, as is
proved by our old charters and legal documents. A
given tree, hung with trophies offered to god or
spirit, would be known long after the heathen abominations had been removed; marks and carvings were
often allowed to remain upon it. Thus Kemble[2]
thinks that the *earnes béam* in Kent, mentioned in an
old document, was probably "a tree marked with the
figure of an eagle." A full description of heathen
rites practised at such a tree is quoted by Grimm
from the life of St. Barbatus (602–683),[3] with the
somewhat damaging remark that "it may be accurate." The Lombards had been baptized, but still
held to heathenish customs; and not far from the
walls of Beneventum, they were in the habit of wor-
shipping a "sacrilegious" tree, in which was hung
the hide of a beast. The men rode a race under the
tree, during which they hurled spears through the
hide; and this had to be done backwards, making
the affair a feat of strength and dexterity. The
piece of skin thus cut out was eaten as an especial
part of the rite. Here, moreover, persons were
wont to fulfil vows, and the whole place was held
sacred. We are elsewhere distinctly told that the
Lombards worshipped a "blood-tree" or "sacred
tree."[4]

[1] Leo, *Rectitud. Singul. Person.* p. 14.

[2] *Saxons in England*, I. 480 (appendix).

[3] *D. M.*[4] 541. A good survival of tree-worship is the case of the
Stock am Eisen in Vienna, into which every apprentice, before setting
out on his *Wanderjahre*, drove a nail for luck. "For luck" is generally what is left of the older notion of divine aid. See Fergusson,
Tree and Serpent Worship, p. 21.   [4] *D. M.*[4] 83.

First of trees in point of sacred character stood the oak. We remember, of course, Glasgerion's oath, " by oak and ash and thorn," where, in original rites, the sacred tree in question was touched by him who swore.[1] The village May-pole must be no more than mentioned, and even the great world-tree, Yggdrasill, may be left to controversy with a general feeling that between heathendom and Christianity, neither one can be claimed for its origin to the exclusion of the other;[2] in any event, we see a support for the supreme importance of tree-cult. Whether we be justified or not in assuming a Germanic "world-tree," there is no doubt of the old Germanic association of trees with the source of existence. About the guardian-tree Swedish women twine their arms in order to insure easy delivery in the pangs of childbirth;[3] and we remember how in our English ballads women in like time of need "set their backs against an oak." Other trees are noted as affording help in like circumstances. Eating the fruit of certain trees may make women pregnant; and when May Margret pulls the nuts in Hind Etin's wood, plainly a sacred region, and so comes into his power, we may perhaps assume a kindred tradition based upon older cult.[4] Indeed, in many a tale, the babies are fetched directly from or out of this or that tree;[5] and we hear of children being drawn through a split sapling in order to cure them of a deformity or a disease. It is in close connection with the use of trees as a place of offering and sacrifice that courts were so often held beneath a

---

[1] Child, Ballads,[2] III. 137; Grimm, R. A. 896 f.
[2] Bugge, *Studier*, pp. 393–529.   [3] Ibid. 512.
[4] Child, Ballads,[2] II. 360 ff.
[5] Bugge, *Studier*, 514. Common belief in Frisia and Holland.

tree;[1] justice was originally divine in every sense.
It is significant that in one of these courts "the oath
was taken with a stick of holly held in the hand."[2]
Down to modern times, certain traditional trees are
held in awe, and the rudest village hind will not
break or mar them.[3]

Our best account of such a sacred tree in the old
heathen days is the well-known story of Boniface
and the "oak of Jove." It is told in Willibald's life
of the saint.[4] He had come to the land of the Hessians, and many of these accepted the laying-on of
hands; "but others, whose minds were not yet
strengthened (*nondum animo confortati*), refused to
accept the truths of the pure faith; some, moreover,
made in secret their offerings and sacrifice, . . .
others openly; some publicly, some privately, carried
on auspices and divinations, magic and incantations;
others again auspices and auguries and divers sacrificial rites; but others, of saner mind, who had renounced all heathen worship, did none of these
things. With help and counsel of these latter,
[Boniface] undertook, with the servants of God
standing about him, to cut down an immense oak-
tree, which was called by its old heathen name, the
Jupiter Oak (*robur Jovis*),[5] in a place known as
Gæsmere.[6] When, resolute of mind, he had begun
to fell the tree, the great crowd of heathen who had
come up cursed him as an enemy of their gods; but

[1] *R. A.* 794 ff.   Gomme, *Prim. Folk-Moots, passim.*   [2] Ibid. 145.
[3] See some verses in Gomme's book, p. 257, about Langley Bush in
Staffordshire.
[4] *Geschichtschreiber d. deutschen Vorzeit,* "Willibald," p. 27 f.
[5] *Interpretatio Romana;* probably Jovis = Thor, Thunor.
[6] Geismar on the Edder.

nevertheless, when he had cut the tree only a little, the huge mass of the oak, moved by a divine blast from above, fell with shattered top ; and as if by command of a higher power, burst asunder into four parts, and four equal fragments of huge bulk lay revealed without any effort of the brothers who stood round about." With the wood of this oak, Boniface built a church.

Spirits of the water are plentiful in Germanic mythology, and had a special cult which survived into modern superstition. Plutarch, in his " Cæsar," has an interesting and valuable passage which not only shows us the prophetic functions of the German woman, but gives us positive evidence of Germanic religious ceremonies in their primitive form. When Cæsar suddenly appeared with his soldiers before the army of Ariovistus, the barbarian host was in consternation. " They were still more discouraged by the prophecies of their holy women, who foretell the future by observing the eddies of rivers, and taking signs from the windings and noise of streams, and who now warned them not to engage before the next new moon appeared." [1] J. Grimm explains the divination from an eddy or whirlpool by the theory that such movements were caused by the spirits who dwelt in the water.[2] Besides this official divination, from the murmur and windings of the watercourses, there was direct worship of the spirits who haunted spring and fountain. True, we are told that it was worship *at* the fountain, *at* the stream; and many modern writers insist that these were simply hallowed places meet for the worship of the dead. But fountains, like trees, with

[1] Clough's Plutarch, IV. 276 [Boston ed. of 1859].   [2] *D. M.*[4] 492.

all the mystery of rippling living waters, or the life-like murmur of foliage, were very different places from the dull stone above a grave; and much of the worship must have been directed to the informing and potent spirit of the place, to a personality which neither stood out from its haunt as a distinct ancestral soul, nor yet merged entirely in the element; it was an animating presence, holding border-ground between individuality and a vaguely felt natural power.

Water-worship is almost universal, found in every place and time, from the river-god of classical lore down to the sacred well of the superstitious European peasant.[1] Worship at springs and wells, as we have seen, is repeatedly forbidden in the canons; Anglo-Saxon decrees forbid the bringing of candle or offering to these once sacred places, and prayers and vigils at the fountain are likewise put under ban.[2] The same holds good of all Germanic races. For the Scandinavians we have testimony of Ari. "Thorstan Rednebb was a great sacrificer; he worshipped the waterfall . . . and used to have all the leavings taken to the waterfall; he was a great prophet."[3] So Gregory of Tours tells about offerings and sacrifices made by the people to a certain lake;[4] cheese was one of the offerings, and this reminds us of the "Cheesewell" of our own traditions, which had its name from the same custom. Belief in the curative property of certain holy wells is common enough down to the present time; a heathen well of repute easily turned Christian with the country, took a saint as patron, and went on curing and blessing as before.

---

[1] Tylor, *P. C.* II. 213 f.
[2] *D. M.*⁴ 484 ff.
[3] *C. P. B.* I. 421, quoted from *Landn.* V. 5.
[4] *D. M.*⁴ 496.

Tales of such are abundant; one well in England is
celebrated by Roger of Hoveden as making the blind
see, the deaf hear, the dumb talk, and the lame receive
power of limb. A woman far gone in dropsy went to
this well by advice of an abbot, drank, and vomited
two huge black toads, which changed into immense
dogs of the same color and then into asses. They
were driven off, and the woman recovered her health.[1]
Strip away the monkish wrappings, and we have the
virtue of a good old heathen well. The dualism which
was partly original and partly owing to the discredit
of heathen worship, shows us another sort of cult in
this domain; for evil and malicious spirits haunted
the water, and worked endless mischief among the
sons of men. Now magic, a very old affair, could be
put into operation against these evil powers, or else
they might be propitiated by a sacrifice of some sort.
Cases of the latter method we shall presently consider; the former is illustrated by the custom of
throwing metallic objects, preferably of iron or steel,
into the well or the stream, and thus binding or para-
lyzing the power of the water-spirit. Iron and steel
were supposed to limit spiritual agencies; and here,
says Liebrecht, is the real explanation of our maxim
that lovers or friends should not make mutual presents of knife or scissors or anything of the sort.[2]
Cornish folk, says Tylor, drop pins and nails into
their holy wells.[3] All manner of curious customs
were associated with the search for cure or blessing
at these holy wells, and some are collected by Brand.[4]

---

[1] Liebrecht, *Otia Imperialia of Gerv. Tilb.* p. 103.
[2] *Otia Imp.* p. 101.   [3] *P. C.* II. 214.
[4] *Antiquities,* "Customs and Superstitions concerning Wells and
Fountains."

Divination was practised, as where people dropped pebbles into the water, or provoked the rising of bubbles, and interpreted the signs according to a traditional code. More direct was the usage at the " wishing-well," where the supplicant threw into the water a piece of gold and then made his prayer. Fountains were known to foretell plague or famine, or. in less sweeping fashion, the approach of a tempest. Wells were decorated with flowers; in one English village, on a certain day, the clergyman and choristers were wont " to pray and sing psalms at the wells."

The notion of " healing springs " is, of course, no vulgar superstition. From oldest times the virtues of certain waters must have been known; and with our Germanic forefathers the salt-springs had precedence, and were brought into close connection with the cult. .The famous passage of Tacitus,[1] which tells how two Germanic tribes struggled for such a dear possession, also informs us that these Germans believed the place itself to be of unusual sanctity, and thought the salt was produced by the direct and gracious intervention of the divinities. When water was thrown upon burning logs, the rude method employed to make the salt, that precious substance was produced by divine agency from these opposing elements of fire and water.

The purifying functions of water bring it into connection with a great variety of ceremonies. Lustration is found in all directions.[2] Sacred rivers meet us in every land, and every village has its haunted brook or spring. The rain itself is holy, and when it

---

[1] *Ann.* XIII. 57.   [2] Tylor, *P. C.* II. 429 ff.

falls into an open grave, it is a sign that the soul of
the dead is already among the blessed;[1] it is God's
benediction. "In olden time," begins the first Helgi-
Lay, "in olden time when eagles were calling on
high, and *holy streams* poured down from the heights
of heaven. . . ." In stress of drought men sought
by magic to bring down the rain, and the church con-
demns those "qui mergunt imagines in aquam pro
pluvia obtinenda."[2] Holy-water itself is a concession of the church to the old well and fountain worship; but whether, as many have claimed, baptism
and the use of water in sprinkling and purifying
were known to heathen custom, is a disputed point.
Mention is made of them in Old Norse annals; but
while Müllenhoff defends their heathen origin, Maurer thinks they were imitated from the rites of the
church, and has secured for his theory the emphatic
approval of Bugge.[3] But even if the rite of sprinkling was taken from the church, a custom of dipping
or otherwise bathing new-born children in running
water, which prevailed among the ancient Germans,
was surely more than a mere "bath," and had ritual
significance. Moreover, when we find this saying of
Odin's: "If I pour water upon the young thane, he
falls not, though he go to battle; he sinks not under
the sword,"[4] even if we admit the influence of bap-

---

[1] Wolf, *Beiträge*, I. 216.

[2] Wolf, *Beitr.* I. 237. Grimm gives several other ceremonies practised by European peasants for the same purpose. *D. M.*[4] 493 ff.

[3] Konrad Maurer, *Ueber die Wasserweihe d. germ. Heidenthumes*,
1880; Müllenhoff in the "Anzeiger" of *Haupt's Zst.*, Bd. VII.; Bugge,
Studier, 371 ff. A comprehensive review of the general subject is Pfannenschmid, *Das Weihwasser im heidnischen u. christlichen Cultus*,
Hanover, 1869.   [4] Bugge, p. 376 f.

tismal rites, we must suppose something in the old heathen ceremonial to which this act bore some resemblance. Running water seems to have had special virtue. We may work backwards from Tam o' Shanter and his Meg to the leechdoms of Anglo-Saxon folk-lore, surely full of heathen reminiscence, where we find as cure for erysipelas on man or horse, a charm, to be sung over the man's head or in the horse's left ear, in running water, and with the head against the stream.[1] In Norway and Sweden, land of cataracts, the virtues of running water would naturally find ample recognition. The spirit who haunts the waterfall is helpful or harmful, and can be cajoled into imparting valuable knowledge, or else must be propitiated by sacrifice to avert the consequences of his ill-favor. He has power to teach men music and magic, and Henrik Ibsen's poem, *Spillemænd*, will occur to lovers of modern Scandinavian literature. We have already heard from Ari of a man who was careful to sacrifice to the cataract. This was for general prosperity; but particularly the art of music is best learned from such a master. To learn to play the harp, says Swedish folk-lore, offer a black lamb to the spirit of the waterfall; while in Norway, the Fossegrim teaches one to play the fiddle. He grasps the learner's right hand and sways it about so long that blood starts from every finger-tip; after that, one can play so that the very trees will dance. Finer yet is the touch of blended old and new belief in the folk's tradition that Nix would gladly purchase im-

[1] F. Grendon, *Journ. American Folk-Lore*, XXII (1909), 172, 173 (A. 11), 219 (notes); cf. p. 213 (E. 13).

mortality and salvation by thus teaching the Christian how to play the violin.[1]

Loveliest of all water-spirits, and brought into manifold touch with old and later cult, are the swan-maidens. One of the finest passages of the Nibelungen Lay is where Hagen surprises these wise women of the flood, and forces them to uncover the secrets of the future. Here it is not the mortal watching from the bank who foretells things to come as he watches the ripples of the stream; it is the creatures of the flood itself.

Both up and down the river he sought the ferryman;[2]
He heard the plash of water: to listen he began.
'Twas wise-women who caused it; all in a fountain fair
They made them fain to dally and cool and bathe them there.

When Hagen had espied them, he stole in silence near,
And when they marked his coming, right mickle was their fear:
That they outran, escaped him, them seemed a mighty joy.
The hero took their garments, nor made them more annoy.

Spake one of the mere-women, — Hadburg was her name, —
"Here will we tell you, Hagen, O noble knight of fame,
If you now, gallant swordsman, our raiment but restore,
Your journey into Hunland, and all that waits you more."

Like birds they swept and hovered before him on the flood,
Wherefore him seemed their wisdom must mickle be and good. . . .

She said: "To Etzel's kingdom ye do right well to fare;
Be witness my assurance of all I now declare:
To no realm ever heroes have better ta'en their way,
To such a noble welcome! — Believe me what I say."

---

[1] *D. M.*[4] 408; Matthew Arnold's poem *Neckan.* Deadly water-spirits are plentiful, but the catalogue belongs to mythology. The *Nicor* is Anglo-Saxon ancestor of "Nick."

[2] To convey the Burgundians over the river.

Her words were good to Hagen and made his spirit glad.
He gave them back their raiment. No sooner were they clad
In all their magic garments, they made him understand
In truth the fate that waited his ride to Etzel's land.

It was the second mere-wife, Sigelind, who spake:
" O son of Aldriane, Hagen, my warning take!
'Twas yearning for the raiment my sister's falsehood made;
And if thou goest to Hunland, Lord Hagen, thou'rt betrayed!" [1]

Hereupon they tell him the true fate of the expedition. An army of similar water-spirits with prophetic powers could be marshalled from oldest times down to Scott's " White Lady " in the *Monastery.*

Whatever may be said of these mild types of water-cult, there is no doubt in regard to the worship of spirits which rule over flood and tempest. Our own ancestors who dwelt by the North Sea, and their neighbors the Danes, knew this cult. Sometimes the evil spirit was propitiated with a sacrifice; sometimes a god of light and cheer was appealed to and made to conquer the demon. Such is the fate of Grendel in our *Béowulf;* and it is significant that an English local name, *Grendlesmere,* has preserved a distinct piece of testimony to the spirit and his cult.[2] Folklore tells many a tale to illustrate the other method. A legend of the Danish coast runs as follows:[3] On the west coast of Jylland it is said that the sea will have his yearly sacrifice in return for not breaking in upon the country; and that therefore in the old times people had a custom of exposing every year a little child in a barrel, since otherwise, oftener than not,

[1] *N. L.* 1473 ff.
[2] Document of Æthelstan's time (931) in *Cod. Dip.* II. 72.
[3] Thiele, *Danmarks Folkesagn,* II. 3.

there followed great ruin and destruction.[1] A milder
rite was the yearly bath of the women of Cologne on
the eve of St. John, by which they sought to avoid
evil and bad luck for the coming year; it seems to
have been a real Rhine-cult, and aroused great interest
in the poet Petrarch, who saw it in the year 1330 and
described it in a letter to a friend.[2] Finally, we come
to the victim seized by the nix, or anticipated by
sacrifice of some beast; folk-lore is full of these
tragedies, and the legends about the water-spirits fill
volumes. Nix is mostly cruel and vindictive. Often
he appears as a black horse or a bull, climbing from
stream or lake to carry off his victim; what is no
longer given he must take. Here, too, belong the
rites at the opening of a bridge, — a live cock built
into the wall in lieu of the victim, and so shading
back into human sacrifice. The bather seized by
cramp or caught in an eddy of the stream, believes
that he is pulled down by a demon of the flood.
To-day we have a dozen superstitions about bather's
cramp; one wears an amulet, or even goes through
some absurd performance to ward off the danger.[3]

Dwarfs have been mentioned; we must not forget
the giants. While these are mostly represented as
foes of man and hated by the gods, the nimble and
keen-witted divinities of a new order of things, while
they are held up to ridicule as a heavy race, dull as
the stones of their native mountains, none the less
we may discover probable traces [4] of a cult directed
to these same stupidities. Offerings to giants occur

[1] See also " Odense Aamand's Offer," II. 17.   [2] D. M.⁴ 489.
[3] Details in Tylor, P. C. II. 209 ff.
[4] " Kaum Spuren," says, however, J. Grimm, D. M.⁴ 461.

in legend and superstition. Like Milton's "lubbar
fiend," such a being will plough and thresh and do
other services for men, in order "to earn his cream-
bowl duly set." In the *Kormakssaga* occurs the
word *blôtrisi*, "giant to whom one makes sacrifice";
but Vigfusson in his Dictionary defines it "an enchanted champion," with a mark of doubt. Stones
smeared with butter may have been, as Grimm remarks, a compliment to the giants. Worship at
the huge stone tombs, believed to be the sepulchres
of a giant race, must have been in a manner worship
of the giant-spirits which haunted the place. The
old homilies explain the heathen gods as "giants,"
and "men who were very mighty."[1] Certain gods
are called directly giants, — "Mercury the giant."

Such ceremonies as we have hitherto described
were of an intimate and personal character, and
limited to a narrow round of domestic life; but we
must now broaden our view, and, first of all, in
addition to the cult of spirits who dwelt in the different elements, and at bidding would take human
form and appear to the mortal who knew the way to
summon them, we must admit a direct worship of
the elements themselves. It was a vague personality
which seemed in the storm-wind to prostrate the
giant oak and hew a path through the forest, out it
was a personality none the less. Human power could
never compass such destruction, and the ancestral
spirits were out of the question; with the evidence of
earliest language, and a careful study of modern
savage reasoning, we come to the assurance that our
remote forefathers must have worshipped from the

[1] Kemble, *Salomon and Saturn*, p. 120 ff.

outset the animated forces of nature. These were
spoken of as persons, and in most cases were regular
divinities, — a heaven-god, a thunder-god, a wind-god.
Before, however, we approach the cult of these
deities, we must trace the more direct worship of the
elements.

Cæsar says [1] of the Germans that they have no gods
save those whom their perceptions reveal to them and
by whose agency they have material profit, such as
Sun, Moon, and Fire: "Solem et Vulcanum et Lu-
nam." Cæsar was undoubtedly wrong [2] in his limitation; but his positive testimony is of value. He
shows a tendency of the Germans to worship deities
which were intimately connected with powers of
nature, as well as the Germanic veneration for these
powers in and for themselves. Let us take for the
first an element which Cæsar does not name, — water.
We have already seen how fain our ancestors were
to worship at wells and springs, and how wide was
the power of healing which they attributed to the
agency of any sacred fountain. But the element
itself was held in highest veneration, and this is particularly manifest in the old leechdoms. "Let the
woman," runs an Anglo-Saxon specimen, [3] "who cannot bring forth [or feed, nourish?] her child, take in
her hand milk from a cow of one color, and then sup
it with her mouth, and then go to running water and
dip up with the same hand a mouthful of the water
and swallow it: then let her speak these words. . . ."
How to get the water is more important than its
source: — at midnight or before dawn, in absolute

---

[1] *B. G.* VI. 21.   [2] *D. M.* 85.
[3] Grendon, *art. cit.*, pp. 206—209. 234 (notes).

silence, with one's hand scooping up the water against or with the stream and turning towards the east, taking the water from three separate brooks, and what not.[1] Celtic water-worship was pronounced; in a certain well a broken sword is made whole, and "the spring that turneth wood to stone," mentioned by the king to Laertes in *Hamlet*, had doubtless something more than chemical traditions.[2]

Fire in many ways resembles water;[3] it is full of motion, capricious, serviceable, destructive. Tylor divides fire-cult into two varieties, — worship of the actual flame before the devotee, and worship of any fire as manifestation of the fire-god.[4] While the orient is the peculiar home of this cult, we find ample evidence of it among the races of Europe; Slavonic tribes are perhaps most prominent. The fire upon the hearth is of course the centre of all domestic ceremony of the sort; brides on entering their new home were once led about the hearth, then central in the hall; and nowadays an Esthonian bride throws money into the flames, or else a live offering, such as a chicken.[5] A devouring and greedy monster, fire is appeased by such gifts and does not fall upon house or barn. Worship of fire is forbidden in the Anglo-Saxon laws and decrees. Cnut's definition of heathendom included the cult of "sun and moon, fire and flood-water," but Grimm can find little else to testify to a regular cult of fire among the Germans. Probably it was a prevailing sentiment rather than a special cult. There is a certain gratitude for the

---

[1] *Leechdoms, passim.*   [2] *D. M.* 487.
[3] Etymology helps us with our English *burn* and German *Bronnen.*
[4] *P. C.* II. 277 ff.   [5] Ibid. II. 285; *D. M.* 501.

benefits of fire, natural to inhabitants of a cold country, as where the Edda, in different mood from Pindar's, says that fire is the best thing for mortals;[1]
while in the cosmogony of the Scandinavian myths
the same element plays a great part in the bringing
forth of life. The assumption that primitive Germanic faith looked forward to a great fire which
should end the world, — that from Muspellsheim came
the creative warmth, and thence also shall come the
element of universal destruction, — is not now held by
all mythologists. It is disputed by Bugge,[2] who refers
to Christian influences this whole notion of the end of
the world; and he is joined by other authorities.[3]

The survivals mostly show us fire as object of worship on account of its purifying and healing properties, — a desperate but potent cure. In the Mark of
Brandenburg we find traces of what was doubtless,
in old times, a far more terrible rite. Until lately,
peasants of that neighborhood were wont to meet
sickness in swine by driving them through a fire,
made under the most careful conditions, by the fric-
tion of a rope, or similar device. In other places, and
under the same circumstances, a similar sacred fire is
prepared; all other fires in the village being meanwhile extinguished, and swine, cattle, poultry even,
are driven through the healing flame.[4] We could
collect a number of similar survivals in which fire
plays this purifying and healing part.[5] It is sig-

---

[1] *D. M.* 500.   [2] *Studier*, p. 419 f.

[3] Meyer, *Völuspa*, p. 182, says that this Norse and sporadically German doctrine of the world's end "has not been proved to be primitive
German belief."   [4] *D. M.* 503 f.

[5] The smoke of these fires is beneficent. If it passed over and
through the branches of fruit trees, it ensured a heavy crop.

nificant — one thinks of the Roman custom — that in
many of these village rites only persons of a pure
life are allowed to take a leading part; and the
favorite fashion of kindling the so-called *neid-fire*,[1]
by the rubbing of sticks, could be matched by similar
restrictions in rites of other races. A double sanctity
must have informed the ceremony when the "neid-
fire" was used to heat water, which one proceeded to
sprinkle over cattle afflicted with the murrain.[2] Fire
played a great part in the midsummer festivals of the
heathen; and held through later times, as at Easter,
or at St. John's day, when great fires were lighted
on the mountains and hilltops, and the whole coun-
try-side seemed to be ablaze. Around these fires.
the people danced and sported, jumped over and
through the flames, and thus kept up in traditional
forms of merry-making the old severities of their
forefathers' cult. A rude sort of divination was
practised with this aid. Wheels bound with straw,
and so set on fire, were rolled down the hillside, into
the river below; if the fire held till it touched the
water, a good vintage was foretold that year.[3] Elsewhere the wheel takes away all ill-luck from the
people of the village.[4] We hear of all manner of
fires at this season; "made of bones," one sort, — the
modern bon-fire, according to a half-parlous etymology;[5] fire of "clean wood"; fire of wood and bones

---

[1] This form is Scotch. The German form is much older. It is mentioned in 742, and forbidden as a heathen rite, — "illos sacrilegos
ignes." The Indiculus speaks, "de igne fricato de ligno, id est, nod-
fyr." *D. M.* 502. See Mannhardt, *Baumk*. p. 518 ff.

[2] *D. M.* 507.   [3] Ibid. 514 ff.

[4] Brand, *Antiquities*, "Summer Solstice."

[5] Skeat, *Dict.*, and Brand as quoted above.

mixed.   Mention is made in an obscure poem quoted
by Brand, but charged with classical allusions, of the
habit of "*casting mylk* to the Bonefyre."   Farmers
were wont to go around their cornfields with burning torches; [1] and in every way a superfluity of heat
and light seems to have been in order.   At the
opposite season of the year, the winter solstice, we
find fire in the same popularity, — witness the Yule
Log and its train of ceremonies.   It is hard, however,
in this case to disentangle the ceremonial from the
practical uses of fire.   Michaelmas, too, had its fires;
then, as in midsummer, blazed the torch, and the
straw-covered wheel rolled down the hillside with a
crowd of torch-bearers rushing after it; by the brook,
the goal of the wild chase, peasant-girls waited for
the runners, and gave them cakes and wine, as prologue to the dance.   Many of these rites survived,
even into our century, and are beyond all reasonable
doubt relics of heathen ceremony.[2]   A little later
than Michaelmas, on St. Martin's day, fires blazed in
even more persistent fashion; torches were borne
about, fields and orchards were visited, and in many
places, baskets of grain or fruit were cast directly
into the flames, — an evident sacrifice.[3]

In short, not to multiply examples of this sort,
still less, to lose ourselves in speculations about
symbols, it is evident that fire survives in all these
ceremonies partly as a once universal means of worship offered to various powers, and partly as an ele-

---

[1] In one German village the burning wheel of St. John's eve is called
the "Hail-Wheel," and Pfannenschmid (*Erntefeste*, pp. 67, 384; Mannhardt, *Baumk.* p. 500) concludes that the rite was meant to defend
crops from the ravages of hail.

[2] Pfannenschmid, *Erntefeste*, pp. 117, 491.   [3] Ibid. 210 ff.

ment which found its own cult among people who wished its beneficence and feared its dangers, — recognizing it doubtless as the most important factor ever added to the progress of civilization. But even in fire-worship we cannot fail to find the trace of manes-cult. The soul was fancied as flame, and about the dead man's barrow hovered an uncanny fire. As usual, the popular belief is perverted into superstition of wiser ages, and only the evil and grosser souls suffer this fiery imprisonment. Such are the dismal lights of the churchyard.

Direct cult of the wind is not illogical; for the storm has its terrors to be averted, and milder breezes bring clouds and fertilizing rain. Feeding the wind is a rite which we have already noticed; Tylor quotes a charm from New Zealand, where, however, the element seems to be personified.[1] The air, like water and fire, is a purifying agent; but it is hard to tell what logic of ceremony survives in the odd notion of a Danish huntsman that to obtain charmed bullets and sure aim (*frit skud*) he must let the wind of a Thursday morning blow into his gun-barrel. Thiele says it means a pact with the Wild Huntsman, who is ruler of the air.[2] Superstition has much to say about witches who can raise the wind, cause storms, and the like. This is black magic; but more legitimate are the ceremonies, once part of a cult, now mostly broken and silly remnants, which avert the harmful agency of storm and flood and hail. These ceremonies were either public or private, and, judging by the survivals,[3] of the most

[1] *P. C.* II. 378.   [2] Thiele, *Danmarks Folkesagn*, II. 112.
[3] A list of these, too long to quote, in Pfannenschmid, *Erntefeste*, p. 373 f.

varied character. Direct testimony of our heathen ancestors' doings in this particular cult is given by a decree of Charlemagne against the custom of "baptizing" bells to act as prevention of the hail, or of writing upon cards and attaching the latter to poles set up in the fields. The "runes" were undoubtedly forbidden because of their heathenish nature; for we read of a case where a bishop took a piece of wax from the grave of a saint, fastened it to one of the highest trees, and so drove away the hailstorms that had before laid waste his fields.[1]

As to the earth, the "mother" of so many myths, we shall have difficulty in separating any direct cult from the worship of an earth-goddess. A long charm of Anglo-Saxon origin[2] contains amid a mass of clerical superstition a few fragments of older heathenism. It runs as follows: "Here is the remedy how thou canst remedy thy fields if they will not bear well, or if any improper thing is done thereupon in the way of magic, or of bewitching by drugs. Take thou by night, before daybreak, four pieces of turf on the four sides of the land, and note how they previously stood. Take then oil and honey and barm and milk of all cattle that may be on the land, and part of every kind of tree that may grow on the land except hard trees,[3] and part of every known herb except burdock[4] alone, and put holy water thereon, and drop thrice on the place of

1 References in Pfann. *Erntef.* p. 57 ff.

2 British Museum, *MS. Cotton Caligula A, VII*, printed in Grein-Wülker, *Bibl. d. angel. Poesie*, I, 312—316; *D. M.⁴*, 1033; and most recently by Grendon, *Journ. American. Folk-Lore*, XXII (1909), 172—177, 219—220 (notes), and pp. 155, 156 (analytic comment).

3 Oak and beech. Grimm, *D. M.* 1035; *R. A.* 506.

4 Çockayne says "buckbean" with (?).

the pieces of turf, and say then these words: ' *Crescite*, wax, *et multiplicamini*, and multiply, *et replete*, and fill, *terram*, this earth. *In nomine patris et filii et spiritus sancti sint*[1] *benedicti.*' And *Pater Noster* as often as the other. And then take the turves to church, and let the mass-priest sing four masses over the turves and let the green part be turned towards the altar, and afterwards, before sunset, take back the turves thither where they were. And have wrought of live tree four signs[2] of Christ and write, on each end, Matthew and Mark, Luke and John. Lay the sign of Christ on the bottom of the pit and then say: *Crux Mattheus, crux Marcus, crux Lucas, crux sanctus Johannes.* Take then the turves and set them there above, and say then nine times these words: *Crescite* and as often *Pater Noster*, and turn thee then eastward, and bow nine times humbly and say these words: —

> " Eastward I stand, I ask for my welfare,
> ask I the Mighty Lord, ask I the Mickle God,
> ask I the holy Heavenly Warder, —
> Earth I ask and Up-Heaven[3]
> and the sooth Sancta Maria
> and heaven's might and high palace,[4]
> that I this charm by the Chieftain's[5] gift,
> may open with[6] teeth in earnest mind,
> waken these fruits for our worldly use,
> till these fields with firm belief,
> make splendid this turf, — as spake the prophet,
> that he speeds on earth who alms divideth,
> well and willingly by will of God.

---

[1] *Sitis?* Wülker.   [2] Crosses.   [3] *Cf.* O. H. G. *ufhimil.*
[4] *Reced* = house, but in Epinal Gloss (Sweet's *O. E. Texts*, p. 83), *ræcedlic* = palatina, " palatial."   [5] *Dryhten,* "leader" = God.
[6] Or "from"; as much as " speak," like the Homeric figure.

"Turn thee then thrice, with the course of the sun, stretch thee then at full length, and say these litanies, and then say *Sanctus, Sanctus, Sanctus,* to the end. Sing then *Benedicite* with outstretched arms, and *Magnificat* and *Pater Noster* thrice, and commit it to the praise and glory of Christ and Sancta Maria, and the Holy Rood and the profit of him who owns thy land and all those that are placed under him. When all this is done, then let unknown seed be taken from beggars, and let there be given to these twice as much as one takes from them, and gather together all the ploughing utensils; then bore in the plowtree and [place in the hole] incense and fennel and hallowed soap and hallowed salt. Take then the seed, set it in the body of the plow, and say : —

> "Erce, Erce, Erce, earth's mother,[1]
> grant thee the Almighty, Master Eternal,
> acres waxing and waving in bloom,
> big with increase, brave to see,
> store of stalks, standing corn,[2]
> broad-leaved barley's bountiful fruit,
> eke the white of the wheat in plenty,
> and likewise all the earth's abundance.
> Grant to him, God eternal,
> and his holy saints which in heaven be,
> that his earth be defended from every foe,
> be safe from every ill and drug
> thrown by magic athwart the land!
> Now bid I the Wielder, this world who made,
> no woman so word-strong,[3] no man be so mighty,
> to turn away these words here said!

[1] Cockayne makes *eorþan* a locative.

[2] A desperate translation of a difficult line. Readings differ, and the text is corrupt.

[3] We notice throughout the charm that chief fear is of women and also chief hope of aid from women, — "mother of earth," or "mother earth," as the case may be.

"Then drive the plow and make the first furrow. Say then: —

> "Hail to thee, Earth, all men's mother,
> be thou growing in God's protection,
> filled with food for feeding of men!

"Take then meal of every kind and bake a loaf, 'as big as will lie within his two hands,'[1] and knead it with milk and with holy-water, and lay it under the first furrow. Say then: —

> "Full field of food for folk of men,
> brightly blooming, blessed be thou,
> in the name of the holy one, heaven's maker,
> and earth's also, whereon we live;
> God, world-maker, grant growing gifts,
> that all our corn may come to our use!

Say then thrice *Crescite in nomine patris, sint benedicti. Amen* and *Pater Noster* thrice."[2]

The value of this charm is evident; for all the expenditure of clerical forms of benediction, there is plenty of the old heathen rite left in full view. Who "Erce" may be is question for the mythologists;[3] but her title as "mother of earth" (or mother earth?) gives us sufficient standing-ground in the matter of cult.[4] As Grimm remarks, earth itself was "holy," and by simple logic any familiar spot of earth had its sacred character. Whoso abode long time away from his land, kissed the earth by way of greeting on his return; while Brutus, in the legend, took the wider

---

[1] Cockayne.   [2] For a few kindred rites, see Grimm, *D. M.* 1035 f.
[3] For which consult the passages noted by Wülker in his *Grundriss*, p. 349.   [4] Myths exist in plenty. See Tylor, *P. C.* I. 326 f.

view of his relation.[1] To die was, according to Scandinavian phrase, "falling to mother earth." Turf cut with its grass fresh upon it plays an important part in the charm just given; and it is perhaps not too fanciful to see in the ceremony of entering upon blood-brotherhood,[2] an assumption of common maternity on the part of the earth in which the two streams of blood flow together. Creeping under the raised sod was also part of various rites;[3] and oaths were made, as by holy trees, so also by turf and grass.

Partly in honor of the gods and goddesses of fertility, partly in honor of the sacred earth herself, were the manifold processions and ceremonies in field and garden. In the tenth century we find a German abbess establishing certain ceremonies which are to take the place of the former "heathen processions about the fields."[4] This was at Whitsuntide; there was to be watching through the night, a solemn procession at morning, and relics were to be borne about the fields. From these substitutions we can in some measure divine the heathen rites. Offerings and feast were in a manner continued, and survive to this day in some parts of Germany as a general feeding of the poor of the parish, often in the churchyard itself. In other places we hear of games and sport, which are forbidden by the synods;[5] but in countless villages of the Continent, as well as in England, the chief elements of these solemn processions have been retained.

---

[1] *D. M.* 534 f.　　　　　[2] Above, p. 173.

[3] *R. A.* 118 f. Other symbolic uses of turf are given in the same place.

[4] In 936. See Pfannenschmid, *Erntefeste*, p. 50 ff., 84 ff. Much material is. of course, collected by Mannhardt, *Feldkulte*.

[5] Pfannenschmidt. p. 53.

In the classical cosmogonies, Tellus must have her Uranus, and a heaven-god is familiar enough in mythology; but the cult[1] of overarching sky seems to have left few traces in our popular customs. The conception is too indefinite; but no such vagueness has hindered the worship of sun, moon, and stars. For the cult and adoration of sun and moon by heathen Germany, Cæsar gives explicit evidence; and from many other writers, as well as plentiful survival, we know what extraordinary efforts were made to help one of these heavenly bodies when it came into eclipse. The notion was common to Roman and barbarian. " Vince Luna! " was the cry, and all manner of noise was made to drive away the monster who was thought to be on the point of devouring its victim.[2] The heading of the twenty-first chapter of the *Indiculus*, to which we have so often alluded and whose loss as a whole is to be so heartily deplored, runs: "De lunæ defectione, quod dicunt *Vinceluna*." The cult of clamor and terror lasted in distorted fashions into the seventeenth century, where cases are on record for England as well as Germany.[3]

Direct worship of sun and moon is found among barbarous tribes of the present day, and to a candid judgment must seem to have been one of the most certain and clearly primitive inferences of the human mind. As J. Grimm hints,[4] people with any beginnings of agriculture, and especially those living in cold or temperate climates, would have a definite cult

---

[1] Myths, however, seem plentiful. See Tylor, *P. C.* I. 322 ff.

[2] The well-known classical reference is Juvenal, VI. 442. See also Tacitus, *Ann.* I. 28.

[3] Tylor, *P. C.* I. 333 f.   [4] *G. D. S.*[3] 51.

of the sun. The universal doctrine that sunrise is
fatal to evil spirits of every sort,[1] is itself ample evidence of this cult. Tylor has plentiful material for
the ceremonies of savage tribes.[2] Corresponding to
his account of the Samoyed woman who bowed morning and evening to the sun, we have the interesting
fact that in the Upper Palatinate people doff the hat
at sunrise.[3] The same thing is done in honor of the
moon ; while the peasant of that region is fain to ask
the sun to come and take away the " seventy-seven
fevers " with which he is afflicted. So, in Lucian's
time, the peasant kissed his hand " as an act of worship to the rising sun."[4] In a note to his *Volkslieder,*[5]
Uhland gives some verses which show in quaint confusion a mingling of Christian and heathen ideas.
with definite survival of element-worship : —

> God bless thee, moon and sun,
> And likewise leaf and grass. . . .
> *   *   *   *   *
> When he came to the hilltop,
> He looked wide around :
> " God bless thee, sun and moon,
> And all my loving friends ! "

Naturally, many of the festal fires which we have
noticed, perhaps those of Eastertide, belong to the
cult of the sun. Tylor reminds us that Aurelian instituted about the time of our Christmas a pagan
festival for " the birthday of the unconquered sun."[6]

[1] In Norse tradition if a troll is smitten by the rising sun, he is
turned to stone ; see *Alvismál,* st. 35 (Bellows, p. 194, Hollander, p.135).

[2] *P. C.* II. 287 ff.   [3] Wuttke, *Aberglaub.* p. 12.

[4] Tylor, *P. C.* II. 296.   [5] *Kl. Schr.* IV. 148.

[6] *P. C.* II. 297. A minor survival of sun-cult is found in the custom
of orientation. See Tylor, *P. C.* II. 296, 421 ff.

As to the midsummer festival, which occurs at the
summer solstice and was called by the Germans
"*sonnewende*," we may safely connect the fires and
wheels with some phase of sun-cult. The further
north we go, the more obvious this relation; and we
are told how after their long night the inhabitants of
" Thule " climbed the peaks to catch the first glimpse
of the sun, and then fell to celebrating their most
sacred festival.[1]

Cult of the moon is familiar in magic and witchcraft. Potent is the time of eclipse, and our Shaks-
perian almanac advises us that then is the season to
get in our slips of yew; leave root of hemlock for
a moonless night. Manifold superstitions about the
moon go back to heathen rites, and against some of
these the church made successful front. " No Christian man," says Beda in one of his treatises,[2] "shall
do anything of witchery by the moon." This is the
rationalism of the new order; but presently inherited
superstition peeps through, for he tells us he has no
doubt whatever that trees which be hewn at full
moon are harder against worm-eating and longer lasting than they which are hewn at the new moon.[3]
Indeed, the moon is more important in superstition
than the sun; it waxes and wanes, and in its setting
of night offers the desirable elements of mystery. It
is the most ancient timepiece, and we have seen that

[1] *D. M.* 601.

[2] *De Temporibus*, Anglo-Saxon trans. said to be by Ælfric, Cockayne, *Leechdoms*, III. 232 ff.

[3] Ibid. 266, 268. A later superstition demanded that trees should be
hewn down in the wane of the moon. *D. M.* 596. Cockayne gives a
leechdom which is to be taken " when the moon is on the wane."
Leechdoms I. 98, 100 (for loss of appetite and for lunacy).

Germanic popular government appointed its assemblies at the full moon,[1] and waited with awe upon the omens of its change.[2] Peace, of course, to the countless superstitions; but we may note that the Esthonian greets a new moon with the words: " Hail, moon! Mayst thou grow old, and may I grow young! "[3] It is an interesting parallel when Congo folk say: "So may I renew my life as thou art renewed! "[4]

The stars are too numerous and too distant for much worship; superstitions like that of the peasant who says a prayer when he spies a falling star, may have some precedent in ceremonial worship, and so may the advice to any wife, that if she wishes the hawks to keep away from her chickens, she must " greet the stars " when she goes to bed.[5]

Prayers to day and night — palpable conceptions, however indefinite and vast — are recorded in Germanic tradition, although it is myth rather than cult which has claimed these provinces. Day is sacred, holy; oaths are made by it;[6] and the same is true of night. In the Edda they are both invoked: —

> Hail, O Day!
> Hail, Day's sons!
> Hail, Night and Sister!
> With gracious eyes gaze on us,
> Give us victory![7]

A later bit from the German, —

> God greet thee, holy Sunday;
> I see thee ride this way!

---

[1] Tac. *Germ.* XI.   [2] Cæsar and Plutarch, as quoted above.
[3] *D. M.* 595, note.   [4] *P. C.* II. 300.
[5] *D. M.* III.; *Aberglaube*, 595, 112.
[6] *D. M.* 614 f. [7] *Sigdr.*, 2 Hollander, p. 274, Bellows, p. 389.

is a personification, and seems perilously near a mere poetic figure, though quoted from a form of blessing;[1] indeed, it is but ill-paying trouble to collect these doubtful relics. The worship of day is not a very evident inference ; rather some more concrete, compact and direct object would have been chosen, — like the sun.

In the same way we find traces of season-cult, especially of spring and summer. The chief trace of this cult, faint enough, is the personification of the season in question, on which we must be careful not to lay overmuch stress. That "May stands at the door" is evidence of poetry and myth; so is Shakspere's jubilant tribute,

> —jocund day
> Stands tiptoe on the misty mountain tops;

or, in soberer vein, —

> The morn, in russet mantle clad,
> Walks o'er the dew of yon high eastern hill.[2]

This personification is common with the seasons, as in the old English lays to spring : —

> Sumer is icumen in, —

or the less famous, —

> Lenten is come with loue to toune.[3]

---

[1] *D. M.* 615.

[2] Another pendant is Milton's exquisite picture : —
> Gray-hooded Even,
> Like a sad votarist in palmer's weed.

[3] Printed in Morris and Skeat's *Specimens of Early English,* II. 48. It dates from the thirteenth century. The same phrase is used in the *Menologium* or Anglo-Saxon Calendar, where heathen forms occur throughout; *e.g.* þæs þe lencten on tun geliden hæfde, werum to wicum. "Since spring ('Lent') had come to town, to the dwellings of men."

This phrase, that spring or any one of the months, is "come to town" that is, "come to the country," occurs constantly in our old literature; and it is matched by an expression in *Béowulf*, where "year" is used for "spring": —

> winter locked them [*sc.* the waves]
> in icy fetters. Then fared another
> year to men's dwellings ...[1]

On the other hand, the approach of winter is expressed with great power in an often-quoted Frisian law: "Si illa tenebrosa nebula et frigidissima hiems *in hortos et in sepes descendit*."[2] Winter — a cruel warrior, giant, or monster; summer or spring — a jocund youth: between these must be strife, and here indeed we find some rites which are doubly interesting since they point backward to Germanic worship and forward to Germanic drama.[3] A ballad printed by Uhland[4] gives the dialogue of such a contest as peasants would perform it, each figure clad in the proper symbolic costume; while J. Grimm collects a number of parallel survivals. A heading of the *Indiculus*[5] may refer to this as a heathen custom which the church abolished as worship and tolerated as amusement. The strife of winter and summer was presented in old England, and the merriment of May Day, with its pole and boughs and dancings, seems to have some connection with the old cult of summer and spring.[6]

"Town," as in the case of Chaucer's "persone of a town," is not our word, but a parish, a district, as it is still used in New England for "township."

[1] *Beow.* 1134; cf. *Anglia*, XL (1928), 81, 82.

[2] See *D. M.* 635.   [3] Ibid. 654.

[4] *Volkslieder*, I. 23. See also the notes.   [5] Cap. 27.

[6] *D. M.* 649. Grimm sums up the four fashions of celebrating this festival which still survive in Europe. See also 657.

CHAPTER XIV

THE WORSHIP OF GODS

Germanic gods and goddesses — Evidence of their cult — The days of the week — Woden — Thunor — Tius — Nerthus, and the Ingævonic group — Other deities.

THE rise and progress of a Germanic family, from mere communal life in the bounds of a narrow canton to the power of a dynasty and the range of a kingdom, were accompanied, we may well believe, by a corresponding development of the ancestral spirits. Where once the shade of the dead man walked protecting and helpful about the limits of his old home, there must now rule a gigantic spirit, fettered to no single habitation, but throned high in air or dwelling in remote and inaccessible places. Meanwhile the ancestral idea became blurred; the god was vaguely known as progenitor of the race.

Parallel with this process ran a sharpening and clarifying of the notions about natural forces. Curiosity, advancing further upon the outer world, reduced its conclusions to a system and made far more distinct the personality which had been so vague to the earlier inquirer. Definite biographies, one may say, were published about the elemental gods, and formed along with heroic legend the staple of primitive poetry. What adjustments were made between ancestral and elemental worship it is difficult to say, though it is clear that the latter would be more public, the former more of a household and peculiar duty. We must content ourselves with an outline of the worship paid in late heathen days to the gods of Germanic tradition.

Monotheism, as we understand it, was unknown to the Germans; but they had the usual tendency towards Henotheism, the worship of one favorite god. Such in early Scandinavia seems to have been the position of Thor. Forms like "*got unde mir willekomen*"[1] do not show any monotheistic spirit; they may refer to the household deity, the Lar. Certainly they do not express our modern notion of God. As for the All-Father of Scandinavian mythology, we may even exclude the very probable Christian influence, and still find ample explanation in the phrases of ancestor-worship. Ancestor-worship, however, had little or nothing to do with the actual Germanic gods, who haunted no barrows, were cabined, cribbed, confined in no hut or village, but

As broad and general as the casing air,

housed in the far-off regions of the north. So ran popular belief; and northward, with outstretched hands, our forefathers turned, when they engaged in ceremonial worship. With the introduction of Christianity, the east became cardinal point of prayer, and the north, as we might expect, was banned as unlucky

[1] *D. M.* 13.

and a place of devils.[1] Who were, then, the dwellers of that cold Germanic Olympus?

Some definite evidence on this point seems to meet us in the names given to our days of the week.[2] The Germans were still of heathen faith when they took the names of these days from Rome and translated them into terms of their own mythology. The week of seven days is naturally given by the changes of the moon, its so-called "quarters"; but we seem to have traces[3] of a week made up of five days only. Of the individual days, Sunday and Monday are obvious translations. But Tuesday, *dies Martis*, is credibly traced to the Germanic god Tius. Wednesday, *dies Mercurii*, has the stamp of Woden plain to see; and old Thor, our Saxon Thunor, is as evident in the name of Thursday,[4] *dies Jovis*. *Frige dæg* is good Anglo-Saxon for the *dies Veneris*.[5] Saturday is Anglo-Saxon *Sæteres dæg*, but also *Sæternes dæg*, evident translation of *dies Saturni*. The other form is not so easy to explain. *Sætere* means a seducer; and there may have been a deity with that by-name, — Loki, the Scandinavian, has been desperately sug-

---

[1] *R. A.* 808; *G. D. S.* 681. In the *Haverford College Studies*, No. 1, "On the Symbolic Use of Black and White," I have collected some material on this subject. It is very significant that an Anglo-Saxon charm against wens conjures the evil *into the north and to the mountains* (*Haupt's Z.* xxxi. 45 ff., printed by Professor Zupitza); and a Finnish charm sends the pestilence to the same place. In old judicial forms this dislike of the north is evident: criminals were hanged on a northward tree. In the *Frere's Tale* of Chaucer the fiend (in disguise) tells that he lives "in the north contre." Much more could be quoted to the same effect.

[2] The général question is discussed, *D. M.* 101 ff. See also *C. P. B.* I. 427 f. For *Frisia* see Richthofen, *Fries. Rechtsges.* II. 431 f.

[3] Ibid.   [4] Old Frisian *Thunresdei*.

[5] Confusion of Frigg and Freyja meets us in Norse tradition. *D. M.* 251.

gested, with a shy look at Danish Lørdag as corruption from the name of the god, — though this seems unlikely. Kemble suggests *settere*, "one who arranges or orders"; but the analogy with Saturn is after all so near as to save us much guessing.

Evidence of cult lies, further, in those names of places which have their origin in the name of a god. For example, the strongest presumption in favor of a god Sætere would spring from such cases as the mention of *Sæteres byrig* in an Anglo-Saxon document under date of the year 1062;[1] and in Scandinavia the popularity of Thor and his worship is abundantly proved by similar means. Petersen[2] shows that the sturdy old god entirely distances all the other Scandinavian deities, and even in Normandy and the Danish parts of England, the name of Thor has left its mark. As with places, so with persons; and here again, so far as Scandinavia is concerned, we find Thor overwhelmingly the favorite,[3] though Odin and Freyr are not neglected. It was customary there for a man to give his son to the service of the god, and to name the former from the latter. We have, in fact, two sorts of names derived in this fashion among Scandinavians of the heathen period. In the first instance any name might be combined with the name of deity in general, such as the Norse *Ass* or *Goð*. "Thus King Raum gave his son Brand to the gods,[4] and thereupon called him Godbrand."[5] Or, on the other hand, the parent

---

[1] Kemble, *Cod. Dip.* IV. 457. There is a plant *sattorlaðe*, "the common crowfoot."

[2] *Om Nordboernes Gudedyrkelse og Gudetro i Hedenold*, p. 46 f.

[3] Ibid. 41, and also Vigfusson, Icelandic Dict. *s.v.* Þórr.

[4] Probably a substitution-survival of the hideous old rite of actual sacrifice of one's children.   [5] Petersen, p. 39 f.

chose the name and service of some special god; and here again we find old Thor by far the most honored among all Scandinavian deities. Such a name was Thorgrim.

The chief god of the Germans when the Roman came in contact with them, seems to have been Woden.[1] This is the English form of the name, although some of our early homilies, evidently under Danish influence, call him Othon or Othin. The meaning of the name is not certain; some connect it with the Old English "wood," — "enraged," "furious;"[2] some with the notion of "wandering," with evident application to the Scandinavian myths which tell about Odin's travels and disguises; and others, again, see in the name a reflection of the god's intellectual qualities.[3] Certain, however, is the fact that Woden is the wind-god, the deity of heaven in the literal sense, the prince of the powers of the air, although he is not the original ruler of Germanic deities; he has taken the place of an older heaven-god, Tius, and seems to have got the latter's wife in the bargain. This, however, is matter for mythology; let us turn to the cult.

In the first place, it is of great significance that we find this god in the genealogy of Anglo-Saxon kings; he is ancestor of the monarchs of Kent, Essex, East Anglia, Mercia, Deira, Bernicia, Wessex, and the

[1] The old German form is Wuotan, or among the Saxons, Wôdan; the Scandinavian form was Oðinn, now commonly called Odin; and in oldest English men said Wôden. The use of Odin in these pages indicates allusion to the Scandinavian god.

[2] "Wodan, id est furor." Adam of Bremen.

[3] D. M.' 109. Wóden (Scan. Óðinn, Germ. Wōtan) is doubtless derived from wód "raging" and presents a god (of death) at the head of a "raging army" (cf. Germ. das wütende Heer). See NED. under "Wednesday".

Lindesfaran.[1] Beda speaks of Hengest and Horsa
as descendants of Woden.[2] Names of places in England and elsewhere bear the same testimony,[3] and not
only places, but animals and plants as well. The
annalists are apt to take Woden as a king who afterwards was deified: "Woden," says one, "whom the
Angles worship as chief god, and from whom they derive their origin, was a mortal man, and king of the
Saxons, and father of many races."[4] The explanation of this supremacy of Woden in the later heathen
times lies in his double attribute of intellectual skill [5]
— he is said to have "invented" runes — and love of
war. Hence the fitness of his place as begetter of
kings, and hence the later tendency to exalt him
above all the gods. The constant warfare of these
times made *Othinus armipotens*[6] easily the central
figure. Here, too, he seems to have taken the place
of Tius, the older "Mars." To Odin the Scandinavians ascribed the invention of their mode of attack
in battle, the wedge-shaped column, really of far
greater antiquity than Germanic warriors ever knew,
and known to these Norsemen as the Boar's Head.
Moreover, Odin was father of war itself; when he
threw his spear, battle was born in the world.[7] The

---

[1] *D. M.* III. 377.

[2] *Hist. Ecc.* I. 15. "Erant autem filii Victgilsi, cuius pater Vitta,
cuius pater Vecta, cuius pater Voden, de cuius stirpe multarum prouin-
ciarum regium genus originem ducit."

[3] *D. M.* 126 f., 131 f.; Grimm, *Kl. Schr.* II. 58 ff. Names of places
compounded with names of this god are comparatively rare in Scandinavia, where Thor is overwhelmingly the favorite. See Petersen, p. 43 f.

[4] *Vita S. Kentigerni*, quoted by Holtzmann, *Germ. Alt.* p. 251.

[5] In Roman interpretation he is called Mercurius; and in *Sal. and
Sat.* the question "Who invented letters?" is answered, "Mercury the
Giant." See also *D. M.* 126.

[6] So Saxo calls him.   *Voluspá*, st. 16.

spear was his peculiar weapon, and was still the chief
arm of Germanic soldiers in the time of Tacitus.
Scandinavian cult, in spite of Viking fashions which
set so mightily toward the god of wisdom and warfare, clung grimly to old Thor; but it bowed enough
to new ways to change several of its great festivals
and in them to honor Odin, giver of victory, as well
as Thor, the protector of house and home. Such a
feast in honor of Odin was held about the beginning
of summer, when the campaign opened, and ways
whether of land or of sea, became easy of passage.[1]
We may suppose this habit to have been Germanic
as well as Scandinavian. Paul the Deacon's famous
story shows two rival tribes asking "Wodan" for
victory. Of course each army promised sacrifice —
its slain enemies — in return for such a gift; and we
find in the Norse sagas this or that hero hurling his
spear over the heads of the hostile band, and crying:
"Odin have you all!" The wolf is Woden's beast,
and the raven is his bird; the latter is also a sign of
victory, not at all the thing of evil it became in later
times. Even as a commonplace of diction the raven
has joyous meaning, as in the lines of *Béowulf:* —

> till a raven black the rapture-of-heaven
> blithe-heart boded.[2]

Another feature of his cult which connects Odin
or Woden with the new Germanic period, is the fact
that he was looked upon as a protector of the merchant and sailor;[3] he aided the bargaining of the
former, and to the latter he gave a favorable wind.[4]

---

[1] Petersen, p. 88.   [2] 1801 f.   [3] See material in Müller's *System*, p. 187.
[4] Grimm's god "Wish" is now generally rejected. It was a personification in mediæval poetry.

THE WORSHIP OF GODS

Moreover, since he was the god that sent forth pestilence and disease, heathen logic inferred that he could best rescue from these ills; as the Scandinavian cried, in moments of sudden danger, " Help me, Odin ! " so in the time of sickness. Luckily we have a genuine relic of the old Woden cult, an incantation preserved in widely sundered dialects, and of undoubted Germanic origin. It is the companion charm to that which invoked the Valkyrias,[1] and was found with it in the library at Merseburg :[2] —

> Phol and Wodan fared to the holt :
> then Balder's foal's foot was wrenched.
> Then Sinthgunt [3] besang it and Sunna her sister :
> then Fria besang it and Volla her sister :
> then Wodan besang it, who well knew how,
> the wrenching of bone, the wrenching of blood,[4]
> the wrenching of limb :
> bone to bone, blood to blood,
> limb to limb, as if they were limed ![5]

Even if we admit Bugge's theories, and let Phol mean the apostle Paul, and Balder mean " the Lord," we have nevertheless plenty of heathendom left. Woden is undoubtedly central figure; and whatever elements have been introduced from Christian sources, they have been obviously substituted, for the older heathen fashion.[6] What makes this charm of supreme importance is the great number of variations found in the different Germanic countries. It appears in Norway and Sweden, in Scotland, in

[1] See above, p. 376.   [2] MS. of the tenth century.
[3] Sinhtgunt, says Bugge, *Studier*, p. 297.   [4] *I.e.* of *veins*. Bugge.
[5] Glued together.
[6] Bugge suggests " Frija and Wodan," p. 307 of the German trans. of the *Studier*.

Flanders, and elsewhere.[1] As Scherer says, Woden is
"supreme physician,"— and here is need of the best.

Still another charm, this time from the Anglo-
Saxon, shows us Woden as final appeal in a somewhat similar emergency.   In the charm of Nine
Worts to be used against poisons,[2] we have a list of
the virtuous herbs, with one or two probable heathen
references.   Then follows: —

> These nine are opposed to poisons nine.
> Sneaking came snake, tore asunder a man.
> Then took Woden nine Wonder-Twigs:
> he smote the Nadder,[3] in nine [pieces] it flew. . . .

Thus Woden, in this place, performs an act of sorcery; and the twigs are in direct accord with the
Germanic method of casting lots described by Tacitus.[4]   These charms are of great interest.   Less
important, however, though not without bearing on
our subject, are the many customs of peasant-life
which seem to point back to an older worship of
Woden.   In some of the German cornfields it was
the habit at harvest-time to leave a heap of corn "for
Woden's horse."   A writer living in Rostock in
1593 describes the custom of Mecklenburg at rye-
harvest, when they gave grain to the god, with the
rhyme: —

> Wode, give thy horse fodder.
> Now thistle and thorn,
> Next year, better corn![5]

---

[1] See *D. M.* 1030 ff.; Bugge, *Studier* (Germ. trans.), 301 ff.; Rochholz. *Deutscher Glaube.* I. 281.

[2] Grendon, *Journ. Amer. Folk-Lore*, XXII (1909), 193, 226—229.

[3] Adder.   [4] *Germ.* X. See below, p. 467.

[5] *D. M.* 128 f. Grimm gives a number of parallel cases. See also
Mannhardt's *Feldculte;* Pfannenschmidt, p. 107 ff.

Trees were sacred to him, and in his grove offerings were made of captives, criminals, or even beasts. His worship was widespread and deeply rooted; when the heathen, by a specified oath, renounced their old faith and joined the church, they were compelled to name Woden as one of the devils and monsters.[1] In Scandinavia he seems to have received, in Viking days, supreme honors; but, as we shall presently see, Thor was the real god of the Northmen. Still, in the famous temple at Upsala in Sweden, described by Adam of Bremen, Odin was represented by an image "like to Mars," — that is to say, fully armed.[2] He it was who received the soul of the warrior in the new-fashioned heaven of Viking Scandinavia, Valhalla; and to him the men of war everywhere — and war was everywhere — put up their prayers and in stress of battle offered service, child, or proper life. By the *Interpretatio Romana* he was called Mercury.

To Thunor, as the Anglo-Saxon called him, the Thor of the Scandinavian peasant, there must have belonged a widespread Germanic cult. Especially was this the case among the Norsemen, where, as Petersen's book shows beyond doubt, Thor "the land-god" was worshipped above all other deities. He was called Jupiter by the Romans, and that not solely, we may imagine, on account of his thunderbolts. It is probable, however, that in the *Germania*,[3]

---

[1] Renunciation used under Boniface by Saxons and Thuringians: "Ec forsacho allum diaboles wercum and wordum, Thunær ende Woden ende Saxnote ende allum them unholdum the hira genotas sint." "I forsake all devil's works and words, and Thuner and Woden and Saxnot and all the monsters who are their companions."

[2] "Wodanem armatum sculpunt." Adam Br. IV. 26.

[3] Cap. IX. See also Zeuss, *die Deutschen*, p. 25.

Tacitus calls him Hercules; for Müllenhoff reminds us that with the Romans Hercules was not only a hero, but also a god. Additional testimony to Thor's or Thunor's importance is the fact that the arch-fiend of Christian times, the devil himself, takes the place of the old thunder-god.[1] In Scandinavia men made most solemn oaths in calling upon Thor, and they celebrated his feast at the sacred time of Yule.[2] As god of the home and all that belongs to it, he was worshipped first and foremost of the deities ; and we may be sure that the rough satire of the Harbards Lay, where Odin boasts of his own amorous and warlike feats, mocks Thor for his homely ways, and generally plays the *miles gloriosus*, was not meant for the ears of peasants. They prayed to him for a mild winter, an early spring, and generous crops; his first thunderings heralded return of warmth and vegetation.[3] As late as the eighteenth century a Scandinavian woman was known to pray regularly to Thor;[4] and the Anglo-Saxon homilies bear witness to the stubbornness of Thunor's cult on English soil.

Thor's thunder, audible sign that he and his hammer were fighting ice-giants and obstinate spirits of the northern hills, was regarded as more a benefit than a terror. It symbolized fertility; and we find several plants named after the thunder.[5] The wood of a tree which had been struck by lightning was good for many purposes, and toothpicks made of it

---

[1] *D. M.* 151, and Chap. XXXIII. throughout. See also Roskoff, *Geschichte des Teufels.* In favorable matters he is represented by Elias.

[2] Petersen, p. 63.

[3] Unowned or lordless land was given to Thor. Grimm, *Kl. Schr.* II. 56 ff.

[4] Holtzmann's *D. M.* 67.   [5] *D. M.* 152 f.

are still thought to cure the toothache.[1] Any man who was smitten by the bolt was regarded as particularly happy in his taking-off.[2] Of trees, the oak was dedicated to the thunder-god, — a bold and not ignoble piece of religious invention. His day was Thursday, still in every regard a lucky day ; in Scandinavia the traditional day for a wedding, and of good right, if we consider that it was Thor's hammer which " hallowed " every bride.[3] The public assembly was held in most Scandinavian districts on the Thursday ; and we must remember the hammer-cast which marked out the borders of a judicial court, as well as the fact that Thor was the patron and god of such an assembly. Most significant is the vast number of Scandinavian names which are compounded with the name of Thor ; places — where we may compare the German Donnersberg — and people abound in proof of this favorite patron ; while but few can be found which bear the stamp of other gods or goddesses.[4] Indeed, some of the names are directly associated with the processes of cult ; Thorkell, for example, from Thorketill, and probably Thurston from Thor's stone.[5] Not only these names ; the kennings which express the god himself, are full of significance for his worship.[6]

Almost alone of Scandinavian gods, Thor found lasting representation in a rude picture carved on stock and stone,[7] even on ships,[8] — " a long-bearded face,

[1] Wuttke, *Aberglauben*, p. 93. [2] *D. M.* 145.
[3] Petersen, p. 70 f. [4] Petersen, p. 41 f.
[5] *D. M.* 155 ff. [6] *C. P. B.* II. 464 f.
[7] Petersen, p. 33 f.
[8] Ibid. 84. It is probable he was once god of battles.

with the hammer hung beneath ";[1] while his actual image was adorned with gold and silver, and set up in the holy places. Runes, moreover, add their testimony to the universal nature of Thor's cult in Scandinavia.[2] Even the vanity of our Germanic ancestors took a religious bent, or more correctly went hand in hand with superstition, inasmuch as their ornaments were often made in the shape of Thor's famous hammer.   Some of these ornaments are of striking beauty,[3] and were meant to hang as charms or amulets about the neck; for to Thor men prayed in times of sudden danger, as well as in sickness and want.[4] He was chief guardian of the home; and on the posts of the high-seat, where sat the master of the Norse household, was carved the face of Thor. Viking belief assigned the souls of dead warriors to Odin, while "Thor has the thralls";—yet not as god of the thralls did he take them, but rather because the servants were part and parcel of the household.[5]

The god whose old Germanic and Gothic name must have been Tîus, Old High German Zio, Scandinavian Týr, but in English was known as Tîw, was once worshipped as the heaven-god, but seems to have been the war-god as well. A gloss of the Epinal *MS.*, which goes back to the seventh century, a most venerable witness, makes Tiig the same as Mars.[6]

---

[1] *C. P. B.* II. 464.   [2] Petersen, p. 51 ff.   [3] Ibid. p. 75.

[4] Ibid. 56, and Adam of Bremen says of the Thor image at Upsala: " Si pestis et famis imminet Thor ydolo lybatur."

[5] Ibid. 62. A mass of information about Thor may be found not only in Petersen's work, but in the brilliant piece of investigation by Uhland, *Der Mythus von Thor*. While the bulk of the book is taken up with theories about the "meanings" of myths, there is much solid material.   [6] The *g* in this form shows it to be of Mercian origin.

As with the other gods, places were named after
him;[1] and songs of battle were chanted in his honor.[2]
It is supposed that he was the deity worshipped in
the grove of the Semnones [3] with such strenuous rites.
Tacitus tells us that human sacrifices were offered to
Mercury and Mars, — that is, to Woden and to Tius;
and similar offerings to a war-god are related by
the historian Procopius.[4] The sword-dance described
above[5] was doubtless in honor of this god, and Grimm
connects with him the worship of swords recorded by
old historians.[6] At the time of Tacitus and in the
neighborhood of central and northern Germany, Tius
seems to have held the place taken in later times by
Woden. His day, Tuesday, has a few superstitions
connected with it which point to older cult; for
instance, it must be on the Tuesday that the plant is
gathered which warriors use for crown.[7]

In Scandinavian cult we find not only a Tyr, but
a god who is really a "hypostasis" of Tyr or Tius, —
Heimdall, "the world-glad." Rams were sacrificed
to him. Another hypostasis of Tius, and more interesting to us, is Saxnéat or Saxnôt, "the sword-companion" or brother in arms,[8] who figures above as
one of the gods to be abjured in the Old German
renunciation, and is undoubtedly Tius under another
name.[9] Saxneat plays an important part in the

---

[1] D. M. 164 ff.   [2] Ibid. 171.
[3] See below, p. 441, and Tac. Germ. XXXIX.; Ann. IV. 64.
[4] Gesch. d. d. Vorzeit, Procop. p. 124.   [5] Above, p. 198.
[6] D. M. 169; Simrock, Mythol. 272 f.   [7] Grimm, G. D. S.[2] 88.
[8] Zeuss, p. 25; W. Müller, System, p. 226 f.
[9] These names indicate various phases of warfare, as Müllenhoff
notes in his important paper in Schmidt's Zeitschrift f. Geschichte,
Vol. VIII.

Anglo-Saxon genealogies, — for example in the royal ancestry of Wessex.

Two inscriptions which Scherer laid in 1884 before the Berlin Academy, would seem co show that Tius even acted as guardian and god of the popular legal assembly. He appears as "Mars Thingsus," *thing* being the Germanic term, still used in Scandinavian tongues, for a legislative body. The inscriptions were found in 1883 on two large votive altars near the old Hadrian's wall in Great Britain, at a place called Housesteads; they show that the altars were erected by a division of Frisian cavalry serving as part of the imperial army under Alexander Severus (222–235), and for some special aid or favor were dedicated to Germanic deities, — Mars Thingsus and the so-called *Alaisiagae*, Bede and Fimmilene, — as well as to the Roman imperial family. F. Kauffmann[1] asserts that Mars Thingsus, while undoubtedly Tius, is not addressed as a god of popular assemblies, but as the patron deity of that battalion or division; for the Germanic army was arranged by clans, and the name of a tribal assembly could be transferred to a military brigade. However that may be, here is Tius worshipped by very near relatives of our own ancestors, whether or not as god of the popular gathering. We may remember that these meetings were under the special protection of a god, and hence were always controlled by the priests, who alone had power to command silence and to punish offenders.[2]

Another god is called in Scandinavian myths Freyr. He is interesting to us as the probable god whose worship was most popular among our coast-

---

[1] *P. B. Beiträge*, XIV. 200 ff.   [2] Tac. *Germ.* XI.

dwelling ancestors by the German Ocean. In the opinion of certain scholars, Freyr and Béowulf, the hero of our old epic, are one and the same god, and with Scandinavian Freyja and Niörthr represented a brother and a sister who were worshipped by the Ingævonic race as far back as the time of Tacitus. The female was then known, in Roman transliteration, as Nerthus,[1] and her cult is described by the historian. In this worship were bound together Reudigni, Aviones, Anglii, Varini, Eudoses,[2] Suardones, Nuithones, — all of them tribes which lived in Schleswig, Holstein, and about Elbe mouth. Nerthus, explains Tacitus,[3] is Mother Earth, and these people " believe that she enters into human affairs, and travels about among the people. In an island of the ocean there is a sacred grove, and in it a holy chariot covered with a cloth. Only the priest is allowed to touch it. He knows when the goddess is present in her consecrated place, and in all reverence accompanies her as she is drawn about by cows. These are joyful times and places which the goddess honors with her presence, and her visit makes holiday. People begin no war, do not take up arms, all weapons are put away; peace and quiet only are then known and welcome, until the priest leads back to her holy place the goddess, now wearied of mortal fellowship. Then the wagon, the covering-cloths, and, — if one cares to believe it, — the divinity herself, are washed in a hidden lake. These services are performed by slaves whom the same lake presently

---

[1] She is not mentioned in the Edda.

[2] On a possible connection with the Jutes, see Hoops' *Reallexikon* under "Eudoses" and "Jüten".

swallows up. Hence spring the secret terror and the
sacred ignorance about something which is seen by
those alone who are doomed to immediate death."
This is the oldest detailed account of Germanic worship, and its subject is a goddess of peace and plenty,
who makes for the promotion of agriculture, trade,
and the arts of civilization. In Scandinavia, centuries later, we find a god Niörthr who loves the water,
and especially the swan's song, and is worshipped by
seafaring folk as the protector of traders and trades.
The fact that our old Germanic goddess was worshipped in a season of general peace points to mer-
cantile opportunities; and the meeting of the related
tribes under such a sanction was doubtless the occasion of barter and trade, — like the Easter or Michaelmas *messe* of mediæval Germany. That trade was an
object of these meetings is proved by the account of
the Suiones in Tacitus,[1] by the religious gatherings
at Upsala in Sweden described by the later historian,
and by the story of places like Lethra in Denmark,
and Throndhjem in Norway, where trade and cult
went together hand in hand. Hence the gods of
traffic, agriculture, peace. The cult of Nerthus, says
Müllenhoff,[2] arose in commerce with foreign sailors
and tradesmen, and naturally was full of associations
with the sea. A few vague allusions and survivals,
such as the ship drawn by German weavers in the
neighborhood of Cologne, or the mention of a ship
in connection with the worship of " Isis " — the *Interpretatio Romana* again — may help to strengthen our
notion of this old cult.[3]

---

[1] *Germ.* XLIV.   [2] *Haupt Z. N. F.* XI. 11 f.
[3] *D. M.* 214 ff.; *Germ.* IX.; Simrock, *Mythol.* p. 369 f.

The name of Nerthus, which suggests a Celtic word meaning "strength," is evidently to be connected with the later Scandinavian Niörthr, who in the Edda is father of Freyr: they were originally one and the same person. Corresponding to Freyr and Freyja in the Norse system, scnolars have assumed a Niörthr and Nerthus, the same pair under other names. In Sweden, Freyr was a very prominent god, and his image stood beside the images of Thor and Odin. Freyr, like the older Nerthus, had a chariot which was drawn about the countryside every spring, while the glad people worshipped and made holiday. In the chariot was a young and beautiful priestess, answering to the priest who went about with the wagon of Nerthus.[1] Here, too, was a time of peace; and Freyr was asked to give rain and sunshine, fertile soil, and a prosperous year.[2] He presided over marriages; and Adam of Bremen speaks of his image as a god of fecundity. The boar was sacred to him, and was not only sacrificed to him, but is said to have drawn his wagon; while even in recent times, Swedish folk were wont to bake cakes in the shape of a boar, remnant of the old Freyr-offering.[3] Curiously enough, in the account of the Æstii, whom he evidently takes to be Germanic,[4] Tacitus says they worship a *Mater Deum* and wear figures of the boar.[5] These were probably made not of metal, but of wood, or of an even softer material. As the military spirit waxed with conquest, the peace-

---

[1] *D. M.* 208.   [2] Ibid. 176.
[3] Ibid. 41.   [4] Müllenhoff, *D. A.* II. 29.
[5] The wagon is a conspicuous thing in the cult of the Phrygian *magna deum mater.* Lucret. *de rer. nat.* II. 597 ff., and *D. M.* 211.

ful emblem served as warlike decoration; Anglo-Saxon warriors wore the boar upon their helmets; and the boar's head, on which Scandinavian warriors took oath, is known in the Christmas feasts of England. Oxen, too, we find used for this sacrificial purpose, and hear of them occasionally under the poetical name of Freyr.[1] Horses, too, were sacrificed to this god; and in Sweden on solemn occasions the slave, the captive, or even the citizen, was offered as a last resort.

Petersen gives a few Scandinavian proper names, which were compounded with the name of Freyr.[2] This, itself, means simply "prince," "lord," "master," and is familiar to us in its feminine form, as the German "Frau." Freyr and Freyja are simply "the lord" and "the lady"; they could appear under different names, as in Anglo-Saxon the god Ing, mentioned by a poem known as the "Rune Lay," and evidently the ancestral god of the Ingævonic race, is undoubtedly none other than Freyr.[3] Significant in this reference of the Rune Lay is the mention of Ing's chariot, which, as Müllenhoff remarks, is assigned only to the highest gods: —

> Ing was erst with Eastern Danes
> seen on earth, but eastward since
> o'er the wave he went; his wain ran after.
> Thus did Hardings the hero call.

Ing is further mentioned in our Anglo-Saxon genealogies;[4] and in *Béowulf* we have the *fréa Ingwina*, "lord of the Ingwine." Béowulf himself, as has been said above, is assumed by many as another

---

[1] *D. M.* 176, 179.   For other survivals of the cult, see *D. M.* III. 76 f.
[2] *Gud.* p. 42 f.   [3] Bugge, *Studier*, p. 2.   [4] *D. M.* III. 384 f.

phase of the same deity.[1] There is no doubt that
the cult of this divinity or group of divinities, çen-
tred near the North Sea, and attested from earliest
times, is for us the most interesting fragment in all
Germanic mythology; it is an authentic, even if
blurred and rapid glimpse, at the religion of our
own forefathers.[2]

Let us now look for a moment at the Scandinavian
Freyja, the later representative of Nerthus. Unfortunately, she has been confused with Frigg (this is
the Norse form, as is also Freyja), the wife of Odin.
Thus in Anglo-Saxon genealogies, we have " Frea "
set down as Woden's wife, whereas the proper name
in Anglo-Saxon would be Fricg.[3] In all Norse cult,
Freyja is abundantly worshipped, and in close relation to the cult of Freyr. She gave men fertility,
peace, and happy wedlock. Boar and ox were sacrificed to her;[4] she has, like Nerthus, the chariot of
highest divinity. Connection with ancestor-worship
is found in the widespread belief that a woman fared
directly to her after death; in Christian times, the
legend ran that souls spent their first night after
death with her successor, St. Gertrude, the second
with the archangels, but on the third went as their
doom directed.[5] The cat was sacred to her ; a happy
recognition of her manifold connection with household
blessings, and not, perhaps, without influence on the
later belief about witches.[6] As Grimm remarks, when

[1] See the preface to Mannhardt's *Mythol. Forschungen*, in Q. F., LI.
p. xi.
[2] Have we a phase of the Terra Mater in that mention of Erce, and
the *folde, fira modor*, of the Anglo-Saxon charm ?
[3] *D. M.* 250.   [4] For oxen, see *C. P. B.* I. 228; *Hyndlul.* v. 36 f.
[5] *D. M.* 50.   [6] Ibid. 254.

a bride goes to marriage in fair weather, folk say that
she "has fed the cat well." Lovers prayed to Freyja,
and for the purposes of cult, as well as by the traditions of mythology, she is in every way Germanic
goddess of love.

Probably Freyja and Frigg, Fréa and Fricg, were
originally one and the same goddess; and furthermore, Bugge[1] may be right in ascribing many of the
tales about Freyja, to the stories heard by Vikings,
and less truculent travellers, about the classical
Venus. As Lady of the Gods, however, Fricg, the
wife of Woden, must go back to an older consort of
the older god, — Tius, we may conjecture. Remains
of the cult of Fricg are collected by Grimm.[2] As
wife of Odin, she was worshipped in Scandinavia,
and like Freyja — one may almost say *as* Freyja —
she presided over marriages, and was called upon for
help by barren women. J. M. Kemble has found
relics of Fricg cult in England; and they have been
noted in Lower Saxony.[3] Perhaps the local name
Freckenhorst is derived from her worship.

Near the mouth of the Scheldt were discovered, in
1647, numerous altars and other stones containing
inscriptions to one Nehalennia; and similar inscriptions have since been found at Deutz on the Rhine.
The goddess is represented "in costume like a Roman
matron"; a dog is often near her, as well as baskets
of fruit. Sometimes she appears with Neptune, and
has her foot upon the bow of a ship. Kauffmann
sees in her a goddess of sailors, explains the name
Nehalennia itself as ultimately based on the Germanic word for "ship," and, as others have done,

[1] *Studier*, p. 10.   [2] *D. M.* 252 f.   [3] Ibid.

brings her cult into connection with the account given
by Tacitus of the Germanic worship of Isis.   As Isis,
this Germanic goddess was worshipped by the foreigners who thronged the border regions, or came
hither in the Roman ships; for Tacitus speaks of the
Frisian waters as thickly navigated by such craft.
So far Kauffmann.   Grimm thought the name was
Celtic and connected with the word for "spinning."[1]
    Another cult is mentioned by Tacitus, — that of the
goddess Tanfana.   While the deities mentioned above
belonged to the circle of Ingævonic religion, this goddess seems to have been best known to the Istævones;
and since it was among these tribes that the worship
of Woden began and grew into such stately proportion, scholars have conjectured that Tanfana was his
companion.   Let us hear Tacitus.[2]   The legions
made a night attack upon the Marsi, who were
encamped not far from the modern Dortmund, holding festival, "lying upon their beds or about the tables,
care-free, not even with their sentinels posted . . .
there was no fear of battle, and yet no peace, unless
it were the languid and disordered peace of drunk-
ards. . . .   A space of fifty miles [the Cæsar] lays
waste with sword and flame.   Not sex, not age, were
spared, things public nor things sacred (*profana simul
ac sacra*); even the temple which is most famous
among those races, which they call the temple of
Tanfana, — all was levelled with the ground."   An inscription has also been discovered, — *Tanfanæ sacrum;*
but its genuineness is denied.[3]   Another deity casually

---

[1] *D. M.*[4] 347, 404; Simrock, *D. M.* 373, 576; Kauffmann in *P. B. Beit.*
XIV. 210 ff.
[2] *Ann.* I. 50 f.   It is the year 14 A.D.   [3] *D. M.* 64, note[2].

mentioned by **Tacitus,** and of probable Germanic
belongings and Celtic origin, is Baduhenna;[1] and an
inscription to a goddess Hludana has been connected
with the Scandinavian Hlothyn, — a connection
stoutly denied by Sophus Bugge.[2]

We are concerned here not with myth but with
actual worship, and cannot delay over names like that
of Balder. Even if Balder was a real Germanic god,
we have no traces of his cult, save in the charm given
above — where Bugge contends that Balder is simply a
title, "the lord,"[3] — and in the names of a few places.
He had a son, Forseti, "foresitter," president of a
court, the ideal judge; and Grimm connects this son
with the Frisian god Fosite.[4] Of this god's cult some
account has been preserved. Liudger, a Christian
missionary preaching the gospel among his heathen
brethren, sailed to the island Helgoland (holy isle),[5]
on the borders of the Danish and Frisian folk, called
after the name of the god Fosetesland (a nomine dei
falsi Fosete Foseteslant est appellata). Another holy
man, Willibrord, visited this island; and we are told
that it was entirely dedicated to the service of the god.
A well or spring was sacred to him, from which none
durst drink save in utter silence. Temples — whatever we are to understand by the term — were erected
in his honor; treasure was gathered there; and flocks
and herds grazed about the place, not to be touched

---

[1] *Ann.* IV. 73.   [2] *Studier*, p. 574.
[3] On the other hand, J. Grimm thinks Phol a familiar form of Balder.
D. M. III. 80.   [4] *Fana Fosetis.* See *D. M.* 190, III. 80.
[5] Möller, *Altengl. Volksep.* p. 91, note, thinks that Helgoland was the
sacred isle of the Saxons south of the Eider, and not to be identified
with the holy isle of the North Anglians, described by Tacitus, *Germania,* XL. 40.

by mortal. It was believed that death or madness would fall upon the wretch who desecrated any of these things; moreover, the king was wont to punish such offenders in the direst fashion (atrocissima morte). Willibrord baptized three persons in the well, and his men killed some of the sacred animals; hence lots were cast by the outraged heathen to see if the Christians should die. One man was thus marked for vengeance, but favoring lots allowed the saint and his other companions to go free. When Liudger came, he destroyed temples, groves, and whatever savored of the heathen cult. The name, Fosetesland, was of course consigned to silence; but "Helgoland" preserves the memory of ancient sanctity. Adam of Bremen says the place was especially venerated by sailors and pirates, "whence it takes the name Heiligland." As late as the eleventh century, superstition maintained its old terrors; and it was believed that if any one committed robbery on the island, even in regard to the meanest object, he would suffer shipwreck or a violent death. To the hermits who were settled about the place. pirates brought a tenth part of their gains. There is no doubt that this island was a chief sanctuary of our heathendom, and Richthofen is inclined to see in Fosite the "president" of the gods, Woden himself.[1]

[1] In his book on *Friesische Rechtsgeschichte*, II. 399 ff., 424 f., 431 f., 434 ff., Richthofen has collected the material used above, — the lives of the two saints, the account of Adam, etc.

CHAPTER XV

FORM AND CEREMONY

Places of worship — Temples — Images and columns — Priest and priestess — Prayer, offering and sacrifice — Survivals — Divination and auguries — Runes.

WHERE did the Germans worship? According to Tacitus,[1] who indulges here in a bit of rhetoric, they think it unbecoming the greatness of the gods to shut them in with walls or to image them in human shapes. This delicate reasoning never occurred to a German; but it is evident that, as a fact, he had no temples such as the Romans had, no statues of the classical sort, and, of course, nothing of that art which lent itself so readily to the purposes of sacred decoration. But places of worship he must have had; and these, as we are told in a somewhat obscure passage of the *Germania*,[2] were groves. Islands seem to have been favorite places for the purposes of a cult; and, as we have just seen, all of Helgoland was given up to such a use. Still, groves were the best-loved temples. The house of gods, like the house of men, could be built about a tree; and we cannot altogether reject the romantic reason, added by Jacob Grimm, that something oracular and divine attracted the early

---

[1] *Germ.* IX.   [2] Ibid. "Lucos et nemora."

worshipper in the swaying of branches and the low
murmur of the leaves. We may suspect from the
exquisite tortures which tradition assigned to him
who injured a tree, that it was once a question of
divine as well as human property, — like the Jupiter-
Oak which Boniface cut down. Mention is made
repeatedly of these sacred groves among the Germans.
Such was the grove of the Semnones, described as
follows by Tacitus.[1] "At a specified time, representatives of all the clans of this race assemble in a
forest which is sanctified by ancestral auguries and
immemorial fear, formally offer up a human sacrifice,
and celebrate their awful and barbaric rites. A peculiar reverence attaches to this grove. No one enters
it unless bound with fetters, in order to show his own
humble case and the power of the divinity; and if he
chances to fall, he is not allowed to rise and stand
up; prone as he is, he must roll along the ground.
The whole superstition implies that in this grove is
the origin of the race, here lives the deity who rules
them all, while all the rest are but subject and tribu-
tary." Mention is also made of a *silva Herculi sacra,*
and of a *lucus Baduhennæ.*[2] The grove of Nerthus is
another example; and even the "temple" at Upsala,
described by Adam of Bremen, seems to have been
originally a grove. Moreover, we know that there
were places of sacrifice in these primitive temples —
barbaræ aræ is what Tacitus calls them.[3] The simple
forest fashion, however, seems hardly to have required
an altar, and in its early simplicity Germanic worship
was doubtless content to hang the victim, or parts of
it, directly upon the sacred tree itself. Around this

[1] *Germ.* XXXIX.   [2] Tac. *Ann.* II. 12, III. 73.   [3] See *Ann.* I. 61.

sacred tree, with its fresh hung offering, marched or danced the worshippers, singing as they moved, and dedicating their gift to the local deity.[1] Müllenhoff refers to a dialogue of Gregory the Great, where the heathens are described as running in this fashion about a goat sacrified "to the devil," with dedication of song and dance.[2]

It is not improbable that this place of worship was at the same time a place of burial, and in many cases may have been fixed originally by the tomb of a powerful ancestor, the founder of the race. Scattered branches of such a race would naturally unite at stated times about this centre of sacred tradition. Trees are planted at the place of burial, or a grove is chosen at the outset. " Each grove," says Tacitus, "is named after the god to whom it is sacred"; and it is not unreasonable to apply this to ancestral as well as to elemental worship. Such a tomb as is described at the end of *Béowulf* may well have been a typical place of worship for Ingævonic tribes ; and the mingling of human legend with myth pure and simple — for Béowulf is as much god as hero — agrees in all probability with the confusion of two forms of worship. Lippert would refer to a similar origin the mediæval association

---

[1] " Germani ea, quæ diis offerebant, non cremebant neque aras neque altaria more græco ac romano habebant, sed capita abscissa et exuvias victimarum similiter et homines diis dicatos, sacris arboribus suspendebant; his quoque ferro cædere et scrobibus, aqua ac cœno mergere solebant." Müllenhoff, *de antiq. German. poesi*, pp. 11, 12.

[2] Ibid. Salt springs were also sacred places, for, as we saw above (p. 69), the god was thought to help the process of salt-making. *Ann.* XIII. 57, and *Amm. Marc.* XXVIII. 5.

of sanctified bones and other relics with the church itself.[1]

Very early in its development, this Germanic place of worship would have a formal enclosure, made by ditch or wall or hedge; and of course the inmost part of the primitive "temple" would need all possible privacy — *secretum illud*, as Tacitus calls it.[2] Progress from such an enclosure to walls and formal building would be a matter partly of development, partly of influence from the pagan world. We should like to know how the English "fane" appeared which High-Priest Coifi helped to demolish. Beda[3] speaks of the *aras et fana idolorum cum septis, quibus erant circumdata*, and says that Coifi, lance in hand, went up to the idols. This would indicate buildings and images.

Jacob Grimm insisted upon the existence of temples of elaborate fashion, and cited that "templum . . . Tanfanæ" which the Romans razed to the ground. Moreover, he called attention to the Frisian law of later times, which imposed penalties for the violation of a temple.[4] In Scandinavia, at least for the later period, we must allow temples in the modern sense. The Norwegian emigrants who went to Iceland took with them materials of their old heathen temples, as

[1] *Rel. d. eur. Culturvölker*, p. 169.

[2] *Germ*. IX. Arminius speaks of the gods who dwelt within these *penetralia* as unseen by the people, and seen only by the priests. *Ann*. II. 10. [3] *Hist. Ecc*. II. 13.

[4] " Qui fanum effregit . . . immolatur diis quorum templa violavit." See also Holtzmann, *Germ. Alt*. 176. The Germans seem to have thought that "death or madness" would fall upon the profaner; when the god did not punish, his priest or king took the task. See the account of the sacred place on Helgoland, p. 438, and Richthofen, *Fries. Recht*. p. 401.

well as earth from under the altars.   In the *Eyrbyg-giasaga* we are told of a definite case,[1] where it is the caretaker of a temple sacred to Thor, who emigrates. When he rebuilds in Iceland, whither he had carried "most of the woodwork," the new structure is "a great house, with doors in the side walls and near one end.   Inside were the pillars for the high-seats, and in them nails called the gods' nails."   It is evidently an exact imitation of the old temple in Norway. This heathen temple of Scandinavia seems to have been a rectangular building, rounded at one end, after the manner of an apse or choir in certain Christian churches, and running from west to east.[2]   Besides this, there occurs a round temple, which may have been the more primitive form.[3]   The material was doubtless timber.   Decoration and metal work were matter of imitation and opportunities; the lavish use of gold, which makes Adam of Bremen speak of the temple at Upsala as *totum ex auro paratum*, is not a characteristic of early Germanic fanes.   Neverthe-less, we hear of great treasure found in the temples of the heathen Frisians.[4]   In the primitive grove, with rough enclosure, there was doubtless ornament, but of a more barbarous fashion, — emblems and mystic signs, approaching the fetishistic order.   In the "apse" were set up the images, such as there

[1] P. E. Müller, *Sagabibliothek*, I. 190 f.; Maurer *Bek. d. Norw. St.* II. 190, note.

[2] This explains the advice of Pope Gregory to use the English temples as Christian places of worship. See Petersen, p. 20, from whom much of this summary is borrowed.

[3] Petersen, p. 23.   Dimensions of the other kind of temple are noted; in one case, 120 by 60 feet.

[4] Richthofen, II. 379. "Magnum thesaurum quem in delubris inve-

were; and before them was a sort of altar covered with iron, whereupon burned a fire that durst not be extinguished, — "the sacred fire." [1] Here lay the ring, dipped by the priest in sacrificial blood, and upon which all oaths were sworn; but when the chieftain presided at popular meetings, he wore this ring upon his hand.[2] On this altar, moreover, stood the vessel which held the blood of sacrifice. No one was allowed to carry arms within the temple.

We have spoken of images set up in the "apse" of this later Scandinavian temple. What were they? Evidently in Scandinavia these were direct portrayals of the gods, as is clearly proved by the account so often quoted from Adam of Bremen. For older stages of our culture, we must observe great caution; and if we find mention of images, we must ascertain definitely what we are to understand. In the *Germania*,[3] a sanctuary of "Castor and Pollux," so called, is said to have no images, *nulla simulacra;* but the Germans, as Tacitus elsewhere informs us, were wont to bear into the battle *signa deorum,* — *effigies et signa.* What are *effigies et signa?* The school of anthropologists who lately have been picking our poor Germanic myths to mere shreds and tatters, tell us in their *interpretatio Africana* that the emblems in question were nothing more than fetishes, — old weapons with the head of a beast.[4] Better is the theory of Müllenhoff,[5] though after all the differ-

---

[1] Petersen, p. 24. [2] Maurer, *Bek. d. Norw. St.* II. 190.
[3] Cap. XLIII. [4] *Rel. d. eur. Cult.* 121.
[5] *De antiq. German. poesi,* p. 13. Holtzmann refers to the later use of animals in coats of arms. See also Tac. *Hist.* IV. 22, for the *effigies.* Müllenhoff's words are: "signa . . . arma et instrumenta, quæ a mythologis nostris attribuita dicuntur, e.g. lancea Mercurii (Wôdani)

ence is nominal, that the *signa* were sundry signs or attributes of the gods, as the lance of Woden or Thor's hammer; while the *effigies* were figures of animals, like Woden's wolf or the goat of Thor. We hear of a bull among the Cimbrians, and of a snake among the Lombards, used for such a *signum*. The moment when line of battle was formed and the attack was begun, counted among the most sacred occasions possible in Germanic life; and these *signa* doubtless meant for the soldier the presence and aid of the deity invoked. They were borne into battle by the priests, and doubtless had been adored and consecrated during the night in their sacred grove, amid rites of the cult and that indispensable banquet "per noctem" which always preceded a Germanic fight.[1] We must also bear in mind another sort of images, which could have analogy with these "signs," — the posts of the high-seats, carved with the image of a god or his symbol. After a great victory over their rivals, the Saxons[2] set up a column with an "effigy" of one of their gods. Much has been disputed about this triumphal affair; but it seems to have been not so much an image as a huge pillar with rude carvings of a head and the usual symbols. Another and later account is more explicit. In 772 Charlemagne waged war against the Saxons, who were stubborn to desperation in their heathen faith; and he destroyed a

malleus Herculis (Tonantis, Thunaris), gladius Martis (Tivi), phallus Liberi . . . sed effigies secundum ipsum Tacitum (Hist. IV. 22) imagines erant ferarum quæ symbolice deos ipsos indicabant ut anguis . . . et lupus Mercurium, ursus et caper Tonantem. . . ."

[1] Müllenhoff, work quoted, p. 13; Tac. *Ann.* I. 65, II. 12; *Hist.* IV. 14.

[2] In 530 A.D. The account is given by Widukind of Corvey, I. 12.

sacred place of theirs which contained an *Irminsul*, a column standing in the midst of a sacred grove, and held by all the neighboring tribes in boundless veneration. This *Irminsul* is called now the "fane," now the "idol"; we shall hardly err in explaining it as a column more or less carved. The annals speak of masses of treasure which Charles carried away from this "temple," a trait which Grimm thinks quite legendary, the flourish of a chronicler, but which Richthofen defends as historical.[1] It seems reasonably sure that, whatever the nature of this *Irminsul*, the heathen Frisians — they were our nearest continental relatives — had regular idols or images. The missionaries speak with horror of a heathendom which can seek help from stones and from deaf and dumb images, "*a lapidibus . . . et a simulacris mutis et surdis;*" and Richthofen's defence of this and other testimony seems to be valid.[2]

In Iceland and the Norse realm generally we find regular images of the gods. Adam of Bremen distinctly testifies to the three images at Upsala in Sweden, — Odin, Thor, and Freyr (Fricco); Odin as a warrior in mail, Thor, with sceptre, holding the middle place as greatest god, Freyr with the customary phallic symbols of fecundity and peace. Direct testimony about similar images in various parts of Scandinavia is collected by Petersen.[3] Maurer says that little images of the gods were carried, amulet fashion, in the pocket of the pious Norsemen.[4] Figure-

---

[1] Grimm, *D. M.*[4] 95 ff. Richthofen, p. 381 ff.

[2] Ibid. 421 ff., 448 f. No image of Foseti is mentioned in the account of Helgoland.

[3] Work quoted, p. 33 ff.   [4] *Bek. d. Norw. St.* II. 231.

heads of the Norse ship are probably to be referred to a similar origin. We hear, moreover, of prayer where the Norseman bowed before his images, or even threw himself on the floor of the fane; he did not look at the images, but held his hands before his eyes "in order to shut out the blinding glare of deity."

Priests were a Germanic institution known in all the tribes;[1] but it is better not to lay too much stress upon a priesthood. Cæsar, denying a priesthood, really concedes German priests;[2] the Cimbrians in Italy had priestesses; and Tacitus goes so far as to define priestly duties among the tribes of which he writes.[3] In public life the German priest played a leading part, and, aside from times of war, seems to have had more civil power than even the head of the state; indeed, Scherer thinks[4] that Munch and Maurer were right, against Waitz, in attributing priestly power to the chieftains. This assumption, as we shall see, derives its strongest support from the practice of Scandinavia; though there is an extreme case of priestly authority mentioned by Ammianus in his account of the Burgundians. The king, he says, may be deposed, if fortune desert the tribe in its campaigns or in its crops; but the priest (sinistus) may not be deposed.[5] If we are only willing to waive the question of identity and not to consider too curi-

---

[1] W. Müller, *System*, p. 82.

[2] VI. 21. His denial is based on comparison with an elaborate system like that of the Druids. Grimm, *D. M.* 73.

[3] *Minister deorum* is his term for priest. [4] *Anzeiger H. Z.* IV. 100.

[5] "Nam sacerdos apud Burgundios omnium maximus vocatur Sinistus et est perpetuus, obnoxius discriminibus nullis ut reges." Am. Mar. 28, 5, 14.

ously the personality of the priest, we may find a clear and definite summary of his functions in the account of Tacitus, who tells us that a public priest casts the lots; accompanies the progress of a goddess; has charge of the sacred things — *effigies et signa;* is present at the great assemblies of the people, commanding silence and invoking divine protection; and, when sentence has been pronounced upon criminals, is entrusted with execution of the sentence.[1] In heathen Scandinavia it is a positive principle that all details of worship are closely connected with the administration of affairs in general, and testify to a union of church and state.[2] The king is high priest; and where a " jarl " acts as viceroy, he performs the king's duty at sacrifice and banquet. In Iceland, the judicial districts were each under control of an officer who was at once judge and priest; and Maurer seems to assume that this custom was common to all Germanic races.[3] The place of justice, of oath and trial and lawsuit, was the place of prayer and sacrifice. It was also, in all probability, a place of trade, as is proved by the history of many a holy resort which develops into a centre of trade, the capital city of the land. Trade and justice demand peace; and peace was only possible under the awful sanctions of a present god.

Little information reaches us in regard to the dress and habits of a Germanic priest. Beda says that Anglo-Saxon priests bore no weapons and rode upon mares, which as late as Chaucer's time was deemed a disreputable mount.[4] It is probable that the official

<hr />

[1] *Germ.* X., XI., XL., etc.   [2] Petersen, p. 1 ff.
[3] *Bek. d. Norw. St.* II. 210.   [4] *D. M.* 75; *R. A.* 86 ff.

robe of a priest was white,[1] and we hear of Gothic priests "with hats," in distinction to the ordinary freemen with flowing locks. Striking is the costume of the Cimbrian sibyls, — gray-haired women dressed in white, with red over-garment and metallic girdle, but bare of foot. They cut the throats of the captives, and let the blood flow into a brazen kettle, — evidently priestly functions; while the wise-woman, of whom much has already been said,[2] was doubtless held in reverence little inferior to that felt towards the priests themselves.

Conjecture and uncertainty surround our efforts to discover the details of private or public rite conducted by these priests, and we must content ourselves with what we know of their ceremony as a whole. To us, perhaps, the simplest form of worship is adoration; but already in this " adoration " we have the notion of prayer and of the movement of the lips. Prayer, a crude desire for good to the person who is praying, may be attributed in some form to primitive races; but it is not the initial act of religious ceremony. Grimm distinguishes three periods of worship; the first knew only sacrifice, the second combined sacrifice and prayer, the third had prayer alone.[3] But Tylor, who remarks that even the rude charm is really a prayer, seems to reject this classification;[4] and we may allow some form of prayer in the rudest cult. Prayer was undoubtedly a matter of bended knee, crossed hands, and uplifted eye. Tacitus tells us

---

[1] D. M. III. 39.
[2] Above, p. 141. See also Cæsar B. G. I. 50.
[3] J. Grimm, über das Gebet, Kl. Schr. II. 460.
[4] P. C. II. 364, 373 f.

that the priest who cast lots glanced towards heaven as he took up the kevils ;[1] while from other sources and survivals it has been surmised that the German looked in supplication towards the north as the home of his gods. As to the words or form, it is significant that Old Germanic poetry, while it contains plenty of greeting and invocation, does not preserve us a single prayer; and it is supposed by Meyer that this omission is made purposely.[2]

But the simplest form of worship is not a definite prayer, as we understand the word—a desire for good expressed to a power capable of granting what we wish. The primitive act is prostration as if before an earthly king, the sign of surrender and absolute submission.[3] To fling one's self on the ground, or to bow neck or head, expresses the elementary act of religion. But after submission comes tribute, and indeed this is the main fact which proved submission, just as prostration symbolized it. Tribute to a heavenly power, whether conceived as ancestor or as personal power of nature, took a form which we call sacrifice. Of this presently.

Solemn chant and hymn, with dance, are among the earliest symbolic acts of worship. Scherer in his *Poetik* is at considerable pains to show why men should have hit upon these expressions of emotion, and sees erotic excitement as one of the leading causes.[4] Devil-dancers and medicine-men testify to

---

[1] *Germ.* X.   [2] R. M. Meyer, *Altgerm. Poesie*, p. 389.

[3] We have many of these symbolic motions in the submission of mediæval vassals to their masters. Pretty is the passage in the Anglo-Saxon *Wanderer*, when the exile dreams he is once more laying his head between his master's hands, and on his knee, and is " clipped " and kissed.   [4] *Poetik*, Berlin, 1888.

the connection of dancing with religious excitement;
and we may imagine that the pleasure of muscular
exertion, analogous to the delights of feast and revel,
was once thought to be shared by the spirits and the
gods themselves.   Dancing was a common occurrence
in the rites of field and harvest.   About the last load
of grain, or the figure set up in the yard, the peasants
form a ring and dance.[1]   Dancing on and by the ancestral graves has been mentioned already,[2] and the
village dance-place, undoubtedly a survival of the
older place of sacrifice, is in some places still consecrated with great pomp and ceremony.[3]   Even the
Christian church took over from heathendom this
custom of dancing as a part of religious ceremony,
and it would seem that the councils were forced to
take measures against the abuse;[4] so firmly was the
practice fixed in popular tradition, that we hear of
nuns dancing in a church—this in the eighth and
ninth centuries—and of repeated rebukes from the
clergy.[5]   The word *lác* means in Anglo-Saxon both
a religious ceremony and a game or play, a dance
or "leaping"; the second syllable of "wedlock" is
the same word, and points to a religious ceremony.
Altogether, we may be sure of the great importance of
dancing in the ceremonies of our heathen forefathers.

Undoubtedly, however, sacrifice was the central
fact, and Grimm remarks that many of the words
used for prayer go back to the notion of an offering.[6]
Symbolic acts such as the already-mentioned prostration in the grove of the Semnones, are, of course,

---

[1] Pfannenschmidt, pp. 38, 99.   [2] Ibid. 166.   [3] Ibid. 286 f.
[4] Probably in the Council of 742, held under Boniface.
[5] Pfannenschmidt, p. 489 f.   [6] *Ueber das Gebet*, Kl. Schr. II. 461.

ancient enough; and we know that in Scandinavia men bowed before the images on ordinary occasions, but in formal prayer threw themselves down and prayed in the dust. Still, all this was only an outward flourish of the sacrifice. Religion was ceremonial and a bargain ; the gods were not thought to give blessings *pour les beaux yeux* of their worshippers.

We have all grades of importance in the nature of the offering, from a simple gift of milk or flesh or grain carried out to a grave, or set in the corner of the house, up to the sacrifice of human beings. The German word for offering, and that for sacrifice, have disappeared : both expressions are now of Latin origin.[1] We may suppose that there were several words corresponding to the several kinds of offering, since we know that there was, in the first place, food given directly to the spirits of the dead, and that there was food or drink set out for the spirits connected with one of the elements. Out of this simple notion may grow an elaborate cult, such as the one found on the island of Rügen and described — perhaps seen [2] — by Saxo Grammaticus. The rites are Slavonic, but are probably not very different from the Germanic fashion. On the northernmost cliff of the island, with three sides of rock falling sheer to the sea, the fourth side an artificial barrier, lay the sanctuary. It was a wooden temple with double enclosure. Within was an enormous image which had four heads and was invested with a sword. In its right hand it held a horn made of different metals,

---

[1] For connection of *bless* and *blood*, see Skeat, *s.v.*, and Sweet in *Anglia*, III. 156.

[2] Lippert, *Relig. d. eur. Cult.* p. 92 ; Saxo, XIV. II. 319.

which the priest annually filled with wine, wherein
he read the prosperity of the coming year. The cult
was very simple. After harvest of each year, all
people of the island came together at this temple,
sacrificed certain animals, and celebrated a great
feast. Before this, however, the priest was expected
to sweep out the precincts of the temple with a sacred
broom, taking care not to breathe while within, but
running outside as often as he was forced to draw fresh
breath. On the day of the feast, the horn of wine is
examined, and emptied at the feet of the image; new
wine is then poured into the vessel, while the priest
drinks to the god. A great cake is laid upon the
altar, which must vanish before another year. Prayers
are made for a good crop, and then the priest dis-
misses the people to their feast. All this is merely
an expansion of the primitive and simple rites of
element and spirit cult.

The libation is a detached ceremony of these early
rites, with evident origin in the worship of the dead.
The early missionaries speak of a drink-offering (*dia-
boli in amorem vinum bibere*) which they met in
heathen ceremonies; in simplest form it is the *minne-
drink* to a dead relative and so ranging up to the
Odin's minne itself. An interesting passage in the
life of St. Columbanus by Jonas Bobbiensis, early
in the seventh century, tells of a group of Suevi
gathered about an immense vessel full of beer, with
which they were about to sacrifice (*litare*) to their
god Mercury, whom they called Wodan. The vessel
was probably an "offering kettle," and the rites were
unmixed with severer features, — merely a libation.[1]

[1] Grimm, *D. M.* 46, 51.

The saint blew (literally) the cask to pieces. Of course, all this holy fervor did not drive the drink-offering into absolute disuse; there came the usual substitution of saints for heathen gods in the matter of libation, the drinking of St. John's or St. Gertrude's *minne* in a Christian church, as well as the survival in social customs, the loving-cup and the toast.

Mention is frequently made of milk, honey, fruit, even flowers, as offering in family worship. Yet it is probable that most of these offerings are compromises; they represent ancient rites of a far sterner character, and the blood of a victim slain upon the tomb. Heathen Germans of the early historical period had a few of these compromises, concessions to advancing culture; the *Indiculus* forbids, among other things, the baking of cake and bread in form of some animal — doubtless the beast ordinarily sacrificed to the god in question. In a Norse saga we find this mentioned as a part of formal worship: men "baked images of the gods;"[1] and there are many survivals known to students of folk-lore as well as to the youthful purchaser of a gingerbread horse. Other compromises for ancient sacrifices are the usages of field and harvest to which we have frequently referred. Reapers leave a few stalks of grain standing in the field and still declare that it is for Wode or some other disguised deity of old; while the Holstein peasant will not pick the last half-dozen apples from his tree.[2]

The sacrifice of animals themselves may have been at one time a compromise for more horrid rites, but

---

[1] *Frithiofs.* and *D. M.* 51.   [2] *D. M.* 47.

this is to consider too curiously for our purposes. In animal sacrifice, blood plays its great part; for it has always been matter of popular belief that the gods hold with Mephistopheles : —

Blut ist ein ganz besondrer Saft;

and the shade of an ancestor, the spirits of the dead, are thought to love nothing so much as the warm, red sap of life. Blood was the original savor and charm of sacrifice, the most grateful part of the offering

The sacrifice of animals was conducted with deliberate pomp. Horns of the victim were gilded, and garlands were hung about its neck and " silken flanks." It was led thrice about the altar or else about the whole assembly ; and was killed by the altar-stone amid song and dance of the worshippers, who were themselves decked out in festal array. The blood was caught in vessels or in a pit, and with this blood priests smeared sacred trees, altar and walls of the holy place, and sprinkled the assembled multitude. Entrails, heart, liver, lungs, were devoted to the gods ; the rest was devoured by the people.[1] The cost of such a sacrifice was defrayed out of public funds, and was a state affair. Fire played its part, as usual, in ceremonial as well as practical purpose ; and we may fancy that natural desire would prompt the association of a liberal drink-offering.

Sacrifice differed according to its purpose and occasion. It might be a matter of joy, revel, and feasting, or it might be the sterner rite to expiate a sin or avert some pestilence ; in the former case, deity

---

[1] Pfannenschmid, p. 38 f.

would be an honored guest, but in the latter, the
god would appear as an angry and exacting master.
The latter would be extraordinary; the former a
matter of regular recurrence, like the festal dates of
Midsummer, Easter, and Yule, or the more frequent
celebration of full or new moon. Feasts of this sort
are to the present day bound up with religion; we
hold them in our houses, and leave the church to
provide for more purely devotional ceremonies.[1]

The favorite animal for sacrifice seems to have
been the horse, though ox, boar, and ram, were often
used;[2] and the cock must have played a brave part.[3]
Color was of great importance, and the male sex was
alone accepted. White horses, white cattle, were
special favorites; and a host of cases could be cited
where folk-lore has preserved this prejudice for the
white.[4] On the other hand, black animals — without
speck of other color — were also chosen for sacrifice,
and in witchcraft, residuary legatee of much old
sacrifice-lore, black cats, cocks, and so on, are particularly popular. But the horse was prime favorite for
sacrifice.[5] In the famous passage of Tacitus[6] which
describes a battle between two German tribes for the
possession of a salt-spring, we are told that the victors
"had dedicated their opponents to Mars and Mercury;[7]
and in accordance with this vow, horses, men, all that

---

[1] The councils forbade "convivia in ecclesia preparare." See Pfannenschmid, p. 341.

[2] *D. M.* 40 ff.   [3] Hehn[s], 336f.

[4] I have examined this peculiarity at some length in a paper "On
the Symbolic Use of the Colors White and Black in Germanic Tradition," *Haverford College Studies,* I. Philadelphia, 1889. See also Simrock, *Mythol.* 510 f.

[5] See above, p. 40.   [6] *Ann.* XIII. 57.

[7] All prisoners were to be sacrificed to Tius and Woden.

the conquered possessed, were given to destruction."
Here we have a sacrifice in the grand style; while
"horses and men" has the true nomadic ring. A
valued article of food, the horse must be a gracious
offering to the gods, and was held as sacred among
the Germans as it had been among the inhabitants of
ancient Persia. Its use for sacrifice and for divinations continued down to modern times, witness two
striking survivals, — one from Denmark, and one
from Switzerland. In Thiele's Folk-Tales of Denmark,[1] we are told of a peasant who has a changeling
foisted upon him, and cannot tell his own baby from
the intruder. He takes a wild colt, and lays before
it on the ground the two children in question. Looking at one child, the horse is fain to stroke it and
remains very quiet; looking at the other, it rages
and tries to trample the changeling to death. This
is exactly in line with the statement of Tacitus[2] that
the horse was used for divination, and that particular
attention was paid to his neighings; while yet another parallel to the Danish anecdote is a ceremony
of Slavonic worship practised on the island of Rügen
nearly a thousand years ago, in which white horses
sacred to the god Svantohvit were used as oracles
after the following fashion. Before the temple was
laid a triple row of lances, and it was noted whether
the sacred horse first crossed the line with his left
or his right foot.[3] The second survival comes from
Switzerland.[4] In 1815, a peasant girl had St. Vitus'
dance and, despite all ordinary remedies, failed to im-

---

[1] *Danmarks Folkesagn*, II. 276.   [2] *Germ.* X.
[3] See Lippert, *Rel. d. eur. Cult.* p. 99.
[4] H. Runge in *Zst. f. Mythol.* IV. 5.

prove under treatment. At last, the parents took a
horse, burned a quantity of straw which was fastened
to its neck, and then buried the horse alive in a deep
pit along with a number of household implements.
This was expected to cure the girl, no matter how
desperate her case; it was a last appeal. A more
agreeable form of this cult, however, was the sacrificial banquet, a highly popular festivity; as result,
the eating of horse-flesh was sign of heathendom,
and remains taboo down to the present. Heathen
Swedes were called " horse-eaters " by their converted brethren.[1] Heads of horses and other sacrificial beasts, often the hides as well, were hung on
trees as an offering to the gods.[2]

But it was not only horses that figured in the Tacitean account; men were included, as they were in
all highly important sacrificial rites. Here, indeed,
we enter the chamber of horrors in ethnology; for
human sacrifice, to quote the words of Victor Hehn,
" peers uncannily from the dark past of every Aryan
race."[3] To offer the dearest, the best, is a logical
outcome of the doctrine of sacrifice; but the anthropologists tell us that the custom opens the door upon
a passage which leads back to cannibalism itself.
Originally a simple matter of give and take, sacrifice
became later an act of propitiation or thanksgiving,
with some faint ethical notions, perverted enough,
shimmering about it. The Germans appear in history
with sufficiently marked love of human sacrifice —
witness the Cimbrians in Italy, the wholesale sacrifices
among warring German tribes, and the direct testi-

[1] *D. M.* 38 f.. 877.   [2] See Rochholz, *Glaube,* I. 251 f., II. 145 ff.
[3] *Kulturpfl.*[3], pp. 538 ff.

mony of Tacitus, who gives us specific cases and a
general summary. Of these instances, besides some
already given, we may note the visit of Germanicus
to the battle-field where Varus had been routed with
his legions.[1] "There lay broken weapons, limbs of
horses; on tree-trunks hung the heads. In neighboring groves were the barbarian altars whereon they
had sacrificed the tribunes and centurions of the first
rank;" while prisoners who had escaped the fate of
that terrible day point out to Germanicus how many
gallows were set up for the prisoners, and how many
pits had been prepared. These pits were probably
places in which the captives were buried alive. In
the *Germania*,[2] Tacitus makes some general statements, and tells us that on "certain occasions"[3]
human victims are offered to "Mercury," while
"Mars" and "Hercules" must content themselves
with animals; and in the passage quoted above, he
speaks with some abhorrence of the bloody[4] and
barbarous rites of the grove of the Semnones. A
chain of evidence reaches from Tacitus down to the
borders of the middle ages. In the fifth century, a
king of the Goths, attacking Italy, vows, if he shall
be favored with victory, to offer the conquered Christians to his god. Jordanis, in his history of the
Goths,[5] after saying that the race was so famous, men
actually believed the god Mars to have been born
among them, narrates concerning the worship of this
deity that prisoners of war were sacrificed to him "in
the belief that one who disposes the fortune of war
ought to be propitiated by human blood." Moreover,

[1] *Ann.* I. 61.   [2] IX., XXXIX.   [3] *Certis diebus.*
[4] " cæsoque publice homine."   [5] Cap. V.

to this "Mars" men promised a part of the booty, and captured weapons were hung upon trees in his honor. Procopius says that the Franks, in the year 539, after they had crossed the Po in their invasion of Italy, slew the women and children of the Goths and hurled their bodies into the river as first offerings of the war. "For," says Procopius, in pious and patriotic horror, "though these barbarians have become Christians, they still keep up many of their heathen customs, such as human sacrifice and other horrible offerings. . . ."[1] The Saxons, says the Roman writer Sidonius Apollinaris,[2] when they were about to leave the coast of Gaul and sail for home, sacrificed the tenth part of their captives, — with torture; and this is confirmed by later accounts. We have already noted a law of the heathen Frisians that whoso broke into a fane or sacred place should be sacrificed to the gods whose temples (*templa*) he had violated.[3] Dietmar of Merseburg relates that every ninth year the Danes celebrated a great festival at Lethra, their chief city, early in January, and sacrificed ninety-nine men and as many horses, — the "equi, viri," of Tacitus once more. Adam of Bremen tells of the sacrifice of men made at Upsala in Sweden, and of the corpses hung up in the sacred grove.[4]

However, on occasion, "the dearest" could mean more than any of these things. In times of great distress, private or general, in sickness, danger, famine, pestilence, the alarm might rise to a point where no alien sacrifice could measure the height of calamity,

---

[1] Procop. *d. bell. Goth.* II. 25. [2] VIII. 6.
[3] *Lex Fris.* add. sap. tit. 12. Other cases, Richthofen, II. 454 f.
[4] *D. M.* 39 ff.; Adam Br. IV. 27.

and some "dearest" thing of family or race must be
offered to the god. Dearest of the dearest was the
king. In olden times the sacrifice of the first-born
seems to have been more or less common; and survivals meet us in Scandinavian legend, where the old
ferocity lingered longest. Kings offer their sons. A
certain monarch, in order to secure length of days,
sacrifices one after another his nine sons to Odin.[1]
In a time of famine, the Swedes sacrificed oxen the
first year, without relief; then they took men; but
the third year bringing no help, they offered up their
king, Dômaldi. In the *Hervararsaga*[2] we are told the
following story of the brave but evil-minded Heidrek: "In a year of famine, the wise men, after they
had made a sacrifice, said that the noblest child in
the land would have to be offered. Heidrek promised to give his son on condition that every alternate
man in the whole population should swear obedience
to him; but with this great army he attacked King
Harek and offered him and his men to Odin." To
be sure, this was *niddingsværk*, clear treason; but
the gods were apparently satisfied. P. E. Müller,
mentioning the story that King Hakon offered up
his son, refers to a number of similar cases.[3] We
have elsewhere occasion to note the custom of sacrifice at funerals,[4] — slave, subject, wife, and friend.

The usual human sacrifice, however, was of captives, criminals, or slaves. The slaves who are em-

---

[1] See also *Ynglingatal*, in *C. P. B.* I. 247; Tylor, *P. C.* II. 403.
[2] P. E. Müller, *Sagabibliothek*, II. 559 f.   [3] *Sagabibliothek*, III. 93.
[4] See p. 319 f.   The sacrifice of Odin "himself to himself" is usually
put under this head; but, in spite of a writer in P. B. *Beitr.* Vol. XV.,
I think the arguments of Bugge convincing to the extent of regarding
this episode as an imitation of the Christian account of the crucifixion.

ployed about the grove of Nerthus, Tacitus reminds
us, are drowned in the lake ; and the Roman's reason
of secrecy is quite fanciful. It was probably an
ordinary sacrifice. In the same way, when Alaric
died and was buried in the Italian river-bed, such
slaves as did the work were killed.[1] The execution
of a criminal was originally a sacrifice to the god
whose peculiar cult had been offended by the crime
in question. Boundaries, as we have seen, were
sacred places ; and thither criminals were brought for
execution.[2]

Everywhere survivals meet us based on the notion
that a human life must be sacrificed at the beginning
of any important piece of work. We have seen what
the Franks, converted as they were, thought necessary before they crossed the Po in their invasion of
Italy. The Vikings of Scandinavia, when they
launched a new ship, would bind a victim to the
"rollers" on which the vessel slipped into the sea, and
thus redden the keel with sacrificial blood.[3] That
the doctrine of souls and manes-cult generally played
its part in many of these rites, is quite beyond question. Lippert relates[4] the story of a king of Siam
who had built a new gate. He chose three men, set
before them a sumptuous meal, gave them peculiar
instructions about their ghostly watch by the gate,
and forthwith had them beheaded and walled into
the new structure.[5] A modern shudder is all very

[1] Jordan. 29; and Hehn, p. 443.
[2] See the quotation from *Juliana*, 635, given p. 55, above; and
Grimm, *Kl. Schr.* II. 74.
[3] The so-called *Hlunn-rod*, *C. P. B.* I. 410, ref. II. 349. See word in
Cleasby-Vigfusson Lex. [4] *C. V. V.* p. 457.
[5] Other instances, Tylor, *P. C.* I. 106 ff. and note 1. I quote the
second ed., London, 1873.

well; but in 1843 when a new bridge was to be built at Halle, the good folk vainly insisted that a child ought to be walled into it in order to insure good luck.[1] Legends are told of children who were thus sacrificed; and we hear of music to drown their cries, and caresses to soothe them in their last moments, that their angry spirits might not harbor spite against the survivors.

The horror of these things shades away, under Christian influence, into many a harmless superstition;[2] a lamb is built into the altar of a Danish church, a chicken is forced to run first over a new bridge and is then killed, and even in our own day it is best to send cat or dog into one's new house, before a member of the family enter. A gingerbread horse, eaten at a given time, replaces the sacrifice; and even the harmless bottle of champagne broken over the bow of a new-launched ship is not without relation to that victim once bound to the rollers of a Viking launch.

Some account of the details of human sacrifice is preserved to us from Scandinavian heathendom. Ari, born in 1067, was as near to the old Scandinavian rites as Beda was to the Anglo-Saxon,[3] — about seventy years from the arrival of the first Christian missionary. The altar, he tells us, was of stone, and had to be kept red and gleaming with sacrificial blood. "There is still to be seen the doom-ring wherein men were doomed to sacrifice. Inside the ring stands Thor's stone whereon those men who

---

[1] *D. M.* 956.   [2] Ibid. 956 ff.; Simrock, *Mythol.* 508.
[3] This remark, and the quotation, are taken from *C. P. B.* I. 403. See also Petersen, 26 ff.

were kept for the sacrifice had their backs broken,
and the blood is still to be seen in the stone." The
blood was caught in kettles, and in old times may
have been mixed with the beer or other drink of the
assembly; sometimes it was baked in bread or cakes.
The "kettles" were also used for boiling the flesh
of cattle and similar offerings; and Grimm mentions
the witches' kettle of later times. A homely superstition makes such a witches' kettle out of that reflection of a fire or a light which one sees through
the window: —

Under the tree,
When fire out doors burns merrily,
There the witches are making tea.[1]

Finally,— putting aside the hideous hints of cannibalism which ethnology thrusts upon us, — we must
assume that the modern banquet, dinner, collation,
whatever savor of food or drink is deemed indispensable for the beginning of any scheme, the welcome
or despatching of any great personage, the celebration of any event, — all go back to the sacrificial feast.
A fair measure of "heathendom" lurks in everybody,
— not to speak of certain other instincts familiar to
the savage mind.

Such were the gifts and fees which immortals had
of man; in return they were expected to give him
not only present help, but counsel and warning for
the future, and this in oracular answer to his query.
Much has been said already, in an incidental fashion,
of the heathen ways of divination and auguries; a
few words must be added, in this place, with regard

---

[1] Whittier, *Snowbound.*

to the distinctly religious ceremony. Casting lots
was an appeal to the gods, and was carried into the
daily round of life, being as applicable to the merest
domestic details as to the greater problems. As regards the latter, tradition tells us that our forefathers
in their German home cast lots to see what part of
the crowded population should emigrate to Britain.
Says one of them: —

> In our fatherland
> are curious customs.
> Every fifteen years
> is the folk assembled, . . .
> and lots are thrown then.
> On whom they fall
> he shall fare from the land.
> Five shall linger ;
> the sixth shall leave,
> out from his kin
> to a land he kens not.[1]

Further back in the history of our race, we meet an
authentic instance of the ceremony, preserved by the
pen of Cæsar. While Ariovistus and his army lay in
camp, Cæsar sent to him certain envoys, C. Valerius
Procillus and M. Mettius, to learn his intentions.
But as they entered the camp of the German leader,
he called out before all his host, and asked what
the strangers had in view, — if they were come to
spy? Scarcely had they begun to answer, when he
ordered them to be flung in chains. After this, Cæsar
offered battle daily, but Ariovistus would not respond
except by skirmishes. Asking certain German prisoners the cause of this delay, Cæsar was told that the

---

[1] Layamon's *Brut*, Ms. Cot. Cal. 13, 654 ff.

women had declared, as result of the lots and divination, that if Ariovistus hoped for victory he must not give battle before the new moon. Cæsar forced a battle, and won it. The envoy Procillus, whom the Germans were carrying away in their flight, broke from his captors, and meeting Cæsar, told of a perilous sojourn in the barbarian camp. Thrice the lots had been cast in his presence to determine whether he should be put to death by fire, or kept until another occasion; and each time the lots were in his favor.[1] It is important to note that here, as among the Cimbrians, women — *matresfamilias* — determine and announce the decree of fate.

Most valuable is the information given us by Tacitus in regard to the process itself. Blocks are cut from the wood of a fruit-bearing tree, — one may think of the beech,[2] — marked with certain signs (*notæ*), and scattered at random on a white[3] cloth; then they are picked up — that is, three of them, one by one — by the state-priest or by the father of the family, according as the ceremony is public or private, and the marks are interpreted. This interpretation gives a favorable or unfavorable answer to the question.[4] Tacitus goes on to say that the noise and flight of birds are used here for divination as in other

[1] Cæs. *B. G.* I. 47–54. The same story is told of S. Willehad, who preached to the heathen Frisians in the eighth century. Lots were cast to decide whether he was to be punished by death or to be set free. On Heligoland, S. Willebrord had a like experience. Richthofen, *Fries. Rechtsgesch.* II. 375, 401.

[2] On the relation of "book" and "beech" see S. Feist, *Etymologisches Wörterbuch d. gotisch. Sprache* (2d ed., 1923), under "*bōka*".

[3] The color is to be noted.

[4] *Germ.* C. 10. Similar rites, partly Christianized, abound in the middle ages. See Richthofen, *Fries. Rechtsges.* II. 451.

countries; but peculiar to Germany is the custom of divining by means of horses, which are kept at public cost in the groves, and must be of snow-white color as well as spared from all ordinary work. When they draw the sacred chariot, either the king or the prince, along with the priest, accompanies them and marks the manner of their neighings. As yet another means of divination, the duel is mentioned which serves as a sign of the outcome of battle.[1]

Returning to the bits of wood and the white cloth, we ask whether these mysterious marks (*notæ*) were, as scholars have assumed, the runes of which we hear and see so much in later times. Wimmer, in his great work on runes,[2] has shown that we have to deal with an imported alphabet, based on the Latin of the empire, and introduced into Germany about the end of the second century of our era. This would exclude the time of which Tacitus is writing. But it is quite possible that certain signs were in vogue among the Germans, imported from Roman or other neighbors and used purely for these purposes of divination; possible, too, that certain originally Germanic signs, rude pictures, or what not, which were called runes, were afterwards discarded for the wonderful Roman symbols. Indeed, as Sievers says,[3] it is quite possible that the Roman alphabet was used in this hieratic fashion as early as the time of Tacitus. Roman coins were familiar enough; and it is significant that "rune" means the same as "mystery."

The runes were cut — "written" — in the wood,

---

[1] See above, p. 184.

[2] The German edition, 1887, contains the author's latest corrections.

[3] Paul's *Grundriss*², I, 249.

and in the first instance have a magic signification. We are told that the Alans used twigs which they marked with incantations;[1] and ample evidence is forthcoming for Germanic tribes, especially in Scandinavia. Müllenhoff[2] explained the process of divination by the fact that these runes were symbols of initial sounds, and it was the business of the priest to make out of his runes an alliterating verse which gave answer to the question of the hour. An Anglo-Saxon gloss translates *sortilegus* by *tanhlyta*,[3] where *tan* is, of course, the "twig" of wood which Tacitus describes. But as the use of runes increased, they were carved on objects with the idea of an enduring magic, as upon the sword which should thus make the wound it gave a mortal one ; or in different purpose, another inscription on a hostile sword would cause it to lose all virtue of destruction.[4]

These magic processes were forbidden by the church, and, coming thus under ban, laid the foundations of witchcraft and the black art generally. Enchanted cup and potion played a great part. It is significant that when Ælfric translates portions of the Bible into his native tongue, he omits that verse in the story of Joseph which points to divination on the part of the hero.[5] Sometimes, however, the church allowed a harmless substitution, as when a leechdom directs the peasant how to cure his cattle. "Take two four-edged

[1] Amm. Marc. 31, 2.

[2] In *Zur Runenlehre*, Halle, 1852, by himself and R. v. Liliencron.

[3] Wright-Wülker, Col. 189.

[4] See *C. P. B.* II. 704. For women as workers of runes, see Wackernagel-Martin, *Ges. deutsch. Lit.* I. 14 and notes. For the whole subject, see *Hovomál*, st. 139 ff. (so-called "Rune Poem"); Hollander. pp. 42 ff.

[5] Genesis, xliv. 4.

sticks "—evidently the old rite — " and write on either
stick, on each edge, the paternoster to the end. . . . "[1]
Saints' names, as was shown by the charm for barren
fields, were used for a similar purpose. Parallel to
the course from coaxing processes into modern magic,
runs the path by which the old hostile incantation
was developed into the dreaded " curse " of mediæval
superstition. A curse which is meant to cut off the
sufferer from all joys and privileges of life is preserved in Norse poetry, where the maiden Gerthr,
beloved of Freyr, at first rejects his embassy of love,
and is threatened with dire calamities ; if she will not
send the wished reply, then may so-and-so happen.
Frightened at the sweep of this Ernulphian terror,
the maid relents.[2] It would be of infinite value to
the historian if he could win back the popular literature of England in the time of conversion and the
early days of the church. It is recorded of Dunstan
that " he loved the vain songs of ancient heathendom,
the trifling legends, the funeral chants " ; and it is
said that he was accused of " sorcery." What we
call " sorcery," the charming of person, of weapon,
of place, the spell which brought ruin to all that
touched the accursed object, — like the famous gold
of the Nibelungs, — all this must have lain heavily
on Germanic life. In what race has not the same
period of development found itself clogged with this
weight of superstition?

The chant, or singing, which lingers in these
names of charm and incantation, is certainly a relic
of the old choral ceremony about a heathen altar.
Poetry begins as handmaid of religion, and the

---

[1] Cockayne, I. 387.   [2] *Skirnismál*, 25 ff.

rhythmic element lives yet in our commonest survivals, — as when children determine who shall be
the mysterious "It" of a game. So the song or
even the murmur of sorcery; so the "backward mutter of dissevering power" to undo the operation of
magic itself. If we could only trace aright historical connections, we should find everywhere about
us, imbedded in custom or tradition, the shards of
our broken heathendom. Of these, the saddest to
study are those that come under the head of witchcraft, — a subject that lies quite aside from our present purposes.

CHAPTER XVI

THE HIGHER MOOD

Public and private standard of morals — Ideals of the race — Æsthetics — Germanic faith — Notions about a future life — Conclusion.

CONDUCT is of prime importance in any modern notion of religion, — that is to say, the conduct of each individual. Early religion looks to the conduct of a tribe or race in its relation to ancestral spirits or protecting gods; grave and altar must be served after the established form. So, too, the family must, as a family, observe the rites of traditional cult. Standards of conduct for persons would therefore take this collective and formal character, and the ideal virtues of our forefathers must have followed the same broad way.

To be sure, this statement will not go unchallenged. Professor Robertson Smith, in his book on *Early Semitic Religion*,[1] assumes not the family, but the kin as social unit, and says that the earliest kin-bond was maternal. Hence was developed the origin of personal ethics; while, on the other hand, religion itself " arose out of a perception of the rela-

[1] Unfortunately, only a summary can be used here, taken from *The Spectator* for October 11, 1890.

tions of the community to its environment animate and inanimate"; nor was it originally "a trembling worship of dismal and malevolent deities," but rather was addressed to friendly gods.

However all this may be, a study of Germanic traditions and literature will show us that such scheme of ethics as our ancestors possessed was what we have supposed would naturally result from a state founded on the family basis. Of this foundation we have abundant evidence; and the ethical system is in full harmony with the constitution of the state. The heroic legends of Germany will help us in this respect; for here shine in a setting of poetry the ideals of the race itself. Poetry gives us just the necessary mixture of imagination working in lines laid down by the development of the race, and facts which are taken from the records of its best moments. Hence the ideal virtues in the ideal figures of the song. Such is the view of Uhland in his valuable researches;[1] and with this purpose we examine the records. As most conspicuous among the private virtues we find generosity, hospitality,[2] and chastity. Chastity is eminently an individual virtue; but a moment's reflection will show that it is absolutely bound up with the prosperity of such a family life as Tacitus describes to us. As the standing reproach of a man is cowardice, so we find that when women are reviled, like the goddesses in the *Lokasenna*, it is for unchastity. The actual evidence for the virtue of Germanic

---

[1] *Kl. Schr.* I. 211 ff. may be found a succinct statement of his views.

[2] As to hospitality combined with sense of national honor, see the account of the Gepidæ, who refused to give up a guest at the command of Justinian, and so went to certain ruin. See also Dahn, *Urgeschichte d. germ. und rom. Völker*, I. 39.

women is strong, and has been discussed above; for
manly purity, as well as the innocent frankness which
governed the relations of younger men and women,
Cæsar gives some valuable testimony. Along with
this must go the fact that indecency has almost
no footing whatever in Germanic literature of the
heathen type.[1] When obscenities occur, they are put
in the mouth of giants, uncouth, raw, and despicable
creatures. Some of this freedom from indecency, indeed, may go to the credit of monkish scribes; but
not all of it. A stern purity, native and rough, is
the note of old Germanic song.

Softness of temper was not a Germanic virtue.
Béowulf is extraordinarily mild and patient, as befits
a hero-god of such sunny origins; but much nearer
to the Germanic heart was Thor, "impiger, iracun-
dus, inexorabilis, acer," with those knuckles whiten-
ing as he grasps the hammer in rage, — a touch that
mightily pleased Carlyle. We therefore exclude patience from our eulogy, but all the more strenuously
may we insist upon Germanic loyalty and faithfulness. Germanic family-life, as Uhland remarks,[2] had
two periods. First is the settled or partly settled life
described by Tacitus; the group of buildings by and
for themselves, isolated, the abode of a single family
or minor clan. Second is the artificial family of the
period of conquest, the chieftain and his followers
forming a new relation. In both cases, however, loyalty is the cardinal virtue. We have seen above how
stern were the demands upon this loyalty in the case
of blood-relationship, and how equally binding was

[1] See *Literaturblatt f. germ. und rom. Phil.*, February, 1891, sp. 47.
[2] *Kl. Schr.* I. 214 ff.

the obligation when leader and vassal took the place
of kin and kin.[1] Loyalty is the key-note of Germanic
life and Germanic virtue; but it is a collective rather
than an individual characteristic, and expresses itself
in literature not by sharply drawn men and women,
but by types. Not only do we miss the devotion of
mediæval chivalry and the tenderness of modern love,
but even the charms of friendship find no room in
hearts filled with the obligations of the warrior and
the clansman; Germanic traditions tell us no tale of
Orestes and Pylades. So, too, with the other graces
of life. The remorseless strain and struggle of that
time left little or no leisure, even if they had found
the desire, for one to cultivate the sense of beauty
or any other of those feelings which we comprehend
under the modern name of æsthetics. Crude forms
of art, like the paint upon a house or the woven lines
of an arm-ring, incipient adornment of person or of
weapon, — these the German knew; but the sense of
quiet beauty was foreign to his mind. In his poetry,
in those kennings which gave him almost his only
chance for description, we get a few glimpses at the
nature which surrounded him; but it is the dash of
waves, the hiss of hail and snow upon a wintry ocean,
howl of wind and storm, sweep of huge bird of prey
hovering " dewy-feathered " in the air and eager for
carrion, — battle-pieces, we must call them, but no
still-life at all. Save in one timid and perhaps inter-
polated picture of a sunny landscape, the quiet which
reigns in the Germanic description of nature is a
quiet of desolation. Such is the powerful passage in

[1] " Die Treue, der Grundtrieb des germanischen Lebens." Uhland,
p. 221.

which Hrothgar describes to Béowulf the haunt of
Grendel,[1] —

> Untrod is their home;
> by wolf-cliffs haunt they and windy headlands,
> fenways fearful, where flows the stream
> from mountains gliding to gloom of the rocks,
> underground flood. Not far is it hence
> in measure of miles that the mere expands,
> and o'er it the frost-bound forest hanging,
> sturdily rooted, shadows the wave.
> By night is a wonder weird to see,
> fire on the waters. So wise lived none
> of the sons of men, to search those depths.
> Nay, though the heath-rover, harried by dogs,
> the horn-proud hart, this holt should seek,
> long distance driven, his dear life first
> on the brink he yields ere he brave the plunge
> to hide his head:

Moreover, the placid beauty of harvest seems to
have been as unfamiliar as the fruits which it is
meant to bring; "they know," says Tacitus, "as
little of the name as of the bounties of Autumn."
Vernon Lee, in her *Euphorion*,[2] points out that this
ignoring of autumnal beauty continued through the
middle ages, despite their extravagant and ceaseless
laud of spring: "Of autumn . . . of the standing
corn, the ripening fruit of summer, . . . the middle
ages seem to know nothing." But we must return
to our study of Germanic ethics.

As we approach modern times, the primitive
ideals, while not removed, are changed. The heroic
stature is lost, and we begin to meet maxims of
prudence, bits of shrewd advice, canny standards of

---

[1] *Béow.* 1357 ff.   [2] I. 119.

action where the right is the practical. Even impulsive Scandinavia shows this. Maurer, in his well-known work,[1] gives a summary of Norse ethics in the heathen age. He finds on the one hand prudence, shrewdness, every-day wisdom; on the other, a sense of duty and the necessity of following this line irrespective of consequences. Maxims of life begin to meet us, even in this period, of a character surprisingly like the philosophical wisdom of the middle ages, with its passion for the golden mean. Prudence is extolled with the fervor of a Juvenal. Keep the "mean"; avoid gluttony and drunkenness (a parlous reference); trust not in riches; do not talk with fools; never confide in women;[2] and above all, remember that nothing can turn aside the weapon of fate. Vengeance is a religion, and human suffering excites little pity; it was treachery that called for actual disgrace and blame. Cruelty was not so bad if it were only open; although the fearful scenes at the court of Ermanric, so famous in our old heroic legends, seem to have roused a shudder in all Germanic bosoms. The little poem about Déor, our oldest English lyric, speaks of Ermanric's "wolfish" disposition. The sneak, the secret foe, is detestable; and hidden treachery is crime of crimes. Steal if you can and must; but steal openly. Generosity and hospitality are, of course, cardinal virtues. Most important of all, we must note that these various virtues stand in almost no connection with the re-

---

[1] *Bek. d. Norw. St.* II. 148 ff. Gnomic poetry was very popular in Germanic literature, and is evidently based on old traditions. Several poems of the sort are to be found in Norse and Anglo-Saxon.

[2] *Havamál*, 83-89. Mostly, as Meyer remarks (*Altgerm. Poesie*, p. 44), the Gnomic poetry describes rather than commands.

ligion of the day, which was a matter of ceremony and ritual.[1]

What has been said of Norse ethics will largely apply to our Anglo-Saxon ancestors. As time goes on, our laws betray the increase of that sense for practical things and that thrifty independence which have clung to the Englishman everywhere. To mend bridges and roads, to pay taxes, to fight in the militia, to be allowed to rule unimpeded over his private affairs, — this standard of duty develops itself early in English history. For the more personal side of ethics, it is under Christian influences that we get our first full view of the Englishman; nevertheless, if the tender shoot is to be judged by the sturdy tree, the story of such a man as King Alfred is enough to shed back a flood of light and praise upon the earliest growth of English character.

Aside from ethics proper, there was a decided vein of philosophy in the old Germanic temperament. The German loved to moralize, to point out the ways of fate, to summarize existence; after his rude fashion he made epigrams, and these strung together in poetical form[2] were doubtless a favorite department of his literature. Such a recitation, by some graver minstrel, took the place of a later court-sermon.

When restraint of human passion, or extraordinary effort of human will, is to be obtained, ethics must

---

[1] Maurer, II. 188.

[2] With critical reserve we may consider in this light the so-called "Sermon" of Hrothgar in *Béowulf*, as well as the poems on "Man's Fate," "Man's Gifts," and the like, to be found in Grein's *Bibliothek d. Ags. Poesie.*

lean more or less upon religious sanctions; and on
the border-land of cult and myth we find the province
of belief in some adjustment of human history, even
in some scheme of reward or punishment, expected
in a life to come. Much of this belongs to the doctrine of the soul-land, elsewhere treated.[1] It is our
place to look at the wider conception of a continued
responsibility for acts of this life. The notion of
future punishment is nowhere sharply defined;[2]
gloom and desolation are recognized by our forefathers as characteristic of Hel's kingdom, but it is
no place of torture. Dietrich, indeed, insisted on
the Scandinavian water-hell, and based his belief on
these lines of the sibyl's prophecy where she sees
"a hall . . . by the corpse-strand," where poisondrops fall through the roof and the walls are made
of serpents' backs; and where she sees, "wading
through raging streams treacherous men and murder-
ous," and the wolf tearing men asunder. But there
are strong reasons against accepting this conclusion.
For a general objection, it may be urged that dualism
is foreign to the spirit of Germanic heathendom; and
that evil powers, as Jacob Grimm remarks, are not
classified and set in order against the powers of good.
For a specific reason, we may call in question the
originality of the quotation just made from the
Voluspa. Bugge is by no means alone in his attack,
and a defence by Müllenhoff, the strongest of his

---

[1] See p. 326 f.

[2] Maurer denies it altogether for Scandinavian heathendom. *Bek. d.
Norw. St.* II. 74. That "general Germanic belief" in the end of the
world by fire, the Muspelli, is now asserted by Bugge to have been
imported along with other scraps of the new faith. For the older view,
see Müllenhoff, *Deutsche Alterthumskunde*, V. I. 66 f.

faith, has failed to convince the best critics that in
the Voluspa we are dealing with untainted Germanic
heathendom. E. H. Meyer in his book on this subject,[1] has come to conclusions as fatal as those of
Bugge. So we are forced to reject this part of the
sibyl's prophecy from our notion of Germanic faith.
The make-up of the picture, and the conception of
misery as united with darkness, wet, and cold, are
undoubtedly genuine; but the moral assumption is
not so.

It is true, however, that our ancestors, like their
Aryan kinsmen the world over, believed in an underworld.[2] The literal caves of the dead were extended
into a figurative kingdom of the dead, the realm of
Hel, the "concealing" goddess. Dark, cheerless, cold,
this was no place of torture.[3] She herself is relentless,
and gives up no soul that once enters her domain;
but punishments — and the Germanic mind would
have been quick enough to heap them in fullest
measure, had they belonged to the conception of the
place — are nowhere to be found. So, too, with
rewards. Under the stress of Viking life, with its
ceaseless brawls and revel, its courage and danger,
grew up a belief which has been sung and told into
a system, and now stands in most people's eyes as
the corner-stone of old Norse faith, — the belief in
that Valhalla whither Odin's maidens led the slain,
where fight and feast alternated in an agreeable perspective down the future, and whither no thrall or
man of peace might win. In point of fact, much of

[1] *Völuspa*, Berlin, 1888.
[2] Schullerus, *Zur Kritik d. Valhollglaubens*, P. B. *Beitr.* XII. 258.
[3] *D. M.* 667.

this amiable belief is of foreign, or at least of very
late origin.[1] The oldest lays of the Edda know
nothing about it; the old sagas know nothing about
it.[2] It is a strange medley, like the life that gave it
currency, and was fashioned into its present shape in
the ninth or tenth century. The wandering seamen
and warriors brought back scraps of foreign lore,
incongruous and wonderful bits of legend; as they
told their tales, huge temples or churches which
they had actually seen, blended in memory with
half-understood teachings of the new religion, and
all was set in the Norse framework, Norse verse,
and Norse manner. One writer goes so far as to
say that the Valhalla, a golden hall with countless doors and stately outline, is a loan from the
Revelation of St. John, — is the New Jerusalem
in Scandinavian disguise.[3] One suggestion, however, made long ago by Wilhelm Müller,[4] deserves
respectful mention. He regards Valhalla as the type
of a palace where earthly kings of that period were
wont to dwell, surrounded by their retainers. In
this new Valhalla would be a "magnified and non-
natural" Germanic hall, embellished by the dazzled
and confused fancy, the half-comprehended world-
lore, of the Viking age.

But let us go back to our primitive German.
What faith had he about a hereafter? Vaguely, —
as indeed all his philosophy lacked sharp definitions, — the German believed in a future world of

[1] Schullerus and H. Petersen, work quoted, p. 98 f.
[2] Schullerus, p. 241.
[3] Schullerus, p. 267. He assumes oral tradition, not book-lore, as
source of the borrowing. [4] *System*, p. 394.

spirits.[1]　Of his own doing in that world he had very dim notions; his care during life was to soothe and coax his future fellow-citizens who had gone before him. Without talent or taste for introspection, he nevertheless began in the earliest moments of awakening thought to muse about the issues of life and death. In his rough, blundering way, he doubtless did what De Quincey in a memorable passage declares all men must do who think at all about these things, — he must have held "some tranquillizing belief as to the future balances and the hieroglyphic meanings of human suffering." That is all we can say.

In speaking of Germanic belief, we have already crossed that border which separates the real from the ideal. But further we may not follow our ancestors into the ideal world which every active and aspiring race has fashioned, — the world of poetry and legend and myth. Such a subject demands a volume for itself, and needs to be studied with more than ordinary care. So far as explanation and interpretation are concerned, it is easy to make the shattered relics of Germanic myth tell almost any tale we may desire to hear. Inexorable criticism and thorough philological knowledge of this material, joined with the insight, imagination, and wide comparative glances of a master of literary history, are indispensable for the man who at this late hour is fain to tread in the path marked out by Jacob Grimm and almost untrodden since his day. Myth-mongers there have been in plenty, — men with "interpretations," who will

---

[1] There is no doubt of this. See Müllenhoff, *Deutsche Alterth.* V. I. 69.

tell us that Norse Idun was grass, or hay, or a star, or poetry; but men who sought the heart of Germanic myth itself have not appeared, — save one. Irascible, arrogant, Müllenhoff nevertheless redeemed his many faults by dint of labor, strength, and a rugged loyalty to his own ideals. He was of the old breed of scholars; he loved poetry as well as paradigms; and no keener or more loving glance than his ever sought to pierce the mist of our Germanic origins.

SUPPLEMENTARY NOTES

CHAPTER I. INTRODUCTION

For a general survey of the anthropological and ethnological background of the English people see R. B. Dixon, *The Racial History of Man* (N. Y., Scribners, 1923, bibliogr.), W. Z. Ripley, *The Races of Europe* (N. Y., 1899 and later issues, bibliogr.), and more briefly in article "Races of Man", *Encyc. Britan.*, 14th ed. On the Celtic and pre-Celtic inhabitants of Britain, see Sir John Rhŷs and D. Brynmor Jones, *The Welsh People* (4th ed., London, 1906), chap. i (Ethnology of Ancient Wales); G. Dottin, *Les anciens peuples de l'Europe*, I (Paris, 1916), 201 ff. ("Les Celtes"); on Roman Britain see T. Rice-Holmes, *Ancient Britain and the Invasions of Julius Caesar* (Oxford, 1907), pp. 375 ff. ("The Ethnology of Ancient Britain"). Cf. also, F. Haverfield, *The Romanization of Roman Britain* (4th ed., revised G. Macdonald, Oxford, 1923).

For an attempted analysis of the endebtedness of Anglo-Saxon literature to the racial elements present in the population, see H. O. Taylor, *Mediaeval Mind* (4th ed., Macmillan, 1927), Vol. I, chap. vii-ix.

On the early history of the Germanic peoples, their expansion from Germany over the Roman Empire, and the name "Germani", see Hoops under "Germanen" and "Stamm"; Fr. Kauffmann, *Deutsche Altertumskunde*, I (Munich, 1913), 63 ff.; H. M. Chadwick, *Origin of the English People* (Camb. Univ. Press, 1924 impression), pp. 166—219; O. Bremer, "Ethnographie der

german. Stämme" in Hermann Paul's *Grundriss*², III, 735 ff.;
article "Teutonic Peoples", *Encycl. Britan.*, 14 th ed.; K. Müllenhoff, *Die Germania des Tacitus* (rev. ed. M. Rödiger, Berlin, 1920),
pp. 100 ff. (= *Deutsche Altertumskunde*, IV); E. Wadsteen,
Norden och Västeuropa i gammal Tid (Stockholm, 1925; concise;
admirable notes); G. Schütte, *Vor Folkegruppe*, Vol. I (Copenhagen, 1926; compendious, original, useful). On Angles, Saxons,
and Jutes, Kauffmann, *op. cit.*, II, 136; Chadwick, *op. cit.*,
pp. 85 ff.; on Ingvaeones, see Hoops under "Germanen", § 18,
Chadwick, pp. 220 ff. (Nerthus Peoples), and T. E. Karsten, *Die
Germanen* (Berlin, 1928), pp. 231 ff. On the Romans in Germany,
see Fr. Koepp, *Die Römer in Deutschland* (3 d ed., Bielefeld,
1926). P. 27: on the ultimate disappearance of the Chauci as
a nation see Chadwick, *Origin*, p. 197.

On the sources mentioned on p. 5 above the following references may be added: on Tacitus' *Germania* the critical editions
by H. Goelzer in *Tacite: Dialogue des Orateurs, Vie d'Agricole,
La Germanie* (Paris, 1922), pp. [150] ff., and A. Gudeman in
Tacitus: De Vita Iulii Agricolae and De Germania (revised ed.,
Boston, 1928). Commentaries of importance for Germanic antiquities are K. Müllenhoff, *Die Germania des Tacitus* (revised ed.
by M. Roediger = *Deutsche Altertumskunde*, Vol. IV, Berlin,
1920); E. Norden, *Die germanische Urgeschichte in Tacitus' Germania* (3rd issue with additions, Berlin, 1923), and Meyer, "Das
antike Idealbild von den Naturvölkern and die Nachrichten des
Caesar und Tacitus", *Zs. f. deutsch. Altertum*, LXII (1925),
226 ff. (on Tacitus' comparative independence of classical tradition). On *Beowulf* note the editions of Fr. Klaeber (2nd ed.,
Boston, 1928), R. W. Chambers (rev. ed., Cambridge, Eng.,
1920), L. L. Schücking (11th and 12th ed. of M. Heyne, Pader-
born, 1918), and F. Holthausen (6th ed., Heidelberg, 1929);
also the commentaries by Klaeber (introduction to his *ed. cit.*),
R. W. Chambers in *Beowulf: an Introduction* (Cambridge, Eng.,
1921; new ed. in preparation), and W. W. Lawrence in *Beowulf
and Epic Tradition* (Cambridge, Mass., 1928).

On All-Souls' see notes under Chapter XII, p. 496 below.

On Germanic Heroic Legend see A. Heusler, *Die altgermanische
Dichtung* (Berlin, 1923 = Vol. XI of *Handbuch der Literatur-
wissenschaft*, ed. O. Walzel); *idem* in Hoops under "Helden-

sage"; and H. M. Chadwick, *The Heroic Age* (Cambridge, Eng., 1912).

On the *Widsið* mentioned p. 6, note edition and elaborate commentary of R. W. Chambers (Cambridge, Eng., 1912), also R. Jordan in Hoops under "Widsith".

CHAPTER II. LAND AND PEOPLE

The older traditional view that Asia was the original home of the Indo-Europeans has now been generally abandoned in favor of some region in Central Europe, placed variously in the valley of the Vistula, the Danube, or the litoral of the Black Sea. For an account (with bibliography) of twentieth-century scholarship on this and other aspects of Germanic antiquities, see T. Bieder, *Geschichte der Germanenforschung*, III (Leipzig, 1925), 91—195 ("Heimat — Arbeiten von 1901 bis zur Gegenwart"), to be supplemented by F. R. Schröder, "Neuere Forschungen zur german. Altertumskunde u. Religionsgeschichte", *German.-Roman. Monatsschr.*, XVII (1929), 177—192 (antiquities). The northern reaches of the Vistula is urged by H. H. Bender, *The Home of the Indoeuropeans* (Princeton, N. J., 1922), esp. pp. 56, 57; the general region of Austria-Hungary by Peter Giles, *Encycl. Britan.* 14th ed., XII, 263b; the Black Sea litoral by A. Carnoy, *Les Indo-Européens* (Brussels, 1921), p.75. On primitive Indo-European culture see H. Hirt, *Die Indo-Germanen* (Strassburg, 1905), I, 202ff., Otto Schrader, *Reallexikon der indogermanischen Altertumskunde* (2d ed., Berlin, 1917—29), and also M. Ebert's monumental *Reallexikon der Vorgeschichte* (Berlin, 1924—29) under various objects, institutions, animals, etc.; Carnoy, *op. cit.*, esp. bibliography, pp. 245, 246; and Giles, *art. cit.* In general it may be remarked that the postulation of a single Indo-European type can scarcely stand today.

On the primitive Germans see Kauffmann, *op. cit.*, I, 63ff.; S. Feist, *Indogermanen und Germanen* (Berlin, 1919), Hoops *passim*, Bieder, *loc. cit.* and Ebert under "Germanen"

The mythological interpretation of the *Beowulf*, especially that of Karl Müllenhoff, accepted on p. 36 above, is now all but universally rejected; see Chambers, *op. cit.*, pp. 291 ff., and Lawrence, pp. 145 ff. On Sceaf's genealogy discussed pp. 48 ff. above see now R. W. Chambers, *Beowulf: an Introduction* (Cambridge, 1921; new ed. in prep.), pp. 89 ff., 311 ff.; W.W. Lawrence, *Beowulf and Epic Tradition* (Cambridge, Mass., 1929), p. 138; A. Olrik - L. M. Hollander, *The Heroic Legends of Denmark* (New York, 1919), pp. 396 ff.

On land-tenure see Hoops under "Flureinteilung"; H. M. Chadwick, *Studies on Anglo-Saxon Institutions* (Cambridge, 1905), pp. 367 ff. ("The Tenure of Land in Prehistoric Times"); K. von Amira, *Germanisches Recht* (in Paul's *Grundriss*³, Strassburg, 1913), §§ 27—32; and P. Vinogradoff, "The Transfer of Land in Old English Law", *Harvard Law Review*, XX (1906—07). 532 ff. Note also L. Brentano, *Eine Geschichte d. wirtschaftl. Entwicklung Englands*, I (Jena. 1927), 48—128, on general economic problems of A. S. period.

CHAPTER III. MEN AND WOMEN

On this chapter in general see M. Heyne, *Körperpflege und Kleidung bei den Deutschen von den ältesten geschichtlichen Zeiten bis zum 16. Jahrhundert* (= Vol. III of *Fünf Bücher deutscher Hausaltertümer*, Leipzig, 1903). On the pronounced mediaeval preference for blond vs. brunette type of beauty see W. Hertz, *Spielmannsbuch* (3rd ed., 1904), pp. 377—378; K. Wienhold, *Die deutschen Frauen in dem Mittelalter* (3d ed., 1897), I, 198—212 (literature cited); and W. C. Curry, *The Middle English Ideal of Personal Beauty* (Baltimore, 1916). Pp. 66 ff.: on foodstuffs see Hoops under "Fleischspeise", "Gemüse", and "Getreide"; on domestic plants and vegetables in A. S. England see J. Hoops, *Waldbäume und Kulturpflanzen im germanischen Altertum* (Strassburg, 1905), pp. 590 ff. P. 70: on the A. S. *corsnæd* see Hoops under "Gottesurteil", p. 321 e, 322 (literature). P. 71: on Bede and A. S. May (*þrimilce*) see Hoops under "Zeitmessung", p. 585, col. 1, and Bilfinger's study cited. P. 71 ff.: see Hoops under "Bier", "Met". P. 77: on baths see Hoops under "Badewesen"; literature cited by L. Thorndike, *Speculum*, III (1928), 197, n. 2. P. 78 ff.: on clothing see Hoops under

'Kleidung" for reference to pertinent articles, especially to "Kleiderstoffe" and "Trachten". P. 81: Müllenhoff, *Germania*, pp. 293, 294, would now translate "an (not *the*) undergarment". P. 84ff.: on ornamentation see Hoops under "Ornamentik" (Plates) and "Armring" (Plates); further Sophus Müller. transl. O. Jiriczek, *Nordische Altertumskunde nach Funden und Denkmälern aus Dänemark und Schleswig*, II (Strassburg, 1898), 101 ff. (Migration period), and for England N. Åberg, *The Anglo-Saxons in England during the Early Centuries after the Invasion* (Heffner: Cambridge, 1926) (richly illustrated). Note article by G. Baldwin Brown, "Was the Anglo Saxon an Artist ?" *Journ. of the Brit. Archaeolog. Ass'n*, N. Ser., XXIII (1916), 171—194.

CHAPTER IV. THE HOME

P. 91: on the fate of Roman towns see, e. g., F. Haverfield, "The Last Days of Silchester [Calleva Atrebatum]", *English Histor. Rev.* XX (1904), 625ff., and L. Gomme, *The Making of London* (Oxford, 1912), pp. 50, 79ff. for the continuity of life and activity on the London site. P. 91, n. 1: on the general plausibility of identifying the scene of the A. S. *Ruin* with Bath, see E. Sieper, *Die altenglische Elegie* (Strassburg, 1915). pp. 226ff. ("Die Ruine"), also *Cambridge History of Engl. Lit.*, I (1907), 43.

On A. S. architecture see Gerard Baldwin Brown, *The Arts of Early England*, I (2d ed., 1926), 52ff. and *idem* in Hoops under "Holzbau" and "Englische (Angelsächsische) Baukunst"; also Hoops under "Flett" and "Königshöfe", and "Fenster" (on lack of glass-windows); M. Heyne, *Das deutsche Wohnungswesen* (= Vol. I of *Fünf Bücher deutscher Hausaltertümer*, Leipzig. 1899), pp. 13ff., 71ff.; W. Schulz-Minden, *Das germanische Haus in vorgeschichtlicher Zeit* (Würzburg, 1912); and Harry Jacobs, *Die Namen der profanen Wohn- und Wirtschaftsgebäude und Gebäudeteile im Altenglischen* (Kiel diss., 1911). All the above but Jacobs are richly illustrated. On the use of stone in A. S. buildings see Hoops under "Steinbau". P. 96: on historical parallels to the burning of Heorot, see *Modern Lang. Notes*. XLII (1927), 173, 174.

P. 101: on the A. S. *burh* as a fortified dwelling and a repaired and adapted Roman ruin see C. Stephenson, "The Origin of the English Towns", *American Histor. Review*, XXXII (1926), 10—21. P. 104 ff.: for literature on Heorot, see E. Björkmann, *Studien über die Eigennamen im Beowulf* (Halle, 1920), p. 62; on the site of Leire see A. Olrik - L. M. Hollander, *Heroic Legends of Denmark* (New York, 1919), pp. 324—347.

P.105: on riding into the hall, see additionally Child, *Ballads*, IV, 510d and VI, 508b (notes on *King Estmere* by G. L. Kittredge).

On early tapestries see Hoops under "Webstuhl" and K. G. Stephani, *Der älteste deutsche Wohnbau und seine Einrichtung* (Leipzig, 1902—03), II, 376 ff. Pp. 119 ff.: on feast and revelry see Hoops under "Geselligkeit", *q. v.* also for sports and gaming, as well as under "Leibesübungen" and "Kinderspielzeug"; articles on "Sport" and "Spiel" are to appear in the supplementary volume to Hoops. For sports and pastimes in A. S. England see W. Pfändler, *Anglia*, XXIX (1906), 417—524. P. 124: on the chase see Hoops under "Jagd"

CHAPTER V. HUSBAND AND WIFE

For comprehensive discussions of marriage and marital relations see Hoops under "Ehe", "Ehegüterrecht", "Ehescheidung", and "Eheschliessung" with full literature; see also von Amira in Paul's *Grundriss*³, pp. 177—183, F. Roeder, *Die Familie bei den Angelsachsen*, 1: *Mann und Frau* (Göttingen diss. — no more published), and E. Westermark, *History of Human Marriage* (5th ed. rev., London, 1921), Index, under "Germans, the ancient". P. 139: for the Germanic conception of the prophetic endowment of women see Hoops under "Weise Frauen" and "Veleda". P. 143: on the prevelance of witchcraft in Anglo-Saxon England see G. L. Kittredge, *Witchcraft in Old and New England* (Cambridge, Mass., 1929), pp. 27 ff. P. 156: on Thor's Mjollnir see Munch-Olsen (cited Chap. XII below), pp. 76 ff., 320, 321.

Note A. Broch, *Die Stellung der Frau in der ags. Poesie* (Zurich diss., 1902) and G. F. von Schwerin, "Women in the Germanic Hero Sagas", *Journ. Engl. German. Philol.*, VIII (1909), 501-512 (very modest beginning).

CHAPTER VI. THE FAMILY

See in general H. M. Chadwick's chapter "Society in the Heroic Age", *Heroic Age*, pp. 344 ff. On the laws of hospitality in Germanic territory see Hoops under "Fremde" and the articles there cited. P. 166: on gift-giving see Hoops under "Schenkung". P. 167: on arm-rings see Hoops under "Armring" (Plates). P. 171: for a classic instance of merry-making over serious battle-wounds see *Waltharius*, 1. 1421 ff. (ed. H. Althof, Pt. ii, pp. 363, 364, note to 1. 1436). P. 173: on the A. S. names of relationship see C. D. Campbell, *The Names of Relationship in English* (Strassburg diss., 1905), and on blood-brotherhood, Althof, *loc. cit.*, pp. 367, 368 (note to 1. 1443 — *pactum cruentum*), Hoops under "Blutbrüderschaft" (universality of custom) and literature cited (for "Pflegebrüderschaft" read "Pflegekindschaft"); "Brotherhood (artificial)" in Hastings' *Encyc. Religion and Ethics;* and as a manifestation of homoeopathic magic J. G. Frazer, *Golden Bough — Spirits of the Corn*, II (London, 1912), 154 ff. P. 182: on the Anglo-Saxon feud see Hoops under "Fehde". P. 183: on the ordeal see Hoops under "Gottesurteil" and "Zweikampf" (for Scandinavian *holmganga* and *einvigi*). Pp. 185 ff.: on slavery see P. Vinogradoff in Hoops under "Unfreie" and among the Anglo-Saxons Fr. Pollock, *Engl. Histor. Review*, VIII (1893), 247 ff. P. 186: on corporal chastisement see Hoops under "Leibesstrafen".

P. 193: on the bestowal of names see von Amira, Paul's *Grundriss*[3], p. 183; on early Teutonic names see M. Schönfeld, *Wörterbuch der altgerman. Personen- und Völkernamen* (Heidelberg, 1911) and literature there cited p. xxxiv; Much in Hoops under "Völkernamen"; E. Björkmann, *op. cit.* Chap. IV above for ample literature; and A. Mawer, F. M. Stenton, edd. *Introduction to the Survey of English Place-Names* (Cambridge, Eng., 1924), *passim*. P. 197: on education see notes on sports and gymnastics cited Chap. IV above and on the practice of fosterage F. Roeder, *Über die Erziehung der vornehmen angelsächsischen Jugend in fremden Häusern* (Halle, 1910).

F. 201 ff.: on the putting to death of aged people, cf. J. G. Frazer, *The Golden Bough — The Dying God* (London, 1911), pp. 10 ff.

CHAPTER VII. TRADE AND COMMERCE

In general see A. Bugge's substantial article "Handel" in Hoops; A. Bugge, Fr. Scheel, et al., *Den Norske Sjøfarts Historie fra de aeldste Tider til vore Dage*, Vol. I (Oslo, 1923); and E. Wadsteen, *Norden och Västeuropa i gammal Tid* (Stockholm, 1925), pp. 90 ff. ("Gamla nordiska Handelsvägar"); on the closely related question of travel see Hoops under "Verkehrswesen" (pp. 399 ff. for England). On weaving see Hoops under "Webstuhl"; on smithing Gerard Baldwin Brown, *The Arts of Early England*, III, 201 ff. and Hoops under "Goldschmiedekunst". See also notes on Ornamentation in Chap. III above. P. 215: the basis of the Runic alphabet is now generally held to be second-century Greek cursive script with some use of the Roman alphabet: see O. von Friesen in Hoops under "Runenschrift"; *ibid.* in *Encycl. Britan.*, 14th ed., under "Runes", and F. R. Schröder "Neuere Runenforschung", *German.-Roman. Monatsschr.* X (1922), 4—16. On the sea in *Beowulf* see F. Klaeber's ed., p. 257 for analysis, and on the kennings for the sea in A. S. poetry H. van der Merwe Scholtz, *The Kenning in Anglo-Saxon and Old-Norse Poetry* (Utrecht, 1928), pp. 65, 152.

CHAPTER VIII. THE WARRIOR

P. 226: on the so-called *trinoda necessitas* (Gummere's "three obligations") see Hoops *s. v.*; on the military in Tacitus see Müllenhoff, *Germania* (*cit. supr.*), pp. 255 ff. Pp. 228, 229: see notes on sport and revelry Chap. IV above. P. 230: on the reality of "bearsark (berserk) frenzy" see Mogk in Hoops under "Berserker". P. 235: on Germanic fatalism see Hoops under "Fatalismus" and "Nornen"; F. Kauffmann, "Über den Schicksalsglauben der Germanen", *Zs. f. deutsch. Philol.*, L (1926), 361—406; in England, G. Ehrismann "Religionsgeschichtliche Beiträge zum germanischen Frühchristentum", Paul and Braune's *Beiträge*, XXXV (1909), 209 ff.; and R. Jente, *Mythologische Ausdrücke*, pp. 196—223 ("Schicksal"). P. 244: on the divinity Saxnôt (Saxnéat), see R. M. Meyer, *Altgermanische Religionsgeschichte* (Leipzig, 1910), p. 196. Pp. 242 ff.: on military equipment see Hoops under "Bewaffnung", and G. B. Brown, *The Arts of Early England*, III, 92 ff. Pp. 254 ff.: on military arrangements see Hoops under "Kriegführung" and "Heerwesen", and in England P. Vinogradoff, *English Society in the Eleventh Century* (Oxford, 1908), pp. 14 ff., and *idem* in Hoops under "Wehrverfassung, *C*.".

On Saxo's story of Hadingus see P. Herrmann, *Die Heldensagen des Saxo Grammaticus*, II (Leipzig, 1922), 89 ff. P. 261: on the *comitatus* see Hoops under "Gefolgschaft"; G. Neckel, "Adel und Gefolgschaft", Paul and Braune's *Beiträge*, XLI (1916), 385—436; and von Amira, Paul's *Grundriss*[3], pp. 188 ff. P. 268: the tentatively given etymology of *comes* may be accepted.

CHAPTER IX. SOCIAL ORDER

On the Germanic ruler see von Amira, Paul's *Grundriss*[3], pp. 148 ff.; A. Bartels, *Rechtsaltertümer in der angelsächsischen Dichtung* (Kiel diss., 1913), pp. 19 ff.; Müllenhoff's *Germania*[2], pp. 182 ff. ("von Führerschaft"), and H. M. Chadwick, *Heroic Age*, pp. 367 ff. ("Government in the Heroic Age"). On the inheritance and (or) election of Anglo-Saxon kings see Chadwick, *Studies on Anglo-Saxon Institutions*, pp. 355 ff., and on the origin of the nobility, *ibid.*, pp. 378 ff.; for later times in England, P. Vinogradoff, *op. cit. supra;* also see Hoops under "Ständewesen".

CHAPTER X. GOVERNMENT AND LAW

In general see references given in the preceeding chapter. Pp. 301 ff.: on the ordeal see notes to Chap. VI above. P. 303 on the *corsnæd* see von Amira in Paul's *Grundriss*[3], pp. 277 ff., also pp. 250, 251.

CHAPTER XI. THE FUNERAL

In the Scandinavian north in the later Bronze Age it is now generally believed that cremation and interment alternated, the former being the practice in viking times; see H. M. Chadwick, *Cult of Othin* (Cambridge, 1899), pp. 40, 59, 64; K. Stjerna, *Essays on Questions connected with the Old English Poem of Beowulf* (London, 1912), pp. 208 ff. for details of finds; Seger's splendidly illustrated survey in Hoops under "Totenbestattung" and headings listed *s. v.*, pp. 603, 605; *Osebergfundet*, I, 210 ff. (English résumé, pp. 395 ff.), 365, 366 (bibliography); and H. Shetelig, *Norges Fornhistorie* (Oslo, 1925), pp. 194 ff. ("Skibsgravene", etc.). On the funeral customs of the Celts, especially the Gauls, see G. Dottin, *Manuel pour servir à l'Etude de l'Antiquité Celtique* (2d ed., Paris, 1915), Index général under "Incinération" and "Inhumation".

Both methods of burial prevailed among the Anglo-Saxons until their conversion when, of course, cremation was abandoned with the adoption of Christianity (Chadwick, *Origin of the English Nation*, pp. 73 ff.); see Gerard Baldwin Brown, *Arts in Early England*, I, 263, III, 114 ff., IV, 627 ff., on A. S. cemeteries (often correcting Kemble). On the burnings of Hnæf and Beowulf see Klaeber, *Beowulf*, pp. 216, 435 n. to l. 3137 ff., and especially Klaeber, "Attila's and Beowulf's Funeral", *Publ. Mod. Lang. Ass'n*, XLII (1927), 255—267. On the burial of precious objects with the dead see Hoops under "Grabbeigaben" and Mogk in Paul's *Grundriss*[2], III, 252 ff. on the religious significance of this practice.

On the special subject of ship-burials see Stjerna, *op. cit.*, pp. 97 ff., and of King Scyld in particular, Stjerna, *loc. cit.*, Klaeber, *Beowulf*, pp. 121 ff. esp. footnotes, and R. W. Chamber's *Beowulf: an Introduction*, pp. 68 ff. for further illustration of parallels noted by Gummere, pp. 323 ff. above.

Note, too, R. Leicher, *Die Totenklage in der deutschen Epik von der ältesten Zeit bis zur Nibelungen-Klage* (Germanist. Abh., No. 58, 1927).

Pp. 330 ff.: of the famous "solitary survivor" passage (*Beowulf*, ll. 2247 ff.) it may be said that this is no longer regarded as a reference to "self-burial"; see illuminating discussion (with references) by W. W. Lawrence, *Beowulf and Epic Tradition* (Cambridge, Mass., 1928), pp. 219—221. On possible influences behind the A. S. elegaic spirit see E. Sieper, *Die altenglische Elegie* (Strassburg, 1915), "Einleitung", pp. 1—122.

CHAPTER XII. THE WORSHIP OF THE DEAD

On Germanic religion in general the following works may be noted: histories of religion cited on p. 279 of S. B. Hustvedt's translation of P. A. Munch and M. Olsen, *Norse Mythology* (American Scandinavian Foundation, New York, 1926), and J. A. Mac Culloch, *Eddic (Mythology) (= Mythology of All Races,* II, Boston, 1930), esp. pp. 393—398, both works dealing rather with mythology than religon. Note especially the following: Karl Helm, *Altgermanische Religionsgeschichte,* Vol. I (Heidelberg, 1913), states the general questions at issue and discusses in detail the prehistoric and Roman period (cited below as Helm); A. Heusler, "Altgermanische Religion" in *Kultur der Gegenwart,* I, iii, 1 (2d ed., Leipzig, 1913); K. Helm, "Die Entwicklung der germanischen Religion" in *Germanische Wiedererstehung* (Heidelberg, 1926), pp. 292 ff. (semi-popular but excellent); Mogk's article "Religion" in Hoops; B. Phillpotts, "Germanic Heathenism" in *Cambridge Medieval History,* II (1913), 480 ff. (slight sketch), 786—790 (excellent bibliographies); the section "Religion" by H. M. Chadwick under "Teutonic Peoples", *Encycl. Britan.,* 14 th ed.; P. Herrman, *Deutsche Mythologie in gemeinverständlicher Darstellung* (Leipzig, 1906) and *Nordische Mythologie in gemeinverständlicher Darstellung* (Leipzig, 1903) (the plan of both of these excellent semi-popular works excludes critical apparatus); K. Krohn, *Skandinavisk Mythologi* (Helsingfors, 1922 — uses in part the results of Finnish scholarship; emphasizes Christian influence); C. Clemen, *Religionsgeschichte Europas,* I (Heidelberg, 1926), 335—368 ("Die Germanen"); H. M. Chadwick, *Heroic Age* (Cambridge, 1912), pp. 393 ff. ("Religion in the Heroic Age"). Note, too, F. R. Schröder, "Neuere Forschungen zur germanischen Religionsgesch.", *German.-Roman. Monatsschr.,* XVII (1929), 241 ff. For an interesting and suggestive discussion of Southern influence see F. R. Schröder, *Germanentum und Hellenismus* (Heidelberg, 1924). Carl Clemen has published a most convenient collection of important passages in Greek and Latin, Classical and Mediaeval, which treat of Germanic religion (*Fontes Religionis Germanicae,* Berlin, 1928), E. A. Philippson, *Germanisches Heidentum bei den Angelsachsen (= Kölner Anglist. Arbeiten, No. 4),*

Leipzig, 1929. Chantepie de la Saussaye's *Religion of the Teutons* (1902), should be used with caution.

On the spread of Christianity in the Germanic world see Kahle's comprehensive article "Bekehrungsgeschichte" in Hoops; for England and Germany, J. P. Whitney, "Conversion of the Teutons", *Cambridge Medieval History*, II (1913), 515—543, 793—797 (bibliogr.); and H. Naumann, "Christentum und deutscher Volksglaube", *Zs. f. Deutschkunde*, XLII (1928), 321—37 (excellent semi-popular summary of survivals).

Pp. 343 ff.: on immortality and death among primitive peoples see J. G. Frazer, *The Belief in Immortality* (3 vols., London, 1913—1922); on life after death among the Germanic peoples G. Neckel, *Walhall: Studien über germanischen Jenseitsglauben* (Dortmund, 1913), pp. 34 ff., and Schröder, *op. cit.*, pp. 20 ff. (modification of Neckel on Valhalla); among the Celts, G. Dottin, *Manuel (cit. supr.)*, pp. 351 ff. (with references).

On the worship of the dead (Totenkult) see Helm, pp. 132 ff., 246, and R. M. Meyer, pp. 89 ff.; for Scandinavia G. Neckel, *Walhall (cit. supr.)*, and W. von Unwerth, *Untersuchungen über Totenkult und Odinverehrung bei Nordgermanen und Lappen* Germanist. Abh., No. 37, 1911); for England the collectanea of R. Jente, *Mytholog. Ausdrücke*, pp. 223 ff. ("Tod und Totenwelt").

On tombs and gift-offerings see notes to Chap. XI above.

On the abode of the dead in Hekla in Iceland see von Maurer, *Zs. d. Vereins f. Volksglaube*, IV (1894), 267 f.

On the pagan origin of the Feasts of All Souls', see J. G. Frazer, *The Golden Bough — Adonis, Attis, Osiris* (3d ed., London, 1914), I, 51 ff.

P. 361: on the Scandinavian *fylgja* see Munch-Olsen, p. 302 ("Familiar Spirits"), and Hoops under "Fylgjen".

CHAPTER XIII. THE WORSHIP OF NATURE

The present chapter touches a multitude of matters concerning nature-worship, most of which can be examined in the general works cited under the preceding. E. g. see R. M. Meyer, pp. 23 ff. (Naturverehrung), 92 ff. (Naturgeister). P. 369: on "house spirits" see Meyer, p. 109, Mogk, p. 297 and *idem* in Hoops under "Hausgeister". On spirits of the air see, further,

G. L. Kittredge, *Witchcraft in Old and New England* (Cambridge, Mass., 1929), pp. 152 ff. ("Wind and Weather"). P. 370: on the Scandinavian *disir* see Munch-Olsen, pp. 33, 304. Pp. 375, 376: for the so-called first Merseburg Charm, see W. Braune-K. Helm, *Althochdeutsches Lesebuch* (9th rev. ed., Halle, 1928), p. 88 (text), pp. 201, 202 (bibliogr.). P. 378: on elves see Meyer, pp. 115, Hoops under "Elvenkult", and in England Jente, p. 167. On dwarfs see Meyer, pp. 128 ff.; Munch-Olsen, pp. 41, 309 ff.; Hoops under "Zwerg"; and especially C. N. Gould, "Dwarf-Names: a Study in Old Icelandic Religion", *Publ. Mod. Lang. Ass'n*, XLIV (1929), 939 ff., esp. p. 959, n. 68 for useful bibliogr. P. 381: on European vegetation dieties and cults, see Frazer, *Spirits of the Corn (cit. supra), passim*. On Anglo-Saxon "wood-elves" see R. Jente, *Mythol. Ausdrücke im altenglischen Wortschatz*, pp. 170, 173 (§ 113).

On tree-worship see Mogk in Hoops under "Baumkult": for Celts Mac Culloch, *Celtic (Mythology)*, pp. 198 ff.; Frazer, *Golden Bough — The Magic Art*, II (London, 1911), 8 ff.; Schröder, *op. cit.*, esp. pp. 39 ff. (Vegetationskulte). P. 387: on Yggdrasil, the world-tree, see Munch-Olsen, p. 298. P. 390: on sacred springs see K. Weinhold, "Die Verehrung der Quellen in Deutschland", Berlin Acad., *Abhandl.*, phil.-histor. Kl. (1898), Abh. I, pp. 1—69. P. 395: on the passage cited from the *Nibelungenlied* see A. H. Krappe, *Neophilologus*, XLV (1929), 42—49, for the underlying folk-tale type. P. 396: on the name Grendel as not being necessarily the Grendel of *Béowulf*, see R. W. Chambers, *Beowulf: an Introduction* (Cambridge, Eng., 1921 — new ed. in prep.), pp. 304 ff. P. 397: on giants in England see Jente, pp. 180 ff. P. 400: On fire-festivals see J. G. Frazer, *The Golden Bough — Balder the Beautiful* (London, 1913), I, 106 ff., for wealth of instances and literature. P. 401: on "Ragnarök" see Hoops *s. v.*, and A. Olrik, W. Ranisch, transl., *Ragnarök: die Sagen vom Weltuntergang* (Berlin, 1922).

CHAPTER XIV. THE WORSHIP OF THE GODS

For detailed information on the deities mentioned in this chapter see the general works cited under Chap. XII. Additionally note the following: P. 418: on the days of the week see

Munch-Olsen, p. 290, and the *New English Dictionary, s. vv.*
"Saturday" is now generally regarded as a half-translated adoption
of Latin *Saturni dies.*

On Woden, Thunor, and Freyr in Scandinavian place-names
see references in Munch-Olsen, pp. 10, 11, 12, n. 2, 16, n. 1.
P. 420: on Woden see Hoops under "Wodan"; in English place-
names Jente, pp. 77, 78; on Woden in the A. S. dynastic genealogies see H. M. Chadwick, *Origin of the English Nation* (1924
impression), p. 252. Pp. 423 ff.: on the so-called second Merseburg Charm see Braune-Helm (*op. cit.* Chap. XIII above), p. 88
(text), pp. 201, 202 (bibliogr.); and according to the *interpretatio
romana*, Helm, p. 259.

Pp. 425 ff.: on Thunor according to the *interpretatio romana*
see Helm pp. 193, 194, 274 ff.; Hoops under "Thor" and "Donar".
Pp. 428 ff.: on Týr see Helm, pp. 270 ff., 366 (Mars Thincsus).
Heimdall is no longer generally regarded as an hypostasis of
Týr. Pp. 430 ff.: on Nerthus, father of Freyr and Freya see
Helm, pp. 311 ff., and Chadwick, *Origin,* pp. 221 ("The Cult of
Nerthus"). The divinity of Beowulf and the equation Beowulf =
(Ingvi-)Freyr is now generally abandoned; see W.W. Lawrence,
Beowulf and Epic Tradition, pp. 142, 143 and notes. On *Isis,*
p. 432, see Müllenhoff, *Germania,* p. 218 ff., esp. 219 where he
withdraws earlier views on the association with Nerthus, and
Helm, pp. 309, 310. P. 434: on Ing see: A. Olrik - L. M. Hollander,
Heroic Legends of Denmark (N. Y., 1919), pp. 416 ff., and Chad-
wick, *Origin,* pp. 216, 217. Freyr and Freya are not identified
outside of Scandinavia. On the wide-spread cult of Frigg in
Sweden see H. Jungner, *Gudinnan Frigg och als Häred* (Uppsala,
1922), esp. pp. 108 ff., and in England Jente, *op. cit.,* pp. 107 ff.

On the dieties Nehalennia (p. 436) and Hludana (p. 438)
existing only in *interpretatio romana* and hence scarcely identifi-
able with other Germanic deities see Helm, pp. 383 ff. and
pp. 380 ff. (relationship between Hludana and Hlóðyn urged).
On the apparently local deities Tanfanna and Baduhenna see
Helm, pp. 299, 300, and 303 ff.; on Baduhenna also Hoops *s.v.*
In Hoops (*s. v.*) Mogk identifies the Scandinavian Forseti with
the Frisian Foseti. On Balder see, of course, inter alia Frazer,
Golden Bough — Balder the Beautiful II (1913), 76—94 (Balder
and the Mistletoe); G. Neckel, *Die Überlieferungen vom Gotte*

Balder dargestellt und vergleichend untersucht (Dortmund, 1920), Schröder, *op. cit.*, pp. 68 ff., and Hoops under "Balder".

CHAPTER XV. FORM AND CEREMONY

On early Germanic worship see Helm, pp. 44 ff., 231 ff. and B. Kummer, *Germanischer Kult und Glaube in den letzten heidnischen Jahrhunderten* (Leipzig diss., 1926); in Scandinavia see Munch-Olsen, pp. 267 ff. and notes, and in general the works cited under Chap. XII. On Celtic temples see Mac Culloch, *Celtic (Mythology)*, pp. 279 ff. Pp. 446, 447: on the Irminsul see H. M. Chadwick, *Origin*, pp. 213, 214; Hoops, *s. v.*; Helm, pp. 370—372, opposes F. Hertlein's identification with the "Juppitersäulen", q. v. in Hoops *s. v.* P. 454: on libation see M. Cahen, *La Libation* (Paris, 1921). On human sacrifice see Kummer, *op. cit.*, pp. 105 ff. (Menschenopfer) and ample literature there cited; for human sacrifice among the Celts see F. N. Robinson in *Anniversary Papers by Colleagues and Pupils of George Lyman Kittredge* (1913), pp. 185—197. Pp. 454 ff.: on lot-casting and divination see Helm, pp. 279 ff. (Wahrsagung); Mogk in Hoops under "Weissagung". P. 462, n. 4: as a modification of Bugge, see, e. g., H. M. Chadwick, *Cult of Othin*, pp. 72—82. P. 468: on runes see notes to Chap. VII above; on runes and magic much has recently been written, of which most must be treated with extreme caution: Magnus Olsen, "Om Troldruner", *Edda*, V (1916), 225—245 (reserved); F. R. Schröder, *Germanentum u. Hellenismus* (1924), pp. 4 ff.; S. Agrell, "Der Ursprung der Runenschrift und die Magie", *Arkiv för nordisk Filol.*, XLIII (1927), 97—109, and more elaborately in his *Runornas Talmystik och dess antika Förbild* (Lund, 1927) (influence of Mithraism; over intricate arithmetical calculations).

INDEX

485

[1] The statement of the text is little, if at all, affected by such a case as that of Walter and Hagen in the Waltharius Lay. For the sake of their old friendship, Hagen long refuses, even at the bidding of his king, to fight Walter; and the latter does his best in the combat to spare Hagen's nephew. The sentiment of the situation, however, is largely due to the poet, who had plenty of classical models to influence him; and the facts are easily referred to the blood-brotherhood, upon which, as Grimm points out (*Lateinische Gedichte des X und XI JH.*— p. 78), the heroes had long before entered.